# RECOVERY FROM SCHIZOPHRENIA

KU-196-252

£7.50

## The Author

Richard Warner graduated from King's College Hospital Medical School, London, and trained at Littlemore Hospital, Oxford, and Dingleton Hospital, Melrose, both innovative social psychiatry centers. He subsequently earned a degree in anthropology from the University of Colorado. He has practised community psychiatry in the Denver area since 1971, and is Medical director of the Mental Health Center of Boulder County. He is also on the faculty of the Departments of Anthropology and Psychiatry of the University of Colorado.

# RECOVERY FROM SCHIZOPHRENIA

*Psychiatry and Political Economy*

## RICHARD WARNER

Medical Director, Mental Health Center of Boulder
County, Boulder, Colorado; and Associate
Professor-Adjunct, University of Colorado, Boulder

ROUTLEDGE & KEGAN PAUL
London and New York

First published in 1985
First published as paperback 1987
by Routledge & Kegan Paul Ltd
11 New Fetter Lane, London, EC4P 4EE

Published in the USA by
Routledge and Kegan Paul Inc.
in association with Methuen Inc.
29 West 35th St., New York, NY10001

Set in Ehrhardt
by Hope Services, Abingdon, Oxon
and printed in Great Britain
by T. J. Press (Padstow) Ltd
Padstow, Cornwall

© Richard Warner 1985

No part of this book may be reproduced in
any form without permission from the publisher,
except for the quotation of brief passages
in criticism

Library of Congress Cataloging in Publication Data

Warner, Richard, 1943–

Recovery from schizophrenia
Bibliography: p.
Includes index
1. Schizophrenia—Treatment—Political aspects.
2. Schizophrenia—Treatment—Economic aspects.
3. Schizophrenia—Treatment. I. Title. [DNLM:
1. Deinstitutionalization—history. 2. Psychotropic
Drugs—therapeutic use. 3. Schizophrenia—drug therapy
4. Schizophrenia—history. 5. Socioeconomic Factors.
WM 11.1 W28r]
RC514.W24    1985          362.2          85–2199

British Library CIP data also available

ISBN 0–7100–9979–7
     0–7102–1392–6 (pb)

*To those who suffer from schizophrenia*

# Contents

# Acknowledgments

Several people were kind enough to give me useful criticism and encouragement when some of the ideas in this book were first drafted in the form of a long article. Among these reviewers were John Strauss, John Wing, Loren Mosher, Solomon Goldberg, Lewis Wolberg, Bernard Bloom and Maxwell Jones. I am most grateful for their advice and direction.

I am also greatly indebted to those who have discussed this research with me and reviewed sections of the book. I have received valuable critiques from the following colleagues in various departments of the University of Colorado: Robert Freedman, Thomas Mayer, Edward Greenberg, Gary Kiger and Paul Shankman. At the Mental Health Center of Boulder County, my associates Phoebe Norton and Ruth Arnold have made useful comments on sections of the manuscript. Julian Leff and Andrew Scull have carefully reviewed large sections of the work and have made many helpful suggestions. I have benefited a great deal from my correspondence with H.B.M. Murphy and discussions with Loren Mosher.

Much credit is due to Marilyn Rogers-Rothman, the librarian whose energy and skill enabled the many sources cited in this work to be assembled. I am especially grateful to my wife, Lucy Warner, whose consistent support and encouragement have been invaluable; her skillful editing and astute criticism have improved the book considerably. I appreciate also the fine job of manuscript preparation done by Gladys Bloedow.

The following figures are reprinted from other sources by permission of the publisher or author. Figure 2.1 is taken from Brenner, M. H., 'Fetal, infant and maternal mortality during periods of economic instability,' *International Journal of Health Services*, 3: 145–59, 1973, p. 153, © 1973, Baywood Publishing, Farmingdale, New York. Figure 5.1 is taken from Bockoven, J. S., *Moral Treatment in Community Mental Health*, New York: Springer, 1972, p. 56, © 1972, J. Sanbourne Bockoven.

Material in chapters 3 and 6 has previously been published in Warner, R., 'The influence of economic factors on outcome in schizophrenia,' *Psychiatry and Social Science*, 1: 79–106, 1981, © 1981 Universitetsforlaget, Oslo. The research at the end of chapter 4 has previously been published in Warner,

ACKNOWLEDGMENTS

R., 'The effect of the labor market on mental hospital and prison use: an international comparison,' *Administration in Mental Health*, 10: 239–58, 1983, © 1983 Human Sciences Press, New York. Chapter 7 has previously appeared in essentially similar form as Warner, R., 'Recovery from schizophrenia in the Third World,' *Psychiatry*, 46: 197–212, 1983, © 1983 William Alanson White Psychiatric Foundation, Washington, D.C.

# Introduction

Does the way we make our living or the form of government under which we live affect whether or not we become insane? Does social class or the state of the economy influence whether schizophrenics recover from their illness? Has industrial development affected the number of schizophrenics who become permanently and severely disabled—lost to their families, costly to the community and leading lives of emptiness and degradation? These questions are at the heart of this book.

My original intent was to uncover what the natural course of schizophrenia had been before the antipsychotic drugs were introduced, but this simple goal led to the realization that some current beliefs about the illness, widely accepted in psychiatry, are not accurate. We may well have been too pessimistic about the course of untreated schizophrenia and overconfident about the benefits of modern treatment. The antipsychotic drugs, it emerges, have not appreciably improved the long-term outcome from the illness; these drugs alone did not unlock the doors of our mental institutions and make possible the community treatment of psychotics. Despite a massive annual investment in the treatment of schizophrenia, the outcome from the illness in modern industrial society is no better than in the Third World.

Each change in our treatment approach to schizophrenia, moreover, is not necessarily an advance. A treatment method of demonstrated effectiveness—moral management—was laid to rest in the mid-nineteenth century only to be resurrected in a similar form nearly a hundred years later. Much of what today is called community treatment is, in fact, the antithesis of treatment: psychotics are consigned to a sordid, impoverished existence in which even basic needs, such as food and shelter, are not met. To understand how such aberrations and misconceptions have come about, to appreciate what has shaped the course and occurrence of schizophrenia, and to see what has molded psychiatric ideology and the social response to the schizophrenic, we need to step outside psychiatry. We have to venture into the territory of the sociologist, the anthropologist and the historian; we must enter the province of epidemiologists, social psychologists, economists and political scientists.

1

# A Note on Theory

The materialist theoretical approach I have used throughout this book is not commonly applied to questions in psychiatry. The central premise of the approach is that in order to understand human thought and behavior it is essential to begin with the material conditions of mankind's existence and productive processes. The origins of philosophical and social change, the materialist argues, are likely to be found in changes in technology. Values, attitudes and ideology are likely to be shaped by political and domestic economy (for example, family patterns, social stratification and political organization); and these aspects of society, in turn, tend to be molded by the forces of production and reproduction, by the technology of subsistence and population control and by labor requirements.[1]

A materialist research strategy, for example, allows us to generate the hypothesis that social attitudes towards the insane partly reflect the usefulness of the psychotic in the productive process; that psychiatric ideology is influenced by economic conditions; that the course of schizophrenia is influenced by class status, sex roles and labor dynamics; or that variations in the prevalence of the illness may reflect differences in modes of subsistence and production. Such hypotheses, of course, must be tested against alternative explanations, and that is what this book sets out to do.

I do not wish to suggest that material conditions *create* schizophrenia in any simple, deterministic way, but rather that they *mold* the course and outcome of the illness and *influence*, along with other factors, its prevalence. Psychiatric ideology is obviously not wholly determined by the economy, but it could be significantly affected by such factors. The materialist perspective allows for the operation of any number of causes besides technological, environmental and production-related forces. People in similar environmental settings will not all develop schizophrenia; biology must be crucial in determining who becomes psychotic. Inbreeding could produce isolated populations with an increased genetic predisposition to schizophrenia. Individual psychology is also relevant; the psychotic or pre-psychotic person's behavior or response to circumstances may sometimes create the stresses which precipitate or worsen his or her illness. The materialist researcher would expect, however, that if we look at a large number of instances we will often find material forces to be important. It is not only biological, genetic or psychological factors which determine the distribution and course of schizophrenia. We should be prepared to expand our concern with social factors, beyond family dynamics and socio-economic status. It is in the relationship between all of these potential causes and the economic, technological and environmental facts of our existence that we may gain the broadest understanding of why some people become schizophrenic and why some of them never recover.

2

## Chapter Topics

The opening chapters of the book establish the background for the subsequent analysis. The first chapter outlines what is known about the factors that promote the appearance of schizophrenia and that shape the course of the illness. The material is presented in such a way that readers who are not already familiar with the facts and features of the illness will learn enough to understand the rest of the book. The next chapter provides details of the ways in which mental and physical health are influenced by the economy, by social class and by the conditions of labor.

The middle section of the book looks at the impact of political economy on schizophrenia. Chapter 3 is an analysis of outcome studies of schizophrenia since the turn of the century and tries to establish whether changes in the long-term course of the illness are linked to large-scale fluctuations in the economy. The extent to which political, economic and labor market forces shaped the postwar policy of deinstitutionalization is examined in Chapter 4; and the role of similar forces in the development of institutions for the insane in the eighteenth and nineteenth centuries and in molding the treatment philosophy of the period is discussed in the following chapter.

Chapter 6 looks at possible reasons for the link between the economy and outcome from schizophrenia, and Chapter 7 attempts to explain why schizophrenia is a less malignant condition in the Third World. The plight of the Western schizophrenic and the way in which the social role and alienation of the psychotic shape the course of the illness is examined in Chapter 8. Moving from the course of schizophrenia to its prevalence, Chapter 9 analyses how social stratification, labor dynamics and subsistence patterns influence the appearance of the illness.

The final section deals with treatment issues. Chapter 10 evaluates the limitations of the antipsychotic drugs and the place of drug-free treatment. The importance of work, status issues and community support in the management of psychosis is covered in the final two chapters.

*Part 1*
*Background*

# 1　What is Schizophrenia?

Schizophrenia is an illness which is shaped, to a large extent, by political economy. The thrust of the following chapters will be to document this claim. First, though, we must be clear what it means. What is political economy? What is schizophrenia, and how can it be 'shaped'?

## What Is Political Economy?

All social groups survive by exploiting their environment and by limiting their population size to whatever their technology and the environment can sustain. The !Kung Bushmen subsist in the arid Kalahari Desert by camping in small bands near the few waterholes that exist and foraging over wide areas for nuts, berries, roots and melons.[1] Industrial societies sustain dense populations through increasingly intensive exploitation of land and sea for food, fuel and raw materials by means of elaborate forms of technology. Whatever the level of complexity of a society, however, it must possess a social structure which regulates the basic mechanisms of production and reproduction—a structure which governs the relationships among the productive and non-productive members of the society; which controls population size; and which regulates the distribution of labor power and energy in the society. All these functions may be subsumed under the term *economy*. Where the social structure is primarily seen as influencing domestic roles and relationships we speak of *domestic economy*. When we are considering larger political groupings (clans, bands, classes, castes and nations) we refer to *political economy*.[2]

We shall be looking, then, for influences on the occurence and course of schizophrenia which lie in differences in the modes of production of various societies—hunting and gathering, subsistence farming and industrial capitalism, for example. What was the impact of the Industrial Revolution upon insanity and the insane? How is schizophrenia affected by styles of labor use, by Third World migrant labor patterns, by unemployment, by land-tenure arrangements, by the social stratification of class and caste, by the fluctuations of the business cycle, by poverty, and by variations in marriage practices and family organization which are consequences of political-economic forces?

## What Is Schizophrenia?

Schizophrenia is an illness (or, equally, a group of illnesses). Psychiatrist Thomas Szasz would disagree, arguing that the whole concept of mental illness is a fabrication—scientifically worthless and socially harmful.[3] Indeed there are many conditions treated as illnesses by psychiatrists which might more logically be considered as non-medical forms of social deviance—for instance, alcohol abuse, transvestism and conduct disorder of childhood (to name but a few), all mental disorders listed in the third edition of the American Psychiatric Association *Diagnostic and Statistical Manual* (DSM-III).[4] Schizophrenia, nevertheless, fulfills any criteria we might wish to establish to define an illness. It is a non-volitional and generally maladaptive condition which decreases the person's functional capacity and which may be identified by a reasonably circumscribed set of characteristic features. Within rather broad limits, the age of onset and the expected course of the condition may be specified. Researchers are beginning to identify anatomical, physiological and biochemical abnormalities in the brains of people exhibiting features of schizophrenia. The predisposition to develop the condition appears to be, to a certain extent, inherited, and in essentially similar forms the disorder is universally identifiable in all societies around the globe (although, as we shall see, in Chapter 9, the prevalence may vary significantly). We may regard schizophrenia as an illness, but it will be apparent that it is an illness which is strongly affected by the patient's environment.

Schizophrenia is a *psychosis*. That is to say, it is a severe mental disorder in which the person's ability to recognize reality and his or her emotional responses, thinking processes, judgment and ability to communicate are so affected that his or her functioning is seriously impaired. Hallucinations and delusions are common features of psychosis.

Schizophrenia is one of the *functional* psychoses. These are the disorders in which the changes in functioning cannot definitely be attributed to any specific organic abnormality in the brain. As more is learned of brain pathology in mental illness this distinction will, no doubt, become less relevant. At the present time, however, it allows us to distinguish certain mental illnesses from such organic mental disorders as the pre-senile dementias (like Huntington's chorea), drug-induced psychoses (such as those the amphetamines may cause) or delirium tremens (secondary to alcohol withdrawal).

The two most common functional psychoses are schizophrenia and manic-depressive illness (also known as bipolar affective disorder). The distinction between the two is often not easy to make and, as we shall see, psychiatrists in different parts of the world at different times have not drawn the boundaries in the same way. In essence, however, manic-depressive illness is an episodic and recurrent disorder in which the psychotic symptoms are associated with severe alterations in mood—at times elated, agitated episodes of *mania*, at other times *depression*, with physical and mental slowing, despair, guilt feelings and low self-esteem.

Schizophrenia, on the other hand, while it may be episodic, will tend to relapse at irregular intervals, unlike the regular, cyclical pattern of manic-depressive psychosis; or it will demonstrate a continuous but fluctuating course. Furthermore, although schizophrenia may be associated with depression, elation or agitation at times, it is often free of these features and the mood is likely, instead, to be blunted, lacking in spontaneity or incongruous. Markedly illogical thinking is common in schizophrenia. Auditory hallucinations may occur in either manic-depressive illness or schizophrenia, but in the latter they are more likely to be commenting on the patient's thoughts and actions or to be conversing one with another. Delusions, also, can occur in both conditions; in schizophrenia they may give the individual the sense that he or she is being controlled by outside forces or that his or her thoughts are being broadcast or interfered with. Both manic-depressive illness and schizophrenia are most likely to begin in late adolescence or in early adult life.

Despite common features, different forms of schizophrenia can appear quite dissimilar. One patient, for example, may be paranoid and hostile in certain circumstances but show good judgment and high functioning in many areas of life. Another may be bizarre in manner and appearance, preoccupied with delusions of bodily disorder, passive and withdrawn. So marked are these differences, in fact, that many psychiatrists believe that, when the underlying neurophysiological and biochemical mechanisms of schizophrenia are worked out, the illness will prove to be a set of different but related conditions which lead, *via* a final common pathway of biochemical interactions, to a similar series of consequences. This view of schizophrenia as a federation of states has been present from the time of its earliest conception. To understand why these conditions were united in the first instance we must look at the history of the development of the idea.

## Emil Kraepelin

The concept of schizophrenia was formulated by the German psychiatrist Emil Kraepelin. Studying, over the course of years, patients admitted to the insane asylums of the late nineteenth century, he observed that certain types of insanity with an onset in early adult life and initially rather varied features seemed to progress ultimately to a similar deteriorated condition. To accentuate the progressive destruction of mental abilities, emotional responses and the integrity of the personality which he saw as central to this condition, Professor Kraepelin termed it dementia praecox—dementia of early life. Against considerable professional opposition, he took the position in 1887 that three conditions, previously considered separate, were in fact subtypes of this single disease entity. These conditions were hebephrenia, marked by aimless, disorganized and incongruous behavior; catatonia, in which the individual might be negativistic, motionless or even stuporose or, at other times, extremely agitated and incoherent; and finally, dementia paranoides, in which delusions of persecution and grandeur were predominant.

In defining dementia praecox, Kraepelin was particularly concerned to show how it differed from other forms of insanity and from idiocy. Unlike cerebral syphilis, no specific cause of the condition could be identified; in contrast to the psychogenic psychoses, dementia praecox did not appear to be an acute response to stress; and it was to be distinguished from manic-depressive insanity by its progressive deteriorating course and by the absence of clear-cut mood swings from elation to melancholia.

Emil Kraepelin's description of dementia praecox continues to serve us well, with some exceptions, as a picture of modern-day schizophrenia. Some of the characteristic features which he identified are listed in Table 1.1. Where his obervations no longer appear relevant is in his description of the symptoms associated with catatonic schizophrenia—automatic obedience, stereotypic movements, waxy flexibility, echolalia and echopraxia (see Table

**Table 1.1 Features of dementia praecox identified by Emil Kraepelin**

| FEATURE | DESCRIPTION |
| --- | --- |
| *Hallucinations:* | |
| Auditory | At the beginning these are usually simple noises, rustling, buzzing, ringing in the ears (p. 7). Then there develops . . . the *hearing of voices.* Sometimes it is only whispering (p. 7). |
| | What the voices say is, as a rule, *unpleasant* and *disturbing* (p. 9). Many of the voices make remarks about the thoughts and doings of the patient (p. 10). |
| | It is quite specially peculiar to dementia praecox that the patients' own *thoughts appear to them to be spoken aloud* (p. 12). |
| Visual | Everything looks awry and wrong (p. 14). People appear who are not there (p. 14). |

*Delusions:*

| | |
|---|---|
| Paranoia | The patient notices that he is looked at in a peculiar way, laughed at, scoffed at ... People spy on him ... persecute him, poison the atmosphere (p. 27). |
| Guilt | The patient has by a sinful life he believes destroyed his health of body and mind (p. 27). |
| Grandiosity | The patient is 'something better,' born to a higher place, ... an inventor, a great singer, can do what he will (p. 29). |
| Ideas of influence | Characteristic of the disease ... is the feeling of one's thoughts being influenced (p. 12). |
| Thought transference | The patient sometimes *knows the thoughts of other people* (p. 13). |
| Ideas of reference | Indifferent remarks and chance looks, the whispering of other people, appear suspicious to the patient (p. 31). |

*Thought disorder:*

| | |
|---|---|
| Poverty of thought | There is invariably at first a *loss of mental activity* and therewith a certain poverty of thought (p. 19). |
| Loose associations | The patients lose in a most striking way the faculty of *logical ordering* of their trains of thought. ... The most self-evident and familiar associations with the given ideas are absent (p.19). |
| Incoherence | By these disorders, which ... remind one of thinking in a dream, the patients' mental associations often have that peculiarly bewildering incomprehensibility. ... It constitutes the essential foundation of *incoherence of thought* (p. 20). |
| Thought block | There can be a sudden 'blocking' of their thought, producing a painful interruption in a series of ideas (p. 22). |

*Affect (emotional expression):*

| | |
|---|---|
| Blunting | Singular indifference ... towards their former emotional relations, the extinction of affection for relatives and friends. ... 'No grief and no joy' (p. 33). |

11

| FEATURE | DESCRIPTION |
|---|---|
| Inappropriateness | One of the most characteristic features of the disease is a frequent, causeless, sudden outburst of laughter (p. 33). |
| Lability | *Sudden oscillations of emotional equilibrium* of extraordinary violence may be developed (p. 35). |
| *Speech:*<br>Abnormal flow | The patients become monosyllabic, sparing of their words, speak hesitatingly, suddenly become mute ... let all answers be laboriously pressed out of them (p. 56). In states of excitement ... a prodigious *flow of talk* may appear (p. 56). |
| Neologisms | There may be produced ... quite senseless collections of syllables, here and there still having a sound reminiscent of real words (p. 68). |
| *Autism:* | Patients with dementia praecox are more or less inaccessible, ... they shut themselves off from the outside world (p. 49). |
| *Stupor:* | The rigid, impenetrable shutting up of themselves from all outer influences (p. 50). |
| *Negativism:* | Stubborn opposition to interference of all sorts (p. 47). |
| *Lack of drive:* | The patients have lost every independent inclination for work or action (p. 37). |
| *Automatic obedience:*<br>Waxy flexibility | The preservation of whatever positions the patient may be put in, even although they may be very uncomfortable (p. 38). |
| Echolalia | The involuntary repetition of words said to them (p. 39). |
| Echopraxia | The imitation of movements made in front of them (p. 39). |

12

| *Mannerisms:* | They add flourishes by which the movements become unnatural, affected and manneristic (p. 45). |
|---|---|
| *Stereotypy:* | Continuance in the *same positions* as well as ... the reception of the *same movements* or *actions* (p. 43). |
| *Intellectual deterioration:* | The patients are distracted, inattentive, tired, dull, ... their mind wanders, they have no perseverance (p. 23). |
| *Deterioration of judgment:* | The faculty of judgment in the patient suffers without exception severe injury (p. 25). |
| *Personality deterioration:* | Their thinking, feeling, and acting have lost the unity ... of the psychic personality, which provides the healthy human being with the feeling of inner freedom (p. 53). |

Source: Kraepelin, E., *Dementia Praecox and Paraphrenia,* Edinburgh: Livingstone, 1919.

1.1). Kraepelin's treatise on dementia praecox is illustrated with photographs of catatonic patients sitting and standing rigidly in bizarre and contorted postures, preserving poses into which they were set by the photographer. It was not unusual for Kraepelin's patients to repeat involuntarily the words and movements of those around them or to stand or kneel for days or longer in the same spot.[5] Patients with such features could still be seen on the wards of old-style institutions after the Second World War, but they are now very rarely seen in the industrial world. Catatonic schizophrenia, however, is still one of the commonest forms of the disorder in the Third World.

It is possible, as social psychiatrist Julian Leff argues, that these catatonic symptoms are a somatic expression of delusions of influence, symbolic thinking and pathological fear, much as the bodily symptoms of hysteria are a somatic conversion of anxiety. Both hysteria and catatonic symptoms have receded in the West, Dr Leff sugggests, as the population has developed a capacity for expressing emotions in verbal and psychological terms rather than as somatic symptoms.[6] It may also be true that the harsh and regressive conditions of asylums around the turn of the century tended to provoke and worsen catatonic symptoms which persisted as a physical expression of the patient's dependent status and barren existence.

Even more probable, these same asylum conditions may have brought about the deteriorating course which Kraepelin saw as central to his concept of the illness. Therapeutic nihilism, extended hospital stays and coercive

13

management within the asylum walls, and poverty and unemployment beyond them, during these years of the late nineteenth-century Great Depression combined to limit the chances of recovery from dementia praecox. Few psychiatrists since Kraepelin, as we shall see in Chapter 3, have found the course of schizophrenia to be so malignant as originally portrayed. As Kraepelin's classification was adopted around the world, nevertheless, so was the impression that the illness was inevitably progressive and incurable. To varying degrees the same view holds sway today—that without treatment the outlook is hopeless—despite considerable evidence to the contrary.

## Eugen Bleuler

Twelve per cent of Emil Kraepelin's patients with dementia praecox recovered more or less completely—few enough, but a sufficient number to cause concern about the central diagnostic criterion being poor outcome. In the more prosperous years of the early twentieth century in Switzerland and in the therapeutically progressive atmosphere of the renowned Burgholzi Hospital, psychiatrist Eugen Bleuler presented a more optimistic view of the outcome from the illness. Stimulated by the psychoanalytic theories of his assistant, Carl Jung, Dr Bleuler formulated a new unifying concept for the condition and gave it a new name. To Dr Bleuler the identifying characteristic of the illness was not poor outcome but a specific psychological picture—a lack of continuity in the associations between the patient's thoughts and a restricted or incongruous expression of emotion. Other symptoms which he regarded as fundamental were ambivalence and autism (a preoccupation with the inner world leading to detachment from reality). From the fragmentation of thinking and feeling, Eugen Bleuler derived the term *schizophrenia*—split mind. The hallucinations and delusions which were commonly part of the psychotic picture, Dr Bleuler considered to be merely secondary to the more fundamental defects.[7]

Dr Bleuler's 1911 monograph, *Dementia Praecox or the Group of Schizophrenias*, contains many examples of patients who fail to show Kraepelin's progressive deterioration and who often recover a high level of functioning.

A young farm girl, age seventeen, has been catatonic for a period of two years. Then she became a nursing attendant. Two years later she was released. She then became a midwife. She married, her husband had a difficult time with her. For example, she would not permit him to sing while he worked. She formed strong unfounded sympathies and antipathies. At the age of thirty-eight, she was again mildly catatonic for some six months. Since then she has been working for eight years outside the hospital, but not as a midwife.[8]

Another of Bleuler's examples:

> Physician: Neurasthenia at twenty-nine. Then at thirty-one after typhoid fever, catatonic. At forty-seven, apparently 'cured'. He then resumes his practice, marries. Has been well for the past two years.[9]

Bleuler's impression was that few, if any, of his schizophrenic patients completely recovered without some vestige of their illness remaining. Far-reaching improvement, however, was common. Fully 60 per cent of his patients recovered sufficiently from their first schizophrenic episode to return to work and support themselves.[10] Such 'social recoveries' cannot be directly compared with Kraepelin's 12 per cent of patients, who may well have shown signs of more complete symptomatic recovery. There can be no doubt, though, that the course of the illness in Bleuler's patients was much more benign than in Kraepelin's hospital in Munich. So much so, that Bleuler was able to assert that

> the therapy of schizophrenia is one of the most rewarding for the physician who does not ascribe the results of the natural healing processes of psychosis to his own intervention.[11]

It would be hard to find in modern psychiatry such an optimistic view of the natural course of schizophrenia.

## Bleuler's Treatment Methods

Why should the outcome for Bleuler's patients have been so superior? He may well have broadened the diagnosis of schizophrenia to include some less severely disturbed patients. But it is also likely that Bleuler was too modest about the value of treatment, and that his methods of management maximized the chances of his patients' recovery. The description of his treatment methods from the first decade of the twentieth century reads like a model of the approaches introduced a half-century later in the social-psychiatry revolution of postwar northern Europe (to be described in Chapter 4) or like the principles of humane care abandoned half a century earlier at the end of the moral-treatment era (described in Chapter 5).

Institutional care, for instance, was to be minimized. 'It is preferable to treat these patients under their usual conditions and within their habitual surroundings,' Dr Bleuler insisted. 'The patient should not be admitted to hospital just because he suffers from schizophrenia, but only when there is a definite indication for hospitalization.' Furthermore, 'one can consider it an established rule that earlier release produces better results.'[12] If the patient cannot return to his own family, 'the care he may receive from a strange family often serves as an adequate substitute.'[13] In pursuing this policy of active community rehabilitation Bleuler may have been aided by the low

15

levels of poverty and unemployment in Switzerland at that time. It is certain, at any rate, that his discharge policies were much more liberal than those of Kraepelin.

The return to an appropriate occupation, Bleuler believed, was vital to the patient's health. 'Idleness facilitates the predomination by the complexes over the personality,' he argued, 'whereas regulated work maintains the activity of normal thinking.'[14] But he emphasized that 'faultless performance can hardly be expected and the unavoidable rebukes can greatly endanger the entire pleasure that the patients take in their work.'[15] Dr Bleuler recognized that a number of other stresses might threaten the patient's recovery—too much responsibility at work, for example, family troubles or a sense of failure.

Within the institution close attention was to be given to the quality of the patient's environment. 'Good surroundings have a very different influence on the patient than unpleasant and noisy ones.'[16] The use of mechanical restraints was limited. Patient self-reliance was encouraged and occupational therapy was considered essential. 'Every mental institution should have the kind of set-up that will make it possible to offer every patient some kind of work at all times.'[17] On Sundays, 'generally a bad day' for the patients as there was no work, 'special care should be taken to provide sufficient opportunity for entertainment.'[18]

Although Bleuler demonstrated that the outcome of schizophrenia was often benign, Kraepelin's more pessimistic view has proven more popular. why should this have been so? Partly, perhaps, because patient management, economic conditions and community acceptance of the mentally ill in most places through many of the subsequent years have been sufficiently poor that outcome from the illness has seemed closer to Kraepelin's experience than to Bleuler's. (This possibility will be examined in some detail in subsequent chapters.) In part, the modern pessimistic view of the untreated course of schizophrenia may have developed because the introduction of the antipsychotic drugs in the mid-1950s and their subsequent, virtually universal, employment in the treatment of psychosis has masked what was previously known of the natural history of the illness. Finally, some diagnostic reforms have tended to follow Kraepelin's lead in attempting to limit the use of the term schizophrenia to only those cases which do not recover.

## Diagnosis

It is by no means universally clear what is schizophrenia and what is not, and before we can study the course of the illness in more detail it will be necessary to examine the different approaches to defining its boundaries.

Scandinavian psychiatrists have tended to use a rather narrow definition

16

of schizophrenia in an attempt to adhere to Kraepelin's emphasis on poor outcome. In this they have followed the course set by psychiatrist G. Langfeldt in 1937. He distinguished between a core group of *process* or *nuclear* schizophrenics, on the one hand, who demonstrated an insidious onset of illness and a deteriorating course and, on the other, a *reactive* group, who tended to show signs of better social functioning before becoming psychotic, to have a more acute onset and to display a better prognosis. The reactive psychotics, for whom the outlook is brighter, have been separated from 'true' schizophrenics in Scandinavian psychiatric terminology and labeled as suffering from *schizophreniform psychoses*.[19] In Britain this approach has not been generally adopted, nor was it much used in the United States until very recently.

Russian psychiatrists, particularly in Moscow, have also emphasized the course of the illness in developing their classification of schizophrenia. In this instance, however, the result is a broad definition. The Moscow-school psychiatrists speak of *periodic* schizophrenia, consisting of acute episodes with normal remission; *stepwise* schizophrenia, in which each acute espisode leads to a period of lowered social functioning; and *sluggish* schizophrenia, with a course of progressive deterioration. Among the periodic schizophrenics are to be found patients who would probably be diagnosed in Western Europe as suffering from manic-depressive psychosis. The Soviet emphasis on social adjustment in diagnosing schizophrenia, in a society where dissidence and non-comformity are seen as pathological, has sometimes led to the use of the label schizophrenia for individuals who might elsewhere have been considered neurotic, eccentric or iconoclastic.[20]

In the United States, until the mid-1970s, the diagnostic approach to schizophrenia was also extremely broad, leading to the labeling of many patients as schizophrenic who in Europe would have been considered manic-depressive or non-psychotic. This diagnostic practice came about not through an emphasis on the course of the illness but as a result of giving weight to certain intrapsychic mechanisms (under the influence of psycho-analytic theory) which were thought to be basic to schizophrenia. Thus, American psychiatry, like the Russian system, expanded the concept of schizophrenia to include patients with no clear psychotic features. In the United States these patients were labeled *latent* and *pseudoneurotic* schizo-phrenics.

In the 1960s a research project used a standardized method of diagnosis (built around British criteria) to compare the diagnostic approaches of psychiatrists in New York and London. Comparing the hospital diagnoses given to hundreds of patients admitted in these two cities on opposite sides of the Atlantic, it was found that American psychiatrists were roughly twice as likely to diagnose schizophrenia, compared with the research team's standardized approach, four times *less* likely to diagnose psychotic depression and ten times *less* likely to label a psychotic patient as suffering from mania. The diagnoses given by the psychiatrists working in London hospitals, as might be expected, were very close to those of the project psychiatrists (who were using a British diagnostic approach).[21] Plainly, at this time, American psychiatrists were labeling patients as schizophrenic who would have been considered manic-depressive in Britain.

The underlying problem was that schizophrenia and manic-depressive illness share many common symptoms. During an acute episode it may not be possible to tell them apart. The distinguishing feature is often likely to be the prior history of the illness. The records of patients with manic-depressive illness (unless they are too early in the course of the illness) should reveal prior episodes of depression and mania with interludes of normal functioning. From 1950 until the mid-1970s, however, American psychiatrists paid little attention to the course of the psychosis in diagnosing schizophrenia and emphasized instead the presence of supposedly 'schizo-phrenic' symptoms and defects. The result was an over-inclusive pattern of diagnosis in comparison with European approaches.

We may view the problem of the diagnosis of schizophrenia in even broader cross-cultural perspective through the findings of the International Pilot Study of Schizophrenia. This large-scale project of the World Health Organization looked at two issues—the diagnosis of schizophrenia around the world (which is what concerns us here) and the course and outcome of the illness. Their findings on the latter question will be discussed later in the book. Using a standardized, British diagnostic approach (incorporated in a computer program), the project evaluated the symptoms of psychotic patients admitted to treatment in nine centers in the developed and developing world—in cities in Colombia, Czechoslovakia, Denmark, India, Nigeria, Taiwan, UK, USA and the USSR.

Comparing the diagnoses made by the local hospital psychiatrists and the uniform research method, the project revealed that the diagnosis of psychosis, in general, and schizophrenia, in particular, was reasonably similar in the European and Third World centers. The serious discrepancies lay in the Russian and American diagnostic approaches. A large proportion of the patients who were labeled schizophrenic by psychiatrists in Moscow and Washington, DC did not meet the research definition and would have been diagnosed as suffering from manic-depressive psychosis or a neurosis elsewhere in the world.[22]

The diagnostic approaches of American psychiatrists changed suddenly and radically in the late 1970s. Much greater attention was paid to discriminating manic-depressive illness from schizophrenia. The stimulus to this movement was clearly the introduction of lithium carbonate to US psychiatry. This drug, a simple salt, is highly effective in the control of manic-depressive illness in many patients and it is more pleasant and probably less potentially harmful to use than the most common alternative category of drugs, the antipsychotics. Lithium carbonate, however, is generally not beneficial for schizophrenic patients.

Research published as early as 1949 in Australia[23] and in 1954 by researchers in Scandinavia[24] demonstrated the effectiveness of lithium salts in manic-depressive illness, and the use of the drug was widespread in Europe and other countries throughout the 1960s. Despite these facts, lithium carbonate was not commonly used in the United States until the mid-1970s. This delay of ten years or more is usually attributed to the concern over accidental poisonings resulting from the use of lithium chloride as a salt substitute for cardiac patients in the United States during the 1940s. Lithium was taken off the market until the US Food and Drug Administration gave permission for its use in the treatment of mania in 1970.[25]

Some observers, however, have suggested that the delay in the marketing of lithium in the United States was due to a lack of enthusiasm on the part of the major pharmaceutical companies. Lithium carbonate is such a simple substance that it cannot be patented. Nor can patentable alternatives be developed from it (as is common with psychiatric medications). Lithium carbonate, consequently, sells for only slightly more than the cost of aspirin. The profit margin for manufacturers is therefore a good deal lower than with other products. (As an illustration of this point, most psychiatrists in the United States receive several visits a month from representatives of pharmaceutical companies marketing patented antipsychotic or antidepressant drugs, but salesmen for lithium carbonate are not seen from one year to the next.)

Whatever the reasons for the delay in the introduction of lithium to the United States, the advent of the drug was followed within a few years by a major revision of the US classification system for mental disorders. These changes meant more for the diagnosis of schizophrenia, however, than a tightening of the criteria to exclude manic-depressive illness. The concept of schizophrenia was narrowed down to include only those patients with the worst prognostic outlook. With the publication in 1980 of the third edition of the American Psychiatric Association *Diagnostic and Statistical Manual* (DSM-III), American psychiatry switched from one of the broadest concepts of schizophrenia in the world to one of the narrowest—a diagnostic approach similar to the Scandinavian system. No psychotic patient, for example, could any longer be labeled as suffering from schizophrenia if he or she had been continuously disturbed for less than six months. Thus, a patient who had experienced several schizophrenic-like episodes, each briefer than six months, was not to be considered schizophrenic. Nor was a patient who did not show a clear deterioration in functioning. Patients who failed to meet these criteria but appeared schizophrenic in other ways were to be diagnosed

19

as suffering from brief reactive psychosis, schizophreniform disorder or atypical psychosis. Those patients who could not be definitely diagnosed as either manic-depressive or schizophrenic, having features of both conditions, were previously labeled schizoaffective and included within the schizophrenia category; now they were to be excluded.[26]

A number of practical implications flow from these geographic and temporal variations in the diagnosis of schizophrenia. In particular, whatever we have to say about the prevalence and course of the illness has meaning only if we define which diagnostic approach is being used. For every narrowly defined case of schizophrenia in the population there are at least four more people who meet broadly defined criteria for the illness.[27] Where the diagnostic concept is deliberately shaped to exclude patients who recover, we must expect the outcome to be worse. In this book, the term schizophrenia, unless otherwise qualified, refers to a middle-of-the-road definition—not as exclusive as the Scandinavian or modern American approach, nor as broad as the Russian or earlier American systems. The definition used here will essentially be the one in use in British psychiatry and the one which, as the WHO Pilot Study shows, is most commonly used around the world. This definition, while clearly differentiating cases of manic-depressive illness, does not exclude psychoses of short duration or those with features of good prognosis. It does, however, exclude patients who fail to show clear-cut psychotic sysmptoms.

## Course and Outcome of Schizophrenia

A thorough analysis of the outcome of schizophrenic illness will be attempted in Chapter 3. At this point it is necessary to give an idea of the wide variation which occurs in the course of the condition. A Swiss psychiatrist, Professor Luc Ciompi, provides a useful analysis of the course of schizophrenia followed into old age. In the late 1960s Dr Ciompi traced 289 patients, all more than 65 years of age, who had been admitted for treatment of schizophrenia to the University Psychiatric Clinic of Lausanne at various times throughout the century. For most·of these patients the history of the illness extended back for more than thirty-five years, in many cases for more than fifty years. This is one of the longest follow-up studies in the literature. Dr Ciompi describes in detail his diagnostic criteria, which are those of Emil Kraepelin and Eugen Bleuler—neither particularly narrow nor broad.

Figure 1.1 is a diagrammatic representation (adapted from Dr Ciompi's paper) of the onset, course and outcome of the illness in the 228 patients for whom the information could be determined with certainty. Dr Ciompi found that the onset of the illness had been either acute (with less than six months from first symptoms to full-blown psychosis) or, conversely, insidious, in

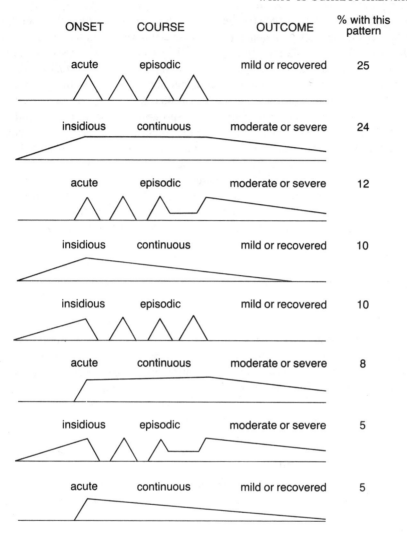

| ONSET | COURSE | OUTCOME | % with this pattern |
|---|---|---|---|
| acute | episodic | mild or recovered | 25 |
| insidious | continuous | moderate or severe | 24 |
| acute | episodic | moderate or severe | 12 |
| insidious | continuous | mild or recovered | 10 |
| insidious | episodic | mild or recovered | 10 |
| acute | continuous | moderate or severe | 8 |
| insidious | episodic | moderate or severe | 5 |
| acute | continuous | mild or recovered | 5 |

*Figure 1.1   The long-term course of schizophrenia in 228 patients*

Source: Ciompi, L., 'Catamnestic long-term study on the course of life and aging of schizophrenics,' *Schizophrenia Bulletin*, 6: 606–18, 1980.

roughly equal numbers of cases. Similarly, the course of the condition was episodic or continuous in approximately equal numbers of patients; and the outcome was moderate to severe disability in half the cases and mild disability or full recovery in the other half. Full recovery was noted in more than a quarter of the patients.[28] The outcome from schizophrenia varies from one period to another and from place to place. These results, like

21

Eugen Bleuler's, are somewhat better than average and, as we shall see (in Chapter 6), this may be a consequence of the superior economic conditions in Switzerland throughout the century. We can see from these results, nevertheless, that the course of schizophrenia varies a good deal between patients and that the outcome is often favourable—regardless of treatment.

Many attempts have been made to predict which patients will have a benign course and a good outcome—good-prognosis schizophrenia—and to identify the features which will distinguish them from patients with poor-prognosis schizophrenia. (This distinction is similar to Dr Langfeldt's differentiation of process and reactive schizophrenia mentioned earlier.) The results of this work will be discussed in some detail in Chapter 10. Here we may briefly state that it is the patients with the higher levels of functioning (social, sexual and vocational) before becoming psychotic who tend to do better. A sudden onset to the illness and an onset late in life are also good prognostic features.

## How Widespread Is Schizophrenia?

Results of prevalence studies range from as few as one schizophrenic for every 2,000 adults in one community to one for each 100 adults in others. This wide variation is in part due, as we have seen, to differences in diagnostic practices and, in part, to variations in the true frequency of occurrence of the illness. Chapter 9 attempts to go beyond diagnostic variability and to look for possible environmental causes of some of the differences in the prevalence of schizophrenia. The studies analysed in that chapter provide an impression of the most common frequency of occurrence of the illness: in many industrial world settings the prevalence of schizophrenia, identified and diagnosed by a variety of approaches, is quite close to one in every 200 adults.

Schizophrenia is found in every culture. The content of the patient's hallucinations and delusions varies from one social group to another—the delusions of villagers living in the north of Ghana are associated with the local fetish system, for example, but among the city dwellers of Accra in the south of that country ideas of influence and control by electricity and radio are more common.[29] The form and basic features of schizophrenia, nevertheless, are similar around the world, as the WHO Pilot Study exemplifies. There is some disagreement as to whether schizophrenia is as common in Third World settings as it is in the West. This question will be studied in Chapter 9.

## What Causes Schizophrenia?

Tuberculosis is the result of an infection by a bacillus. In the early decades of the century, however, when the disease was widespread, although a huge proportion of the population became infected with the organism, only a relatively small number went on to develop clinically recognizable evidence of the disease. What caused the manifest symptoms of the illness to appear in those few, in some cases years after the initial infection? Poor social conditions were known to increase the susceptibility to the illness, and improvements in diet and housing were linked to a decline in the death rate from tuberculosis long before effective drug treatment was introduced. The irritant effects of coal dust on miners, pregnancy in women and the debilitating influence of secondary illnesses, all could reduce an individual's resistance to the disease. What, then, is the cause of tuberculosis? The tubercle bacillus? Overcrowding? Poor diet? The stresses of lower-class living? Or any of the other environmental, occupational or constitutional factors which increase the individual's susceptibility? Clearly any and all of these factors may be considered contributory, and the reduction in the prevalence of the illness had as much to do with elimination of some of the social causes and with the increase in the resistance of the population by vaccination as with the direct attack on the infective organism by chemotherapy.

The same principles apply to schizophrenia. We do not know with certainty of a specific organic defect or infective agent which is critical in the development of schizophrenia (although there are a number of theories and there has been an expansion of knowledge in this area). We do know, however, of several factors which increase the susceptibility to this illness and which may provoke its appearance. To grasp how these factors may influence the development and the course of schizophrenia we need to use an interactive conceptual model such as the one proposed by American psychiatrists John Strauss and William Carpenter.

An adaptation of the conceptual scheme offered by these authors[30] is given in Figure 1.2. An interactional model allows for various types of explanation to assume importance at different stages in the individual's development. The genetic contribution, the intrauterine environment and birth trauma might each play a part in forming the newborn infant's predisposition to developing schizophrenia. The vulnerability to the illness might theoretically be heightened during development by brain damage, for example, or by unusual family communication patterns.

Whether or not the illness becomes manifest in later life will depend upon the extent of the vulnerability and the subsequent exposure to a variety of stresses. Precipitating stresses may be biological in nature (such as hallucinogenic drug abuse), or psychosocial. In the latter category are life events (such as starting work, leaving home or bereavement), environmental influences (criticism or intrusiveness at home, for example) or existential concerns (loss of a sense of purpose or belonging).

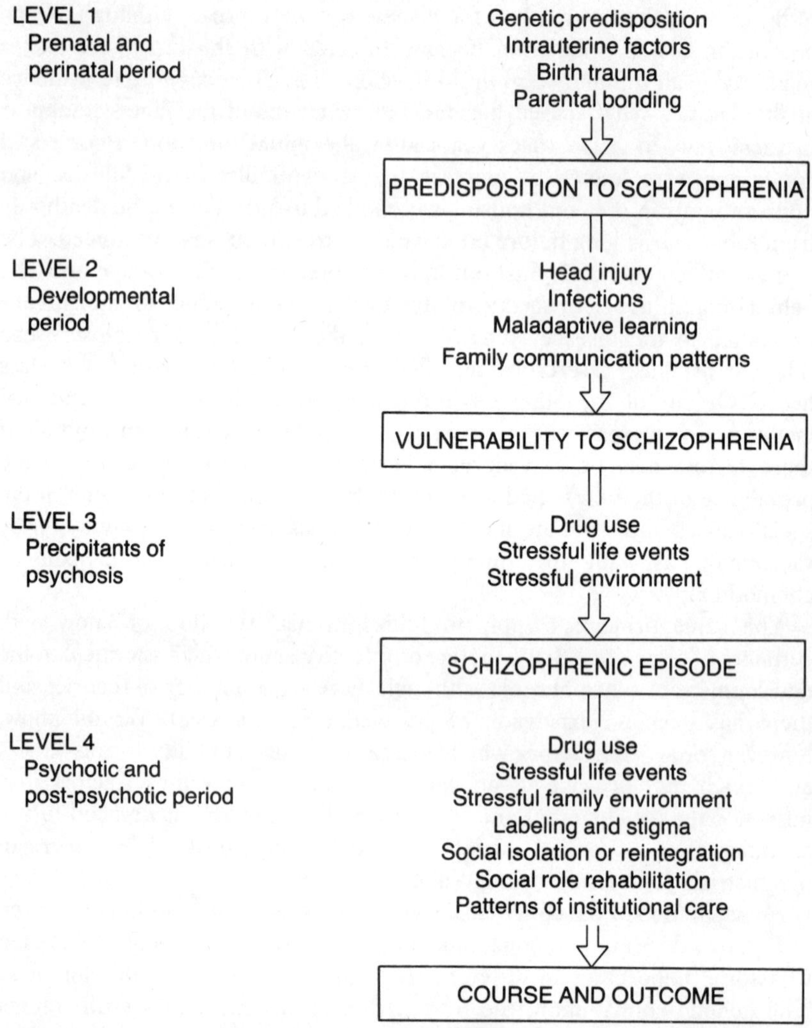

LEVEL 1
Prenatal and
perinatal period

Genetic predisposition
Intrauterine factors
Birth trauma
Parental bonding

⇓

| PREDISPOSITION TO SCHIZOPHRENIA |

LEVEL 2
Developmental
period

Head injury
Infections
Maladaptive learning
Family communication patterns

⇓

| VULNERABILITY TO SCHIZOPHRENIA |

LEVEL 3
Precipitants of
psychosis

Drug use
Stressful life events
Stressful environment

⇓

| SCHIZOPHRENIC EPISODE |

LEVEL 4
Psychotic and
post-psychotic period

Drug use
Stressful life events
Stressful family environment
Labeling and stigma
Social isolation or reintegration
Social role rehabilitation
Patterns of institutional care

⇓

| COURSE AND OUTCOME |

*Figure 1.2    Interactional model for factors possibly affecting the onset, course, and outcome of schizophrenia*

Once an episode of psychosis has begun, these same stressors and new ones, together with the degree of vulnerability, will determine the subsequent course and outcome of the illness. Labeling and social stigma may well affect the individual's sense of self-worth, as may his or her success in reintegrating with the social group and in returning to a valued social role. Criticism, rejection, restriction, confinement or idleness might well limit the individual's capacity for recovery from schizophrenia.

24

The strength of some of these potential causes of vulnerability and precipitants of psychosis has been better demonstrated than others. On the following pages a few of the more important will be briefly outlined.

## Inheritance

Relatives of schizophrenics have a greater risk of developing the illness than others. The prevalence of schizophrenia in the general population varies, as we have seen, depending on such factors as diagnostic criteria; but it is generally less than 1 per cent. The prevalence of the condition in the brothers and sisters of schizophrenics also varies quite widely in different studies— ranging from 3 per cent to 14 per cent, however, the risk is considerably higher than usual. For those with one schizophrenic parent, the risk of developing schizophrenia is between 8 per cent and 18 per cent. Among the children of two schizophrenic parents, the prevalence ranges from 15 per cent to 55 per cent.[31]

Studies of people adopted in infancy suggest that this increased risk of schizophrenia in the relatives of identified cases is related to inheritance rather than environment. The children of schizophrenics have a similar increased prevalence of the illness whether they are raised by their biological parents or by adoptive parents. Likewise, the family history of schizophrenics brought up by adoptive parents reveals an increased prevalence of the illness among their biological relatives but not among their relatives by adoption.[32]

If one of a pair of non-identical twins suffers from schizophrenia, the chance that the other twin will develop the condition is roughly the same as in siblings who are not twins—in the region of 10 per cent. When one *identical* twin is schizophrenic the likelihood of finding the illness in the other twin is around 50 per cent.[33] Thus, although identical twins have exactly the same genetic make-up, they do not have an identical risk of developing schizophrenia. One may reasonably conclude from these figures, then, that genetic factors play a major part in establishing the vulnerability to the illness but that environmental factors (including the intrauterine experience, theoretically) must also play important roles before schizophrenia becomes manifest.

The twins studies reveal other useful pieces of information about the inheritance of schizophrenic vulnerability. When one of a pair of identical twins has a severe and deteriorating form of schizophrenia, then it is virtually certain that the other twin will show signs of the illness; but if one identical twin has a mild form of the psychosis, the chances of the other twin developing schizophrenia are very much lower—around 25 per cent.[34] This observation suggests that the genetic vulnerability influences both the onset and the course of the illness. The identical twins of schizophrenics, furthermore, if they do not develop schizophrenia, run an increased risk of developing other psychiatric disorders—alcoholism, neurosis or personality

25

problems.[35] What is inherited is, perhaps, not specifically a vulnerability to schizophrenia but, instead, an underlying biochemical and functional disturbance which may express itself in somewhat different ways under the influence of environmental stresses.

Just what is the deficit which might be inherited?

## Brain Chemistry

Emotions and thought processes are regulated by the complex interaction of systems of nerve cells throughout the brain. Each nerve cell (or neuron) exerts its effect by the release of a chemical mediator at the synapse—the point of contact, with another neuron. Biochemical theories attempting to explain the appearance of schizophrenic symptoms have focused on abnormalities in the action of some of these chemical neurotransmitters. Such theories remain speculative in nature, however, and are only modestly supported, so far, by research evidence.

The predominant biochemical theory of schizophrenia—the dopamine hypothesis—suggests that the underlying abnormality may be a relative overactivity of tracts of neurons in which dopamine is the chemical mediator. Acute stress, leading to sudden increases in dopamine turnover, could thus precipitate an episode of psychosis in a vulnerable individual.[36] The dopamine hypothesis is dealt with in some detail in Chapter 10. An alternative theory—the transmethylation hypothesis—stresses that certain neurotransmitters (dopamine, norepinephrine and serotonin) may be broken down into compounds which are very similar to mescaline, LSD and psilocybin. Neurotransmitters being pathologically converted into hallucinogens in the brain could theoretically account for the appearance of schizophrenic symptoms.[37]

Other pieces of research have variously suggested abnormalities in an enzyme whose function is to destroy certain neurotransmitters (monoamine oxidase), abnormalities in the functioning of naturally occurring brain opiates (endorphins), and abnormalities in the production of various proteins and from the action of slow viruses.[38] The large number of such theories is perhaps an indication of the inadequacy of any one hypothesis and of our relative ignorance, despite impressive recent advances, of the biochemistry of the brain.

## Brain Structure

That there *are* biochemical differences in schizophrenia is certain—just as certain as that there are biochemical correlates in the brain to rage, anxiety and learning Spanish. That there are *anatomical* differences in the brains of schizophrenics (as in some organic brain disorders) is by no means definite, however, and in fact the evidence for such abnormalities in the structure of the brain is quite sparse. Decades of post-mortem study of the brains of schizophrenics has failed to produce agreement on any neuroanatomical changes specific to the illness. Recent research using advanced staining techniques, nevertheless, has shown indications of injury in an area of the brain known as the limbic system. These changes were found in a large proportion (but not all) of a sample of severely ill, institutionalized schizophrenics—changes which were not evident in non-schizophrenic psychiatric patients.[39] This study is of interest as it suggests the possibility of abnormality in the same area of the brain (the limbic system) that neurochemical research has incriminated as functioning abnormally in schizophrenia. This interconnecting network of terminals and tracts is believed to be central to the regulation of emotion and to the individual's response to stress.

Perhaps the most important recent evidence, however, for anatomical changes in the brain in schizophrenia has been provided by computed tomographic (CT) scans. Most studies using such brain scans have found evidence of mild cerebral atrophy in a proportion of schizophrenic patients.[40] The changes, which include enlargement of the fluid containing ventricles of the brain and widening of the fissures between folds of brain tissue, are not generally found in other psychiatric patients unless they have organic brain damage, nor are they found in normal people.

The cause of such cerebral atrophy is not known. Since the abnormalities are found equally in first-break, acute schizophrenics and in chronic patients, it is scarcely possible that the changes are due to treatment.[41] The cerebral atrophy might be considered evidence that schizophrenia is a degenerative brain disease, but since the changes occur in only about a quarter of cases, this could only apply to a subtype of the illness. Such a possibility is rendered unlikely by the finding that the CT scan abnormalities are not confined to one specific clinical subgroup.[42] Nor is there one well-defined group of patients with enlarged cerebral ventricles and another with normal-size ventricles; the CT-scan changes are distributed along a smooth gradient from normal to large.[43] Perhaps the most probable explanation is that the cerebral atrophy found in some schizophrenics is an indicator of some earlier brain injury which is not specific to schizophrenia but which increases the vulnerability to developing the illness. Such brain damage might result, for example, from intrauterine drug effects, birth trauma, infections or one of a list of similar assaults.

## Brain Functioning
Vulnerability to schizophrenia, then, may have a number of biological sources. How it is expressed as abnormal brain *functioning* has also been studied. Some research workers have examined the level of arousal in schizophrenics through such measures as heart rate, pupil size and skin conductance. Others have measured differences between people from the

27

general population and those with a high risk of developing schizophrenia in their response to such stimuli as audible clicks and flashing lights. Computerized averaging of multiple electroencephalograph tracings of subjects' responses to these stimuli (evoked potentials) has been used in this work. The overall impression from such reasearch is that schizophrenics, as well as some of their relatives presumed to have a high risk of developing the illness, have an abnormal pattern of response to environmental stimuli. They may be overly responsive to pieces of sensory information—sights, sounds, smells and touch—and more limited in their ability to blot out irrelevant material.

It is essential to our capacity to concentrate on what is happening to us that we be able to attend to one aspect of our environment at a time and screen out the multiplicity of other bits of sensory data with which we are constantly bombarded. This capacity to discriminate stimuli and to focus attention may be disrupted in those who are vulnerable to schizophrenia. Such a deficit would be a possible result of abnormal functioning in the limbic system. Given sufficient stress the affected individual will become overwhelmed and highly aroused. Withdrawal into an isolated, inner world may thus be a useful maneuver against the effects of the person's excessive vigilance towards irrelevant stimuli.[44]

Such a formulation, although still speculative, fits the available information fairly well and allows us to forge a link between biochemical and anatomical abnormalities, on the one hand, and the symptoms of schizophrenia, on the other. It gives us an understanding of how development and environmental stresses may interact with an individual's physiological response pattern to precipitate an episode of schizophrenia.

## The Family

'In my own very self,' wrote D. H. Lawrence in his last work, 'I am part of my family.'[45] Psychiatrists since Sigmund Freud have regarded the family as crucial to the development of human personality and mental disorder. Anti-psychiatrist David Cooper sees Western family life as a form of imperialism crushing individual autonomy.[46] It is to be expected, therefore, that many will have looked to the family for dynamic forces capable of creating schizophrenia.

In 1948 psychoanalyst Frieda Fromm-Reichmann proposed that some mothers fostered schizophrenia in their offspring through cold and distant parenting.[47] Others have pointed to parental schisms and power imbalances within the family as important in the genesis of the illness.[48] The double-bind theory, put forward by anthropologist Gregory Bateson and his colleagues, postulates that schizophrenia is promoted by contradictory parental injunctions from which the child is unable to escape.[49] Existential psychoanalysts R. D. Laing and Aaron Esterton offer a similar formula for

28

the production of schizophrenia through the mystification of the child with confusing patterns of communication.[50]

While enjoying broad public recognition, such theories have seldom been adequately tested. Recent research has claimed to find abnormalities in the patterns of communication within the families of schizophrenics that are not evident in the families of non-schizophrenics.[51] These findings, not confirmed by later research,[52] have been the subject of controversy.[53] None of the work in this area, furthermore, satisfactorily resolves the question of whether the patterns of deviance alluded to in the families of schizophrenics are the *cause* or the *effect* of psychological abnormalities in the psychotic family member.

While there may well be stresses in the rearing of children which could increase vulnerability to schizophrenia, their nature and existence have not yet been verified. One thing only is certain in this field: thousands, if not millions, of family members of Western schizophrenics have suffered shame, guilt and stigma as a consequence of the widespread acceptance of such theorizing. Parents have not only witnessed their child's personality distorted and his or her ambitions destroyed by illness, they have felt blamed, directly or indirectly, for causing the condition. Family members may carry the burden of living with someone whose actions can be unpredictable and distressing and whose emotional responses are unrewarding, but they may also receive little empathy and support from therapists who are liable to censure and distrust them. The reactions of society to the schizophrenic and his or her relatives may be sufficient, of themselves, to produce distorted patterns of family interaction.

**Stress—Domestic and Non-domestic**

If we study the family, not for formative influences building a vulnerability to schizophrenia, however, but for current household stresses influencing the course of an already established illness, a far more clear-cut picture emerges. Schizophrenics returning to relatives (by birth or marriage) who are critical or smothering have a much higher relapse rate, according to British research, than those who return to relatives who are less hostile or intrusive.[54] Further studies have shown that relatives who are less critical and over-involved exert a positive therapeutic effect on the schizophrenic—their presence leading to a reduction in the patient's level of arousal, while the reverse is true for the more stressful relatives.[55] The benefits of a low-stress household on the relapse rate of these schizophrenics appear to be equally as strong as the effect of antipsychotic drug treatment.

There is no indication that the more critical and over-involved relatives are at all abnormal by everyday Western standards. The evidence suggests, in fact, that the families in which schizophrenics do well have adapted to having a psychotic person in the household by becoming unusually low-key and permissive.[56] In the developing world, however, the picture appears to be different. A study conducted in Chandigarh, India, reveals that few relatives of schizophrenics in this Third World city show the same high levels of criticism and overinvolvement found to be common in the West.[57] These Western responses to mentally disordered family members may be a product of emotional isolation engendered by nuclear-family life, or the result of high achievement expectations placed on the psychotic. The decline of extended-family living is largely a consequence of industrialization, and educational and occupational achievement standards are higher in our advanced technological society. Through such family dynamics as these, political economy may affect the course of schizophrenia.

It is also clear that other forms of stress in the lives of schizophrenics trigger psychotic relapse and influence the course of the illness. In a study conducted in London, 46 per cent of a group of schizophrenic patients experienced a stressful life event which was clearly not a consequence of the illness in the three-week period preceding a psychotic relapse. By contrast, only 12 per cent of a matched group from the general population had experienced such stress. The life events noted included role changes (such as leaving school), change of living arrangements, development of illness, and other disappointments and crises. When life events were included which may not have been independent of the individual's own actions or illness (events such as job loss), nearly two-thirds of the schizophrenics reported experiencing such stress compared with less than a fifth of the general population sample.[58]

A similarly well designed study conducted in New Haven, Connecticut, also found a significantly greater incidence of stressful life events in a group of schizophrenics during the period preceding relapse (in this case, one year) when compared with a matched control group.[59]

It is unclear whether stress can create a vulnerability to schizophrenia during an individual's development[60] (levels 1 and 2 of Figure 1.2) but it *is* clear that stresses of various kinds play a part in triggering psychosis in those who are already vulnerable and in shaping the course of a manifest schizophrenic illness (levels 3 and 4 of Figure 1.2). At these later stages—influencing the vulnerable individual and those already schizophrenic —we may also perceive the prominent effects of political and economic forces. Much that is stressful in life is not covered by such concepts as family hostility or recent life changes. We all need to have the respect of others, for example. Finding value and meaning in life and having a sense of belonging to one's own kind and community are omnipresent existential concerns. Problems arising from these concerns commonly emerge in the lives of schizophrenics—problems (it will be argued here) produced or exacerbated by the political and economic dimensions of the society.

The following chapters will attempt to show that political economy assumes a hitherto underemphasized importance in the production and perpetuation of schizophrenia. Specifically, it not only determines mental-health policy and legislation, it also molds public reaction to insanity and even shapes psychiatric ideology. Political and economic factors influence the social status, social role and social integration of the psychotic—his or her sense of worth, meaning and belonging. Just as the destinies of all in society are shaped by political and economic forces, so too is the course and, perhaps, the occurrence of schizophrenia.

## Summary

- Schizophrenia, originally termed dementia praecox, is a functional psychosis with some unifying features but several distinctly different forms.
- In defining dementia praecox, Emil Kraepelin saw poor outcome as a central feature of the condition.
- Although Eugen Bleuler found outcome from the illness to be good in a majority of cases, Kraepelin's original pessimism has been more widely accepted.
- Bleuler's good results may have been a consequence of his enlightened treatment approach.
- Scandinavian psychiatrists have adopted a narrow diagnostic approach to schizophrenia, emphasizing poor outcome.
- Russian psychiatrists use a broad diagnostic concept which includes patients who would not be considered psychotic elsewhere.
- American psychiatry switched from a similarly broad diagnostic approach to a narrow definition of schizophrenia in 1980.
- The course of schizophrenia is quite variable; the outcome can be mild in half the cases.
- The prevalence of schizophrenia varies widely (partly because of diagnostic differences) but it is often close to 1 schizophrenic for every 200 adults in populations in the industrial world.
- Schizophrenia appears to be universally distributed.
- Multiple social and biological factors interact to produce a vulnerability to schizophrenia, to trigger an episode of psychosis and to shape the course of the illness.
- Genetic predisposition contributes to the vulnerability to schizophrenia but does not alone account for its occurrence.
- An overactivity in tracts of neurons in which the neurotransmitter is dopamine may be the underlying biochemical deficit in schizophrenia.
- Some schizophrenics appear to suffer from mild cerebral atrophy.
- The underlying functional deficit in schizophrenia may be an inability to discriminate relevant from irrelevant environmental stimuli.

31

- Theories which suggest that family communication patterns may produce a vulnerability to schizophrenia remain unverified.
- Evidence that family stresses may trigger relapse in schizophrenics, on the other hand, is strong.
- Life-event stress also appears to trigger episodes of schizophrenia.
- Political economy refers to the part of the social structure which regulates labor, energy, production and reproduction in groups larger in size than the family.
- Political and economic factors, it is argued, are important in influencing the course and, possibly, the appearance of schizophrenia.

# 2 Health, Illness and the Economy

How far do economic factors influence our birth and death, control our health, mold our behavior and identity and affect our sanity? We may look for the answer to these questions by two methods—by studying the differences between social classes and by calculating the human effects of fluctuations in the economy.

## Social Class, Illness and Death

Lower-class people in industrial society die younger. This much was clear to the statisticians of the nineteenth century and continues to be true today. In 1842, the average age of death for different classes in various British centers of trade and manufacturing was estimated to be as follows:

|               | GENTRY | TRADESMEN | LABORERS |
|---------------|--------|-----------|----------|
| Bethnal Green | 45     | 26        | 16       |
| Leeds         | 44     | 27        | 19       |
| Liverpool     | 35     | 22        | 15       |
| Manchester    | 38     | 20        | 17       |

The well-to-do classes enjoyed a lease of life more than double that of the working classes.[1] The dramatic difference was largely accounted for by high infant mortality in the poorer classes and by deaths among adults from consumption, pneumonia, infectious diseases and other conditions associated with poverty, malnutrition and overcrowding.[2]

Class differences in life span persist in modern industrial society. According to the British Registrar General's figures, there is a clearly-defined social-class gradient in mortality rates. British working-class citizens run a greater risk of death at all ages. In adults the difference in death rates is apparent over a wide range of causes from malignancy to heart disease. Where the cause of death is accidental or from respiratory or infectious disease, lower-class mortality rates are most dramatically elevated—from 3 to 5 times greater than for the highest social class.[3]

Throughout the Western world there is a similar relationship between social class and life expectancy. In nineteenth-century America, as in Britain, the ratio of the death rates in the highest and lowest classes was around 2:1. By the 1940s the class gap had closed to 1.4:1 or 1.3:1, but in more recent decades no further progress has been made towards narrowing the class difference.[4] The differential is greatest in the middle years of life and includes deaths from stress-related causes. Several studies have shown, for instance, that sudden death from heart attack is more common in people with lower levels of education. Some researchers attribute this finding to the stress of living in or near poverty.[5]

Sickness rates follow the same pattern as mortality. British unskilled working men, aged 45–64, report four times the number of days of acute sickness as men of the same age in professional jobs, and twice the rate of chronic sickness.[6] In the United States illness of all kinds is more common among the poor. Forty-one per cent of all low-income Americans aged 45–64 have a chronic illness which limits their activity—only 14 per cent of high-income Americans are so afflicted.[7] Multiple studies have reported a close association between high blood pressure and lower-class status,[8] and a county-wide survey of risk factors for illness in Florida found socio-economic status to be the social factor most strongly affecting the incidence of psychosomatic illness.[9]

While material factors such as poor nutrition and poor housing contribute to high rates of illness and death in the lower classes, environmental stress is also important. Migration, unemployment, job turnover, divorce and separation are all more common among the poor.[10] A survey of the Toronto Borough of East York found symptoms of physical and emotional distress to be from 3 to 5 times more common among the poorly-educated and low-income residents. The presence of these symptoms, in turn, was found to be associated with the person's exposure to a recent stressful life event, particularly demotion or job loss.[11] Two studies conducted in New Haven, Connecticut, and another carried out in Manhattan, New York City, have yielded similar results—substantially higher levels of psychological symptoms in working-class subjects than in the upper class. The difference in symptom levels in these studies, as in Toronto, was explained by the larger number of unpleasant life events affecting the working-class members. This finding held true (in the New York City study) when only those life events were counted which were independent of the person's own actions—suggesting that it was indeed the stress which precipitated the symptoms and not the psychological disturbance which led to the stressful events.[12]

A large-scale survey of drinking habits among residents of suburban Chicago offers similar evidence of links between social class, stress and symptoms. Low-income residents and those who reported more economic strain were more likely to have symptoms of anxiety. Lower-class members were also more likely to have low self-esteem and a sense of limited personal control over events. Operating together, these three factors—heightened anxiety, low self-esteem and a limited sense of mastery—were found to increase the individual's inclination to use alcohol to relieve distress.[13] Class status may thus mold personality, coping strategies, emotional symptoms, and alcohol use and indirectly influence physical health.

## Social Class and Mental Illness

The evidence is strong that stresses are greater among the lower working class and that increased ill health and emotional distress are, to a certain extent, a consequence of these stresses. It is also clear that schizophrenia and other mental disorders are more common in the lower classes. In the Great Depression sociologists Robert Faris and Warren Dunham found that the highest rates for treated schizophrenia were concentrated in Chicago's slum areas. From a rate of over 7 cases per 1,000 adults in these central districts the prevalence of treated schizophrenia declined gradually through the more prosperous sections of the city to the lowest rates of below 2.5 per 1,000 adults in the most affluent areas.[14] Since the publication of this pioneer work, a number of other epidemiological studies have confirmed that high rates of mental disorder, particularly schizophrenia, are concentrated in centrally-located, low socio-economic districts in many American and European cities—Peoria, Illinois; Kansas City, Missouri; St Louis, Missouri; Milwaukee, Wisconsin; Omaha, Nebraska;[15] Worcester, Massachusetts;[16] Rochester, New York;[17] Baltimore, Maryland;[18] Oslo, Norway;[19] and Bristol, England.[20]

Sociologist Robert Clark demonstrated in the 1940s that Chicago residents in low-status and low-income occupations had a higher incidence of treated schizophrenia than higher-status workers.[21] This observation has also been confirmed by a number of studies. In their survey of New Haven, Connecticut, in the 1950s, August Hollingshead and Frederick Redlich revealed a gradient of progressively greater prevalence of treated schizophrenia in the lower socio-economic classes. The prevalence of the illness was 11 times greater in the lowest class compared with the highest class.[22] Leo Srole and his associates, in a community survey of midtown Manhattan in New York City, which located both treated and untreated cases, found mental disorder to be more common in the lower classes than in the upper classes and more prevalent in those who remained at the same socio-economic level than in the upwardly mobile.[23] Dorothea Leighton and her colleagues, again, found mental disorder to be most frequent in the lowest social class in their comprehensive survey of Stirling County, Nova Scotia.[24] Social psychiatrist Örnulv Ödegard demonstrated that first admissions for schizophrenia to all psychiatric hospitals in Norway were most common among low-status workers, such as ordinary seamen and farm labourers and one-third as

35

frequent among the owners and managers of businesses and others in high-status occupations.[25] In London, Lilli Stein showed that there existed a social-class gradient in the incidence and prevalence of mental illness (with the highest rates in the lowest classes) which was particularly marked for schizophrenia.[26]

## Social Drift or Social Stress?

A reasonable explanation for the social-class gradient in schizophrenia, and one which is commonly given, is that people with the greatest risk of developing the illness drift into lower-status occupations and low-income city areas as a result of their marginal, pre-psychotic levels of functioning. This is known as the social-drift hypothesis. An alternative explanation would be that the stresses of lower-class living, including labor-market stresses, increase the risk of developing schizophrenia. A final, theoretical possibility is that there exists an increased genetic predisposition towards schizophrenia in the lower classes. When we come to look at the prevalence of schizophrenia in the Third World (in Chapter 9), we will find that the relationship between class (and caste) and schizophrenia is reversed. In the developing world it is the *upper*-class, *better*-educated individuals who are more at risk for schizophrenia. As industrialization advances, moreover, this inverted social-class gradient switches around to conform to the pattern found in the West. These phenomena clearly defy explanation by either the social-drift or genetic hypotheses and they invite speculation about possible social and economic causes.

In developing areas of the Third World, the better-educated are more likely to be competing for regular employment in a restricted wage labor market; the lower caste and class members are involved in subsistence activities to a greater extent. The stresses of the labor market, therefore, may account for the inverted class gradient (as we shall see in Chapter 9). In the industrial world, both social drift and social causation could be producing the class gradient for schizophrenia; the two theories are not mutually exclusive. If social drift partly accounts for the relationship, we should expect schizophrenics to be (a) downwardly mobile in occupational status and (b) working in lower-status jobs than their fathers. Sociologist Melvin Kohn, who has reviewed the published research on this topic, argues that neither proposition has been decisively proven. The studies conducted so far offer conflicting results. Dr Kohn concludes:

> The weight of evidence lies against the drift hypothesis providing a sufficient explanation of the class-schizophrenia relationship. In all probability, lower class families produce a disproportionate number of schizophrenics.[27]

The view that schizophrenia may be provoked, even partially, by the stresses of lower-class living, however, is not well accepted by the mainstream of psychiatric writers. Psychiatrist Robert Cancro argues in the American *Comprehensive Textbook of Psychiatry* that such a conclusion is 'premature,' but, he concedes, not yet 'definitively rejected.'[28] In the same textbook, psychiatrist Herbert Weiner contends that 'no simple [causal] relationship between social class and schizophrenia exists.'[29] With such cautious opinions as these, the role of social-class stress is widely discounted in the day-to-day practice of psychiatry. In the light of the information given above on health, mortality and social class, this approach seems blinkered. To accept the conservative view we have to acknowledge, on the one hand, that increased life stresses in the lower classes can account for higher rates of psychological symptoms, stress-related illness and death; but we are obliged to conclude, on the other hand, that these stresses do not contribute to the increased prevalence of another stress-related condition—schizophrenia. Such a conclusion seems implausible.

Why have the findings on social class and schizophrenia had so little impact on psychiatry? American psychiatrists John Strauss and William Carpenter suggest that this neglect

> may . . . reflect the fact that influential research and clinical writing and teaching most often come from persons and institutions with predominantly upper and middle class orientations, while a large number of schizophrenic patients are lower class and unemployed.[30]

To acknowledge the likelihood that social stress provokes the development of schizophrenia is not to deny the possibility that social drift is also important. Indeed, it is not unusual to find schizophrenics who have had marginal levels of social functioning for some years before their first, clear psychotic break. In such cases, downward mobility is unavoidable, and this, in itself, becomes an additional source of stress.

An interesting observation emerges from the research on the social mobility of schizophrenics. While many patients may not show a decline in their occupational status to a level lower than that of their fathers, the occupational level of the general population is sometimes found to have risen around them.[31] Relative to the rest of the population the schizophrenics have lost ground. What is happening, then, is not exactly social *drift* but social *stagnation*. This is what one might expect to see in a group of people who are not high in drive and ambition. For individuals living in some settings this would not be a great weakness. In modern industrial society, however, where to stay at the same level is to lose status, the pre-schizophrenic may be at a disadvantage in comparison to more driven individuals and under greater pressure than he or she would experience in a non-industrial setting.

The link between social class and mental disorders such as schizophrenia, interestingly, has only been conclusively demonstrated for city dwellers. Strongest in large cities, it becomes weaker in smaller cities and most rural areas. In the small town of Hagerstown, Maryland, for example, the prevalence of schizophrenia was not related to social class.[32] Dorothea Leighton and her co-workers did detect a social-class gradient for mental disorder in rural Nova Scotia, but not in rural Sweden.[33] In two British studies, one comparing London women with women in the crofting and fishing community of North Uist in the Outer Hebrides and another comparing women in London with women living in the rural Isle of Wight,[34] the prevalence of mental disorder was found to be highly influenced by class in the urban setting but not at all in the rural communities. On the rural Danish island of Samsö, although mental disorder in general was more frequent among the lower social classes, the prevalence of psychosis in particular was unrelated to class.[35]

The absence of a social-class gradient for schizophrenia for most rural areas can be explained in two ways. Schizophrenics may migrate away from rural areas and become part of the urban under-class. This explanation is a variation of the social-drift hypothesis. Alternatively, the conditions of rural working-class life may be less likely to provoke the onset of schizophrenia than urban lower-class existence. We shall see shortly, when we look at the effects of the business cycle, that there is also a rural-urban difference in the effect of fluctuations in the economy on symptoms of mental disorder just as there is a rural-urban variation in the influence of social class. The rural-urban difference in the effects of economic change cannot be explained by social drift, and if the differential is the result of similar factors in each case (which seems likely), then we must look for real differences in the impact of economic and class-related stress between cities and country towns.

This, then, may be a convenient point to begin to examine the effects of the business cycle on health, illness and mortality.

## Business Cycles

The economy rises and falls with a variety of rhythms. Since the Industrial Revolution, capitalist development has advanced in long phases of growth, interrupted every few decades by great, global depressions marked by industrial stagnation and high rates of unemployment. Each newly-industrialized nation joins in synchrony with the economic pulse of the more developed societies. In Britain, the 'hungry forties' of the last century were followed by the Great Victorian Boom (1850–73). The industrialized economies of Europe and North America all felt the impact of the protracted Great Depression of the late nineteenth century (1873–96) and reeled again in the 1920s and 1930s.[36] (In Europe the great twentieth-century depression began a decade sooner than in the United States.) Faced with this pattern we may be excused for pessimism about the economic outlook for the remainder of the 1980s. Superimposed on the long waves are shorter business cycles of varying amplitude—about two a decade may be identified, for example, in the period since the Second World War.

The social effects of both the long and short business cycles as well as of briefer economic fluctuations have been studied. Researchers have looked for correlations between economic indicators and illness, mortality rates and such social events as marriage, divorce and crime.

As early as 1893, for example, it was noticed that divorce became less common in the depression and more common in the boom.[37] (This phenomenon, which continues to hold true today, may well be a consequence of the greater degree of individual economic independence which becomes possible when more employment—especially women's employment—is available.) By 1901 another researcher identified an increase in marriage rates with periods of prosperity in trade.[38]

More elaborate social studies of the impact of fluctuations in business were carried out in the 1920s. Statisticians William Ogburn and Dorothy Thomas found that the boom brought with it high rates of marriage, divorce, birth, infant mortality and general mortality. Only suicide and (possibly) criminal convictions were found to increase in the depression.[39] A few years later, Dorothy Thomas confirmed these findings (except for divorce and crime) and expanded on them. She noted that beer and spirits consumption, arrests for drunkenness and alcohol-related deaths, all increased in the boom. The only social phenomenon clearly tied to economic recession was suicide.[40]

Recent studies of the business cycle have applied advanced statistical techniques and have concentrated not just on the effects of the boom or bust but also on the impact of *any* economic change, up or down, reasoning that any change can be stressful.

Every week for 16 months from 1971 to 1973, researchers conducted surveys of samples of the population of Kansas City to gather information on recent events in people's lives and to evaluate their mood and stress symptoms. Ralph Catalano and David Dooley subsequently looked for correlations between these survey results and measures of local economic fluctuations. They found that both the local unemployment rate and absolute economic change (up or down) were linked to increases in the number of life events reported by the respondents and to their physical and emotional symptoms of stress. The unemployment rate alone was most closely associated with an increase in reports of depressed mood. The researchers noted that the changes in mood and stress symptoms were sometimes immediate but usually followed the economic change with a lag of 1–3 months.[41] People with low income responded much more severely to economic change than did city residents in the middle-income bracket. The poor, Catalano and Dooley reason,

> have the smallest economic resources with which to cushion any short-term economic setbacks. . . . When the economy improves it may be the low-income group which disproportionately has to pay the psychological price of adapting to new jobs in new locations with new colleagues.[42]

## Rural-Urban Differences

From the large metropolitan area of Kansas City, Catalano and Dooley and their co-workers next turned their attention to small-town Hagerstown, Maryland, and the surrounding rural Washington County. Hagerstown, it will be recalled, was the site of an earlier study which revealed no association between social class and mental illness. At the time of both studies the town population was close to 36,000. For 32 months from 1971 to 1974, the researchers conducted surveys of the small town and rural residents, collecting the same information as in the Kansas City study. The survey of Hagerstown and district, however, revealed none of the associations between economic change, stress and pathology which had been found in Kansas City.[43] The small-town and rural residents appeared to be protected against the psychological impact of both social class and economic change. Why was this so?

The contrast was not due to differences in economic stress, for the local economy of Hagerstown was *less* stable than that of the large city. The difference, report the researchers, may have been a result of the fact that the small-town residents started from a lower baseline of stress. Respondents from the Hagerstown area reported fewer life events and stress symptoms than Kansas City residents, and showed less fluctuation in these variables. The small-town residents, furthermore, may have enjoyed more social support, which acted as a buffer against stress. The Hagerstown residents were more satisfied with their neighborhoods, friendships and marriages than were big-city dwellers, and they were more likely to have multiple social roles beyond marriage and employment.[44] Being an amateur baseball coach or a volunteer fireman, for example, may have minimized the impact of unemployment or demotion.

Another report confirms that rural residents may be protected by social support from some of the health hazards of economic change. Comparing the impact on manufacturing workers of plant closings in two areas—one rural and one urban—Susan Gore found that rural workers enjoyed more social support than urban employees. Unemployed workers who rated their wives, relatives and friends as unsupportive had more severe psychological problems and symptoms of ill-health. They blamed themselves more for being unemployed and felt more economically deprived. Those who feel unsupported, argues Gore, are more dependent on their jobs for self-esteem, and when unemployed they are more likely to lose their sense of worth.[45]

## Boom or Bust?

The early studies of the business cycle, we have seen, implicated the boom in the production of most social pathology, with the one clear exception being suicide. Catalano and Dooley's analysis of short-term economic fluctuations in Kansas City points to absolute economic change (up and down) as a source of stress and stress symptoms and to a link between unemployment and depressed mood. When the news media cite research on the effect of the economy, however, it is always the harmful impact of the depression and deepening unemployment which we hear about—never the boom. Why is this so?

The commonly-cited research which links economic *recession* to multiple social problems is the work of Harvey Brenner, an American statistician. Using complex statistical techniques, Dr Brenner has pursued the hypothesis that the increase in problems during the boom is, in fact, a delayed response to the business decline which precedes it. Thus when the US Congress asked for a report, in 1976, on the *Social Costs of National Economic Policy*, Brenner was able to supply them with a document, more than 200 pages long, which pointed to unemployment as having a profound impact on health and crime.[46] A sustained 1 per cent increase in unemployment, claimed Brenner, has the following effect:

| SOCIAL PHENOMENON | % INCREASE |
|---|---|
| Suicide | 4.1 |
| State mental hospital admissions | 3.4 |
| State prison admissions | 4.0 |
| Homicide | 5.7 |
| Cirrhosis of the liver mortality | 1.9 |
| Cardiovascular-renal disease mortality | 1.9 |
| Total mortality | 1.9 |

These figures have since been widely quoted and widely accepted. But can they be taken at face value? At the crux of this issue is Brenner's heavy reliance on the supposed lag between the initial stress of unemployment and the subsequent appearance of social pathology. Cerebral strokes, for example, are linked to the economic recession, Brenner argues, with a lag of

6–9 years; cardiovascular-renal disease, with a lag of 3–6 years.[47] When the length of the business cycle being studied is only 3–5 years, the use of lags such as these becomes difficult to comprehend. So, too, is a lag of two years behind the recession for arrests for drunkenness.[48] 'The inclusion of a minus one year lag borders on the incredible,' protests epidemiologist Stanislav Kasl about one of Brenner's pieces of research. 'Surely that must undermine and ridicule the investigator's own efforts to suggest unidirectional causal interpretations.'[49]

The problem with Brenner's use of the lag is not merely that a number of absurd and inexplicable correlations is offered (some of the lagged correlations, properly explained, might be reasonable) but that the optimal lag is determined *post hoc* by scanning the data. If a lagged effect is expected, it should be possible to predict in advance roughly what the lag period will be, so that a clear hypothesis may be tested. Brenner does not attempt to do this, however, and little pattern or consistency emerges from the lagged correlations.

Does it matter whether it is the boom or bust which brings more problems? To anyone interested in politics and political theory it does, for it is an issue at the heart of a debate between Marxists and liberals. To the Marxist it is capitalism which is pathogenic; the business cycle is an inherent element of the capitalist economic system—an unavoidable consequence of the production of goods for the market and of the resulting crises of overproduction.[50] The liberal economist sees the business cycle as an unfortunate feature of the industrial economy, but one which can be controlled.[51] He or she favors fiscal and monetary policies which will stimulate the economy and turn away the ugly face of unemployment. Sustained economic growth is seen as feasible and necessary to minimize human suffering. The Marxist does not regard the upsurge in commodity production and consumption and the accompanying mobilization of labor which marks the boom as necessarily beneficent. One cannot imagine even the most liberal wing of the US Congress, however, calling for a report on the harmful social effects of the economic recovery.

Congress, for example, would not be likely to call upon Joseph Eyer. Unlike Brenner, radical social analyst Eyer sees much social pathology and mortality as a direct consequence of the boom. Less than 2 per cent of the death rate in the United States—that for suicide and homicide—he argues, varies directly with unemployment. The general death rate, including such stress-related causes as coronary heart disease, alcoholic cirrhosis and perforated gastric and duodenal ulcers, rises during the boom. Eyer attributes some of the excess mortality of the boom to change in diet, alcohol consumption and cigarette-smoking, but he considers social stress to be the most important cause. Among the stresses of the boom he identifies are social-relationship changes such as rising marriage and divorce rates, fragmentation of the community due to increased migration and such job-related factors as overwork, alienating work processes and industrial disputes. The lag between these stresses and the development of pathology, argues Eyer, pointing to research on the impact of life events, would not be years, as Brenner suggests, but a few days, weeks or months—if the impact were not immediate.[52]

Observing that industrialization brings about an increase in mortality in younger adults at the age of labor-market entry, Eyer sees the development of wage work as central to the disease-producing stresses of our society. He argues, moreover, that the deleterious impact of modern labor conditions may be seen in the high mortality which affects those cohorts of workers who enter the US labor market during the boom to a greater extent than those who enter during the depression.[53]

That this type of cohort analysis may lead to more than one interpretation is evident from economist Alfred Bunn's study of heart-disease mortality in Australia. Bunn traces an epidemic increase in coronary heart disease back to a point source in the Great Depression. Each cohort of Australian citizens born in successive decades experienced a dramatic increase in mortality during the 1930s—an increased risk which was sustained throughout the lives of surviving members of these cohorts. The decline in the death rate from heart disease after 1968—a phenomenon which has not otherwise been adequately explained—is due, Bunn argues, to the eventual death of most of the population who had been of working age during the Great Depression. Immediate and late effects of unemployment and economic stress, suggests Bunn, contribute to heart-disease mortality; the more recent recessions of the early 1960s and late 1970s add their own lesser waves of increased mortality to the parabolic curve of the epidemic initiated by the Great Depression.[54]

To support his case, Bunn offers a correlation analysis of unemployment and annual mortality from coronary heart disease in Australia, similar to Brenner's work with American statistics. Bunn, like Brenner, finds an association between high unemployment rates and mortality, but his analysis is subject to the same criticisms as Brenner's work. The effects appear to be lagged, but inconsistently; the lag varies from zero to five years.[55] Statistical 'detrending' procedures, used by Bunn and Brenner to remove long-term trends in mortality from their analyses, leave only residual variations in mortality to be explained by fluctuations in unemployment. Just what are these 'residual components,' and how important they are is open to question.[56]

Bunn argues that the Australian data do not confirm Joseph Eyer's claim that high mortality is closely related to *low* unemployment and the boom. In testing this hypothesis, however, he does not allow Eyer the possibility of even a slightly lagged effect, such as a year; he tests only for a correlation with zero lag.[57] Brenner, in his more recent work, has looked at the possibility of a connection between the economic upturn and increased mortality and has found, in fact, that such a correlation does exist in the United States. Using fluctuations in income as an indicator, Brenner found that rapid economic growth was as closely correlated with mortality from heart disease and cirrhosis as was unemployment. The effect of economic expansion, moreover, was immediate, while the correlation with unemployment was lagged several years.[58]

Which is more harmful to one's health—the boom or the slump? Both have been incriminated. The case of infant mortality gives us the opportunity to pursue the question further, and to see if prosperity may indeed bring undesired consequences.

## Infant Mortality

Nowhere is the issue of the pathogenic effect of the boom *versus* the bust better illustrated, and nowhere is the question of the use of the lag as a statistical device more central, than when we look at infant mortality. The early studies of the business cycle, as we have seen, found infant deaths to increase in the boom. Predictably, however, when Brenner studied this relationship he found increases in infant mortality to be a response to economic downturn after a lag of varying numbers of years. The death rate of infants aged one month to one year (postneonatal mortality), for example, is said to be related to increases in unemployment with a lag of 3–5 years.[59] Figure 2.1, which is taken from Brenner's article on the topic, illustrates this point. In the figure, percentage changes in postneonatal mortality occurring over five-year intervals are plotted annually for half a century. Brenner has advanced the infant-mortality graph by four years, to match the lag which his statistical analysis reveals, and to show a mirror-image relationship between the lagged graph of infant mortality and an inverted graph of unemployment (i.e., unemployment and lagged infant mortality rise and fall together).

There are problems with this analysis, however. In the first place, if we do away with Brenner's lag and put the graph of postneonatal mortality back where it started, four years later—as in Figure 2.2—we see that there is a respectable fit between the mortality graph and the inverted unemployment rate. In other words, it seems that postneonatal mortality rises when unemployment *falls*. This picture suggests that we should at least look to see if such an inverse correlation is statistically significant—but Brenner does not do so.

In the second place, there is no logical explanation for a four-year lag in postneonatal mortality. Deaths in this age group—one month to one year—are typically related to the immediate environment and are due to such causes as intestinal and respiratory disease, infections and accidents.

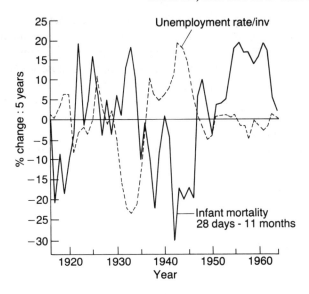

*Figure 2.1    Five-year changes in the US unemployment index (inverted) and the neonatal mortality rate per 1,000 live births. Neonatal mortality is moved forward four years to show the relationship with a four-year lag*

Source: Reproduced from Brenner, M.H.; 'Fetal, infant, and maternal mortality during periods of economic instability,' *International Journal of Health Services*, 3: 145–59, 1973, by permission of the publisher.

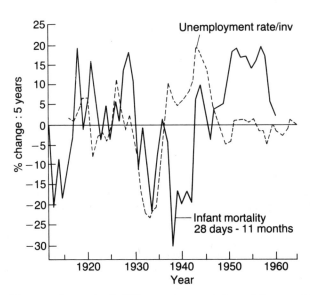

*Figure 2.2    Five-year changes in the US unemployment index and the neonatal mortality rate per 1,000 live births. Neonatal mortality is not lagged*

45

One would predict a lag of no more than a month behind an economic change in most cases. Even if one hypothesized that the infant was at increased risk of death due to economic influences working throughout the mother's pregnancy, then the maximum lag period in those instances would be less than two years. A four-year lag makes no rational sense.

Finally, there exist excellent *a priori* grounds for assuming a direct link between high infant mortality and the boom. Victorian observers were well aware that infant mortality in Britain decreased during crises in trade.[60] Figure 2.3 demonstrates that the contemporary commentators were correct: infant mortality rose and fell with the industrial growth rate through the latter half of the last century.

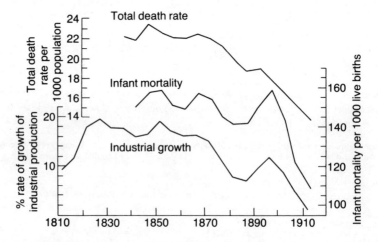

*Figure 2.3   General mortality and infant mortality for England and Wales, and industrial growth for the UK, 1810–1920; expressed as five year averages*

Source of statistics: Mitchell, B.R., *European Historical Statistics 1750–1970*, Abridged edn., New York: Columbia University Press, 1978.

The reason for this effect, maintained the philanthropists and physicians of the time, was the employment of mothers. In the industrial areas of Victorian England a very large proportion of young married women were employed in the factories from dawn to dusk—or longer. Female factory hands returned to work within two weeks of the birth of a child, frequently leaving the infant in the care of elderly childminders or girls as young as seven years of age. Fatal accidents to infants in the care of incompetent minders were not uncommon. Laudanum and other widely-available preparations of morphia were freely used to quiet fractious babies. Early weaning was essential and infants were routinely fed with watered-down and often contaminated milk. Deaths from intestinal infection were prevalent.[61]

46

Physicians pointed out that infant mortality was highest where more women were employed in the factories. Around the Lancashire cotton mills the death rate was particularly high, and the Medical Office of Health for Staffordshire offered the following figures for the 1880s;[62]

| GROUPS OF TOWNS | RATE OF INFANT MORTALITY |
| --- | --- |
| Many women employed | 195 |
| Fewer women employed | 166 |
| Practically no women employed | 152 |

If a correlation exists in modern times between postneonatal mortality and the boom—as appears possible—it may not be a direct consequence any longer of women's employment, but such a hypothesis deserves testing. Child care no longer approximates Victorian conditions and infant mortality is much reduced since those times, but the frequency of breast-feeding might well vary inversely with the employment of mothers and could affect the prevalence of intestinal infections in infants. Such a link opens up the possibility that the drastic slowing of the trend towards lower infant mortality which has occurred in the United States since 1950 may be a consequence of the great postwar increase in the employment of married women. A mechanism of this type would have important public-health implications, but these will not become apparent as long as researchers make the unwarranted assumption that undesirable social phenomena must be traced back to economic decline rather than to economic growth.

*Both* phases of the business cycle may bring problems. This much becomes evident if we return briefly to Brenner's paper on infant mortality. While he unrealistically associates postneonatal mortality and unemployment using a four-year lag, he identifies a much more credible correlation between the death rate for infants less than a month old and the unemployment rate, which requires only a one-year lag.[63] Such deaths in tiny infants, which may often be related to pregnancy factors, could logically be influenced by economic changes occuring months before. Thus, the possibility emerges that early infant mortality may be magnified by economic deprivation and late infant deaths may be affected by the dynamics of the boom. Such an interpretation makes logical sense and moves us further away from overly simplistic assumptions about the nature of the social and economic stresses of modern industrial society.

## Work Stress and Alienation

One source of interest in the debate over the harmful effects of the boom

47

versus the bust is the attempt to evaluate the relative importance of two potential health hazards—the stresses of working and of unemployment. The direct link between the working environment and ill health and death is evident in the statistics on industrial accidents and disease. One estimate reveals that each year in Britain two thousand workers die from an injury sustained on the job, another thousand die from an industrial disease and a million take sick leave because of an industrial illness.[64] Less commonly recognized, women performing housework have a high injury rate, thousands dying in Britain each year as a result of domestic accidents.[65] Not so straightforward to evaluate, however, is the importance of workplace stress in the production of mental and stress-related illness.

We may find evidence of the hazards of work stress in the research on heart attacks. Psychological stress and significant life changes increase the risk of myocardial infarction and sudden cardiac death.[66] A thirty-year follow-up study of healthy Canadian men found that sudden cardiac death was much more common on the first working day of the week. Thirty-five per cent of such deaths in previously healthy men, and 75 per cent of the deaths at work, occurred on a Monday. The researchers point to 'reintroductions to occupational stress, activity or pollutants after a weekend respite' as likely precipitants.[67] A study conducted in the United States similarly has revealed a higher death rate from coronary heart disease on Mondays than on other days of the week.[68]

Pointing to the same source of stress, one study has demonstrated that overwork increases the risk of heart attack in young men more than any of the standard risk factors.[69] Several other pieces of research have shown overtime and increased work load to be correlated with changes in serum cholesterol, cardiac arrhythmias and an elevated frequency of myocardial infarction.[70] American tax accountants, for example, approaching the tax deadline of April 15, show changes in blood-clotting and serum cholesterol which increase their risk of heart attacks and strokes.[71] A study comparing heart-attack victims and a matched control group of healthy people, all of whom were employed in the same Swedish nationwide chain, found that workers suffering heart attacks had experienced many more stressful life events before falling ill—but the events which were more common in the heart-attack victims were all job-related. The stressful events included major changes in working schedule or conditions, undertaking more responsibility at work or having trouble with the boss.[72] The same research group studying members of the Swedish construction workers' trade union found that increased responsibility at work was the only life-change measure among dozens examined which predicted an increased risk of heart attack in this sample.[73]

One important piece of research, the Framingham (Massachusetts) study of risk factors in coronary heart disease, found no correlation between job-related stress and the presence of angina pectoris and other indications of heart disease. This finding may well be due to the fact that all of the heart patients in this study suffered from relatively chronic illness and were heart-attack survivors: sudden-death victims were automatically excluded.[74] On balance, the evidence is strong that the stresses of working are important precipitants of heart attack.

One of the most widely embraced of Karl Marx's theories is his concept of alienation. The concept is well enough accepted, in fact, that the US Senate in 1972, concerned about the apparent spread of job dissatisfaction among workers and the threat of falling productivity, commissioned a study of alienation in the workplace.[75] Illustrated in the popular imagination by the assembly-line worker who is so disgusted and bored that he willfully damages the car on which he is working, Marx's theory of alienation covers this phenomenon and more. Marx described the estrangement of the worker from the creative process and from the product of his or her labors, an alienation from his or her physical and essentially human characteristics, and from his or her fellow human beings. This condition, argued Marx, is the inevitable consequence of commodity production, wage work and the division of labor—a result of converting labor into a commodity.[76]

The experience of working-class men and women offers numerous examples of what Marx meant. Many auto workers despise the cars they build. ' "What'd you buy this piece of shit for?" ' demands a young General Motors worker of author Barbara Garson, kicking her car—a machine he might have helped build himself.[77] The work process may be regarded with derision. ' "There's a lot of variety in the paint shop," ' reports another Lordstown worker. ' "You clip on the color hose, bleed out the old color, and squirt. Clip, bleed, squirt, think; clip, bleed, squirt, yawn; clip, bleed, squirt, scratch your nose." '[78] The boredom can be dehumanizing—' "You forget you're not a machine," '[79] says a copy typist; the close supervision oppressive—a steelworker complains, ' "I would rather work my ass off for eight hours a day with nobody watching me than five minutes with a guy watching me." '[80] Job-status differences estrange co-workers. ' "What is this 'Yes, sir' bullshit?" ' yells the same steelworker at his foreman. ' "I came here to work, I didn't come here to crawl." '[81]

The problems, moreover, are not only to be found in the industrial workplace. Writes Lillian Breslow Rubin:

There is, perhaps, no greater testimony to the deadening and deadly quality of the tasks of the housewife than the fact that so many women find pleasure in working at jobs that by almost any definition would be called alienated labor—low status, low-paying, dead-end work made up of dull, routine tasks; work that often is considered too menial for men who are less educated than these women.[82]

The effort to enforce household labor may distort domestic relations. A working-class husband insists angrily,

> 'A wife's got to learn to be number two. That's the way it is, and that's what she better learn. She's not going to work. She's going to stay home and take care of the family like a wife's supposed to do.'[83]

How widespread is worker alienation? A large majority of workers in many industrialized countries express satisfaction with their work when polled; the size of this majority is always greater in higher-status jobs and older age groups. When asked whether they would prefer another occupation, however, as many as 60 per cent of American workers say yes.[84] Arthur Kornhauser, in his study *Mental Health of the Industrial Worker*, sees the expression of satisfaction with fundamentally unfulfilling jobs as an adaptive response on the part of the workers—a consequence 'of their dwarfed desires and deadened initiative, reduction of their goals and restriction of their efforts to a point where life is relatively empty and only half meaningful.'[85] The extent of alienation, therefore, is hard to measure. Reviewing the research, Marie Jahoda and Harold Rush can only conclude that:

> there exists a stratum of society—its size is hard to determine—of degraded, frustrated, unhappy, psychologically unhealthy people in employment whose personal morale is as low as their productivity, who are unable to provide a constructive environment for their families, [and] whose lack of commitment in employment colours their total life experience.[86]

Can we estimate the psychological impact of alienating work? In his study of Detroit factory workers, Arthur Kornhauser found a clear correlation between the mental health of the worker and the skill of his job. Feelings of inadequacy, anxiety, depression and hostility were greater in those who performed the most routine, repetitive work. These symptoms, Kornhauser demonstrated, were not related to the worker's pre-employment characteristics but were a product of the job itself.[87] More than one study has shown that restricted independence at work is related to poor mental health. A large survey of American men representing a broad range of civilian occupations found low work complexity and close supervision to be associated with the worker's low job satisfaction, low self-esteem and raised level of anxiety.[88] A more recent survey of adults living in Oslo, Norway, extends these findings. The degree of close supervision on the job was found to be correlated with a variety of psychiatric symptoms—a link which was not explained independently by social and demographic factors.[89]

Reviewing the literature widely, Stanislav Kasl concludes that the correlation between measures of mental health and job satisfaction is not a particularly powerful one, though, as we have seen, expressed job satisfaction may not be a good reflection of the actual qualities of the work environment. Kasl finds that the evidence is clearest for the heightened prevalence of mental disorder amongst those performing the most routine, unskilled factory work.[90] For some workers, it is clear, we should not necessarily expect unemployment to be psychologically damaging—it may be a welcome release for those in the most alienating occupations.

## Unemployment

The majority of the research points to serious adverse consequences from unemployment, but there are indications that job loss for some workers under certain circumstances may not be distressing and may even be a positive experience. Blue-collar workers laid off by plant closings showed few lasting psychological or stress-related problems over the two-year period of displacement, unemployment and re-hiring through which they were followed by research workers Stanislav Kasl and Sidney Cobb. The working men in this study generally showed brief, initial responses to stress—increased depression, anxiety and raised blood pressure—most evident during the phase of anticipation prior to unemployment. Kasl suggests that these men showed few damaging effects from unemployment because many had given up the idea that their monotonous jobs were meaningful or important.[91]

Researchers Ramsay Liem and Paula Rayman counter with the suggestion that Kasl and Cobb's findings were undramatic because the unemployment circumstances of the men in their sample were not severe. In his own study of blue-collar and white-collar families in which the husband lost his job, Liem found significant increases in psychiatric symptoms in both the men and their wives and signs of mounting family distress. Symptoms increased as unemployment continued but receded after re-employment. The response to job loss was greater in this sample than in Kasl and Cobb's study, argues Liem, because the period of unemployment was much longer,the local economy was severely depressed and job prospects were poorer. Plant closings such as Kasl and Cobb studied, furthermore, may create a type of unemployment in which self-blame is less prominent.[92]

Liem's interpretation of these findings is borne out by a study of middle-class, unemployed men conducted by sociologist Craig Little. Nearly half of the men in this sample had a somewhat more positive response to unemployment; these were more likely to be the men who were optimistic about re-employment, had not been out of work long and who were in a better financial situation. Kasl's point is also supported, however, since the more positive responses came from men whose prior job satisfaction had been low.[93]

The context in which job loss occurs clearly affects the response of the unemployed. Acknowledging this point, we may also recognize that the consequences of unemployment are usually distinctly harmful. Evidence on the damaging effects of unemployment began to accumulate during the Great Depression. Two researchers reviewing the topic in 1938, after compiling more than a hundred reports, observed that unemployment could lead to emotional instability, depression, hopelessness, distrust, domestic problems, narrowed activities and apathy.[94] More refined modern studies confirm these findings; the introduction of higher levels of financial support for the unemployed does not appear to have reduced the impact of joblessness.

Paula Rayman and Barry Bluestone's study of job loss in the American aircraft industry found unemployment to be linked to serious signs of strain such as alcoholism, raised blood pressure, increased smoking and anxiety.[95] Plant closings in Appalachia brought depression and sickness to the redundant employees.[96] A British study notes increasing general symptomatology in unemployed young men.[97] Older American workers laid off after years of stable employment responded with more ill health than those in a control group, a sense of powerlessness and loss of initiative.[98]

Some studies point to the harmful effects of both job stress and unemployment. The survey of members of the Swedish construction workers' union, mentioned above, found joblessness and dissatisfaction with work to be associated with an increased accident rate; unemployment and changes at work increased the risk of neurosis.[99] In the study of Toronto residents, job loss and demotion at work combined were major risk factors for ill health.[100] We may safely conclude that modern labor dynamics can be unhealthy for both employed and unemployed workers.

## Suicide

Analysis of suicide patterns yields more evidence of the destructive effect of labor dynamics and especially of unemployment. All authorities are agreed that suicide rates peak during economic recessions and have done so throughout the century.[101] The unemployment index is the strongest predictor of changes in the suicide rate, having a substantially greater impact on male suicide rates than on female suicide.[102] One researcher, Albert Pierce, has asserted that suicide statistics show an increase whenever the economy fluctuates up or down,[103] but a later attempt to replicate his work has found unemployment to be more important than absolute economic change.[104] The view of Emile Durkheim, the early French sociologist, that 'fortunate crises ... affect suicide like economic disasters'[105] has not been borne out. His claim, however, that work protects against suicide does appear to be supported by the data.

Throughout the industrial world suicide is more common in the elderly[106] and is higher in retired men than in working men of the same age.[107] The pattern of increasing suicide with age holds true for white Americans; but for blacks and especially American Indians, who experience high levels of unemployment early in life, the suicide rate shows a peak in the young-adult years (see Figure 2.4). The Indian reservations with the highest suicide rates are those with the most severe problems of unemployment, alcoholism and traditional family disintegration.[108] Suicide is more common among those in the lower-income, lower-status jobs where employment is least secure.[109] Economic stress could account for many of these findings, or the absence of a socially-endorsed useful role (in middle-class whites, a problem most common in late life) could be an important precipitant of suicide. That the current picture is a response to changes accompanying the growth of wage work is supported by a study of suicide in Hong Kong. Before industrialization, Chinese suicide was more common in younger adults; industrial development has brought declining prestige, changed roles and a steep rise in suicide to the elderly of the modern city.[110]

The circumstances of individual suicide victims suggest that joblessness, work problems and economic difficulties may all be critical stresses. Studies have generally found around a quarter to a third or more of suicide victims to be unemployed—a substantially higher rate than in the general population or

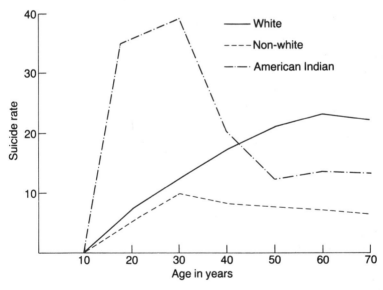

*Figure 2.4    Age-specific suicide rates per 100,000 population for white, American Indian and other non-white groups in the USA, 1969 and 1971 average*

Source of statistics: National Institute of Mental Health, *Suicide, Homicide, and Alcoholism among American Indians*, Washington, DC, Department of Health Education and Welfare, 1973.

53

in control groups.[111] In addition, a pattern of frequent job changes, job dissatisfaction and downward mobility is often uncovered.[112] Which comes first—the emotional problems or the work difficulties? In many cases it is clear that unemployment and job instability is a result of poor physical or mental health;[113] but we should not expect a simple one-way relationship. Impaired performance or loss of work role may well damage self-esteem and increase hopelessness and depression. The central role of the workplace in this relationship for those who are employed is revealed by the repeated finding that suicide (like sudden cardiac death) is most common on Mondays, declining in frequency as the week progresses.[114]

It is clear that the job market and the economy have a direct and decisive impact on our patterns of living, our view of ourselves and our emotions. Since this is so, we might reasonably expect the economy to influence the production of serious mental illness and to affect the rate of admission to psychiatric hospital.

## Mental Hospital Admissions

The first comprehensive attempt to estimate the effect of the economy on mental hospital admissions was Harvey Brenner's *Mental Illness and the Economy*, published in 1973.[115] Earlier researchers had studied the variations in hospital admissions over relatively short periods of time, and some had pointed out that rising admission rates during the Great Depression appeared to correspond to increasing unemployment figures.[116] Brenner's work went a great deal further, however, and is still the most important study of the topic.

Brenner analysed admissions to New York state mental hospitals from the mid-nineteenth century to the late 1960s, looking for correlations with measures of economic activity and employment. From 1910 the data included admissions to public and private hospitals; for the earlier period admissions to one state hospital were examined. Admissions rates regularly increased during economic decline. This relationship was particularly clear for patients with functional psychosis. For schizophrenics from childhood up to the age of around 60 years the relationship was strong, and the finding held true for first admissions and readmissions. The effect of economic change appeared to be more or less immediate; the correlation occurred with no lag but was strengthened by the addition of a (theoretically acceptable) one-year lag.

In select groups of patients the relationship between admission rates and the economy was found to be reversed. Elderly patients with senile brain disease were more commonly admitted during the boom, as were female patients with late-onset involutional psychosis.[117]

Brenner's work on mental hospital admissions has been subject to close scrutiny and has survived the challenge largely undamaged. Statisticians James Marshall and Donna Funch criticized Brenner for his use of statistical detrending procedures and for his failure to make allowances for changes in hospital capacity. Their replication of Brenner's work, taking into account these technical points, essentially confirmed the original findings. The state of the economy, they found, was closely tied to the admission of working-age men and women; but for the young and the aged, hospital capacity was a better predictor of admission rates.[118]

Brenner's principal finding of a link between the recession and mental hospital admissions has since been confirmed by a number of other studies. In Ontario, admissions to a provincial psychiatric hospital for the period from 1960 to 1977 were found to exceed discharges during economic slumps; during the boom the reverse held true.[119] Readmissions to state inpatient and outpatient mental health facilities in Missouri from 1971 to 1979 correlated with the unemployment rate.[120] Community mental health center outpatient admissions in Denver, Colorado, in the 1970s were also linked to the unemployment rate.[121]

What could explain these findings? Brenner examines three theories. Firstly, the tolerance for the dependent mentally ill might decrease as families encounter greater economic stress. The data do not support this hypothesis, for the most dependent—the young and the aged—tend to be hospitalized in the boom and not the recession. It seems likely, in fact, that increased mobility during the boom and expanding exployment opportunities outside of the home for potential care-givers may be stronger factors leading to rejection of the mentally disabled.

A second possibility is that financial destitution may lead patients to seek the shelter of hospital as an almshouse. Again, the explanation is not supported by the statistics. Economically comfortable patients show the same increase in admission rates during the slump as do marginal patients. Admissions to costly private hospitals also increase during recessions—an economic burden rather than a means of support.[122]

We are left with one likely explanation—economic stress and unemployment lead to a true increase in symptoms of psychiatric illness. Much of the research cited in this chapter supports the notion that the economy can lead directly to such changes in psychological symptoms. Why should the impact on hospital admissions occur more in the recession than in the boom? Perhaps because those who are susceptible to serious mental illness are most likely to be functioning marginally on the job and are most likely to be laid off when the economy takes a downturn. The fact that it is principally working-age men and women who show increased hospital admissions during declines in the economy favors this idea. Other research has shown that the admission of unemployed patients and those with job-related difficulties does, in fact, increase during recessions.[123] Overall, we have strong evidence that the production of mental illness increases with each setback in the economy and with the reduction in the call for labor.

Physical and mental diseases, including schizophrenia, are more common in the lower classes and their occurrence fluctuates with the economy. Economic stress, working conditions and unemployment are involved in the creation of this ill health, despair and insanity. In the next chapter we may examine the extent to which the economy and the labor market shape the course of schizophrenia and influence whether it emerges as a benign or a malignant condition.

## Summary

- Illness and death rates are higher in the working classes.
- Stressful life events are more common in the lower classes and contribute to the raised prevalence of stress-related physical and mental illness.
- Mental disorder is concentrated in the lower classes in the industrial world and in the upper castes and classes in the Third World—a pattern which only a theory of social causation can explain.
- Social stress and social drift may operate together to account for the social-class gradient for schizophrenia in urban-industrial areas.
- In large cities, fluctuations in the economy are associated with increased changes in people's lives and with symptoms of psychological distress.
- Residents of rural areas appear to be protected from the adverse effects on physical and mental health of socio-economic status and fluctuations in the economy.
- Early studies of the business cycle found that most social pathology increased in a boom, except suicide which became more common in a slump.
- Research tying social pathology to rising unemployment can often be faulted for over-enthusiastic reliance on the notion of lagged effects.
- Both the stresses of working and unemployment can create significant health hazards.
- Some types of infant mortality may increase in a boom, other types in a recession.
- Work problems, economic stress and unemployment appear to be important in precipitating suicide.
- Mental hospital admissions for working-age people increase in a slump, probably in response to economic and labor-market stresses.

*Part 2*
*The Political Economy of Schizophrenia*

# 3 Recovery from Schizophrenia

Few topics in psychiatry have been researched as frequently over as long a period of time as has recovery from schizophrenia. Ever since Emil Kraepelin focused on the deteriorating course of the illness in defining dementia praecox, psychiatrists throughout the Western world have been interested in comparing the recovery rates of their patients with those of other physicians. More than a hundred long-term outcome studies of schizophrenia have been published in Europe and America during this century and several thousand studies of the short-term effect of different treatment methods have been carried out. Despite this volume of work, however, a clear picture of long-term outcome in schizophrenia has not emerged.

Many researchers have formed the impression that recovery rates in schizophrenia have improved in comparison with earlier times. Their optimistic conclusions have not always been disinterested: often they have attributed the improved outcome to new treatment methods—insulin coma, electro-convulsive therapy and psychosurgery[1] or, more recently, community treatment and the antipsychotic drugs.[2] Heinz Lehmann, an American psychiatrist, writing in a major textbook in 1981, endorses the widespread opinion that modern psychiatric treatment has improved the outlook in schizophrenia. The chances for a favorable outcome from a schizophrenic psychosis, he argues, are four or five times better than they were in the early years of the century. He attributes this change to 'good follow-up therapy and well controlled maintenance drug treatment.'[3] He presents a table of ten follow-up studies of schizophrenia conducted since the 1930s which appear to support his argument and show improving recovery rates.

A number of researchers have arrived at more pessimistic conclusions.[4] Joseph Stephens, a professor of psychiatry at Johns Hopkins University, after reviewing thirty-eight long-term follow-up studies which included data on patients admitted as early as the First World War, remains unimpressed with improvements in recovery rates or the long-term benefits of drug treatment.[5] Swiss psychiatrist, Manfred Bleuler (son of Eugen Bleuler, who coined the term 'schizophrenia') has a particularly interesting perspective. 'During the greater part of my life,' he writes, 'I have lived in hospitals which cared mostly for severe cases of schizophrenia, and from babyhood on through my whole childhood, gravely sick schizophrenics even lived in my parents' family.'[6]

Study of the course of illness in his patients over several decades led him to conclude, in 1968, that little change had occurred in the proportion of patients who deteriorated or who recovered. 'There still exists the sad chronic evolutions to severe chronic conditions, and it is doubtful whether modern therapy has been able much to increase the number of total, life-long recoveries.'[7] The only improvement Manfred Bleuler could detect was a decrease in the severity of chronic schizophrenic deterioration as a result of a reduction in the mishandling and neglect of hospitalized patients that was common earlier in the century. Although not impressed with the results of treatment, Dr Bleuler is less pessimistic about the natural course of the illness. He writes:

> Generations of psychiatrists felt that schizophrenia was a process psychosis progressing to complete deterioration, if life was long enough to allow the process to come to an end. ... I am certain today that the contrary is true.[8]

Dr Bleuler found that many of his chronic patients improved later in life, rather than deteriorating, and that another 25–35 per cent of his schizophrenic patients before the Second World War recovered from their illness after only acute episodes of psychosis.

Which view is correct: that schizophrenia is an inherently catastrophic illness from which only modern psychiatric treatment can afford relief; or that it is a condition with a considerable, spontaneous recovery rate upon which treatment has little long-term effect? The first point of view, without a doubt, is the opinion of the majority of psychiatrists. Taking a deeper look into the storehouse of information on recovery from schizophrenia in the dusty volumes of psychiatric journals going back to the turn of the century may help resolve this issue. If we analyse this material according to time periods that reflect the major changes in the state of the economy, we may also throw some light on another question: to what extent have changes in the economy during the century influenced the outlook for schizophrenics?

## Follow-up Studies

Unfortunately, there are problems involved in comparing the results of the many long-term follow-up studies of schizophrenics. As we have seen in Chapter 1, which patients are labeled schizophrenic varies from country to country, from time to time and from one psychiatrist to another. The patients chosen to be followed may be male or female, adolescent or adult, experiencing their first psychotic break or more chronically ill, or selected by any other criteria the researcher chooses. Any of these factors may affect the course of the psychosis. The patients may be followed for any period of time: one year, ten years or until death. If the illness is progressive, this factor could clearly affect the results. These follow-up studies are obviously not strictly comparable. Any attempt to get useful information from them, then, makes the assumption that the differences between the studies balance out when large numbers of them are collected into groups. If significant changes in outcome are uncovered, it will be necessary to calculate whether the variations may be due to differences in diagnosis, patient characteristics or follow-up methods between the groups.

## Measures of Recovery

One of the crucial variables in these studies is how the psychiatrist chooses to measure the patients' condition at the time of follow-up. The researcher may be most concerned about whether symptoms of the illness are still present but can concentrate on either psychotic features, such as hallucinations or delusions, neurotic symptoms, such as anxiety, or personality defects like withdrawal or eccentric habits. The proportion of patients considered to have recovered will depend on how rigorously recovery is defined. If outcome is measured in terms of social functioning, the investigator may look at any combination of a range of features including the following: working ability, capacity to care for basic needs, abnormal behavior causing distress to others, criminal activity, number of friends, or sexual functioning. Social functioning measures are particularly hard to standardize. A fairly unambiguous measure is whether the patient is in or out of hospital at follow-up; but this is not necessarily, as we shall see, a reliable measure of social functioning.

To impose some consistency on the follow-up results, information has been gathered from studies according to predetermined definitions of terms which have been in use throughout this century:

*Complete recovery:* Loss of psychotic symptoms and return to the pre-illness level of functioning.
*Social recovery:* Economic and residential independence and low social disruption. This means working adequately to provide for oneself and not being dependent on others for basic needs or housing. This term is the one most open to variations in measurement. Since an important part of the definition is employment status we run a risk of tautological reasoning in correlating social recovery with the unemployment rate.
*Hospitalization:* In a psychiatric hospital at the time of follow-up.

Every European and North American follow-up study that was uncovered during a lengthy period of library research and which provided information on one or more of these categories has been included in Table 3.1. The list

## Table 3.1 Recovery and hospitalization rates in 68 outcome studies of schizophrenia

| AUTHORS | COUNTRY | YEARS OF ADMISSION | MEDIAN YEAR OF ADMISSION | FOLLOW-UP YEARS LATER | ORIGINAL COHORT SIZE | NUMBER DEAD AND NOT FOLLOWED-UP | COMPLETE RECOVERY | | | SOCIAL RECOVERY | | | HOSPITALIZED | | | STAGE OR TYPE OF ILLNESS | TREATMENT |
|---|---|---|---|---|---|---|---|---|---|---|---|---|---|---|---|---|---|
| | | | | | | | NUMBER FOLLOWED-UP (+ DEAD) | NUMBER COMPLETELY RECOVERED | % | NUMBER FOLLOWED-UP (+ DEAD) | NUMBER SOCIALLY RECOVERED | % | NUMBER FOLLOWED-UP (+ DEAD) | NUMBER IN HOSPITAL AT FOLLOW-UP | % | | |
| Kraepelin (1919) | Germany | late 1880s | late 1880s | up to 29 or until death | c65 | — | c65 | c12 | 8 | | | | | | | Hebephrenic | |
| Kraepelin (1919) | Germany | late 1880s | late 1880s | up to 29 or until death | c45 | — | c45 | 0 | 0 | | | | | | | Paranoid | |
| Kraepelin (1919) | Germany | late 1880s | late 1880s | up to 29 or until death | c97 | — | c97 | c13 | 13 | | | | | | | Catatonic | |
| Evensen (1904) | Norway | 1888–1897 | 1892 | 5–15 | 182 | 29 | 207 | 25 | 12 | 182 | 27 | 15 | | | | Male, first admission | |
| *1881–1900* | | | | | | *Percentages derived from totals* | | | | | | | | | | | |
| E. Bleuler (1950) | Switzerland | 1898–1905 | 1901 | 3–10 | 515 | 0 | | | | 515 | 307 | 60 | | | | First admission | Early discharge |
| Stearns (1912) | USA | 1901–1905 | 1903 | ? | 395 | 75 | 315 | 16 | 5 | | | | 315 | 202 | 64 | | |
| Rosanoff (1914) | USA | 1907–1908 | 1907 | 5 | 169 | 23 | | | | | | | 169 | 99 | 59 | First admission | |
| Mayer-Gross (1932) | Germany | 1912–1913 | 1912 | 16–17 | 328 | 125 | 294 | 89 | 30 | 294 | 103 | 35 | 294 | 56 | 19 | | |
| Bond (1921) | USA | 1914 | 1914 | 5 | 47 | 3 | 47 | 1 | 2 | 47 | 9 | 19 | 47 | 31 | 66 | Women, mixed duration | |
| Murdoch (1933) | England | 1900–1931 | 1915 | 1–31 | 75 | 11 | 75 | 12 | 16 | | | | | | | Criminal | |
| Müller (1951) | Switzerland | 1917–1918 | 1917 | 5–30 | 100 | 1 | | | | 100 | 28 | 28 | 100 | 33 | 33 | First admission | |
| Rennie (1939) | USA | 1913–1923 | 1918 | 1–26 or until death | 500 | — | 456 | 112 | 25 | 456 | 166 | 36 | 456 | 254 | 56 | Mixed duration | |

| | | | | | | | | | | | | | | | | | |
|---|---|---|---|---|---|---|---|---|---|---|---|---|---|---|---|---|---|
| Strecker & Willey (1927) | USA | prior to 1920 | prior to 1920 | over 5 | 180 | 0 | 180 | 38 | 20 | | | | | | | | |
| Lemke (1935) | Germany | 1918–1923 | 1920 | 15 | 255 | 24 | | | | 126 | 43 | 34 | 126 | 35 | 27 | Male | |
| Freyhan (1955) | USA | 1920 | 1920 | 13 | 100 | 11 | | | | | | | 100 | 65 | 65 | Mixed duration | ECT, insulin coma, psychosurgery, psychotherapy |
| Otto-Martiensen (1921) | Germany | before 1921 | before 1921 | ? | 527 | 98 | | | | 312 | 105 | 34 | 312 | 66 | 21 | | |
| 1901–1920 | | | Percentages derived from totals | | | | 1373 | 268 | 20 | 1850 | 761 | 41 | 1919 | 841 | 44 | | |
| Langfeldt (1939) | Norway | 1926–1929 | 1927 | 7–10 | 100 | 0 | 100 | 17 | 17 | 100 | 21 | 21 | 100 | 46 | 46 | Acute onset | |
| Braatöy (1936) | Norway | 1926–1929 | 1927 | 6–7 | 208 | 15 | 208 | 40 | 19 | 208 | 62 | 30 | 208 | 97 | 47 | First admission | |
| Bond & Braceland (1937) | USA | 1927–1928 | 1927 | 5 | 116 | 10 | 113 | 12 | 11 | | | | | | | Mixed duration | No specific treatment |
| Norton (1961) | England | 1928–1930 | 1929 | 2 | 207 | — | | | | | | | 207 | 122 | 59 | Female, mixed duration | |
| Wooton et al. (1935) | England | 1928–1931 | 1929 | 2–5 | 104 | — | 95 | 18 | 19 | | | | 95 | 64 | 67 | Mixed duration | |
| Fromenty (1937) | France | mid-1920s to mid-1930s | 1930 | up to 15 or until death | 271 | — | 271 | 41 | 15 | | | | | | | Mixed duration | Heavy sedation, 'abcès de fixation' or 'sulfoidol' |
| Cheney & Drewry (1938 | USA | 1926–1935 | 1930 | 1–12 | 500 | 50 | 452 | 51 | 11 | 452 | 112 | 25 | 452 | 197 | 44 | Mixed duration | No specific treatment |
| Hunt et al. (1938) | USA | 1927–1934 | 1930 | 3½–10½ | 677 | 69 | 604 | 82 | 14 | | | | | | | First admission | |
| Rupp & Fletcher (1940) | USA | 1929–1934 | 1931 | 4½–10 | 641 | 89 | 608 | 40 | 7 | 608 | 133 | 22 | 608 | 343 | 56 | First admission | |
| Horwitz & Kleiman (1936) | USA | 1930–1933 | 1931 | 1–3 | 193 | 8 | 170 | 9 | 5 | | | | 170 | 89 | 52 | | Radiothermy $CO_2$ & $O_2$, and psycho-therapy |
| Gerloff (1936) | Germany | 1925–1939 | 1932 | 7–11 | 382 | 52 | | | | 341 | 113 | 33 | | | | | |
| Malamud & Render (1939) | USA | 1929–1936 | 1933 | 2–9 | 344 | 21 | 309 | 53 | 17 | 309 | 94 | 30 | 309 | 155 | 50 | Mixed duration | Psycho-therapy or social re-adjustment |

# Table 3.1 (continued)

| AUTHORS | COUNTRY | YEARS OF ADMISSION | MEDIAN YEAR OF ADMISSION | FOLLOW-UP YEARS LATER | ORIGINAL COHORT SIZE | NUMBER DEAD AND NOT FOLLOWED-UP | COMPLETE RECOVERY NUMBER FOLLOWED-UP (+DEAD) | COMPLETE RECOVERY NUMBER COMPLETELY RECOVERED | % | SOCIAL RECOVERY NUMBER FOLLOWED-UP (+DEAD) | SOCIAL RECOVERY NUMBER SOCIALLY RECOVERED | % | HOSPITALIZED NUMBER FOLLOWED-UP (+DEAD) | HOSPITALIZED NUMBER IN HOSPITAL AT FOLLOW-UP | % | STAGE OR TYPE OF ILLNESS | TREATMENT |
|---|---|---|---|---|---|---|---|---|---|---|---|---|---|---|---|---|---|
| Müller (1951) | Switzerland | 1933 | 1933 | 5–18 or until death | 100 | 5 | | | | 100 | 38 | 38 | 100 | 28 | 28 | First admission | |
| Stalker (1939) | Scotland | 1932–1937 | 1934 | 1–6 | 133 | 0 | 129 | 15 | 12 | 129 | 26 | 20 | 129 | 91 | 71 | First admission | 'Ordinary' methods |
| Fröshaug & Ytrehus (1963) | Norway | 1933–1935 | 1934 | 6–8 | 95 | 3 | | | | 87 | 16 | 18 | 87 | 32 | 37 | First admission | |
| Briner (1939) | Germany | 1933–1936 | 1934 | 2–5 | 267 | 37 | | | | 245 | 111 | 45 | 245 | 64 | 26 | Early | Continuous narcosis or early discharge |
| Romano & Ebaugh (1938) | USA | 1933–1936 | 1934 | 1–4 | 600 | 46 | 442 | 1 | 0 | 442 | 152 | 34 | 442 | 247 | 56 | Mixed duration | |
| Guttman et al. (1939) | England | 1934–1935 | 1934 | 3–4 | 188 | 7 | 184 | 42 | 23 | 184 | 67 | 36 | 184 | 77 | 42 | Early | No drastic treatment |
| Norton (1961) | England | 1934–1936 | 1935 | 2 | 224 | — | | | | | | | 224 | 141 | 63 | Female, mixed duration | |
| Beck (1968) | Canada | 1930–1942 | 1936 | 25–35 | 84 | 0 | 84 | 6 | 7 | 84 | 11 | 13 | 84 | 54 | 64 | First admission | No insulin coma, ECT or psychotherapy |
| Carter (1942) | England | 1935–1937 | 1936 | 3 | 47 | — | 47 | 10 | 21 | 47 | 14 | 30 | | | | Adolescent | No specific treatment |
| Tsuang et al. (1979) | USA | 1934–1944 | 1939 | 30–40 or until death | 200 | — | 186 | 38 | 20 | 186 | 65 | 35 | 186 | 33 | 18 | Mixed duration | |
| Errera (1957) | USA | 1932–1948 | 1940 | 8–24 | 59 | 2 | | | | 54 | 14 | 26 | 54 | 13 | 24 | Ages 15 to 21 | |
| Johanson (1958) | Sweden | 1938–1942 | 1940 | 10–18 | 100 | 16 | 98 | 1 | 1 | 98 | 8 | 8 | | | | Males, first admission | No treatment or lobotomy |
| Freyhan (1955) | USA | 1940 | 1940 | 13 | 100 | 4 | | | | 100 | | | 100 | 42 | 42 | | |
| 1971–1940 | | | | | | | 4100 | 476 | 12 | 3674 | 1057 | 29 | 3084 | 1035 | 49 | | |

Percentages derived from totals

| Reference | Country | Period | Pub. year | Duration (years) | | | | | | | | | | | | Notes | No 'modern' therapies |
|---|---|---|---|---|---|---|---|---|---|---|---|---|---|---|---|---|---|
| Hastings (1958) | USA | 1938–1944 | 1941 | 6–12 | 251 | 9 | 247 | 68 | 28 | 247 | 103 | 42 | | | | Mixed duration | |
| M. Bleuler (1978) | Switzerland | 1942–1943 | 1942 | 20–23 or until death | 208 | — | 208 | 30 | 14 | 208 | 64 | 31 | 208 | 93 | 45 | Mixed duration | |
| Masterson (1956) | USA | 1936–1950 | 1943 | 5–19 | 83 | — | 83 | 15 | 18 | 83 | 27 | 33 | | | | Adolescent | |
| Holmboe & Astrup (1957) | Norway | 1938–1950 | 1944 | 6–18 | 255 | 0 | 255 | 97 | 38 | 255 | 147 | 58 | 255 | 89 | 35 | First admission, acute onset | ECT, insulin coma, and psycho-surgery |
| Astrup et al. (1963) | Norway | 1938–1950 | 1944 | 5–22 | 721 | 32 | 696 | 131 | 19 | 696 | 248 | 36 | 555 | 118 | 21 | Non-acute | ECT, insulin coma, and psycho-surgery |
| Eitinger et al. (1958) | Norway | 1940–1949 | 1944 | 5–15 | 154 | — | 154 | 18 | 12 | 154 | | | | | | | ECT, insulin coma, and lobotomy |
| Harris et al. (1956) | England | 1945–1968 | 1946 | 5 | 126 | 2 | 125 | 37 | 30 | 125 | 61 | 49 | 125 | 42 | 34 | Mixed duration | Insulin coma |
| Vaillant & Funkenstein (1966) | USA | 1948–1950 | 1949 | 2–14 or until death | 72 | — | 70 | | | 70 | 19 | 26 | 70 | 17 | 23 | Mixed duration | ECT, insulin coma |
| Leiberman et al. (1957) | England | 1948–1950 | 1949 | 3 | 156 | 2 | 154 | 49 | 32 | 154 | 85 | 55 | 154 | 44 | 29 | First admission, early | ECT, insulin coma |
| Norton (1961) | England | 1949–1950 | 1949 | 2 | 145 | — | | | | | | | 145 | 53 | 37 | Female, mixed duration | |
| Niskanen & Achté (1971) | Finland | 1950 | 1950 | 5 | 100 | 4 | 100 | 30 | 30 | 100 | 59 | 59 | 100 | 22 | 22 | First admission | |
| Huber et al. (1975) | Germany | 1945–1959 | 1952 | 22 | 502 | — | 502 | 111 | 22 | 502 | 281 | 56 | 502 | 67 | 13 | | |
| Kelly & Sargant (1965) | England | 1950–1955 | 1952 | 2 | 39 | 2 | 39 | 14 | 36 | 39 | 18 | 46 | 39 | 12 | 31 | Selected | Insulin coma |
| Stephens (1970) | USA | 1948–1958 | 1953 | 5–16 | 472 | 17 | 383 | 97 | 25 | | | | | | | First admission | |
| Norton (1961) | England | 1953 | 1953 | 2 | 129 | — | | | | | | | 129 | 26 | 20 | Female, mixed admission | |
| Ackner & Oldham (1962) | England | c1954 | 1954 | 3 | 66 | — | 66 | 27 | 41 | 66 | 38 | 58 | 66 | 14 | 21 | Early | Insulin and barbiturate coma |

# Table 3.1 (continued)

| AUTHORS | COUNTRY | YEARS OF ADMISSION | MEDIAN YEAR OF ADMISSION | FOLLOW-UP YEARS LATER | ORIGINAL COHORT SIZE | NUMBER DEAD AND NOT FOLLOWED-UP | COMPLETE RECOVERY | | | SOCIAL RECOVERY | | | HOSPITALIZED | | | STAGE OR TYPE OF ILLNESS | TREATMENT |
|---|---|---|---|---|---|---|---|---|---|---|---|---|---|---|---|---|---|
| | | | | | | | NUMBER FOLLOWED-UP (+ DEAD) | NUMBER COMPLETELY RECOVERED | % | NUMBER FOLLOWED-UP (+ DEAD) | NUMBER SOCIALLY RECOVERED | % | NUMBER FOLLOWED-UP (+ DEAD) | NUMBER IN HOSPITAL AT FOLLOW-UP | % | | |
| Astrup & Noreik (1966) | Norway | 1951–1957 | 1954 | 5–12 or until death | 273 | — | 273 | 16 | 6 | 273 | 92 | 34 | | | | First admission | ECT, insulin coma, leucotomy and psychotropic drugs |
| 1941–1955 | | | Percentages derived from totals | | | | 3285 | 740 | 23 | 2818 | 1242 | 44 | 2348 | 597 | 25 | | |
| Brown et al. (1966) | England | 1956 | 1956 | 5 | 111 | 3 | 88 | 32 | 36 | 97 | 53 | 55 | 88 | 11 | 12 | First admission | Phenothiazines |
| Brown et al. (1966) | England | 1956 | 1956 | 5 | 228 | 6 | 173 | 32 | 18 | 205 | 79 | 39 | 173 | 47 | 27 | Previous admissions | Phenothiazines |
| Fröshaug & Yrrehus (1963) | Norway | 1953–1959 | 1956 | 3–8 | 103 | 5 | 97 | 23 | 24 | 97 | 35 | 36 | 97 | 17 | 18 | Female, first admission | Phenothiazines |
| [a]Wirt & Simon (1959) | USA | c1956 | 1956 | 1 | 80 | 0 | 79 | 7 | 9 | 79 | 29 | 37 | 79 | 20 | 25 | First admission | Chlorpromazine, reserpine, ECT, insulin coma and psychotherapy |
| Henisz (1966) | Poland | 1956 | 1956 | 7 | 249 | 22 | 230 | 30 | 13 | 230 | 73 | 32 | | | | Early | Chlorpromazine, ECT and insulin coma |
| Mandelbrote & Folkard (1961) | England | 1956–1958 | 1957 | 2–4 | 288 | 8 | | | | 230 | 96 | 42 | 288 | 51 | 18 | Mixed duration | |
| Kelly & Sargant (1965) | England | 1956–1958 | 1957 | 2 | 39 | 0 | 39 | 12 | 31 | 39 | 24 | 61 | 39 | 2 | 5 | Selected | |
| Norton (1961) | England | 1957 | 1957 | 2 | 189 | — | | | | | | | 189 | 19 | 10 | Female, mixed duration | Phenothiazines |
| Cole et al. (1963) | USA | 1957–1959 | 1958 | 3 | 110 | 0 | | | | 108 | 47 | 43 | | | | Male, mixed duration | |

| Author (year) | Country | Period | Year | | | | | | | | | | | | | Admission | Treatment |
|---|---|---|---|---|---|---|---|---|---|---|---|---|---|---|---|---|---|
| … (1966) | | | 1960 | | | | | | | | | | | | | admission, mixed duration | psychotic drugs, ECT and psycho-therapy |
| Kelly & Sargant (1965) | England | 1958–1961 | 1959 | 2 | 45 | 0 | 44 | 14 | 32 | 44 | 32 | 73 | 44 | 3 | 7 | Selected | Phenothiazines |
| Holmboe et al. (1968) | Norway | 1958–1961 | 1959 | 5–7 | 169 | 0 | 169 | 12 | 7 | 169 | 35 | 21 | | | | First admission | Anti-psychotic drugs |
| Niskanen & Achté (1971) | Finland | 1960 | 1960 | 5 | 100 | 5 | 100 | 29 | 29 | 100 | 68 | 68 | 100 | 14 | 14 | First admission | Hospital and community treatment |
| Leyberg (1965) | England | 1960 | 1960 | 3 | 81 | | 81 | 18 | 26 | 81 | 26 | 32 | 81 | 14 | 17 | Mixed duration | Anti-psychotic drugs and psycho-therapy |
| Holmboe et al. (1968) | Norway | 1959–1962 | 1960 | 5–8 | 42 | 0 | 42 | 6 | 14 | 42 | 15 | 36 | | | | First admission | Phenothiazines and psycho-therapy |
| Levenstein et al. (1966) | USA | 1959–1961 | 1960 | 2 | 77 | 1 | 77 | 9 | 12 | 77 | 30 | 34 | | | | Selected | Phenothiazines, ECT and insulin therapy |
| Vaillant et al. (1964) | USA | 1961–1962 | 1961 | 1–2 | 103 | 0 | 100 | 25 | 25 | 100 | 64 | 64 | 100 | 13 | 13 | Mixed duration | Anti-psychotic drugs and ECT |
| Kelly & Sargant (1965) | England | 1960–1963 | 1961 | 2 | 48 | 0 | 48 | 24 | 48 | 48 | 32 | 67 | 48 | 4 | 8 | Selected, mixed duration | Anti-psychotic drugs |
| Hall et al. (1966) | USA | 1961–1962 | 1961 | 1 | 188 | 0 | 188 | c38 | 20 | 188 | 72 | 38 | | | | Acute, first admission | Anti-psychotic drugs |
| Bland et al. (1978) | Canada | 1963 | 1963 | 11–12 | 92 | 0 | 88 | 29 | 33 | 88 | 61 | 69 | | | | First admission | |
| Bland & Orn (1978) | Canada | 1963 | 1963 | 14 | 45 | 2 | 43 | 7 | 16 | 43 | 27 | 63 | 43 | 2 | 5 | First admission | |
| Niskanen & Achté (1971) | Finland | 1965 | 1965 | 5 | 100 | 6 | 100 | 21 | 21 | 100 | 64 | 64 | 100 | 10 | 10 | First admission | |

# Table 3.1 (continued)

| AUTHORS | COUNTRY | YEARS OF ADMISSION | MEDIAN YEAR OF ADMISSION | FOLLOW-UP YEARS LATER | ORIGINAL NUMBER COHORT SIZE | NUMBER DEAD AND NOT FOLLOWED-UP | COMPLETE RECOVERY | | | SOCIAL RECOVERY | | | HOSPITALIZED | | | STAGE OR TYPE OF ILLNESS | TREATMENT |
|---|---|---|---|---|---|---|---|---|---|---|---|---|---|---|---|---|---|
| | | | | | | | NUMBER FOLLOWED-UP (+ DEAD) | NUMBER COMPLETELY RECOVERED | % | NUMBER FOLLOWED-UP (+ DEAD) | NUMBER SOCIALLY RECOVERED | % | NUMBER FOLLOWED-UP (+ DEAD) | NUMBER IN HOSPITAL AT FOLLOW-UP | % | | |
| Cottman & Mezey (1976) | England | 1964–1968 | 1966 | 4–9 | 56 | 1 | 42 | 22 | 52 | 42 | 34 | 81 | 42 | 2 | 5 | First admission | Phenothiazines and community care |
| W.H.O. (1979) | Denmark | 1968–1969 | 1968 | 2 | 48 | — | 48 | 5 | 10 | | | | | | | Mixed duration | |
| W.H.O. (1979) | England | 1968–1969 | 1968 | 2 | 57 | — | 57 | 20 | 35 | | | | | | | Mixed duration | |
| W.H.O. (1979) | USA | 1968–1969 | 1968 | 2 | 38 | — | 38 | 8 | 21 | | | | | | | Mixed duration | |
| W.H.O. (1979) | Czecho-slovakia | 1968–1969 | 1968 | 2 | 53 | — | 53 | 14 | 26 | | | | | | | Mixed duration | |
| Harrow et al. (1978) | USA | after 1970 | after 1970 | 2–3 | 79 | 4 | 79 | 13 | 16 | 79 | 33 | 42 | 79 | 14 | 18 | Acute and chronic | Phenothiazines and psycho-therapy |
| Johnstone et al. (1979) | England | before 1978 | before 1978 | 1 | 45 | 1 | | | | 43 | 15 | 35 | | | | Acute | |
| 1956–present | | | | | | | 2165 | 466 | 22 | 2382 | 1064 | 45 | 1652 | 249 | 15 | | |
| | | | Percentages derived from totals | | | | | | | | | | | | | | |

Note: [a] Year of admission unclear: study included in this section as phenothiazine was used.

68

is certainly not complete: the German literature alone probably contains a great many more suitable studies. The sixty-eight studies which are included, however, form a more comprehensive survey that has previously been made: most importantly they give us a good deal of information about recovery rates for patients admitted in every decade since the turn of the century.[9]

Recovery rates during various time periods were figured by the simple method of adding all patients who achieved each level of recovery in one time period and calculating what percentage they formed of the total group of patients followed up in that period. A point of detail: patients who were dead at the time of follow-up, and for whom there was no information about the state of their illness when they died, could either have been included in the analysis or excluded. In this survey they were included in the total of patients followed up, but, of course, they never contributed to the proportion of recoveries. This tends to reduce the calculated recovery rates for the earlier decades of the century, when institutional death rates were substantially higher, and makes the test of the theory that outcome from schizophrenia was good during those years more severe.

## Periods of Analysis

Each study was assigned to a time period according to the median date of admission of the group of patients. Unavoidably, several patient groups were admitted during one time period and followed up in another. Assigning the group to the earlier time assumes that the conditions in force earlier in the illness are more important in shaping the ultimate course. This limitation suggests, however, that the trends in recovery rates should be analysed only over rather long periods of time.

The periods of analysis selected were as follows.

*1881–1900:* The Great Depression of the late nineteenth century (1873 to 1896 in Britain) ran through most of this period and was a time of severe unemployment throughout the industrial world. Mental institutions were overcrowded and, particularly in Germany, barren and coercive.[10] An aura of pessimism pervaded psychiatry. Kraepelin's patients were admitted at this time, and since only one other study is available for the period, these results are not included in the formal analysis.

*1901–1920:* The period was characterized by improving employment and included the First World War. More active psychiatric treatment methods were established and, in the United States, the mental hygiene movement developed.

*1921–1940:* This was a time of severe economic depression, beginning several years earlier in Europe than in the United States, with unemployment rising to around a quarter of the work force throughout the industrial world.

69

Electro-convulsive therapy, insulin coma and psychosurgery were introduced in the treatment of psychosis.

*1941–1955:* This period saw the Second World War and, particularly in Northern Europe, postwar full employment. A postwar social revolution in psychiatric treatment occurred in Northern Europe, resulting in increased rehabilitative efforts for psychotic patients.

*1956 onwards:* Declining employment and 'stagflation' characterized the economies in most industrial countries. The neuroleptic drugs were introduced into widespread use at the beginning of this period and US community mental health centers began to be established in the mid-1960s.

## Results

The results of the analysis are shown in Figure 3.1. Average figures for unemployment in the United States and the United Kingdom for each time period are also drawn in (inverted) to allow comparison.[11] The figures from the two outcome studies on patients admitted before 1901 are sketched in dotted lines to emphasize that they are not reliable but merely indicative of the general trend.

The picture which emerges is in conflict with some widely held beliefs in psychiatry. In the first place, *recovery rates from schizophrenia are not significantly better now than they were during the first two decades of the century.* The arrival of the antipsychotic drugs shortly before 1955 appears to have had little effect on long-term outcome. Complete recovery rates remain around 20–25 per cent and about 40–45 per cent of schizophrenics are socially recovered at follow-up.

Second, *the state of the economy appears to be linked to outcome in schizophrenia.* During the Great Depression of the 1920s and 1930s, the rate of complete recovery was halved at 12 per cent; social recovery fell to less than 30 per cent. An analysis of variance shows that these changes are greater than would be expected by chance. The little information available for patients admitted during the Great Depression of the late nineteenth century shows the same trend toward low recovery rates. The statistical correlation between changes in the recovery rates and US and UK average unemployment after 1900 (see Table 3.2) is high, but as we are comparing only four periods we should not attach too much significance to this statistic. The more important finding is the variation of complete, symptomatic recovery with unemployment: social recovery may fluctuate with the economy merely because it is itself partly a measure of patient employment. These variations in recovery rates now allow us to explain the conflicting opinions of how outcome in schizophrenia has changed during the century. If we contrast recent rates of recovery with results from the Great Depression of the 1930s or with Kraepelin's figures for patients admitted in

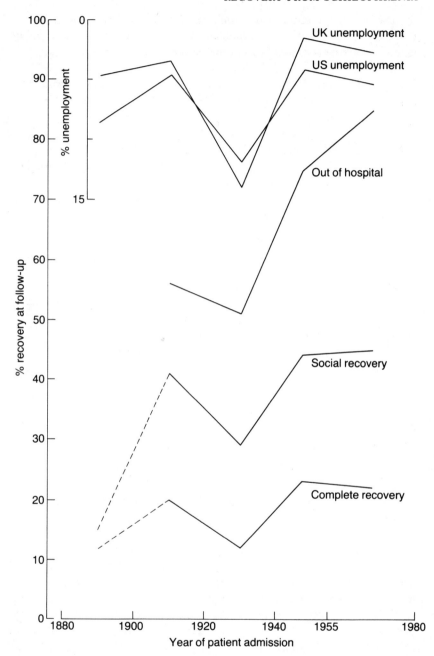

*Figure 3.1   Outcome from schizophrenia in Europe and North America as reflected in 68 studies, and average unemployment (inverted) for the USA and UK for the same time periods*

the 1880s then modern outcome will appear superior. On the other hand, if we include recovery statistics from the two decades between the depressions, recent results do not benefit from the comparison.

**Table 3.2 Correlation of recovery rates in schizophrenia with average unemployment rates in the USA and UK during four periods of the twentieth century**

| ADMISSION PERIOD | COMPLETE RECOVERY % | SOCIAL RECOVERY % | US UNEMPLOYMENT % | UK UNEMPLOYMENT % |
|---|---|---|---|---|
| 1901–20 | 20 | 41 | 4.7 | 3.5 |
| 1921–40 | 12 | 29 | 11.9 | 14.0 |
| 1941–55 | 23 | 44 | 4.1 | 1.5 |
| 1956–present | 22 | 45 | 5.4 | 2.7 |

PEARSON'S CORRELATION COEFFICIENT

|  | US unemployment | | UK unemployment | |
|---|---|---|---|---|
|  | $r$ | $\alpha$ | $r$ | $\alpha$ |
| Complete recovery | 0.97 | 0.05 | 0.99 | 0.01 |
| Social recovery | 0.95 | 0.05 | 0.98 | 0.05 |

Finally, it is clear that *schizophrenics experienced the impact of deinstitutionalization before the antipsychotic drugs were brought into use.* The claim which is commonly heard, particularly in the United States, that the antipsychotic drugs made community treatment of schizophrenics possible is brought into dispute. The proportion of schizophrenics out of hospital at follow-up increased significantly from around 50 or 55 per cent before 1940 to more than 70 per cent in the immediate postwar period. After the antipsychotic drugs were introduced, the proportion of patients out of hospital continued to increase to 85 per cent. One point stands out with regard to this trend towards community treatment; whereas the decrease in hospital use in the postwar years before 1955 was associated with an improvement in the recovery rates of schizophrenics, after the advent of drug treatment deinstitutionalization did not bring any improvement in the symptoms or social functioning of these patients.

Despite the popular view in psychiatry, the antipsychotic drugs have proved to be a critical factor in neither emptying mental hospitals nor achieving modern recovery rates in schizophrenia. Other probable causes of the deinstitutionalization movement will be presented in Chapter 4, and political, economic and social explanations for the variations in recovery from schizophrenia will be offered in Chapters 5, 6, 7 and 8. The reasons for the poor showing of the antipsychotic drugs will be discussed in Chapter 10. It will be argued that, rather than psychiatric treatment having a big impact on schizophrenia, both the course of the illness and the development of psychiatry itself are governed by political economy.

Before going on to this analysis, however, we should see if there are reasons to doubt the accuracy of the findings of the survey of outcome studies of schizophrenia.

## Differences in Diagnosis

Could differences in the diagnosis of schizophrenia between one country or one time period and another have produced these results? We know, for example, that Scandinavian psychiatrists have a narrow concept of schizophrenia which excludes brief illnesses and emphasizes poor outcome. American psychiatry, on the other hand has, until recently, employed a broad concept of schizophrenia, which included much of what European psychiatrists call manic-depressive illness and also some conditions which would not be considered psychoses elsewhere (see Chapter 1). If the sample of outcome studies included proportionally more Scandinavian studies and fewer American studies during the Great Depression, then this bias might account for the low recovery rates found for that time period. As Table 3.3 shows, however, this is not the case. In fact the largest proportion of Scandinavian studies in the survey appears during the period 1941–55, when the overall outcome was best; and the largest proportion of American studies comes during the Great Depression, when outcome was worse. These variations, theoretically, would tend to minimize the changes in outcome which were found, not inflate them.

If the studies for the three geographic areas, Great Britain, the United States and Scandinavia, are plotted separately, as in Figure 3.2, we find that recovery rates are, in fact, worse in Scandinavia and better in Britain. If there were a large proportion of British studies during the period 1941–55, this might account for the good outcome noted at that time. Again, this is not the case. The largest proportion of British studies happens to be in the most recent time period—a variation which should have biased the results in favour of antipsychotic drug treatment. It is true that there were no Scandinavian studies included for the years before 1921, and this fact may have boosted the outcome results for those early decades, but this bias

73

Table 3.3 Recovery rates in the USA, Scandinavia and Britain in 68 outcome studies of schizophrenia. The proportion of total subjects from all countries in each time period upon which the regional recovery rate is based is also shown

| | 1901–20 | | 1921–40 | | 1941–55 | | 1956–PRESENT | |
|---|---|---|---|---|---|---|---|---|
| | RECOVERY RATE % | PROPORTION OF TOTAL GROUP % | RECOVERY RATE % | PROPORTION OF TOTAL GROUP % | RECOVERY RATE % | PROPORTION OF TOTAL GROUP % | RECOVERY RATE % | PROPORTION OF TOTAL GROUP % |
| *USA* | | | | | | | | |
| Complete recovery | 17 | 73 | 10 | 70 | 25 | 22 | 18 | 26 |
| Social recovery | 35 | 27 | 28 | 56 | 37 | 14 | 44 | 26 |
| *Scandinavia* | | | | | | | | |
| Complete recovery | — | 0 | 14 | 10 | 20 | 45 | 17 | 26 |
| Social recovery | — | 0 | 22 | 13 | 41 | 47 | 43 | 21 |
| *Britain* | | | | | | | | |
| Complete recovery | 16 | 5 | 19 | 11 | 33 | 12 | 30 | 29 |
| Social recovery | — | 0 | 30 | 10 | 53 | 14 | 47 | 37 |

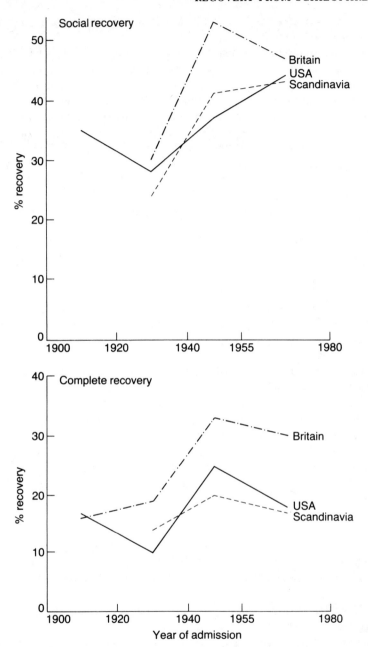

*Figure 3.2 Recovery rates in schizophrenia as shown by studies from Britain, USA and Scandinavia*

should, in theory, have been offset by the small proportion of British studies during the same period.

The most important conclusion to draw from Figure 3.2, however, is that, with some minor exceptions, the same overall pattern of poor outcome in the depression and higher recovery rates during the boom is shown in all three areas. The pattern is not demonstrated for Britain and Scandinavia before 1921, as there is only one British study for that period and none from Scandinavia, but the subsequent relationship to economic fluctuations and the lack of improvement with the arrival of the antipsychotics is clear. Social recovery rates do not appear to have improved as much in the United States immediately after the Second World War as they did in the European countries: this could well be a reflection of the fact that the postwar social psychiatry revolution occurred several years earlier in Northern Europe than it did in the United States.

Diagnostic differences from country to country, then, probably do not account for the observed results. Could the findings be an artefact of changes in diagnostic habits over time? One important historical change was Eugen Bleuler's conception of schizophrenia, introduced in 1911, which attempted to escape Kraepelin's emphasis on inevitable deterioration as a central feature of the illness. Bias from this source is averted in the survey of outcome studies by beginning the formal analysis with Eugen Bleuler's own patients.

Another important historical factor has been the changing American diagnosis of schizophrenia. The broadening of the US concept of schizophrenia may have become most evident after 1950—this is when the incidence of manic-depressive illness appeared to decline in the United States.[12] American psychiatrists began to separate schizophrenia from manic-depressive illness more rigorously again in the mid-1970s, after lithium carbonate was introduced as an effective treatment for the latter condition. American diagnosis became even more narrow in 1980, when it adopted the Scandinavian practice of excluding from the category of schizophrenia brief, 'schizophreniform' psychoses.[13] These developments suggest that American studies between 1950 and the late 1970s might tend to report better outcome and give a false picture of fluctuating recovery rates. Although this is a reasonable concern it does not appear to be a critical factor in shaping the results of this survey in view of the following:

- US results fluctuate according to the same pattern as European results after 1920.
- British outcome figures are better than US results despite a narrower British diagnostic approach.
- US studies account for a relatively small proportion of the results in this survey after 1950.

## Patient Selection

If more chronic, poor-prognosis patients were included in the cohorts studied in the Great Depression, this bias could account for the worse outcome noted at that time. This potential problem does not appear to have occurred. More studies included in the series from 1921 to 1940 were, in fact, of patients with good prognostic features than were included in the periods immediately before or after. Good-prognosis patients were considered to be those designated as 'first admission,' 'early,' 'acute' or 'selected' (see Table 3.4). An even larger proportion of patients in the studies after 1956 had good prognostic features: this could conceivably have led to an over-optimistic estimate of recovery rates since antipsychotic drugs were introduced. Any kind of bias due to patient selection seems to be less important when we compare the actual recovery rates for 'good-prognosis' patients with the total group. The differences, as shown in Figure 3.3, are not particularly great. The interesting possibility emerges however, that the

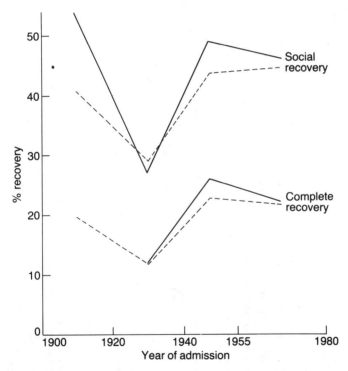

*Figure 3.3   Recovery rates for good-prognosis patients designated as 'first admission,' 'early,' 'acute,' or 'selected' among 68 outcome studies of schizophrenia (solid line). Recovery rates for the total group of patients are added (dotted line) for comparison*

77

Table 3.4 Recovery rates for good-prognosis patients designated as 'first admission,' 'early,' 'acute,' or 'selected' among 68 outcome studies of schizophrenia. The proportion of total subjects with these good-prognosis designations is also shown

| | 1901–20 | | 1921–40 | | 1941–55 | | 1956–PRESENT | |
| --- | --- | --- | --- | --- | --- | --- | --- | --- |
| | RECOVERY RATE % | PROPORTION OF TOTAL GROUP % | RECOVERY RATE % | PROPORTION OF TOTAL GROUP % | RECOVERY RATE % | PROPORTION OF TOTAL GROUP % | RECOVERY RATE % | PROPORTION OF TOTAL GROUP % |
| Complete recovery | — | 0 | 12 | 49 | 26 | 39 | 22 | 71 |
| Social recovery | 54 | 33 | 27 | 50 | 49 | 31 | 46 | 66 |

patients with a potentially favourable outlook only achieve better recovery rates when the economy is thriving.

Although we have to use caution in interpreting the findings of this survey of outcome in schizophrenia, particularly for the early years of the century, the results are by no means invalidated by the limitations of the research material. In fact, most of the possible bias which was detected would tend to downplay the somewhat provocative findings rather than dramatize them.

## Summary

An analysis of sixty-eight follow-up studies of outcome in schizophrenia conducted in Europe and North America since the turn of the century reveals:

- recovery rates for patients admitted since the introduction of the anti-psychotic drugs are no better than for those admitted after the Second World War or during the first two decades of the century.
- Recovery rates were significantly lower during the Great Depression of the 1920s and 1930s.
- The Great Depression excepted, complete recovery occurs in roughly 20–25 per cent of schizophrenics and social recovery in 40–45 per cent.
- The proportion of schizophrenic patients in hospital at follow-up has declined dramatically through the century, most of the decrease having taken place before the advent of the antipsychotic drugs.
- These findings do not appear to be artefacts of variation in diagnosis or selection of patients.

# 4  Deinstitutionalization

What accounts for the finding arrived at in the previous chapter, that the proportion of schizophrenic patients found to be in hospital at follow-up declined dramatically *before* the advent of the antipsychotic drugs? A widely-held belief about modern mental health care is that these drugs, introduced in the mid-1950s, brought a new dawn to psychiatry, making possible effective treatment and community care for psychotic patients. Chlorpromazine, the first of the antipsychotic drugs, initiated a 'therapeutic revolution' in the hospital and community treatment of schizophrenia, argues psychiatrist John Davis in the *Comprehensive Textbook of Psychiatry.* He continues:

> Those changes have resulted in a massive reduction in the number of hospitalized schizophrenic patients, a finding all the more remarkable since, up to the introduction of the new drugs, there had been a steady increase in the number of hospitalized mental patients. The shift in the fate of mental patients is the most convincing proof of the efficacy of those agents.[1]

Dr Davis illustrates the point with a graph showing the rise and fall in the number of residents of US state and county mental hospitals during this century. His graph is essentially similar to the broken line in Figure 4.1, with the addition of the letters CPZ and an arrow pointing to the peak of the graph in the mid-1950s indicating the time chlorpromazine began to be widely used. The observation that the antipsychotic drugs made deinstitution-alization possible has become a truism of modern psychiatric practice. But how accurate is it?

A moment's reflection discloses that the figures relevant to this issue are not the *absolute* numbers of mental hospital residents, but the numbers *as a proportion of the general population.* A graph of the *rate* of mental hospitalization—the continuous line in Figure 4.1—reveals a different picture. Whereas the absolute number of mental hospital residents peaked in 1955, the rate of hospital use peaked in 1945 and never climbed as high again. Although there has been a marked decline in the population of mental hospitals since the introduction of the antipsychotic drugs, it is clear that

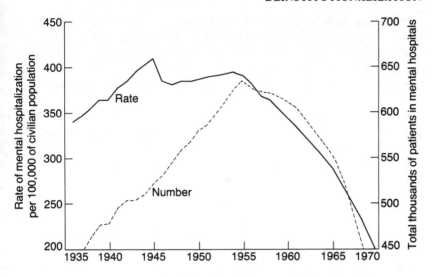

*Figure 4.1   Resident patients in US federal, state, county and private hospitals*

Source of statistics: US Bureau of the Census, *Historical Statistics of the United States: Colonial Times to 1970*, Part I, Washington, DC, 1975, p. 84.

something else was happening in the first postwar decade to alter patterns of psychiatric hospital use.

## The Impact of the Antipsychotics

Several psychiatrists, especially those practicing in northern Europe before and after the Second World War, have remarked that the arrival of the antipsychotic drugs in 1954 had little impact on the discharge rates of many mental hospitals. Örnulv Ödegard studied the figures for patients first admitted to all Norwegian psychiatric hospitals before and after the introduction of the antipsychotics.[2] He found a small increase in discharge rates for patients admitted during 1955–9 compared with those admitted during 1948–52, prior to the use of drugs. But he found a much bigger increase in the discharge rate when he compared the 1948–52 group with patients admitted in the late 1930s. The figures for functionally psychotic patients were:

| ADMISSION DATE | % DISCHARGED AND NOT READMITTED |
|---|---|
| 1936–40 | 52 |
| 1948–52 | 63 |
| 1955–59 | 67 |

In Britain, Alan Norton observed the same pattern at Bexley Hospital in Kent.[3] Although some improvement in discharge rates occurred between 1953 and 1957 with the introduction of drug treatment, a much more dramatic trend of improvement was already under way by the end of the Second World War, as these figures for female schizophrenics show:

| ADMISSION DATE | % IN HOSPITAL 2 YEARS AFTER ADMISSION |
|---|---|
| 1928–30 | 59 |
| 1934–6 | 63 |
| 1949–50 | 37 |
| 1953 | 20 |
| 1957 | 10 |

Michael Shepherd and his colleagues, after studying the discharge rate from St John's Hospital in Stone, Buckinghamshire, between 1954 and 1957, concluded that the introduction of drug treatment after 1954 had made no significant change.[4] Their net release-rate figures (discharges expressed as a proportion of the average number of patients in residence) for schizophrenia were as follows:

| YEAR | NET RELEASE RATE (%) |
|---|---|
| 1954 | 18.4 |
| 1955 | 19.5 |
| 1956 | 15.4 |
| 1957 | 18.8 |

At Mapperley Hospital in Nottingham, the patient population began to decline as early as 1948, from 1,310 patients in that year to 1,060 in 1956, and continued to drop at a similar pace after drugs were brought into use.[5]

Similar examples for the United States are harder to find. The number of patients resident in Massachusetts mental hospitals was already declining in 1954, before chlorpromazine was in use;[6] and at Vermont State Hospital the discharge rate for schizophrenia increased steadily after 1948.[7] Looking only at first-admission, white, male schizophrenics entering California state hospitals, psychiatrist Leon Epstein found that the discharge rate for such patients was already increasing between 1951 and 1954 (the year when drug treatment was introduced). Furthermore, schizophrenic patients first admitted in 1956 and 1957 who were treated with the new drugs showed a *lower* discharge rate than those who were treated without drugs. The discharge rate for this group of patients as a whole (drug-treated and drug-free) nevertheless continued to increase.[8] Erwin Linn demonstrated that the same phenomenon occurred at St Elizabeth's Hospital in Washington DC. Although the discharge rate for functional psychotics increased at this hospital between 1953 and 1956, the release rate for those treated with drugs was again lower than for those treated without drugs.[9] (Such a result, however, would theoretically occur if only the patients with the worst prognosis were given drug treatment.) Overall it seems probable that some other influence besides a purely pharmacological effect was operating to stimulate American deinstitutionalization.

Much more influential than these studies, however, were the figures for New York state mental hospitals presented by Henry Brill and Robert Patton. They noted that the residential population of the state hospitals was increasing by around 2,000 patients each year until 1955. In that year 30,000 cases received the new type of drug treatment, and in the following year the upward trend was converted into an annual *decrease* in the residential population of the following approximate magnitude:

| | |
|---|---|
| 1956 | 500 |
| 1957 | 500 |
| 1958 | 1,200 |
| 1959 | 2,000 |

The authors concluded that 'the abrupt population fall was in material degree due to introduction of the new drugs' because 'no other explanation for the statistical changes could be found.'[10] They were, however, unable to demonstrate a direct cause-and-effect relation between drug treatment and patient discharge although, as sociologist Andrew Scull points out,[11] and as Davis's view at the beginning of this chapter illustrates, their work is often interpreted as having done so. The New York experience was so close to the pattern for the country as a whole that the use of antipsychotic drugs is now inextricably linked in the minds of most American psychiatrists and mental health professionals with the development of community care for psychotics and the radical changes associated with the advent of the deinstitutionalization era. The data from northern Europe, however, make it plain that increased discharge rates, shorter hospital stays, and community treatment for psychotic patients were becoming the rule in many areas well before the antipsychotic drugs arrived on the scene.

If not to the new drugs, to what, then, may we attribute these postwar changes in the management of mental patients?

83

## The Social Psychiatry Revolution

A revolution in the treatment of psychotic patients was taking place in many parts of northern Europe before drugs were available—a revolution which went largely unnoticed in the United States until it was well under way. Mainstream opinion in American psychiatry to this day, in fact, has overlooked the significance of the European social psychiatry revolution and continues to emphasize the central importance of drug treatment. As expressed by John Davis, the advent of chlorpromazine

> created an atmosphere that emphasized positive treatment and led to the vigorous application of other therapies, such as milieu therapy, psycho-therapy, group therapy and occupational therapy. The greater use of those social therapies was made possible by the effective treatment, through medication, of the disruptive and destructive aspects of the patient's illness.[12]

From the American perspective this association of events appeared to be true, but the evidence from northern Europe demonstrates that social therapies, far from being 'made possible' by drug treatment, preceded and rivalled the antipsychotic drugs in their impact on the rehabilitation of psychotic patients.

British psychiatrists at Netherne Hospital, near London, noted a 'greatly improved general pattern of care of the severely ill in hospital' during the period from 1945 to 1948 compared with conditions for those admitted a decade earlier. They saw

> the changes for the better being evident from the larger number of open wards, the increased freedom patients are able to enjoy, the abolition of restraint and strong clothing, and the diminution of seclusion, aggression and incontinence.[13]

The psychiatrists associated these improvements with the introduction of physical therapies (insulin coma and electro-convulsive therapy) and with changes in hospital policy and community attitudes.

In 1949 Dr George Bell unlocked the doors of all the wards of Dingleton Hospital in Melrose, Scotland. In earlier decades physician superintendents of other hospitals had made similar attempts—Rutherford at Lenzie Asylum in 1881, for example, and Saxtby Good at Littlemore Hospital, Oxford, in 1935—but public pressure had always forced the doors closed again. Bell's success, however, heralded an Open Door Movement in psychiatry which swept the Western world in the years which followed. Mapperley Hospital opened its doors in 1953 and Warlingham Park, South London, soon after. Day hospitals for psychotic patients were used extensively in Great Britain in the 1940s and 1950s, and in Amsterdam, Holland, a comprehensive program was developed for the treatment of the mentally ill in their own homes. Not until 1958, when drug treatment was well established, did St Lawrence Hospital, New York, become fully open door.[14] Within the European hospitals, other changes were taking place.

Beginning in 1946, British psychiatrists developed new patterns of institutional living. Termed 'therapeutic communities' by Dr Tom Main, groups of therapists and patients worked together to create a hospital environment where traditional models of institutional authority were broken down, patients participated in the government of their hospital community, staff and patient roles were blurred and open communication was highly valued. Initially, this type of treatment setting was not available for psychotics. Tom Main worked with demoralized ex-soldiers at Northfield Hospital, Birmingham, and Maxwell Jones, foremost in developing the therapeutic community concept, worked with unemployed drifters and, later, patients with character disorders at the Henderson Hospital in South London.[15] In due course the therapeutic community idea was introduced into wards for psychotic patients. At the Littlemore Hospital, Oxford, throughout the 1960s there were therapeutic communities in three different treatment units—for the elderly, for brain-damaged patients and for general adult psychiatric patients. The programs, radical in concept, were established by Dr Ben Pomryn, who had worked with Maxwell Jones at the Henderson Hospital. On the general adult unit—the Phoenix Unit—staff and some 60 acute and chronic psychiatric patients (i.e. 70 or more people) participated in daily community meetings which established ward policy, evaluated new admissions, held interviews with patients' families, prescribed treatment (including drug treatment and electro-convulsive therapy) and authorized discharges. Maxwell Jones introduced similar changes to Dingleton Hospital and turned it into an inovative model drawing staff and visitors from many parts of the world.

The new hospital activity and therapeutic optimism were geared to early discharge, rehabilitation, and treatment in the community. Chronically institutionalized patients developed social competence and were placed in supervised hostels, returned to their families, or were set up in houses of their own, living together in family-like groups. Psychiatrists and nurses left the wards to see patients in their homes and in outpatient clinics and to consult with family physicians and community mental health workers. Sheltered workshops prospered, especially in Holland and, after 1960, in Britain, and produced goods competitive in the industrial market place. Industrial therapy in the United States, meanwhile, lagged a long way behind.[16]

Such radical changes, in several areas pre-dating the introduction of chlorpromazine, explain why drug treatment appeared to have little effect in many hospitals. Professor Ödegard demonstrated that of the seventeen

85

mental hospitals in Norway, those which had previously had a poor discharge record showed the most benefit from the introduction of the antipsychotic drugs; those which already had a higher discharge rate, and were presumably more advanced in social therapeutic techniques, showed no increase in the number of patients discharged and maintained in the community after drugs became available (see Table 4.1). Dr Ödegard concludes that for hospitals where social *milieu* therapy was not well developed 'the drugs were a real blessing,' but that

> in the more privileged institutions the drugs simply meant that one form of therapy was replaced by another and equally efficient one.[17]

Similarly, Dr N. H. Rathod, a psychiatrist at Cane Hill Hospital in Surrey, demonstrated that the effects of the new 'tranquillisers' were very limited on wards where particular attention was paid to the creation of a therapeutic environment.[18]

Table 4.1 Number of patients discharged and not readmitted per 100 admissions for all Norwegian mental hospitals

| HOSPITAL | 1949–53 | 1955–9 | % CHANGE |
|---|---|---|---|
| 1 | 75.7 | 71.6 | −5.4 |
| 2 | 67.1 | 65.5 | −2.4 |
| 3 | 66.5 | 62.3 | −6.3 |
| 4 | 60.2 | 57.6 | −4.3 |
| 5 | 58.4 | 44.9 | −23.1 |
| 6 | 57.0 | 49.8 | −12.6 |
| 7 | 56.6 | 59.6 | +5.3 |
| 8 | 54.4 | 49.0 | −9.9 |
| 9 | 53.8 | 63.9 | +18.8 |
| 10 | 53.6 | 53.6 | 0 |
| 11 | 52.0 | 51.2 | −1.5 |
| 12 | 51.1 | 51.4 | +0.6 |
| 13 | 49.1 | 65.4 | +33.2 |
| 14 | 48.7 | 50.4 | +3.5 |
| 15 | 46.7 | 46.5 | −0.4 |
| 16 | 44.4 | 51.4 | +15.8 |
| 17 | 34.2 | 41.4 | +21.0 |

Source: Ödegard, Ö., 'Pattern of discharge from Norwegian psychiatric hospitals before and after the introduction of the psychotropic drugs,' *American Journal of Psychiatry*, 120: 772–8, 1964.

Antipsychotic drugs, then, appear to be more effective for the psychotic patient who is living in an inadequate setting and to be less valuable where the environment is designed for his or her well-being. This is an important

86

point and one which we will return to later in the book. It is a point which is not readily apparent to mental health professionals who were not practicing before the antipsychotic drugs were in use: and because of the peculiarities of deinstitutionalization in the United States, it is a point scarcely recognized in American psychiatry. In practice, drug treatment is all too often used as a cheap substitute for adequate psycho-social care. As concern grows over the harmful side effects of the antipsychotic drugs and over the social plight of large numbers of poverty-stricken psychotics in the community, this becomes an issue of some consequence.

## Deinstitutionalization in the United States

The antipsychotic drugs had a more revolutionary impact in the United States, where there were relatively more backward asylums in 1955, than in those parts of northern Europe where social therapy prevailed. The subsequent course of deinstitutionalization in America also differed from that in northern Europe. Despite the development in the United States of a network of community mental health centers after 1965, the welfare of the chronically and severely mentally ill has largely been overlooked. A substantial proportion of those discharged from US mental hospitals were merely transferred to another category of institution—nursing homes.

For many patients the switch was to their disadvantage. Nursing-home staff are generally low-paid and have no training in mental health, wards are often locked and overcrowded, the environment is frequently shabby, there are generally no attractive grounds for recreation, and psycho-social treatment and activity programs are deficient or absent. In general, the only treatment offered is drugs: and it was the advent of the antipsychotic drugs, facilitating control of the florid features of patients' psychosis even when the patients are in grossly inadequate settings, which allowed huge numbers of the mentally ill to be shunted to cheaper nursing home care. Thus, although the number of patients in US state and county mental hospitals declined from 504,604 in 1963 to 369,929 in 1969, the number of patients with mental disorders in nursing homes increased to such an extent that the total institutionalized population of the mentally ill was actually *higher* in 1969. Mentally-ill residents of mental hospitals and nursing homes combined rose from 726,325 in 1963 to 796,712 in 1969. Many of these patients were elderly but large numbers of younger adults were also transferred to nursing homes. The number of patients under the age of 65 in state and county mental hospitals fell by nearly 100,000 between 1963 and 1969 but the number of mentally ill patients in this age group in nursing home accommodation increased by more than 25,000 during the same period.[19] Ellen Bassuk and Samuel Gerson point out, however:

Untherapeutic though many nursing homes are, living conditions in most of them are at least tolerable. Conditions may be worse for discharged patients living on their own, without enough money and usually without any possibility of employment. Many of them drift to substandard inner-city housing that is overcrowded, unsafe, dirty and isolated. Often they come together to form a new kind of ghetto subpopulation, a captive market for unscrupulous landlords.[20]

Newspaper reports have exposed the impoverished condition of formerly hospitalized patients leading lives of isolation and fear in the community—100 discharged patients in Washington, DC, without therapeutic rehabilitation programs; 200 ex-patients of Agnews State Hospital in California housed in boarding homes in San Jose with no medical care; 300–1,000 patients in rooming houses and hotels in Long Beach, New York, without supervision. A survey of discharged mental patients conducted in 1970 in California's San Mateo County found 32 per cent living in board and care homes.[21] These 'small wards in the community' are generally sordid and bare establishments in poor, inner-city areas where theft is rampant. One-third of the chronic mental patients in a large sample of residents of board and care homes in Los Angeles had been robbed or assaulted or both during the previous year.[22] Each such establishment houses more than fifty ex-hospital patients, and may accommodate several hundred.[23] The patients often receive no psychiatric treatment other than a supply of drugs and have no employment or worth-while social activity. A typical boarding home resident, report California psychiatrists Theodore Van Putten and James Spar,

> spends 8.46 hours of the day in bed, a time limited primarily by the sponsor's continual efforts to keep him out of his bedroom, and 1.46 hours at the dining table. He spends the rest of the day in virtual solitude, either staring vacantly at television (few residents reported having a favourite television show; most were puzzled at the question), or wandering aimlessly around the neighbourhood, sometimes stopping for a nap on a lawn or park bench.[24]

Patients who suffer a psychotic relapse are likely to be treated briefly in hospital with drugs and may well be discharged again to an inadequate setting or to live on the street. As this cycle repeats itself they become known as 'revolving-door patients.' About half of the patients released from US psychiatric hospitals in the early 1970s were readmitted within a year of discharge.[25] As public mental hospital beds are cut back, it becomes increasingly difficult for acutely psychotic patients to gain readmission. For example, in 1981 the state hospital in Denver, Colorado—Fort Logan Mental Health Center—had a waiting list for admission of more than one hundred adult cases. Since the hospital's discharge rate was around one adult every week or two, patients at the bottom of the waiting list could expect admission within two to four years.

In consequence of the nationwide bed shortage and rapid-discharge policy many psychotics end up in jail, usually charged with offenses associated with trying to survive on the streets without money—trespass (sleeping in the hallway of a public building) or defrauding an innkeeper (eat and run). Around 6–8 per cent of the 147,000 inmates of local jails in the United States are psychotic.[26] Similarly, 8 per cent of a large sample of federal prisoners surveyed in 1969 were diagnosed as psychotic.[27]

Such is the plight of a substantial proportion of the 'deinstitutionalized' mentally ill across the United States. It is scarcely suprising that, as revealed in the last chapter, the overall social functioning of schizophrenics has not improved with the introduction of antipsychotic drugs. But in northern Europe, also, the picture has changed from the early days of the social psychiatry revolution.

## Psychiatric Stagnation

In Britain, the number of mental patients admitted to hospital who had 'no fixed abode' increased threefold between 1959 and 1964. By 1966, 10 per cent of the 30,000 men and women 'sleeping rough' in Britain were thought to be suffering from mental illness.[28] More than 20 per cent of the longer-term residents of the Camberwell Reception Centre for the destitute (a converted Victorian workhouse in South London) were considered mentally ill in the early 1970s.[29] At this time, too, concern developed over the increasing numbers of mentally ill criminal offenders who were committed to hospital or incarcerated in prison or borstal.[30]

The Social Services Act of 1970 transferred the responsibility for many aspects of community care for the mentally ill away from local health authorities and placed it in the Social Services Departments. Many professionals feel this has not been a successful move. In 1976 only 43 per cent of the recommended minimum number of places in hostels and group homes had been established and day facilities were equally scarce. Some local authorities had provided none at all.[31] A survey of the social situation of 190 schizophrenics living in the community in Salford in the late 1970s revealed 30 per cent accommodated in slum housing, 16 per cent with inadequate nutrition and 34 per cent who spent all or most of their time doing absolutely nothing. Among more than 100 largely psychotic patients in the psychiatric wards and day hospital of the London Borough of Camden on a single day in 1976, one-half were known to have been living alone before admission, nearly a third in transitory accommodation (such as abandoned homes, doss houses and reception centers) or sleeping on the streets; two-thirds were totally unemployed, most of them for more than a year; and more than a third of the inpatients received no visitors. Many of these patients, clearly, had no worth-while community links, but despite their obvious social deprivation only 6 per cent of Camden's inpatients were subsequently discharged to any kind of supportive setting, like a hostel or group home.[32] Such 'rehabilitation' was not what the innovative British community psychiatrists of the 1950s had in mind.

Hospital conditions have also deteriorated in Britain. Government reports, covering the period from 1976 to 1982, record the widespread existence of overcrowding, understaffing and custodial attitudes to patients throughout mental hospitals in many counties. Instances of cruelty and neglect are documented.[33]

Why did the deinstitutionalization movement go sour in Britain? Why was it never particularly sweet in the United States? Or, phrasing the questions differently, why was there a golden era of active social and community psychiatry in northern Europe in the immediate post-war years but not in the United States?

## Outdoor Relief

Sociologist Andrew Scull in his book, *Decarceration*, attributes the motivating force for the British and American deinstitutionalization movement to the post-war development of welfare programs which enabled the indigent and the disabled to be maintained more cheaply outside an institution.[34] This form of support, known to the Victorians as 'outdoor relief,' had been drastically reduced in the mid-nineteenth century. The twentieth-century Great Depression increased the pressure for a more comprehensive relief of poverty in the industrial nations, and both Britain and America instituted social-insurance schemes for the totally and permanently disabled in the five years following the Second World War.[35] Scull's analysis has considerable merit. Ödegard has made a similar observation concerning Norway's

> new and improved pension system for persons incapacitated by illness, which was introduced in 1960 and which includes psychotic invalids. . . . This has made possible the discharge of many psychotic invalids and is probably the main reason why the rates of discharge as 'not cured' did not show any great increase until after 1960.[36]

It is also clear, as Andrew Scull has argued, that the American switch to the use of nursing homes is attributable to the health-insurance structure. The state governments are responsible for the cost of maintaining patients in state mental hospitals, but care provided in a private nursing home may be billed to Medicaid (for the indigent) or Medicare (for the elderly). Since the federal government pays a large part of these insurance bills, it rapidly became apparent to state legislators after the inception of these programs in

1965 that they could cut the state budget by transferring mental patients to private-sector care.

Reference to disability pensions and health-insurance schemes, however, does not answer all the questions about the early stages of deinstitutionalization. Looking at disability payments, one would have predicted, for example, a late onset for community care in Norway, and an earlier, roughly simultaneous timing in Britain and America. To understand why the post-war social psychiatric revolution took place in northern Europe and not America, and why it subsequently stagnated in Britain it is necessary to study other political factors.

## Politics and Institutions

Broadly speaking one can set down four possible political motives for a deinstitutional trend:
- cost savings;
- a humanitarian concern for the welfare, liberty and human rights of the institutional inmates which outweighs the fear of their liability to the community;
- a need to put the buildings to a new purpose;
- a need to put the inmates to a new purpose.

Which elements are applicable to the post-war psychiatric deinstitutionalization?

*Cost saving,* as discussed above, has clearly been an important factor behind the emptying of psychiatric institutions, but it does not explain the differences in the characteristics of the process between countries.

*Humanitarian concerns,* while usually part of the rhetoric associated with changes in institutional use, are probably never sufficient cause for such changes. The welfare of the mentally ill was the espoused reason for the nineteenth-century movement to institutionalize massive numbers of the insane and of the reverse trend after the Second World War. The humanitarian concerns of the advocates of deinstitutionalization during the late nineteenth and early twentieth century, however, were never sufficient to halt the expansion of hospital care. Why did their views suddenly become effective after the Second World War? Furthermore, humanitarian considerations can scarcely account for the widespread current practice of maintaining psychotics in poverty, housed in degrading environments in the community, largely without proper care and treatment. On the contrary, it seems more probable that the philosophy of care is a secondary phenomenon, itself shaped by the contemporary patterns of institutional use.

*The conversion of old institutions to new purposes* historically has been very common. Seventeenth-century French leper hospitals became houses of correction,[37] a nineteenth-century British jail was converted into an insane

91

asylum[38] and Victorian workhouses in the twentieth century became general hospitals or reception centers for the destitute. There is no indication, though, that the mentally ill were discharged from mental hospitals after the Second World War to make way for some urgent new function for the buildings. Many of the old hospital wards have been closed and left vacant. More urgent, perhaps, was the need to avoid the capital outlay required to keep the old, Victorian institutions functional.

We must look, then, to a *change in the perceived value of the institutional inmates* themselves to find the stimulus for deinstitutionalization.

## Labor Dynamics

So great was the labor shortage in post-war Britain that *The Times* of January 1947 called for the selective immigration of half a million foreign workers, and economist Lionel Robbins warned that 100,000 foreigners should be recruited to work in the coal mines if the country was not 'to lapse into a position of impotence and economic chaos.' The government launched an attack on non-productive 'spivs and drones,' and the *Daily Mail* argued that if Scotland Yard were used 'to help to round up the work dodgers' one-and-a-half million workers could be added to the labor force. By September of that year the Cabinet was discussing the possibility of banning the football pools to force the redeployment of the women who processed the coupons into the labor-starved textile industry.[39]

A sustained, peacetime labor shortage of these dimensions had not been seen in Britain, or in those other north European nations which experienced the phenomenon, since employment records began or, quite probably, since the beginning of the Industrial Revolution. It seems reasonable to suppose that such a demand for labor, extraordinary also by recent Western standards, was a major stimulus to the effective rehabilitation of the mentally ill. Contemporary observers confirm this view. British social psychiatrist David Clark identifies as major factors which promoted the European Open Door Movement and deinstitutionalization: 'the development of welfare states where the disabled (including the psychiatrically crippled) were supported in their homes, [and] the development of full employment (in northern Europe at least) creating a demand for the labour of impaired people.'[40] Similarly, Professor Ödegard reports of Norway: 'Since the war there has mostly been a certain degree of over-employment, and it has been possible for hospitals to discharge to an independent existence even patients with a borderline working capacity and a questionable social adjustment.'[41] In Massachusetts, one of the few parts of the United States where the mental hospital population began to diminish before antipsychotic drugs were introduced, the decline in hospital use was also seen to be associated with a vigorous demand for labor.[42]

92

The strategic importance of the rehabilitation of large numbers of the mentally ill should not be underestimated. Between the Great Depression and the 1950s the proportion of schizophrenics in Britain who were employed may have increased by as much as twenty percentage points: this estimate is suggested by the improvement in the social recovery rate of British schizophrenics revealed in the last chapter. Since 34 people in every 10,000 of the population were schizophrenic, according to a post-war prevalence study conducted in London,[43] one can estimate that the rehabilitation of schizophrenics alone may have added 30,000 workers to the British labor force.

A number of other reports has confirmed that rehabilitation efforts for the disabled are closely related to the demand for labor. The Heller Committee survey of permanently disabled workers in the San Francisco Bay area in 1942 and 1943 found that wartime labor conditions left virtually none of the disabled unemployed.[44] British and American studies show that the employment of the mentally retarded increased from around 40 per cent in the Great Depression to 80 or 90 per cent during and after the Second World War.[45] Vocational rehabilitation activities are also very highly developed in the full-employment conditions of the Eastern Bloc countries.[46]

Labor dynamics, then, may explain many features of the deinstitution-alization movement. Before the introduction of the antipsychotic drugs, the post-war full employment in northern Europe required the rehabilitation of the marginally employable mentally ill, stimulating the development of more therapeutic styles of hospital care and a policy of early discharge. The move to milieu therapy and community treatment was delayed in the United States, where full employment did not generally develop. The introduction of disability pension schemes made possible the discharge of patients in the absence of employment opportunities, and the advent of the antipsychotic drugs allowed the control of symptoms in patients placed in inadequate and stressful settings. These changes, particularly in the United States, led to a different style of community management—the transfer of patients to low-cost placements, often without genuine attempts at making patients productive, valued and integrated members of society. The steep rise in unemployment in Britain from the late 1960s may go a long way to explain the subsequent stagnation in British psychiatric rehabilitation.

## International Comparisons

The countries which led in the post-war revolution in social psychiatry were, according to Maxwell Jones,[47] Britain, the Netherlands, Norway and Switzerland. Table 4.2 lists post-war unemployment statistics for these countries and other parts of Europe and North America: the unemployment figures have been adjusted[48] to make them reasonably comparable. The four

93

Table 4.2  Unemployment rates in northern Europe and North America

| | HIGH UNEMPLOYMENT | | | | | | LOW UNEMPLOYMENT | | | | | |
|---|---|---|---|---|---|---|---|---|---|---|---|---|
| | BELGIUM | DENMARK | GERMANY | ITALY | CANADA | USA | FRANCE | NETHERLANDS | NORWAY[a] | SWEDEN | SWITZERLAND | UK |
| 1950 | 6.3 | 4.1 | 7.2 | 8.7 | 3.6 | 5.2 | 1.4 | 2.0 | 2.7 | 1.7 | 0.5 | 2.5 |
| 1951 | 5.7 | 4.5 | 6.4 | 9.2 | 2.4 | 3.2 | 1.3 | 2.4 | 3.6 | 1.6 | 0.2 | 2.2 |
| 1952 | 6.8 | 5.9 | 6.1 | 9.8 | 2.9 | 2.9 | 1.3 | 3.5 | 2.4 | 1.7 | 0.3 | 2.9 |
| 1953 | 6.8 | 4.4 | 5.5 | 10.2 | 2.9 | 2.8 | 1.6 | 2.5 | 3.3 | 1.9 | 0.3 | 2.6 |
| 1954 | 6.2 | 3.8 | 5.2 | 8.7 | 4.5 | 5.3 | 1.6 | 1.8 | 2.2 | 1.8 | 0.2 | 2.3 |
| 1955 | 4.7 | 4.7 | 3.8 | 7.5 | 4.3 | 4.2 | 1.5 | 1.3 | 2.5 | 1.8 | 0.1 | 2.1 |

Sources: All unemployment statistics, except those for Norway, have been adjusted to render them comparable, and are taken from Maddison, A., *Economic Growth in the West*, New York: Twentieth Century Fund, 1964, p. 220. Unadjusted figures for Norway are taken from Mitchell, B. R., *European Historical Statistics 1750–1970*, abridged edn, New York: Columbia University Press, 1978, p. 68.

countries which were progressive in psychiatry at that time are among those with low unemployment rates. Countries, like the United States, where the rehabilitative movement was delayed, had higher rates of unemployment. Open-door policies and the deinstitutionalization movement did not reach Italian mental hospitals until the 1960s, arriving in the wake of an economic boom which brought many changes in the social and political climate.[49]

The number of mental hospital beds in use varies substantially from one industrial nation to another. Sweden, in 1974, provided one psychiatric-hospital bed for 250 citizens, for example, whereas in Poland one psychiatric bed served more than 800. A number of economic and political factors might be expected to influence mental hospital use and, if the demand for labor was an important stimulus to deinsitutionalization, then unemployment could prove to be one such influence on psychiatric hospital use. In the mid-1960s, in fact, industrial nations with higher unemployment rates tended to use more mental hospital beds (see Table 4.3). A multiple regression analysis shows that the average national unemployment over a five-year period accounted for 40 per cent of the variance in the provision of psychiatric beds in 1965 in the nine Western industrial nations for which comparable statistics are available (see Table 4.4).[50] This relationship was independent of a number of other economic and demographic variables. After taking into account the influence of per capita gross national product, infant mortality (as an indicator of the national level of health and welfare provisions) and the proportion of elderly in the population, unemployment accounted for 47 per cent of the variance in the use of mental hospital beds. Over the next decade, however, the relationship between mental hospital use and unemployment disappeared. As Table 4.4 shows, by 1974 a combination of two factors—the national infant mortality rate and the proportion of the population over age 65—predicted 71 per cent of the variance in mental hospital beds provided; unemployment accounted for only 1 per cent of the variance.

The link between unemployment and mental-hospital use in 1965 suggests that, until that time, the availability of work may have acted as a control on hospital discharge rates. The correlation disappeared after the 1960s because psychiatric hospital populations continued to shrink in Australia, Canada and the United States in the absence of improvements in employment. Elsewhere mental hospital use increased or remained relatively constant. This divergence may be attributed to the degree to which each country exercised the option, offered by disability benefits and drugs, to maintain psychotics in the community regardless of the availability of employment. In addition, in the United States the advent of Medicaid in 1965 led to massive reductions in mental hospital beds as patients were transferred to nursing homes. No longer is it essential that mental hospitals control and sustain a large segment of the surplus population. Their use has

Table 4.3 Psychiatric hospital beds per 10,000 of the general population, average annual unemployment rates over five-year periods, infant mortality per 1,000 live births, general population over age 65 and per capita gross national product in 1979 US dollars

| | 1965 | | | | | 1974 | | | | |
|---|---|---|---|---|---|---|---|---|---|---|
| | PSYCHIATRIC HOSPITAL BEDS | AVERAGE ANNUAL UNEMPLOYMENT (%) 1961–5[b] | INFANT MORTALITY | ELDERLY POPULATION % | PER CAPITA GNP | PSYCHIATRIC HOSPITAL BEDS | AVERAGE ANNUAL UNEMPLOYMENT (%) 1970–4[b] | INFANT MORTALITY | ELDERLY POPULATION % | PER CAPITA GNP |
| *Western industrial nations* | | | | | | | | | | |
| Japan | 13.3 | 1.3 | 18.5 | 6.4 | 3,633 | 18.4 | 1.3 | 10.8 | 8.0 | 7,425 |
| West Germany | 17.7 | 0.5 | 23.9 | 12.0 | 7,908 | 17.8 | 1.0 | 21.1 | 14.0 | 10,681 |
| France | 20.5 | 1.5 | 21.9 | 12.2 | 6,304 | — | 2.8 | 14.7 | 13.0 | 9,508 |
| Italy | 22.4 | 2.9 | 35.6 | 9.9 | 3,568 | 20.9 | 3.2 | 22.6 | 12.0 | 5,243 |
| Australia | 27.1 | 2.1 | 18.5 | 8.4 | 5,801 | 20.7 | 2.2 | 16.1 | 9.0 | 7,874 |
| UK | 28.5 | 2.6 | 19.0[a] | 12.3 | 5,348 | 31.9[a] | 3.3 | 16.3[a] | 14.0 | 6,529 |
| USA | 31.1 | 5.7 | 24.7 | 9.5 | 7,873 | 14.2 | 5.4 | 16.7 | 11.0 | 9,577 |
| Sweden | 35.4 | 1.5 | 13.3 | 12.8 | 9,374 | 40.5 | 2.3 | 9.2 | 15.0 | 11,835 |
| Canada | 35.9 | 5.4 | 23.6 | 7.6 | 6,070 | 21.8 | 5.8 | 15.0 | 8.0 | 8,497 |

*Centrally planned economies*

| | | | | | | | | | | |
|---|---|---|---|---|---|---|---|---|---|---|
| Hungary | 2.4 | — | 38.8 | 10.2 | 2,335 | — | — | 34.3 | 13.0 | 3,039 |
| Romania | 3.1 | — | 44.1 | 7.6 | 1,824 | 7.0 | — | 35.0 | 9.0 | 2,804 |
| Bulgaria | 4.2 | — | 30.8 | 8.5 | 1,866 | — | — | 25.5 | 11.0 | 2,645 |
| USSR | 9.9 | — | 27.6 | 7.3 | 3,354 | — | — | 27.7 | 9.0 | 4,913 |
| Czechoslovakia | 11.7 | — | 25.5 | 9.9 | 3,567 | 11.3 | — | 20.4 | 12.0 | 4,692 |
| East Germany | 18.2 | — | 24.8 | 14.6 | 3,412 | 18.9 | — | 15.9 | 16.0 | 4,558 |
| Poland | — | — | 41.7 | 7.0 | 2,042 | 12.1 | — | 23.7 | 10.0 | 3,069 |

Sources: Psychiatric hospital beds (except USSR) and infant mortality: World Health Organisation, *World Health Statistics Annuals*, 1964 to 1977, vols I, III, Geneva: 1967–77; USSR psychiatric hospital beds (1962 figure): Field, M. G. and Aronson, J., 'Soviet community mental health services and work therapy,' *Community Mental Health Journal*, 1: 81–90, 1965; Unemployment: Sorrentino, C., 'Unemployment in international perspective,' in B. Showler and A. Sinfield (eds), *The Workless State*, Oxford: Martin Robertson, 1980; Elderly population: World Bank, *World Tables, 2nd edn*, Baltimore: Johns Hopkins University Press, 1980; Per capita GNP: CIA National Foreign Assessment Center, *Handbook of Economic Statistics 1980*, Washington, DC: US Government Printing Office, 1980.

Notes: [a] Figure for England and Wales
[b] Unemployment statistics are adjusted to US concepts to render them comparable
[c] See the appendix for similar data for 1968 and 1971

**Table 4.4 Variance in psychiatric hospital beds provided in nine Western industrial countries accounted for by different social indicators**

|  | % OF VARIANCE ACCOUNTED FOR | CUMULATIVE % OF VARIANCE |
|---|---|---|
| 1965 (N = 9) |  |  |
| Unemployment | 40 | 40 |
| GNP | 25 | 64* |
| Infant mortality | 5 | 70 |
| Elderly in population | 6 | 75 |
| 1965: Entering unemployment as the last step (N = 9) |  |  |
| GNP | 26 | 26 |
| Infant mortality | 0 | 26 |
| Elderly in population | 3 | 28 |
| Unemployment | 47* | 75 |
| 1968 (N = 9) |  |  |
| GNP | 39 | 39 |
| Unemployment | 24 | 63* |
| Infant mortality | 9 | 72 |
| Elderly in population | 3 | 75 |
| 1971 (N = 9) |  |  |
| GNP | 37 | 37 |
| Unemployment | 10 | 47 |
| Infant mortality | 10 | 57 |
| Elderly in population | 8 | 65 |
| 1974 (N = 8) |  |  |
| Elderly in population | 34 | 34 |
| Infant mortality | 36 | 71* |
| GNP | 8 | 79 |
| Unemployment | 1 | 80 |

* Significant at the .05 level (two-tailed test).
Note: Variance statistics were obtained by a stepwise multiple-regression method using the figures in the appendix.

become, to a greater degree, a matter of social policy. The extent of psychiatric institutional care now appears to be largely a reflection of two factors. One is the national, political commitment to the quality and universality of health and welfare provisions (of which infant mortality is an indicator). The other, since the antipsychotic drugs are of little benefit in the care of senile organic psychosis, is the proportion of the elderly in the general population.

Deinstitutionalization, in some circumstances a sign of progressive efforts towards community care and rehabilitation of the mentally ill, may elsewhere indicate the opposite—abrogation of responsibility for the welfare of a segment of the poor. In the United States, where health and welfare provisions for the destitute are not well developed, the small numbers of available mental hospital beds represent a refusal to provide adequate psychiatric treatment for the indigent mentally ill. In Sweden, on the other hand, a political commitment to adequate health and welfare provisions coupled with the existence of a large elderly population leads to a substantially greater use of mental hospitals. Each of the other Scandinavian countries, like Sweden, maintains comprehensive health and welfare services, low infant mortality rates and substantial numbers of psychiatric hospital beds. Of these four countries Denmark and Norway, with the greatest labor shortages until the mid-1970s, preserved relatively low rates of mental hospital use and the most highly developed community treatment programs.[51]

It is evident from the figures in Table 4.3 that it is not only the labor shortage in the Eastern Bloc countries which leads to their minimal use of psychiatric institutions but also the underdevelopment of their health services in general (witness their high infant mortality rates) and the low proportion of the elderly in the general population. Nevertheless, we know that the labor shortage in these countries, particularly Russia and Poland, has led to a very great emphasis on work therapy, intensive community rehabilitation efforts, greater acceptance of the mentally ill in the community and the workplace and efforts to keep the elderly productive.[52]

Full employment, then, may no longer be a major factor determining the size of mental hospital populations but it could be an important influence on the characteristics of community treatment and the adequacy of rehabilitative efforts. Where the surplus population is large, the conditions established for the psychotic patient tend to be least conducive to his or her recovery. Where the labor of the marginally productive is in demand, there shall we find the most highly developed community treatment programs and the most humane hospital conditions. We shall see to what extent these factors influence the course of schizophrenia.

## Summary

- The rate of mental-hospital occupancy as a proportion of the general United States population was declining before the introduction of the antipsychotic drugs.

- Revolutionary changes in hospital and community psychiatry in northern Europe preceded the introduction of antipsychotic drug treatment.
- The discharge rates from progressive hospitals, particularly in northern Europe, were not improved by the arrival of the antipsychotics.
- The delay in the introduction of new social and community psychiatry techniques to the United States created the impression there that drug treatment was vital to community care.
- Deinstitutionalization in the United States has relied heavily on the use of drugs and has led to the placement of large numbers of the mentally ill in low-cost, inadequate settings.
- Community care for the mentally ill in Britain has stagnated since the 1960s.
- The main political and economic driving forces to deinstitutionalization were (a) cost-saving and (b) in northern Europe, the post-war demand for labor.
- Comparing Western industrial nations in 1965, the number of mental-hospital beds in each country was correlated with the national unemployment rate.
- A decade later, mental hospital use appeared to be less influenced by the labor market and more affected by national health and welfare policy.

# 5  Madness and the Industrial Revolution

In the last decade of the eighteenth century a humane method of treating the mentally ill sprang into being in Europe, within a few years came to be adopted in many parts of the civilized world, and after half a century or so faded away. It left in its place restrictive patterns of institutional care of which few people in psychiatry are proud but which persisted until the latter half of the twentieth century. Many psychiatrists have remarked on the common features of moral treatment (as the early movement was called) and the post-Second World War social psychiatry revolution. Were the two movements indeed similar: and, if so, could they have been stimulated by similar political and economic conditions? If not, why did moral treatment come into being when it did? The use of moral management was accompanied by claims of excellent recovery rates in mental illness. Were these claims accurate? If so, why were the methods abandoned and what light does the episode throw on the conventional approach to the history of medicine which shows us always progressing to higher levels of technical achievement through a process of scientific discovery?

## The York Retreat

This house is situated a mile from York, in the midst of a fertile and smiling countryside; it is not at all the idea of a prison that it suggests, but rather that of a large farm; it is surrounded by a great walled garden. No bars, no grilles on the windows.[1]

So runs the description of the York Retreat given by a Swiss visitor in 1798. The name, 'Retreat,' was significant: not a 'hospital' nor an 'asylum' but 'a quiet haven in which the shattered bark might find the means of reparation or safety.'[2] Within this house was developing a mode of care for the mentally ill which was to prove as revolutionary as Pinel's action in striking the chains from the inmates of Bicêtre in 1793.

Like Pinel's work, the York Retreat was a reaction against the inhumanity of the contemporary treatment of the insane. It was founded in 1792 and opened in 1796 by the Society of Friends after one of their members,

101

Hannah Mills, died in the York Asylum under circumstances which suggested neglect or ill treatment. Designed for thirty patients and primarily made available to Quakers, the cost of treatment at the York Retreat ranged from eight to fifteen shillings a week. Accommodation for personal servants was provided at a further fee. The establishment was clearly not intended to be for the poor.

Under the direction of William Tuke, a 60-year-old tea and coffee merchant, a style of non-medical care was developed which, like Pinel's approach, came to be called moral treatment. Believing that most deranged people could be rational if not provoked by harsh treatment or cruelty, the Tukes encouraged the exercise of patients' self-control as an alternative to the use of external restraint. Punishment for inappropriate behavior was avoided, but minor privileges were awarded to those who conformed to the attendants' wishes. Chains were never used and straight waistcoats rarely, and then only to prevent a patient hurting himself or herself or other residents. The iron sashes of the windows were disguised to look like wood. Patients were expected to dress in their best clothes and take part in all usual social activities—tea parties, reading, writing, sewing and gardening. Work was felt to be essential in fostering patients' self-control and self-esteem. Drugs were seldom used, and exercise, warm baths and a generous diet of 'meat, bread and good porter' were felt to be most useful in quieting patients and ensuring good sleep.[3]

## Before Moral Treatment

The revolutionary nature of moral treatment at the York Retreat becomes evident when it is set against conventional care of the time. At the nearby York Asylum, where Hannah Mills had died, abuses were exposed by investigations conducted some years after the opening of the Retreat. 'Flogging and cudgelling' were routine, and patients were 'verminous and filthy.'[4] Behind a partly hidden door, a visitor in 1814 discovered a series of small cells

> in a very horrid and filthy condition ... the walls were daubed with excrement; the air-holes, of which there was one in each cell, were partly filled with it.

Upstairs he found a room

> twelve feet by seven feet ten inches, in which there were thirteen women who, [the keeper] told me, had all come out of those cells that morning. ... I became very sick, and could not remain longer in the room. I vomited.[5]

Charles Dickens characterized asylum care of this period as follows:

Coercion for the outward man, and rabid physicking for the inward man, were the specifics for lunacy. Chains, straw, filthy solitude, darkness, and starvation; jalap, syrup of buckthorn, tartarised antimony, and ipecacuanha administered every spring and fall in fabulous doses to every patient, whether well or ill; spinning in whirligigs, corporal punishment, gagging, 'continued intoxication'; nothing was too wildly extravagant, nothing too monstrously cruel to be prescribed by mad-doctors.

Lest we should consider that these practices were enforced through malice, he continues:

In other respects these physicians were grave men, of mild dispositions, and—in their ample-flapped, ample-cuffed coats, with a certain gravity and air of state in the skirts; with their large buttons and gold-headed canes, their hair-powder and ruffles—were men of benevolent aspects.[6]

Frank abuses (and psychiatrist William Parry-Jones argues that these may well have been overemphasized by historians[7]), Dickens' point is well taken. We should not assume that the eighteenth-century mad-doctors were morally degenerate; chains and flogging were not necessarily maliciously intended. Even George III during his bouts of insanity was chained, beaten, starved and intimidated with threats.[8] The management techniques were those of animal trainers because the insane were regarded as bestial. At the Bicêtre in Paris and the Bethlem Hospital in London, the inmates were exhibited to the public, for a fee, like zoo creatures.[9] The insane were left naked in the cold and damp because they were believed to posses inhuman resistance to the effects of the elements.[10] Both Andrew Scull and French psychologist Michel Foucault have emphasized that the introduction of moral treatment involved a redefinition of the madman's condition from the essence of bestiality to a degree of human rationality.[11] Now the lunatic becomes a fractious child. As the Swiss doctor commented in the visitors' book at the Retreat:

In moral treatment, one does not consider the insane to be completely deprived of reason, out of reach of the influence of fear, hope, affection and honour. Rather one regards them, it seems, like children who have too much energy, and who put it to dangerous uses.[12]

In this redefinition lay the revolutionary impact of moral management.

## The Origins of Moral Treatment

Curiously enough, this fundamentally new approach was not only introduced simultaneously by Pinel and Tuke, but similar humane methods of patient care sprang into being independently at the same point in time in other parts of Europe. In Florence, Vincenzo Chiarugi, the physician in charge of the newly opened Hospital Bonifacio, published regulations for patient care, in 1789, which eliminated the use of physical force or any type of restraint except for the occasional use of the straightjacket. He specified:

> It is a supreme moral duty and medical obligation to respect the insane individual as a person.[13]

Similarly, Joseph Daquin, the physician in charge of the institution at Chambéry in the Savoy region (an independent duchy situated between France and Italy) published, in 1791, a treatise advocating humane care for the mentally ill.[14] Around the same time, Parisian physician and philosopher Georges Cabanis, who arranged Pinel's appointment to the Bicêtre, proposed improved treatment methods for the insane.[15] Physician John Ferriar at the Manchester Lunatic Hospital, although administering such standard medical remedies as blood-letting, blistering and purging,[16] expressed the opinion, in 1795 (the year before the Retreat opened), that the primary goal of treatment lay in 'creating a habit of self-restraint,' not through coercion, but by 'the management of hope and apprehension, . . . small favours, the show of confidence, and apparent distinction.'[17]

For each of these independent innovations, local causes may be found. Psychiatric historian George Mora, for example, suggests that Pinel and the French physicians, in liberating the insane, were reflecting the spirit of freedom and equality of the French Revolution (1789–99); Chiarugi's radical reforms were a product of the revolutionary political and economic reforms of the rule of the Grand Duke Peter Leopold (1747–92); the philosophy of the York Retreat was based on the contemporary British bourgeois ideal of the family.[18] But these individual influences fail to explain the simultaneous but independent origin of the same notion within a five-year period in different parts of Europe.

To call the phenomenon 'a striking example of *zeitgeist* in the history of psychiatry'[19] is to say nothing about causes. To see it as a reflection of the Enlightenment's eighteenth-century ideals of human dignity, worth and freedom is to provide a unifying concept but still only fits one ideology within the broader framework of another. If we examine the political and economic underpinning of Enlightenment thinking, however, we may be in a better position to understand why moral treatment occurred when and where it did. British historian, Eric Hobsbawn, has this to say about the philosophy of the Age of Reason:

> The Great Encyclopaedia of Diderot and d'Alembert was not merely a compendium of progressive social and political thought, but of technological and scientific progress. For indeed the conviction of the progress of human knowledge, rationality, wealth, civilization, and control over

nature with which the eighteenth century was deeply imbued, the "Enlightenment," drew its strength primarily from the evident progress of production, trade, and the economic and scientific rationality believed to be associated inevitably with both. And its greatest champions were the economically most progressive classes, those most directly involved in the tangible advances of the time: the mercantile circles and economically enlightened landlords, financiers, scientifically minded economic and social administrators, the educated middle class, manufacturers, and entrepreneurs.[20]

Revolutionary to the old social and political order, the Enlightenment ideas were central to the capitalist transformation of production. Leaving aside, for the moment, the American Revolution (1776–83), the culmination of eighteenth-century Enlightenment philosophy and its associated political, economic and technological changes was (what Hobsbawm refers to as) the 'dual revolution.'[21] This comprised the French Revolution of 1789 and the contemporaneous British Industrial Revolution (which Hobsbawn dates from the 1780s, when the British economy became 'airborne'[22]).

'It is significant,' writes Hobsbawm,

> that the two chief centres of the [Enlightenment] ideology were also those of the dual revolution, France and England. . . . A secular, rationalist and progressive individualism dominated 'enlightened' thought. To set the individual free from the shackles which fettered him was its chief object. . . . Liberty, equality and (it followed) the fraternity of all men were its slogans.[23]

Enlightenment ideas, then, gave the French Revolution its slogan, the determined capitalist his individualism, and the innovators of moral treatment their philosophical base. Beyond France and England, the sites of origin of the humane treatment methods were also centers of Enlightenment ideology and progressive politics. Savoy, culturally linked to France, instituted enlightened peasant liberation shortly before the French Revolution;[24] and Chiarugi in Florence was under the influence of one of the most remarkable reforming princes of the eighteenth century, Grand Duke Leopold of Tuscany, a man strongly influenced by Enlightenment ideas. Moral treatment, moreover, was most avidly adopted by another enlightened nation—post-revolutionary, industrializing America.

When moral treatment, then, set the insane 'free from the shackles,' the movement was a component of the dual revolution which shook the Western world. This is most compellingly revealed in the image of Pinel, at the height of the French revolution, striking the chains from the insane of Bicêtre and La Salpêtrière. But the essential connection between the Industrial Revolution and the new methods of managing the insane can, similarly, be

105

demonstrated. Central to an understanding of the process are the changes which were taking place in the deployment of labor.

## The Growth of Wage Labor

In 1780, on the eve of the dual revolution, France and Britain were the two economic giants of Europe. In volume of trade they were nearly equal. France's foreign trade had increased fourfold in sixty years and her colonial system in some areas was stronger than that of the British.[25] Each of these countries, like the rest of Europe, was experiencing staggering population growth. In the half century after 1750 the population of France rose by 22 per cent, from 22 million to nearly 27 million; in the United Kingdom population increased 36 per cent, from 10 million to 16 million.[26] In each of the two countries the conditions of the rural poor were harsh and worsening. The great majority of French peasants were landless or had insufficient holdings, oppressed by feudal dues, tithes, taxes and inflation.[27] In Britain, the enclosure of common lands in the eighteenth century deprived cottagers of their subsistence and drove increasing numbers into agricultural wage labor which provided meager and intermittent compensation. The result was destitution for many and an increase in applications for poor relief. Taxes for relief—the poor rate—more than tripled between 1760 and 1801 in Britain, and nearly equaled the entire cost of English national government, excluding the army and navy.[28]

Holding back the onset of the Industrial Revolution, argues British historian T. S. Ashton, were social resistance to change and the lack of skill and adaptability of the workers.[29] But as the population grew, the mass of the landless poor swelled and the ranks of beggars, vagrants and unemployed increased, the diversion of laboring men, women and children into industrial wage work became possible. 'It was not the least of the achievements of the industrial revolution,' writes Ashton, 'that it drew into the economic system part of that legion of the lost, and that it turned many of the irregulars into efficient, if over-regimented, members of an industrial army.'[30] In France,, by way of contrast, the Revolution so far improved the condition of the peasants that the flow of 'landless free labourers merely trickled into the cities' and the 'capitalist transformation . . . was slowed to a crawl.'[31]

Some of the 'irregulars' in Britain, were less readily 'regimented' than others—the insane amongst them. What was to be done with those who would not, or could not, work? In striving to hold down the cost of poor relief the policy makers of the early Industrial Revolution became obsessed with the need to force 'the very great number of lazy People to maintain themselves by their own Industry.' Obligating applicants for relief 'to submit to the Confinement and Labour of the Workhouse'[32] was one such measure. The number of psychotic and mentally deficient confined in poorhouses in

106

England and Wales, however, became considerable—4–5,000 by 1789, estimates Kathleen Jones.[33] Many more were confined for vagrancy in jails and Bridewells (houses of correction), and others were maintained on outdoor relief.[34] Hospitals and asylums were few. Bethlem in London had existed since the twelfth century, and two hospitals were opened through voluntary public subscription in the 1750s—the Manchester Lunatic Hospital and St Luke's in London. In most areas, however, those lunatics who were unmanageable in workhouse and jails were transferred, at public expense, to private madhouses. The number of these private establishments was increasing, and 30–40 licensed houses existed at the end of the eighteenth century.[35] The York Retreat was one such.

## The Asylum Movement

Public responsibility for the care of pauper lunatics could not be avoided, and indeed it became a basic requisite in shaping the new wage labor force (as Andrew Scull has pointed out in his book on this theme, *Museums of Madness*[36]). To separate the employable from the unemployable was essential to the rationalization of poor relief. The able-bodied should not be encouraged to be idle, but the incapacitated had to be accommodated. In an effort to reduce the bill for the care of pauper lunatics in private madhouses, the British County Asylum Act of 1808 recommended the establishment of public specialty hospitals for the insane. The first county asylums to open were in rural districts where pauperism was severe and subsistence farming declining.[37]

Throughout Europe, moral treatment was intimately tied to the development of the new specialty establishments for lunatics. The York Retreat was one of a growing number of private madhouses, and its methods were copied, to a limited degree, by the new county asylums. Bicêtre had become a central institution for the insane alone, only one year before Pinel struck off the fetters. La Salpêtrière was converted to that purpose in the same year. The miscellany of the poor, who had previously been confined there, was released by the revolutionary government 'in order to distribute it to the points where the labor force was rarest.'[38] Criminals, henceforth, were to be housed separately from lunatics.[39] Chiarugi's humane methods were introduced in a newly erected hospital for the insane in Florence. And in the United States, as the first wave of hospitals for the insane began to be opened, moral treatment was the style of management which the new superintendents studied and aimed to establish in their institutions.

## Rehabilitation and Institutionalization

One of the attractions of moral treatment was its curative and rehabilitative emphasis. If patients could be cured and discharged to support themselves, they would cease to be a drain on the public purse. The proprietor of the private Whitchurch Asylum in Herefordshire, for example, played up this point in an advertising handbill. Arguing that patients admitted to his establishment recovered in a matter of days, compared with months and years for a cure in the local county asylums, he estimated that the cost of a cure in his private licensed house was a fraction of the cost in the public asylums.[40] Furthermore, the emphasis in moral management on hard work and self-discipline, as Scull has pointed out, reflected the same attitudes required in shaping the new industrial labor force.[41]

Despite the rehabilitative emphasis in moral treatment, however, the increase in asylum care was rapid. With the growth of wage work and the existence of a large, cheap supply of labor, the marginally functional insane were at a considerable disadvantage. Many of those who might have been fairly productive in working subsistence smallholdings were now unemployable. Labor mobility, long working hours and poverty made it harder for families to support their disabled members at home. It had been difficult enough before, as the following petition from a Lancashire laborer to the Poor Law authorities in 1681 demonstrates:

> John Sandholme of Inskip cum Sowerby humbly sheweth unto your good wor[shi]pps that his wyffe is exterordnary troubled with Melanchollic distemper in soe much that shee is in danger to distroy her selfe if shee should be Left in the house Allone but for the space of halfe an houre and he hath A Child that is but About A munthe Above halfe A yeare old which he nurseth and hee is A very pore Mann and hath nothinge to Maintayne him selfe not his wyffe and Child but his owne hand Laboure & he can not Leave his wyffe to worke unless he hier An able p[er]son to stay & Looke to his wyffe for fear shee distroy her selfe. . . .[42]

Such home care for the insane through outdoor relief diminished as the Industrial Revolution advanced and institutional care expanded. When outdoor relief expenditure was severely restricted in the mid-nineteenth century there was a commensurate increase in the outlay on lunatic asylums and workhouses.[43] The proportion of the population of England and Wales officially identified as insane (including those in workhouses and the community, but largely comprising asylum inmates) grew dramatically during the moral treatment era and the period of establishment of county asylums. In 1807, the official count was 2.3 insane people per 10,000 population; by the time moral treatment had faded away in 1870, there were officially 24.3 per 10,000. Nearly all of the increase (at least after 1844 when the available figures allow a distinction to be made) is in the number of pauper lunatics; the number of private patients remained remarkably small and constant throughout the nineteenth century.[44]

There was clearly a growth in the recognition and confinement of the insane, but did the Industrial Revolution also spawn an actual increase in the occurrence of insanity? Contemporary opinion was divided on this question, the majority arguing that the increase was more apparent than real. As we shall see in Chapter 9, however, there is a distinct possibility that psychosis, and particularly schizophrenia, was indeed becoming more prevalent as the nineteenth century advanced.

## Moral Treatment for the Poor

The treatment methods of the moral-management advocates and of the twentieth-century pioneers of social psychiatry were very similar (see Table 5.1); so, too, was the political function of the movements they created. Just as the post-Second World War social psychiatry revolution legitimized deinstitutionalization, so moral treatment legitimized the growth of institutional care in the nineteenth century. In each case, the ideology of a treatment approach, initially humane and directed towards the patients' benefit, became subtly distorted and was used to serve political ends which were not necessarily in the patients' interests. After the Second World War, the effort to rehabilitate patients to decent living and a useful role in the community

Table 5.1  **Moral treatment and the post-Second World War social psychiatry revolution compared**

| MORAL TREATMENT | POST–SECOND WORLD WAR SOCIAL PSYCHIATRY REVOLUTION |
| --- | --- |
| Non-restraint | Non-restraint |
| Non-confinement | Open door |
| Self-control emphasized | Therapeutic community |
| Privileges - not punishment | Positive reinforcement |
| Small treatment settings | Small units |
| Homelike environment | Less barren wards |
| Warm baths and generous diet | Patient comforts improved |
| Work therapy | Vocational rehabilitation |
| Patients are human | Patients are to be respected |
| Patient seen as child | Patient seen as adult |
| Social activities | Social retraining |
| Drugs seldom used | Drug treatment valued |
| Early discharge | Early discharge |
| Community involvement | Community involvement |
| Legitimized institutional expansion | Legitimized institutional decline |
| Supposed cost savings | Supposed cost savings |

became translated into a rush to dump patients on the street and in nursing homes in order to save money. Similarly, Samuel Tuke's *Description of the Retreat*, published in 1813, encouraged reformers in the belief that asylums could be curative and hastened the expansion of the county asylum system. Moral treatment, as it was offered to paupers in the public asylums, however, bore relatively little resemblance to moral treatment as it was developed for the middle-class clientele of the York Retreat.

At the Retreat, seven staff cared for thirty patients, and, in addition, personal servants lived on the premises. In the county asylums, the generally accepted ratio was one keeper to thirty patients.[45] The early asylums were overcrowded and staffed by unqualified and untrained keepers. Despite the superintendents' promises of improved cure rates, local authorities were unwilling to pay for a decent standard of care. Consequently, many patients slept on straw, mechanical restraints were commonly used and opportunities for patients to work or enjoy social diversion were restricted.[46] The high annual mortality rates at the asylums of Lancaster and the West Riding of Yorkshire (17 per cent and 18 per cent, respectively, of the resident population) were the result, argued John Thurnam, a physician at the York Retreat, of poor nutrition and hygiene. Even greater mortality rates at the Norfolk County Asylum (19 per cent) and at St Peter's Hospital for paupers in Bristol (20 per cent) were the consequence of lack of adequate medical care and 'the want of a proper amount of land for the exercise and employment of the patients.'[47]

By the mid-1840s only five of the seventeen county asylums had abandoned mechanical restraint. Foremost amongst them were Lincoln Asylum, under the direction of Robert Gardiner Hill, and the massive new asylum at Hanwell, Middlesex, where John Conolly was the superintendent. The limited acceptance of moral treatment at that time is illustrated by the fact that Hill was forced to resign his post owing to public opposition; and Conolly was unable to persuade his governing committee to meet the expense of two of his innovative ideas—basic education classes for patients and professional training for the staff. With the restriction of outdoor relief and the great expansion of the asylum system, during the next decade, the situation was reversed. By the mid-1850s, nearly all the thirty county asylums had discarded mechanical restraints and adopted some features of moral management.[48] Staffing patterns, at least in some asylums, improved. At Lancaster Asylum in 1846, on the 'tranquil' wards, there was one attendant for twenty-five patients, and on the more disturbed wards, one attendant to fifteen refractory patients.[49] The value of moral treatment in legitimizing social policy is here illustrated—legitimizing, that is, the Poor Law Commission policy of categorizing the destitute, providing poor relief in specialized institutions and cutting back on outdoor relief. The task accomplished, the cost of care per patient was soon reduced through progressive cheeseparing and expansion of the size of the institutions. Mechanical restraints and solitary confinement returned, and by the late 1860s moral treatment in the public asylums had again become a mere facade.[50]

In his description of nineteenth-century private madhouses, *The Trade in Lunacy*, William Parry-Jones highlights the differences in treatment for the poor (paid out of the public purse) and for private patients. He remarks: 'With regard to the maltreatment of lunatics in madhouses, confined under bad, often appalling, physical conditions, the evidence is . . . substantial and refers, especially to pauper departments during the first half of the nineteenth century.'[51] Again: 'The various factors which operated to keep the charge for paupers as low as possible . . . served to delay the introduction of the non-restraint system and to foster the continuance of the merely custodial confinement of lunatics.'[52] Mechanical restraint was rarely seen in licensed houses receiving only private patients, but was freely used in those houses taking paupers.[53] Some proprietors felt that restraints should not be used on patients from the 'respectable class: their feelings are more acute than those of the humbler grade.'[54] But the fact that non-restraint treatment required more and better trained staff and led to higher charges was generally recognized.[55] Whereas in the pauper establishments one keeper might care for ten or fifteen patients, in the houses for the wealthy the ratio was one attendant or servant for every one or two patients.[56] Moral treatment in Britain, it is clear, was not generally for the poor. As we have seen, for a few years, from the 1850s to the 1860s, during the expansion of the asylum system, a form of moral treatment was made available to paupers in county asylums; but otherwise, humane care was for those who could afford it.

## Cure Rates

Did the class bias in quality of care influence the outcome of insanity? In attempting to answer this question, we have to be very cautious about using the published cure rates of the time. Where one madhouse proprietor talked of patients being 'cured' or 'discharged recovered' another might have used the term 'relieved' or 'improved.' Again, patients admitted to one establishment might have included more who were young and early in the course of a functional psychosis; on the other hand, many of those admitted to county asylums were chronic patients transferred from workhouses or were elderly people with dementia. Bearing these considerations in mind, the statistics published in 1845 by Dr John Thurnam (see Table 5.2) are among the most useful. The figures show that institutions receiving paupers consistently reported lower recovery rates and higher mortality rates. Dr Thurnam argued that these results were not entirely due to the condition of

111

**Table 5.2   Recovery and mortality rates for British mental institutions, comparing private and pauper establishments before 1845**

|  | RECOVERY AS % OF ADMISSIONS | MORTALITY AS % OF NUMBER RESIDENT |
|---|---|---|
| *County asylums* | | |
| Receiving both private and pauper patients (average of 6 asylums, 1812–44) | 46.87 | 10.46 |
| Receiving paupers only (average of 9 asylums, 1812–44) | 36.95 | 13.88 |
| *Metropolitan licensed houses* | | |
| Receiving principally private patients (average of 27 houses, 1839–43) | 30.87 | 6.80 |
| Receiving principally paupers (average of 3 houses, 1839–43) | 23.74 | 18.10 |
| *Provincial licensed houses* | | |
| Receiving principally private patients (average of 41 houses, 1839–43) | 43.50 | 6.57 |
| Receiving principally paupers (average of 44 houses, 1839–43) | 41.50 | 10.56 |

Source: Thurnam, J., *Observations and Essays on the Statistics of Insanity,* London: Simpkin, Marshall, 1845, Table 12.

the patients on admission, but were, in part, a consequence of the differences in their management.[57]

The size of the institution may have been an important factor: asylums and licensed houses receiving private patients were generally a good deal smaller. Metropolitan licensed houses for paupers held an average of 400 patients; those for private patients had an average capacity of 23 residents.[58] For this reason, perhaps, at the model pauper asylum of Hanwell in Middlesex—with a thousand beds, far and away the largest mental institution in the country—the recovery rate was well below average, despite the emphasis on moral management and non-restraint. Daniel Hack Tuke's figures show the recovery rate at Hanwell fluctuating between 25 per cent and 32 per cent of admissions during the first forty-five years of the hospital's operation.[59] At Lancaster Asylum, Britain's rapidly expanding, second largest mental hospital, the introduction of more progressive treatment methods in the early 1840s reduced mortality rates but failed to improve discharge and cure rates; the percentage of recoveries, in fact, declined after the introduction of moral treatment.[60] The social policy which established large, cost-effective asylums

112

and limited expenditure on patient care, reduced the possibility of rehabilitation for the insane poor. The improvements in public mental hospital care made during the expansion of the asylum system in the 1850s and 1860s cannot be shown to have improved cure rates. The smaller size of the private establishments, on the other hand, and the much higher ratio of staff to residents, may well have enhanced the possibility of recovery for wealthier patients.

## Labor in Nineteenth Century Britain

What was the effect of the labor market on policy and practice in nineteenth-century British psychiatry? As we have seen, at no time was there a particularly strong rehabilitative emphasis to public psychiatry. This observation is understandable in view of the exceptionally high levels of unemployment which existed throughout the century. A famous dispute has raged among social historians as to whether living conditions for the working class worsened or improved during the early decades of the British Industrial Revolution.[61] Over one fact, however, there can be little room for debate (although information on the subject is scattered)—prior to 1850 unemployment was substantial. Vagrancy was increasing dramatically, 10 per cent of the population were paupers in the 1840s and, at times, cyclical unemployment reached colossal heights. In the business slumps of 1826 and 1841–2, unemployment in the region of 75 per cent was not uncommon in the hard hit areas of the industrial North and Midlands.[62] A contemporary observer, Henry Mayhew, writing of Londoners in the early nineteenth century, concludes: 'In almost all occupations there is . . . a *superfluity of labourers*. . . . In the generality of trades the calculation is that one-third of the hands are fully employed, one-third partially, and one-third unemployed throughout the year.'[63] Although the availability of employment increased after 1850,[64] unemployment continued to be considerable throughout the Great Victorian Boom (1850–73) and may well have been only moderately better than during the subsequent Great Depression (1873–96).[65] That the heyday of moral treatment in the county asylums occurred in the boom years of the 1850s and 1860s is perhaps not especially relevant (except insofar as improved institutional conditions allowed an increased strictness in the limitation of outdoor relief[66]). There is no evidence, on the one hand, of a labor shortage at that time or, on the other hand, of a stronger rehabilitative effort or increase in discharge rates from the institutions. What is relevant is that the one clearly rehabilitative movement in psychiatry in Britain since the beginning of industrialization and the development of asylums occurred during the only period of significant labor shortage in two centuries—the years immediately following the Second World War.

The labor history of nineteenth-century America is substantially different from that of Britain. How did it influence psychiatry in the United States?

## Industrializing America

Labor was in short supply in industrializing and expanding America during the first half of the nineteenth century.[67] 'English observers in the mid-nineteenth century,' writes historian Daniel Boorstin, 'Admired the ease with which American labourers moved about the country, from one job to another. They were amazed at the general freedom from fear of unemployment. . . .'[68] Real wages, in consequence, were higher in the United States than Europe.[69] The members of the Yates Committee to the New York legislature in 1824, reported:

> In this country the labour of three days will readily supply the wants of seven, while in Europe the labour of the whole week will barely suffice for the maintenance and support of the family of an industrious labourer or peasant.[70]

Pauperism was exceedingly rare by European standards, and what there was existed largely in the maritime cities, where newly arrived immigrants congregated. Less than 1 per cent of the population of Philadelphia were paupers in the 1820s and less than 2 per cent of the population of New York State.[71] Unemployment remained low during much of the antebellum period, becoming more significant from the 1850s onward.[72] Population increase and the late Victorian depressions of 1873, 1884 and 1893, however, brought high unemployment and poverty.[73] Peacetime labor shortage of early nineteenth-century dimensions has not been seen since in the United States.

Was American psychiatry more rehabilitative in its emphasis in the early nineteenth century, in response to the heavy demand for labor? It is certainly true that moral treatment was vigorously adopted by the first corporate asylums which were established (by public subscription) in those years. The founders of these New England hospitals were much influenced by the examples and writing of Tuke and Pinel and applied their methods from the moment the doors were opened—at the Friends' Asylum, Frankford, Pennsylvania (1817), Bloomingdale Asylum, New York (1821), McLean Hospital, Boston, Massachusetts (1818), and the Retreat at Hartford, Connecticut (1824). The independent Pennsylvania Hospital in Philadelphia, which established a separate branch for the insane in 1841, was also a model of progressive care. These hospitals, many of them established by Quakers, were, like the York Retreat, primarily intended for the treatment of private patients. Some, however, like the Hartford Retreat and the Bloomingdale Asylum, took substantial numbers of paupers in return for public funding.

As in the best British private establishments, staffing was comfortably high—one attendant to six patients at the Pennsylvania Hospital, one attendant to two patients at other hospitals. Restraints were very rarely used, and a full, if somewhat over-regimented, schedule of social and work activities was established for all inmates. Such was the success and public good favor of these progressive institutions that they were a major influence in the development of public hospitals for the insane.[74]

## American Public Hospitals

Discussions of this era in American psychiatry often make the point that moral treatment was not generally made available to the poor or that it existed more in the pious mouthings of hospital superintendents than in the actual conditions of patients in the public institutions.[75] This point of view deserves some debate, however, especially if we restrict ourselves to a study of the earliest decades of operation of the public hospitals. George Mora writes, in the *Comprehensive Textbook of Psychiatry*, for instance:

> Among the earliest state-supported institutions were the Eastern State Hospital at Lexington, Kentucky, opened in 1824; the Manhattan State Hospital in New York City, opened in 1825; the Western State Hospital in Staunton, Virginia, opened in 1828; and the South Carolina State Hospital in Columbia, South Carolina, opened in 1828. In contrast with the private or corporate hospitals, in which moral treatment was applied, those state institutions remained largely custodial.[76]

Of the four examples chosen by Dr Mora, two might reasonably be described as 'largely custodial.' The performance of the state asylum in Lexington, Kentucky, was less than creditable. Historian David Rothman considers that it 'had ... become a custodial institution' by 1845;[77] the figures supplied by Gerald Grob in his review of *Mental Institutions in America* suggest that this may have been true as early as 1840 (see Table 5.3). Yet even this institution had high ideals in the early years—the directors insisted, for example, that no restraints be used.[78] In using Manhattan State Hospital as an example, Mora is presumably referring to the New York City Asylum on Blackwell's Island which actually opened in 1839. This institution, as we shall see later, was also clearly custodial, but for special reasons. At the Western Virginia State Hospital, however (according to Norman Dain's study of that state's mental hospitals), moral treatment *was* introduced in 1836 by an enthusiastic young superintendent who so upgraded the quality of the hospital that he was able to attract private, upper-class, white patients, who accounted for a third of the admissions.[79] Social reformers visiting the hospital in 1842 regarded it as excellent, and reported:

**Table 5.3** Patients discharged 'recovered' expressed as a percentage of admissions in selected years for American asylums open before 1845[a]

| | 1820 | 1825 | 1830 | 1835 | 1840 | 1845 | 1850 | 1855 | 1860 | 1865 | 1870 | 1875 |
|---|---|---|---|---|---|---|---|---|---|---|---|---|
| *Corporate and private hospitals* | | | | | | | | | | | | |
| Hartford Retreat, Connecticut | — | 23 | 55 | 50 | 60 | 43 | 47 | 43 | 41 | 37 | 33 | 40 |
| McLean Asylum, Massachusetts | 22 | 36 | 41 | 54 | 48 | 62 | 45 | 46 | 32 | 43 | 42 | 19 |
| Bloomingdale Asylum, New York | — | 46 | 43 | 42 | 53 | 44 | 51 | 49 | 33 | 43 | 39 | 30 |
| Friends' Asylum, Pennsylvania | 20 | —[b] | 44 | 22 | 46 | 52 | 52 | 40 | 40 | 28 | 42 | 32 |
| Pennsylvania Hospital | — | — | — | — | — | 45 | 51 | 57 | 46 | 44 | 36 | 42 |
| *State and city hospitals (northern)* | | | | | | | | | | | | |
| Maine Insane Hospital | — | — | — | — | 28 | 39 | 60 | 32 | 46 | 33 | 37 | 36 |
| Boston Insane Hospital, Mass. | — | — | — | — | 7 | 24 | 51 | 29 | 41 | 25 | 26 | 30 |
| Worcester State Hospital, Mass. | — | — | — | 46 | 51 | 42 | 52 | 55 | 60 | 48 | 41 | 25 |
| New Hampshire Asylum | — | — | — | — | —[b] | 42 | 44 | 53 | 45 | 39 | 28 | 44 |
| New York City Asylum, Blackwell's Is. | — | — | — | — | — | — | — | —[b] | — | — | 27 | 31 |
| Utica State Asylum, New York | — | — | — | — | — | 46 | 47 | 47 | 31 | 32 | 32 | 31 |
| Central Ohio Asylum | — | — | — | — | 52 | 29 | 51 | 63 | 49 | 41 | — | — |
| Vermont Asylum | — | — | — | — | 45 | 29 | 53 | 48 | 41 | 38 | 29 | 25 |
| *State hospitals (southern)* | | | | | | | | | | | | |
| Kentucky Eastern Asylum | — | 44 | — | —[b] | 8 | 37 | 34 | 35 | 46 | 44 | 28 | 60 |
| Maryland State Hospital | — | — | — | 9 | 38 | 44 | 35 | 37 | 50 | 65 | 83 | 16 |
| Tennessee State Hospital | — | — | — | — | —[b] | —[b] | 34 | 46 | 47 | —[b] | 41 | 44 |
| South Carolina Asylum | —[b] | — | — | — | — | 57 | 50 | 31 | 54 | 70 | 29 | 29 |
| Virginia Eastern Asylum | —[b] | —[b] | —[b] | —[b] | —[b] | —[b] | —[b] | —[b] | —[b] | —[b] | —[b] | 46 |
| Virginia Western Asylum | — | — | — | —[b] | —[b] | — | — | — | 41 | 44 | 44 | 40 |

Source: Percentages calculated from data in Grob, G. N., *Mental Institutions in America*, New York: Free Press, 1973, pp. 374–93.
Note: [a] These figures, being calculated on statistics for a single year, are substantially less accurate and more subject to fluctuation than if based on longer time periods.
[b] Hospital open but figures not available.

The employments, recreations, amusements, instructions, and influences are very various, and well fitted to soothe the excited, cheer the desponding, guide the erring, check the vicious, raise the fallen, and restore the insane. The restraints are very few.[80]

Treatment at each of the two Virginia state hospitals was reportedly comparable, and benefited from an exceptionally good level of staffing—one staff member (including slave attendants) for every three patients.[81] South Carolina State Hospital, the last of Dr Mora's examples, far from being custodial had a high patient turnover. From data provided by Gerald Grob, we can calculate that from 1845 (when records became available) to 1865 the number of patients discharged as recovered (and not merely improved) was regularly around 50 per cent of admissions (as shown in Table 5.3) or 20 per cent of the total hospital population.[82]

As we survey the fourteen or so public hospitals which were in operation in the United States by 1845, and recall that non-restraint management had established itself in fewer than a third of the ill-staffed, British county asylums by the mid-1840s, it appears possible that the pauper lunatic in America at this time was the more fortunate. Unsatisfactory hospital conditions were primarily to be found in New York City and in some institutions in the non-industrial South. Besides the two state hospitals in Virginia, we know that progressive and humane measures were practiced in Worcester State Hospital, in Massachusetts; at Utica, in upstate New York; and at the Vermont Asylum, in Brattleboro. The Maine Insane Asylum was in the hands of Isaac Ray, a prominent psychiatrist and moral-treatment advocate.[83] If Worcester State Hospital is a fair illustration, staffing patterns were excellent by contemporary British asylum standards—one attendant to twelve or fifteen patients during the 1830s and 1840s.[84]

Mortality rates (the measure which Dr Thurnam considered the best standard of comparison of the quality of asylum care) were considerably better in American state hospitals than in British county asylums in the 1840s (see Table 5.4). These differences were not due to the admission of more elderly patients to British hospitals—the age distribution of admissions to British and American asylums was quite similar.[85] Since acutely ill patients tended to have a higher death rate, the low mortality might theoretically have been a result of the admission of more chronic patients to the American hospitals. Equally, the lower death rate in the American institutions may well have reflected better conditions for American insane paupers.

In general, David Rothman feels the American public asylums tried to emulate the private institutions but were not able to achieve quite the same standards.

There were lapses and failures, but in the first few years of the asylums they were not gross ones. Most mental hospitals in the 1830s and 1840s

**Table 5.4   Mortality rates in British and American pauper asylums as a percentage of the number resident**

| BRITISH COUNTY ASYLUMS | | AMERICAN STATE AND CITY HOSPITALS | | |
| --- | --- | --- | --- | --- |
| | MEAN ANNUAL MORTALITY 1839–44 % | | ANNUAL MORTALITY 1840 | 1845 |
| *Receiving paupers only* | | *Northern states* | | |
| Bedford | 10.5 | Maine | 10.4 | 8.7 |
| Dorset | 12.2 | Boston, Mass. | 6.2 | 5.8 |
| Kent | 10.7 | Worcester, Mass. | 6.6 | 7.6 |
| Lancaster | 13.2 | New Hampshire | — | 7.9 |
| Middlesex | 9.1 | Utica, New York | — | 7.9 |
| Norfolk | 19.1 | Central Ohio | 10.7 | 10.8 |
| Suffolk | 10.8 | Vermont | 7.4 | 7.6 |
| York | 13.6 | | | |
| *Receiving private and pauper patients* | | *Southern states* | | |
| Chester | 11.8 | Maryland | 10.0 | 9.3 |
| Cornwall | 7.7 | South Carolina | — | 8.4 |
| Gloucester | 10.7 | Virginia Eastern | — | 9.4 |
| Leicester | 11.3 | | | |
| Nottingham | 9.2 | | | |
| Stafford | 13.7 | | | |

Source: British asylums: Thurnam, *Observations and Essays on the Statistics of Insanity.* Table 13. American asylums: mortality rates calculated from statistics in Grob, *Mental Institutions in America*, pp. 374–93.

abolished the whip and the chain and did away with confinement. . . . And often they accomplished more, treating patients with thoughtfulness and humanity.[86]

Charles Dickens, in his *American Notes*, though critical of much that he saw in the New World of 1842, was very favorably impressed by the Boston Insane Hospital for paupers, and devotes several pages to a description of his visit. He was particularly struck by the dignity with which the patients were treated, their freedom from restraint or restrictions in the use of potentially dangerous instruments, their provisions for work and social activity (including sewing circles, balls and carriage rides) and the intimate involvement of the superintendent and his wife in the daily life of the hospital. 'It is obvious,' he concludes, 'that one great feature of the system, is the inculcation and encouragement, even among such unhappy persons, of a decent self-respect.'[87] The Boston Hospital, aside from this report, has never been heralded as an outstandingly progressive hospital by the standards of the times. Dickens also found the private Hartford Retreat to be 'admirably conducted,'[88] but he was severely critical of the recently opened New York City Asylum on Blackwell's Island. At the latter institution: 'I saw nothing of that salutary system which had impressed me so favourably elsewhere; and everything had a lounging, listless, madhouse air.'[89] At last Dickens had come upon an American asylum as depressing as he was to find St Luke's in London a few years later.[90] And the reason for the melancholy conditions at the New York City Asylum? Perhaps, as he says,

> New York, as a great emporium of commerce, and as a place of general resort, not only from all parts of the States, but from most parts of the world, has always a large pauper population to provide for; and labours, therefore, under peculiar difficulties in this respect.[91]

The New York *State* Hospital, over 200 miles north at Utica, escaped the problem of overcrowding with foreign-born paupers from which the city hospital suffered, [92] and became recognized as a model state institution. The rare instance of unenlightened hospital conditions was to be found where poverty and unemployment were beginning to appear within the shores of the United States.

## Rehabilitation

Not only were conditions generally humane in the public institutions, they were also genuinely rehabilitative. Work therapy was strongly emphasized at such state hospitals as Worcester, Massachusetts; Utica, New York; and Brattleboro, Vermont.[93] Patients were released on parole from the Eastern Virginia Asylum to seek work in local towns, and some were also boarded out with families in order that 'the accustomed life of the lunatic shall be less essentially at variance with that pertaining to persons generally of sound mind.'[94] Several hospitals, including Utica, instituted the measure for which Conolly in England was unable to obtain funding—classes for patients. A variety of subjects was taught, including music and drama. Most hospitals had libraries for the patients. In addition, links with the community at large were strengthened by encouraging the participation of teachers, ministers and other visitors in the day-to-day operation of the hospitals.[95]

The rehabilitative emphasis appears to have been associated with reasonably high discharge rates. As Table 5.3 shows, the proportion of patients discharged 'recovered' from public hospitals in different years compared quite well with figures for private hospitals. (No doubt, of course, hospital superintendents attached different meanings to 'recovered,' but there is no reason to believe that public-hospital doctors were particularly optimistic in this respect.) We see very respectable recovery rates not only at

119

South Carolina Asylum, as previously noted, and at such hospitals of repute as Worcester and Utica, but also at the New Hampshire Asylum, the Central Ohio Asylum and the Vermont Asylum. Recovery rates at these hospitals through the 1850s were at least equal to those (given by Thurnam) for the best British county asylums. Table 5.5, drawn from Thurnam's statistics, shows that recovery rates at the American corporate hospitals and at the Worcester Asylum (admittedly the best of the state hospitals) all exceeded average cure rates at British institutions through the mid-1840s. Such direct comparison of overall recovery rates, however, can only yield very crude impressions in view of the probable differences in the patient populations and in measures of recovery. Cure rates in the United States, for example, might have been boosted by the fact that many chronic psychotics, especially blacks, were not admitted to the state hospitals but languished in jails and workhouses. It is not apparent, however, that this occurred more in the

**Table 5.5  Recovery and mortality rates in British and American mental institutions before 1845**

|  | RECOVERY AS % OF ADMISSIONS | MORTALITY AS % OF NUMBER RESIDENT |
|---|---|---|
| *Britain* | | |
| Private and Charitable Asylums (average of 8 asylums, 1766–1843) | 40.94 | 8.93 |
| Metropolitan Licensed Houses (average of 30 houses, 1839–43) | 25.65 | 14.68 |
| Provincial Licensed Houses (average of 85 houses, 1839–43) | 42.24 | 9.85 |
| County Asylums (average of 15 asylums, 1812–44) | 40.25 | 12.79 |
| *United States* | | |
| Corporate Hospitals | | |
| Bloomingdale Asylum, New York, 1821–41 | 46.18 | 10.32 |
| Friends' Asylum, Frankford, Penn., 1817–42 | 44.38 | 10.64 |
| Hartford Retreat, Conn., 1824–43 | 56.29 | — |
| McLean Asylum, Boston, Mass., 1818–43 | 44.95 | 11.07 |
| Average of 4 corporate asylums | 47.41 | 10.65 |
| State Hospitals | | |
| Worcester State Hospital, Mass., 1833–43 | 44.56 | 6.76 |

Source: Thurnam, *Observations and Essays on the Statistics of Insanity,* Table 12.

United States than in Britain; (and, as we have seen, the lower mortality rates in American institutions suggest that the American hospitals were receiving their fair share of chronic patients.) Higher discharge rates from American institutions might partly have reflected a policy of early discharge rather than a real difference in patient outcome. Nevertheless, such figures would still have been an accurate reflection of a greater rehabilitative emphasis in American psychiatry of the period.

## The 'Cult of Curability'

Some contemporary observers formed the impression that American mental-hospital treatment and cure rates were superior to those which existed in Britain. Like Dickens, Captain Basil Hall was a British visitor whose impressions of America were generally somewhat uncomplimentary. In the published account of his travels, however, he waxed lyrical over the patient management at the Hartford Retreat, which he witnessed in 1827, and contrasted the high recovery rates at that hospital with current British results. During the previous year, 25 of the 28 'recent' cases admitted to the Hartford Retreat—89.2 per cent—had recovered, he reported, but 'at two most ancient and celebrated institutions' of the same type in Britain only 25.5 per cent of 'recent' (acute) cases were cured.[96] Hall's claims attracted a great deal of attention on both sides of the Atlantic and were widely quoted in the press. Soon, other American hospital superintendents reported similar rates of success. Samuel Woodward at the Worcester State Hospital claimed recovery rates for 'recent' (acute) cases of 82–91 per cent for the early years of the hospital's operation between 1833 and 1840. John Galt, superintendent at the Eastern Virginia Asylum, announced, in his report of 1842, 92 per cent recovery in acute cases and 53 per cent recovery overall in new admissions. Around the same time, William Awl, superintendent of the Ohio State Asylum, reported cure rates of 80–100 per cent for cases of recent onset, and 48 per cent recovery for all cases of up to ten years duration admitted over a four-year period.[97] Heads of corporate and public asylums alike argued that recovery from insanity was the rule, incurability the exception. As stated by Amariah Brigham of Utica State Hospital: 'No fact relating to insanity appears better established than the general certainty of curing it in its early stage.'[98]

It is easy to dismiss such claims as American bombast and typical of the entrepreneurial audacity of the New Republic. The claims were, indeed, extravagant and clearly motivated, in part, by a wish to impress state legislators with the value of investment in hospital care. Dorothea Dix used these reports of the benefits of modern treatment in her successful campaign to establish public mental hospitals throughout the United States. The episode in American psychiatry has subsequently been disparaged as the

'Cult of Curability.'[99] Obviously, statistics may have been molded somewhat to improve the effect. Galt's 92 per cent recovery figure was, like many other reports, based on a small sample—13 admissions. Criteria for defining 'recent' cases and 'recovery' were subject to manipulation; and patients who relapsed, were readmitted and subsequently discharged again, might be counted as 'recovered' more than once.[100] Despite such statistical flaws, nevertheless, we cannot rule out the possibility that cure rates were outstandingly good at the time. Indeed, it seems quite possible that recovery rates for acutely ill patients admitted to American public and private mental hospitals throughout the first half of the nineteenth century were distinctly better than in the decades which followed or in contemporary Britain. Two points emerge clearly from the reports of the period. The emphasis on curability was largely an American phenomenon, and it pervaded public psychiatry as extensively as it did the private institutions. In Britain, George Burrows reported similarly high recovery rates in 1820 for 'recent' cases admitted to his madhouse, as did the proprietors of other private establishments.[101] The same degree of universal optimism, however, did not develop in British public hospitals of the period.

The enthusiasm of the American hospital superintendents was, in fact, based upon the observation of distinctly superior rates of recovery. Table 5.6 allows us to compare separately the cure rates for acute and chronic patients admitted to several British and American hospitals before 1842. The American recovery rates for acute patients were substantially better than the British. It may reasonably be assumed that these figures for recent cases are more comparable than those for total admissions. Undetermined numbers of chronically psychotic and demented patients, epileptics and mentally retarded amongst the general admissions largely determined the overall recovery rate, which, as we may see in Table 5.6, bore little relationship to the cure rate in acute illness. Significant differences in the causes of acute mental illness, however, could conceivably have accounted for the disparity in recovery rates. Thurnam argued, for example, that more of the American hospital admissions were suffering from alcohol-related psychoses and delirium tremens, which ended either in early recovery or death.[102] If this opinion were correct, we would expect to find higher death rates in the American asylums (in fact, as we have seen, they were lower) and higher recovery rates in male patients (which was true at Bloomingdale Asylum, but not at Worcester[103]). Whatever the causes, it is clear that there was a distinctly better course and outcome to acute mental illnesses in early nineteenth-century America, which needs to be explained.

## The Cover-up

Few physicians care to believe that their methods are not as successful as

**Table 5.6  Percentage of admissions discharged 'recovered' from British and American asylums according to duration of illness**

| | LESS THAN 12 MONTHS DURATION | MORE THAN 12 MONTHS DURATION | ALL CASES |
|---|---|---|---|
| *Britain* | | | |
| Private Hospitals | | | |
| York Retreat, 1796–1843 | 61.87 | 18.88 | 46.94 |
| Asylums for Private and Pauper Patients | | | |
| Bethlem Hospital, 1827–39 | 52.38 | 12.50 | 50.96 |
| Dundee Asylum, 1820–40 | 59.06 | 13.71 | 42.36 |
| Lincoln Asylum | 50.95 | 9.62 | 40.10 |
| St Luke's Hospital, 1751–1834 | 39.71 | — | — |
| County Asylum for Paupers Only | | | |
| Maidstone Asylum, Kent | 49.26 | 4.84 | 20.68 |
| Wakefield Asylum, Yorkshire | 53.74 | 11.50 | 44.18 |
| *United States* | | | |
| Corporate Hospitals | | | |
| Bloomingdale Asylum, New York, 1882–41[a] | 74.85 | 11.57 | 47.19 |
| Friends' Asylum, Frankford, Penn., 1817–38[b] | 58.23 | 25.20 | 45.11 |
| State Hospitals | | | |
| Worcester State Hospital, Mass., 1833–40 | 82.78 | 14.40 | 42.30 |
| Central Ohio Asylum, 1838–42 | 79.53 | 20.20[c] | 47.70[d] |

Source: Thurnam, *Observations and Essays on the Statistics of Insanity.* p. 57. Statistics for Ohio Asylum are added from Grob, *Mental Institutions in America,* p. 182.
Notes: [a] Private patients only.
    [b] Private and pauper patients.
    [c] Cases of 1–10 years duration.
    [d] Cases of up to 10 years duration.

those of others and, still less, that the achievements of their profession are following a progressively downhill course. Such concerns may well explain the intensity and somewhat derisory air with which later American psychiatrists have attempted to refute the curability claims of the moral-treatment era. They have been anxious to see the errors in these reports but less keen to validate any truth within them. Most vigorous and influential of these critics was Pliny Earle, and his work *The Curability of Insanity*, published in 1876, is frequently cited as the definitive debunking of the 'myth of curability.'[104] Dr Earle contended that the excellent recovery rates recorded by Samuel Woodward during the earliest years of the Worcester State Hospital were grossly exaggerated by statistical juggling. He made

123

much of the fact that the same patient might be counted as 'recovered' after every relapse and that percentages of recoveries were calculated on the basis of those discharged, not on the numbers admitted. His conclusion, much more in keeping with the figures for his own institution, late in the century, was that insanity was, in fact, far less curable than had been supposed.

Pliny Earle's attempt to rewrite psychiatric history, however, has itself been exposed as a cover-up. Dr Sanbourne Bockoven, who has reanalyzed Dr Earle's figures and uncovered more material on Samuel Woodward's patients,[105] concludes that Earle himself was guilty of statistical juggling. Dr Earle knew, for example, that the counting of repeated recoveries, which he so criticized and which has been raised by every critic since, made almost no difference to the overall recovery rate of Worcester State Hospital patients—a difference of less than a quarter of a percentage point. Dr Earle also knew of the existence of a comprehensive follow-up study of Samuel Woodward's discharged patients, conducted by Dr John Park, a later superintendent of Worcester State Hospital—a study which showed that outcome was, indeed, so superior in the early decades of the hospital's operation that Dr Park judiciously withheld the results from publication.

At Dr Earle's suggestion, Dr Park had compiled a retroactive review of admissions and discharges since the opening of the hospital in 1833, employing his own criteria for 'recovery,' not Dr Woodward's. His results (continued up to 1950 with modern data), showing the changes in the percentage of admissions discharged as recovered from Worcester State Hospital, are displayed in Figure 5.1 (taken from Dr Bockoven's book). Dr Park, who was as keen as Dr Earle to demonstrate that the early recovery rates were artificially inflated, was unable to reduce Dr Woodward's figures by more than 2 or 3 per cent. Overall recovery rates of 45 per cent in the moral-treatment era, as we can see, fell to 20 per cent in the late Victorian Great Depression and to 10 per cent in the 1930s.

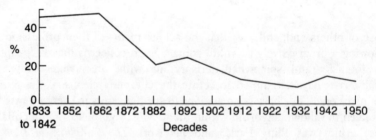

*Figure 5.1 Percentage of admissions discharged as 'recovered' from Worcester State Hospital over successive decades.*

Note: Reprinted by permission of the author. From Bockoven, J. S., *Moral Treatment in Community Mental Health*, New York: Springer, 1972, p. 56. © 1972. J. Sanbourne Bockoven.

124

David Rothman has criticized Dr Bockoven's work on two counts. Rothman argues, in the first place, that the revised recovery rates for Dr Woodward's patients 'are considerably lower than the claims for the 1830's and 1840's.' Here Rothman makes the error of confusing the claimed recovery rates for 'recent' (acute) cases (which were over 80 per cent) with general admissions (45 per cent recovery). Secondly, Rothman claims that Bockoven 'makes no attempt to question just what 'recovery' meant in the original records.'[106] But Rothman is incorrect here, also. Bockoven demonstrates exactly what 'recovery' meant for Woodward's patients by presenting the results of Dr Park's follow-up, 36–60 years after discharge, of all of Woodward's patients who left the hospital, 'recovered,' prior to 1847. There were 1,173 such patients, and information was collected on the condition of 984 of them. This project was both ambitious and successful, and took Dr Park ten years to complete. The study showed that an extraordinary 58 per cent of the patients followed-up never had another relapse in the rest of their lives or until the time of follow-up. Another 8 per cent had relapsed but were well at follow-up. Dr Bockoven draws the conclusion that, during the moral-treatment era,

> the natural history of psychosis in general (including cases due to organic changes of the central nervous system) was such that a large proportion of patients were able to leave the mental hospital, and only a small proportion, perhaps 20–30%, were destined to die in a mental hospital. Favourable outcome was, of course, even more frequent in the functional psychoses considered alone.[107]

A contemporary of Pliny Earle's, Isaac Ray, a psychiatrist of equal stature and experience, rebutted Earle's views in 1879. Dr Ray argued that the early statistical reports were no more biased than recent figures and that recoveries had, in fact, become less frequent. The reasons, he believed, for the decline in recovery rates included a failure to provide an adequate trial of moral treatment to many patients. Latter-day psychiatric historians, however, have generally ignored Dr Ray and repeated Pliny Earle's rather self-serving opinions as accurate.[108] They have, thereby, buried important information— the course of functional psychoses in patients admitted to early nineteenth-century American hospitals was more benign than in the hundred years which followed.

## The Demise of Moral Treatment

It is possible, then, that the labor shortage in the first half of the nineteenth century in America influenced rehabilitative efforts for the insane and elevated recovery rates in psychosis. This notion, however, reverses some of the orthodox explanations for the demise of moral management in the latter part of the century. Thus, it was not so much that the failure of promises of curability led legislators to demand cost-cutting in the institutions; it may have been the diminished need for manpower which reduced the incentive to fund vigorous treatment programs and caused a reduction in cure rates. It was not just a build-up of chronic patients and an increase in hospital size and overcrowding which caused the deteriorating institutional conditions; it was the decline in rehabilitative efforts which created the build-up of chronic patients. And the foreign paupers who filled the asylums and so outraged the sensibilities of the psychiatrists and middle-class clientele—the Irish 'clodhoppers' with their 'filthy habits'—they were not incurable because they had 'scarcely an idea beyond that of . . . manual employment,' as Isaac Ray claimed.[109] They were stuck because there was no employment outside the hspital, and no longer any work therapy within the hospital.[110] (Inmates' work had become too competitive to be tolerated by the unemployed beyond the institutions' walls.) If funding cuts and overcrowding with chronic patients and paupers were the problems, then the affluent private hospitals which selected more 'recent' cases and excluded paupers— Pennsylvania Hospital, the Friends' Asylum, McLean Hospital, Bloomingdale Asylum (which excluded paupers after 1857) and the Hartford Retreat (after 1866)[111]—these hospitals should have experienced few difficulties. As Table 5.3 shows, however, recovery rates deteriorated in these institutions also after 1870. Public and private asylums alike declined from curative to custodial institutions.[112]

Moral treatment reached its zenith in labor-starved, early nineteenth-century America for two reasons. Firstly, given a demand for labor, moral management was a truly rehabilitative measure which could restore the maximum level of functioning to the marginal psychotic patient. Secondly, as in contemporary Britain, it legitimized the establishment of specialized institutions for confirning the unemployable insane. With the inevitable disappearance of the labor shortage, the social-control functions of the institutions overcame their rehabilitative purpose. Where environmental factors had previously been seen as important in causing psychosis, the emphasis now was on heredity. Prevailing concepts of prognosis were pessimistic.[113] At this point in history, in the coercive, prison-like environ-ment of a German asylum[114] during the universal, late nineteenth-century Great Depression, dementia praecox was defined as a progressively deteriorating and all but incurable illness.

When moral treatment returned, a century and a half after its original appearance, its objectives and ideology were similar but the locations were switched. This time it was in labor-short northern Europe that it served (at least initially) a genuinely rehabilitative purpose, but in America it was largely used merely to legitimize the deinstitutionalization movement—the transfer of the indigent mentally ill from indoor to outdoor relief, and from

126

state budget to federal. Both the concept and management of psychosis appear to have been influenced by political and economic factors. Ideology and practice in psychiatry, to a significant extent are at the mercy of material conditions.

## Summary

- Moral treatment was a humane and non-restrictive method of management for psychotics which came into being simultaneously in several parts of Europe in reaction to the eighteenth-century concept of madness as bestial.
- The origins of moral treatment were also those of the French Revolution and the English Industrial Revolution—Enlightenment thinking, dramatic changes in population and labor patterns, and the capitalist transformation of production.
- The treatment method was inextricably tied to the development of mental institutions, and it helped legitimize the public asylum movement.
- A function of the new asylums was to enact the social policy of providing poor relief to the unemployable in institutions and restricting outdoor relief to the employable.
- Moral treatment was little used in British public asylums except for a brief spell during the boom years of the 1850s and 1860s when the asylum system was being expanded.
- Private patients in Britain enjoyed more humane care and better recovery rates than paupers.
- The high levels of unemployment in Britain throughout the nineteenth century may well have limited rehabilitative efforts for the insane poor.
- The labor shortage in early nineteenth-century America was associated with more intense rehabilitative efforts and higher cure rates, especially in acute mental illness, in public asylums.
- Later American psychiatrists attempted to obscure the fact that recovery rates were higher during the moral-treatment era.

# 6  Labor, Poverty and Schizophrenia

Why did fewer schizophrenics recover during the twentieth-century Great Depression? It is, of course, scarcely surprising that social recovery rates in schizophrenia declined at that time since employment is a large part of the measure of social functioning; but why was there a drop in the rate of complete, symptom-free recovery (as revealed by the analysis of follow-up studies in Chapter 3) from an average of 20 per cent to 12 per cent? Which of the following possible explanations is most applicable?

- Government spending on psychiatric treatment decreased during the Depression, resulting in hospital overcrowding and poor quality care.
- The stresses of the Depression, including economic hardship and unemployment, affected patients and their families and prevented recovery or precipitated psychotic relapse.
- The reduced demand for labor led to diminished rehabilitative and reintegrative efforts for schizophrenics, resulting in changes in mental-health policy, psychiatric ideology and social tolerance of the mentally ill.

## Government Spending

Mental hospital admissions, especially for schizophrenics and other functional psychotics, increase during an economic recession (as Harvey Brenner's work, *Mental Illness and the Economy*, has shown). If legislators cut back on funding during the Great Depression, at a time of increasing demand, the result would, presumably, have been overcrowding, deteriorating care and non-therapeutic hospital conditions. Is this what happened? The evidence suggests it is not.

The annual expenditure on psychiatric hospitals in the state of Colorado, for example (as can be seen in Figure 6.1), increased considerably between 1913 and 1955, even after allowance has been made for inflation and state population growth. During the decade of the Great Depression, however, expenditure was consistently well *above* the general trend. Before the 1930s, two other spikes of increased spending are evident during the recessions of 1914–15 and 1920–2. Hospital spending was less than usual during the Second World War, but returned to the general trend after the war.

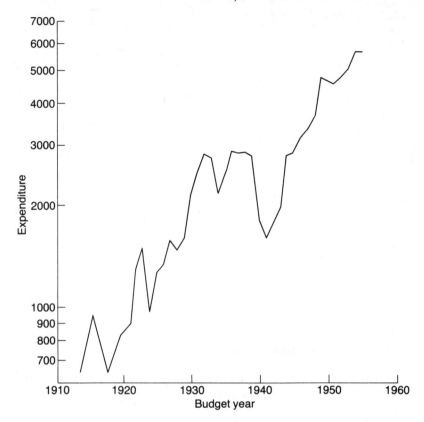

*Figure 6.1  Annual expenditure on Colorado state psychiatric hospitals in constant (1967) dollars per 1,000 population*

Sources: Expenditure: 'State of Colorado Budget Reports, 1923–24 to 1955–56;' inflation factor: 'Bureau of Labor Statistics Wholesale Price Index, All Commodities,' population of Colorado: Decennial US Census with interval year estimates.
Note: Capital outlay is included.

(Spending on mental health services after 1955 is not presented here because of the added complications of alternative sources of revenue—such as federal funding, social security benefits and public health insurance—which became important after the onset of deinstitutionalization.) In this state of the union, at least, psychiatric funding did not decrease during the Depression but, rather, increased at a faster rate than usual in an effort to meet the increased demand for care.

The same spending pattern has held true for England and Wales since the late Victorian era, as Figure 6.2 shows. Here the rate of expenditure on 'lunacy' and lunatic asylums increased during the nineteenth- and twentieth-

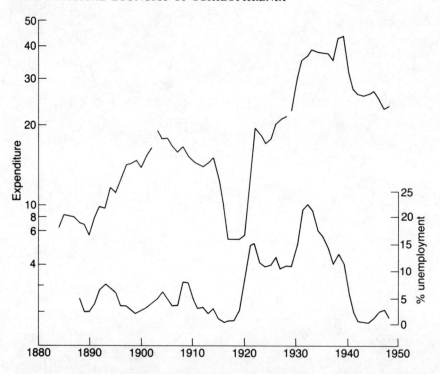

*Figure 6.2   Annual expenditure on 'lunacy' and lunatic asylums in England and Wales in constant (1871) pounds per 100 population: annual unemployment for comparison*

Sources: Expenditure and inflation factor (Sauerbeck–Statist Overall Price Index): Mitchell, B. R. and Deane, P., *Abstract of British Historical Statistics*, Cambridge: Cambridge University Press, 1962; Mitchell B. R. and Jones, H. G., *Second Abstract of British Historical Statistics*, Cambridge: Cambridge University Press, 1971; population: Mitchell, B. R. *European Historical Statistics, 1750–1970*, New York: Columbia University Press, 1978, pp. 25, 32, with interval year estimates.
Notes:  A change in the method of data collection was made in 1903. Capital outlay on asylums is included.

century Great Depressions, decreased slowly during the relatively full employment years after the turn of the century and after the Second World War, and dropped sharply during the two world wars.

It is possible, of course, that the increased use of mental institutions in the Depression outstripped even these inflated hospital expenditures, in which case overcrowding and poor care would still have occurred. This does not seem to have happened, however. Brenner reports, for example, greatly increased capacity at New York state public hospitals during the Great Depression—a 73 per cent increase in available beds between 1929 and 1938. Overcrowding was common at these hospitals before, during and after the Great Depression, but was apparently no worse during the early years of the economic downturn than in the late 1920s or mid-1950s.[1] Figures for

130

the percentage occupancy of Canadian mental hospitals between 1934 and 1960 draw the same picture (see Figure 6.3). Overcrowding in these hospitals was at its lowest in the 1930s and at its highest in the 1950s.

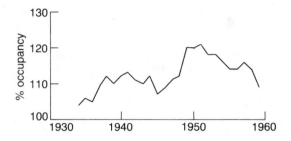

*Figure 6.3   Percentage occupancy of Canadian mental institutions*

Source: Urquhart, M. C. and Buckley, K. A. H., *Historical Statistics of Canada*, Cambridge: Cambridge University Press, 1965.

Decreased government spending and hospital overcrowding, it seems, are not the explanation for the poor outcome in schizophrenia during the Great Depression. Similarly, there is no sign of increased spending after the Second World War to account for the improved recovery rates at that time. The switch to community care was, in fact, considered to be a cost-saving measure. Whether, in actuality, community treatment was cheaper is hard to determine. An analysis of the real cost of such care would have to include the expense of social services provided through several agencies, and of supportive accommodation and disability payments. No such study appears to have been done in Britain. Some American cost and benefit studies of deinstitutionalization were made available in the 1970s. Their value for our purpose is somewhat reduced by unsophisticated analytic methods, small sample size or the inclusion of unrealistic projections of savings and benefits attributed to the patients' employability. All of these studies, however, show community treatment to be significantly cheaper than state hospital care.[2]

It seems that, during the Great Depression, more money was spent on buying more hospital care for schizophrenics and the result was, for whatever reasons, lower recovery rates.

## Economic Stress and Unemployment

Stress may provoke a psychotic relapse in a schizophrenic (as discussed in Chapter 1). Both the boom and bust parts of the business cycle bring their own varieties of stress. In the depression they include loss of status, self-worth and independence for the unemployed, a sense of failure for those who slip down the social ladder, and economic hardship for many.

131

Schizophrenics in the community are exposed to all these possible stresses and those with marginal levels of functioning are particularly at risk when jobs are in short supply.

Clinical experience shows us that economic uncertainty is a serious stress for many patients. As social security regulations were tightened during the early years of the Reagan administration, for example, many stable psychotics whose disability payments were abruptly terminated suffered relapses of their illness. The mental condition of many psychotics similarly becomes worse when their most basic needs are not provided for. In the United States, homeless, male schizophrenic patients are frequently admitted to hospital, hungry, dirty, sleepless and floridly psychotic. When, after some meals and a good night's sleep, their mental state dramatically improves, hospital staff claim that the patient has 'manipulated' his way into free board and accommodation. More benign observers argue that the patient's improvement is evidence of the efficacy of the dose of the antipsychotic medication which he received on admission. In fact, such patients often improve as readily without medication. The florid features of their psychosis on admission are an acute response to the stress of their abject poverty and deprivation.

We can estimate from the social recovery rates in Chapter 3 that 70 per cent of schizophrenics were unemployed at follow-up during the Great Depression—significantly more than after the Second World War. In recent years, again, it has become so common for schizophrenics in the community to be out of work that mental health professionals rarely consider unemployment a significant stress for their patients. For many such psychotic individuals, however, the dreary rounds of days without purposeful activity, lives devoid of meaning and a social existence stripped of status are a constant strain. British unemployed men complain:

> 'You're a drag on everybody else really.'
> 'Sometimes I get to walking up and down on the carpet.'
> '. . . cannot be bothered to dae nowt, just feel like stopping in bed all day.'
> 'When you're out of work you worry and don't feel like eating.'
> 'I go for a walk and try to do some reading if I can, but it's very hard for me to get the brain functioning properly.'
> 'I'm so *moody* you know.'
> 'I thought, "What's the bloody point of it all, anyway? What's the reason for it all?" Then you start to become, well, deranged.'
> 'I think you start to lose your identity in yourself. . . . There's times when, well "What's . . . what am I?" '[3]

Such responses are those of unemployed men who are not particularly susceptible to psychosis. The impact on schizophrenics can scarcely be less severe, and could well affect their recovery and relapse rates.

132

Indeed, the similarity of many features of chronic schizophrenia to the psychological effects of extended unemployment is striking. Anxiety, depression, apathy, irritability, negativity, emotional overdependence, social withdrawal, isolation and loneliness, and a loss of self-respect, identity and a sense of time—all these are common amongst the long-term unemployed.[4] Compare these features, and the words of the British unemployed quoted above, with this description of the chronic schizophrenic:

Anergy, or disturbances of volition, have at times been incorrectly described as apathy. . . . Patients may be abnormally tired, fatigue easily, and experience clinical depression. The chronic schizophrenic may sit blankly for long periods, unaware of the passage of time. . . . He may remain in bed when he intended to look for a job, avoid or put off without reason any activity that is new, unfamiliar or outside of his routine. . . . Life is routine, constricted, empty. He may sleep most of the day, be awake most of the night. The chronic schizophrenic in the community may fear contact with strangers. . . . He may be unable to cope with . . . the complex demands of welfare departments.[5]

Although many of these 'negative' features of schizophrenia are known to be made worse by the social deprivation of institutional care, they are nevertheless seen by psychiatrists as inherent aspects of the illness. (Hence the emphasis on the biological concept of 'anergy' rather than the psychological attribute of 'apathy.') Mental health professionals become frustrated by, and sometimes critical of, their chronic psychotic patients' dependency, incompetence and unreliability. To label such problems as biological deficits helps the professional cope with his or her frustrations, but it also increases the pessimism regarding treatment and the stigma which attaches to the patient. That such deficits are, to a large extent, socially induced becomes apparent, however, when we read the words of this unemployed (non-psychotic) teenager:

'I feel outside of it . . . [unemployment] just makes me feel different. I really admire these guys who can get up and shave, and have breakfast, and make a journey to work, and come home again, and have meals—guys who can do all that in one day! I don't know how they can manage it. When I've got to sign on, or anything like that, just do the one thing, it bugs me all day. . . . Or if I've got anything to do . . . say to catch a bus to go somewhere, it's a real drag. We can't seem to get with it.'[6]

The similarity in the emotional reactions of the unemployed and of psychotic patients was highlighted by a study conducted in the Great Depression. The level of negativity and pessimism about the future in large samples of the Scottish and Lancashire unemployed was found to be greater than that of groups of psychotically depressed and schizophrenic patients.[7] If

133

the unemployed are as distressed as hospitalized psychotics, how can we hope that the unemployed psychotics will return to normal during hard times? In fact we may ask, as does the author of the study of the Scottish and Lancashire jobless, 'why mentally distressed unemployed . . . do not become psychotic.'[8]

The answer is, of course, they may well do so. Brenner found that it was precisely that segment of the population which suffers the greatest relative economic loss during a depression—young and middle-aged males with moderate levels of education—which showed the greatest increase in rates of admission to New York mental hospitals for functional psychosis during an economic downturn. Prominent among these patients were first admissions for schizophrenia.[9] We saw in Chapter 2 that the likeliest explanation for this effect was a true increase in the occurrence of psychosis secondary to the stresses of the economic recession and unemployment. In Chapter 9 we shall explore in more detail whether labor dynamics significantly affect the prevalence of schizophrenia. Here we shall concentrate on how far the labor market influences the course and outcome of the illness.

Unemployment may exert an indirect influence on some psychotics in the community. One stress factor known to be associated with poor outcome in schizophrenia is the effect of living with hostile, critical or emotionally overinvolved relatives. The greater the proportion of time a schizophrenic spends in the company of such a relative, the greater is his or her chance of relapse.[10] During a depression, both the relative and the patient are more likely to be unemployed and at home together. For the minority of schizophrenics who live with such a relative, this may be a serious stress. A successful treatment program which has been developed to reduce the high risk of relapse for such patients uses as one of its techniques efforts to increase the separation of patient and relative by getting one of them out of the house and at work.[11]

On the other hand, the home environment for the unemployed patient may be too under-stimulating. It was found in one five-year follow-up study of schizophrenics in London that for patients who were unemployed and living at home, the length of time spent doing absolutely nothing was similar to that of patients in backward asylums.[12] Such poverty of daily existence is known to be closely allied to the clinical poverty of institutionalism and the negative features of schizophrenia.[13]

To emphasize, thus, the stresses of unemployment for schizophrenics is not to overlook the fact that, for many of these individuals, the stress of employment is also a major difficulty. Schizophrenics experience severe problems, argues psychiatrist Hans Huessy, as a consequence of the 'fabulously highly developed division of labor in industrial society.'[14] Work-related stress is certainly important for these patients. In one group of schizophrenics, for example, 60 per cent had experienced a stressful life

134

event in the three weeks before their psychotic breakdown; of these, the stress for one-third had been related to stopping or starting work, completing job training or changing hours of employment.[15] Starting work, however, is an acute stress which, if weathered, may lead the psychotic to higher functioning. Unemployment, on the other hand, brings the chronic strain of low status and purposelessness, which may prevent recovery. Whichever part of the picture we study, nevertheless, it seems likely that the labor market is closely involved in the social production and perpetuation of psychosis.

## The Industrial Reserve Army

Unemployment, argued Friedrich Engels, is not an aberration but an unavoidable component of capitalist production.

> It is clear that English manufacture must have at all times save the brief periods of highest prosperity, an unemployed reserve army of workers, in order to be able to produce the masses of goods required by the market in the liveliest months.[16]

Karl Marx, like Engels, maintained not only that 'a surplus labouring population is a necessary product of accumulation . . . on a capitalist basis' but that it is also

> a condition of existence of the capitalist mode of production. It forms a disposable industrial reserve army, that belongs to capital quite as absolutely as if the latter had bred it at its own cost.[17]

Marx developed this concept in some detail in *Capital* and distinguished various components of the reserve army of labor. The segment which he labeled the 'stagnant' category of the 'relative surplus population' would these days be called the secondary labor force. It is characterized by

> extremely irregular employment. Hence it furnishes to capital an inexhaustible reservoir of disposable labour-power. Its conditions of life sink below the average normal level of the working class.[18]

Even the most poverty-stricken among them are 'in times of great prosperity . . . speedily and in large numbers enrolled in the active army of labourers.'[19] Many of the marginally functional mentally ill are to be found in this group and in the related category of

> those unable to work, chiefly people who succumb to their incapacity for adaptation, due to the division of labour; . . . the victims of industry, . . . the mutilated, the sickly, the widows, &c. Pauperism is the hospital of the active labour-army and the dead weight of the industrial reserve army.[20]

135

This analysis leads Marx directly to what he terms the 'absolute general law of capitalist accumulation:'

> The greater the social wealth, the functioning capital, the extent and energy of its growth . . . the greater is the industrial reserve army . . . The law that always equilibrates the . . . industrial reserve army to the extent and energy of accumulation . . . establishes an accumulation of misery, corresponding with accumulation of capital.[21]

The view that unemployment and poverty are in proportion to capital growth and accumulation—the rich get richer and the poor get poorer—has been criticized. But the criticism is largely the result of a misunderstanding. Marx was not, as many believe, suggesting that the wages and conditions of workers would deteriorate, but that unemployment and the conditions of the poor, the marginally productive and the dependent would worsen.[22] His assertion that the surplus population would be preserved and expanded by the capitalist mode of production has been vindicated.

The size of the industrial reserve army in modern times is considerable. The ranks of the officially unemployed have to be multiplied several times to include discouraged workers, housewives who wish to work, the under-employed and the disabled (who could be rehabilitated).[23] The true United States unemployment rate during the early 1970s, according to political scientist Charles Anderson, might be realistically estimated at 25 per cent.[24] These days it would be considerably greater. In the 1980s official unemployment in the United States has exceeded 10 per cent, and in Britain is close to 14 per cent. These figures conceal even more massive wastage of human power in certain segments of the population. Official unemployment among adult black men in the United States rose to 45 per cent in 1982; and if black men not counted by the census-takers were included, the figures would indicate that fewer than half of adult black males are employed. Among black teenagers in the United States, unemployment hovers around 50 per cent, but one employment analyst estimates that only a sixth of these adolescents have jobs since so many have dropped out or never joined the labor force. With the definition of 'full employment' being adjusted upwards with some regularity—most recently to 6.5 per cent in the United States; with poverty increasing—nearly a sixth of American families, a third of black families, now living in poverty; who can claim that the industrial reserve army has been demobilized? Its ranks, in fact, are swelling.[25]

## Rehabilitation and Reintegration

Marx's analysis suggests that the treatment of the great majority of the mentally ill will always reflect the condition of the poorest classes of society. In the absence of some powerful political counter-force the outlook in schizophrenia is unlikely to get better. Despite the fact that an improvement in conditions of living and employment for psychotics may yield higher rates of recovery, this consideration will remain secondary. Significant treatment efforts will only be expended on those skilled workers who are acutely mentally ill and whose disappearance from the work force involves the loss of a substantial investment in training. Efforts to rehabilitate and reintegrate the chronically mentally ill will only be seen at times of extreme shortage of labor—after the other battalions of the industrial reserve army have been mobilized. At other times, the primary emphasis will be one of social control. The rate of recovery of those who have an 'incapacity for adaptation' will, then, be a barometer of the extent of poverty and unemployment.

There is evidence to support this interpretation. In the earlier chapters, for example, we have seen that successful rehabilitation and social reintegration of the mentally ill have been closely related to the demand for labor and, in many instances, this success appears to be a reflection of the intensity of the rehabilitative efforts. To recapitulate:

- Rehabilitation of the mentally and physically disabled is more successful in wartime and during periods of labor shortage.
- Deinstitutionalization began, before the introduction of the antipsychotic drugs, in those north European countries that had low unemployment rates.
- The number of mental hospital beds provided in the industrial nations in 1965 was related to the national unemployment rate.
- The proportion of schizophrenics in hospital at follow-up increased during the Great Depression.
- Discharge and recovery rates in labor-starved, early nineteenth-century America may have been higher because of the availability of moral treatment in the public asylums.
- Recovery rates and treatment efforts declined as pauperism and unemployment became more common in the new republic.

Just how does the labor market influence approaches to the mentally ill? Rehabilitative and reintegrative efforts for psychiatric patients are comprised of three inter-related elements:

    (1) political consensus, or state mental health policy;
    (2) professional consensus, or psychiatric ideology; and
    (3) social consensus, or tolerance of the mentally ill.

A speculative attempt to illustrate how these components may vary with the business cycle is set out in Table 6.1. At any one time, both sets of attitudes may be encountered, of course, but as the economic climate changes so does the balance of opinion.

It becomes clear from this formulation that psychiatric ideology may be influenced by changes in the economy—a notion which implies a rejection of the conventional concept of scientific progress inherent in mainstream medical

137

**Table 6.1  Differences in rehabilitative and reintegrative efforts for the mentally ill during the depression and the boom**

| DEPRESSION | BOOM |
| --- | --- |
| *Political Consensus* | |
| Custodial care is necessary to protect the community | Community care is preferable |
| Hospital expansion is required | A cost-benefit analysis of psychiatric rehabilitation must include savings resulting from patients' increased productivity |
| *Professional Consensus* | |
| Schizophrenia is incurable | Schizophrenia is curable |
| Genetic and biological factors are important causes of psychosis | Social factors are important causes of psychosis |
| Hospitals are therapeutic | Mental institutions are harmful |
| Early discharge is dangerous | Psychosocial treatment is valuable in psychosis |
| Physical, surgical and pharmaceutical treatment methods are most valuable | Treatment efforts should be directed towards the most severely mentally ill |
| Neurotic patients are more treatable than psychotics | |
| *Social Consensus* | |
| The mentally ill are dangerous and should be locked up | Anybody can become mentally ill |
| I would not want to work with/live next to/marry a mental patient | |

history. There are certainly grounds for this position. As we have seen, when recovery rates and treatment standards declined at the end of the moral-management era, and at the onset of the Great Victorian Depression, psychiatric philosophy became pessimistic and turned from an interest in social causes of illness to biological and hereditary factors. Kraepelin defined schizophrenia as an incurable disease. Early discharge was considered dangerous. Eugen Bleuler reformulated the concept of schizophrenia as a condition from which many recovered without defect in the sunnier economic climate of Switzerland before the First World War. At this time, he and his colleagues at Burghölzli Hospital in Zurich—Carl Jung and Adolf Meyer—developed psychodynamic theories of schizophrenia. Bleuler encouraged the early discharge of his patients to avoid the dangers of

138

institutionalism. During the twentieth-century Great Depression, physical treatment methods and psychosurgery were emphasized. Psychosis was neglected and psychiatry, especially in America, concentrated upon the long-term, dynamic treatment of less severely disturbed, middle-class and upper-class, neurotic patients. Widespread interest in social factors in mental illness, in the understanding of psychosis and in community care were not to return until 80 or 90 years after moral treatment disappeared— until the boom decades after the Second World War. By contrast, psychiatry in post-revolutionary Russia during the early twentieth century pursued a different course—a method of psychological and social reintegration which evolved from the work of Ivan Pavlov.[26]

Ideological views which emerge counter to the mainstream of psychiatric thought make no headway in the face of a contrary political and social consensus. Critics, in the mid-Victorian era, who objected to the expansion of asylums into mammoth institutions where individual treatment was impossible were ignored by local authorities and a tax-conscious populace concerned to maximize cost-efficiency.[27] Hospital superintendents who attempted to establish open-door policies before the advent of the postwar social psychiatry revolution were defeated by public opinion.[28] Alfred Adler, in the 1930s, gained little recognition for his views on the importance of social factors in psychopathology; and the work of American social scientists in the 1930s on the interaction of culture and mental disorder did not influence psychiatric theory or practice to an appreciable degree.[29]

A recent example further illustrates how psychiatric philosophy is molded by the politics of the period. In 1981, as part of a nationwide trend towards bugetary cuts in human services, the City and County of Denver, Colorado, sharply reduced its allocation to Denver General Hospital. The administrators of the community mental health center, which formed a part of the hospital, responded by drastically cutting their services to their most severely disturbed clients—money-losing outreach services to hundreds of ex-state hospital clients in boarding homes, including a day-care program, alternative supportive housing, sheltered employment and vocational training. A number of these chronically ill clients brought a class action suit against the hospital and its funding agencies, demanding reinstatement of these essential services. The psychiatrists and administrators of the mental health center entered the following defense: there was no evidence to show that the type of community services they had been providing to the chronic psychotic patients were at all effective.[30] Their view was incorrect,[31] but this is incidental. The point of interest here is that less than a decade earlier the Colorado state legislators had been assured that such community-treatment methods were so superior that the state hospitals could be run down and the funds diverted to community mental health centers. From bouyant optimism to the depths of pessimism in less than ten years—from legitimizing the last stages of deinstitutionalization to legitimizing the final abandonment of the same patients to poverty and neglect in their inner-city ghetto. The story of moral treatment is, here, being repeated under similar economic conditions. The cause for mounting pessimism appears the same in each case—governmental indifference leaves the patients stranded in sordid environments, without adequate treatment and without a purpose in life. The victims are blamed each time, however; it is, supposedly, the inherently incurable nature of the patients' condition which indicates that we should not waste time and money treating them.

## Social Tolerance

Can it be shown that public tolerance of the mentally ill is similarly affected by the economic climate? In general, discrimination, prejudice and negative stereotyping are known to increase sharply as competition for scarce jobs increases. Negative attitudes towards ethnic minority groups become more common during hard times.[32] But information about the effect of the economy on attitudes towards the mentally ill is limited. In Britain, many observers noted an improvement in public attitudes towards mental patients at the time of the postwar social psychiatry revolution.[33] As Professor Morris Carstairs wrote in 1961: 'Few would claim that our current "wonder drugs" exercise more than a palliative influence on psychiatric disorders. The big change has been rather one of public opinion.'[34] In America, in line with the higher unemployment, the later onset of deinstitutionalization and the less intense rehabilitative and reintegrative thrust of that movement, public attitudes were slower to change. Community studies from the 1950s reported that attitudes towards the mentally ill were characteristically negative and rejecting.[35] By the 1960s there were indications that the general public was becoming more accepting,[36] but there was no subsequent demonstrable improvement in the status of the mentally ill during the economic stagnation of the 1970s.[37]

## Rehabilitation Efforts—Cause or Effect?

Having seen that both recovery rates in schizophrenia and rehabilitative efforts expended on the mentally ill tend to diminish during the depression, the question of cause and effect remains to be addressed. Do the patients fail to get better because nobody bothers to treat them, or does nobody bother to treat them because they fail to get better? Earlier in this chapter it was suggested that unemployment has a direct psychological impact on those who are out of work, including the mentally ill, and could thus stand in the way of recovery from psychosis. Can we rule out the additional possibility, implicit in Marxist theory, that a labor glut so diminishes the political incentive to rehabilitate the mentally ill that treatment efforts and community integration are discouraged, thereby worsening recovery rates?

Like most 'chicken and egg' questions, this one is probably unanswerable. The events occurring at times of major policy change are so tightly intertwined that no one factor can be recognized as causative. Kathleen Jones, for example, sees three components to the postwar British social psychiatry revolution—the open-door movement, the introduction of the antipsychotic drugs and legislative developments.

> From the point of view of the therapy or of public policy, the coincidence of these three movements was fortunate, since each reinforced the other. From the point of view of social analysis, it was less so, since it made it impossible to trace cause and effect with any confidence. The three strands of development crossed and re-crossed, becoming so interwoven that it will probably never be possible to determine what influence each had.[38]

Certainly there is no indication, in the case of postwar Britain, that psychiatrists, noting greater success rates, dragged politicians unwillingly along. As early as 1948, the National Health Service Act established local authority mental health departments which assumed responsibility for community care for the mentally ill; in 1954 a parliamentary bill pushed for further modernization of mental health services and hospitals; and, in the same year, a Royal Commission was formed to consider legislative reforms which would facilitate community care.[39] All this occurred before the widespread introduction of the antipsychotic drugs and contemporaneous with the earliest moves to open the doors of the psychiatric wards. It seems probable that the political incentive to put into practice advances in psychiatric care and to increase the rehabilitation of the mentally ill was already there—stimulated by the urgent need for labor.

The question of cause and effect has a practical aspect. If it were possible artificially to maintain employment for the mentally disabled during hard times, would recovery rates improve (and admission rates and treatment costs decline), or would the social and political consensus existing during the depression limit the potential for improvement in the course of psychosis? It seems quite possible, in fact, that the effect of the social and political forces would be to obstruct the development of preferential employment for mental patients. Since the earliest days of institutions, workers in the regular labor force have objected to the unfair competition of inmates' labor during periods of unemployment. Charles Dickens illustrates this point by contrasting the prisons of labor-starved America in the 1840s with those of Britain, where a surplus of workers existed.

America, as a new and not over-populated country, has, in all her prisons,

141

the one great advantage, of being able to find useful and profitable work for the inmates; whereas, with us, the prejudice against prison labour is naturally very strong, and almost insurmountable, when honest men who have not offended against the laws are frequently doomed to seek employment in vain. Even in the United States, the principle of bringing convict labour and free labour into a competition which must obviously be to the disadvantage of the latter, has already found many opponents, whose number is not likely to diminish with access of years.[40]

Here, in a nutshell, is the antagonism between unemployment and rehabilitation and recovery in mental illness.

More recent examples may readily be found. In the 1930s, efforts were made to introduce into British psychiatric hospitals methods of work therapy designed (by Dr Herman Simon of Gütersloh, Germany) to discourage 'idleness or fatuous madness.' The failure of these efforts is explained by David Clark: 'The world-wide depression of the 1930s may have made it difficult to justify diverting work to hospital patients when fit men outside were unemployed.'[41] In modern times, sheltered workshops in the United States, which generally provide employment for the disabled by contracting for piece-work with industry, face similar difficulties. During a business recession, fewer contracts are available and disabled workers have to be laid off. Alternatively, the workshops can bid to complete contracts for less than the actual cost. This makes them reliant upon government subsidies which are liable to be cut back as the depression deepens. Some workshops go bankrupt, others find that their attempts to subsidize their programs and under-bid for contracts are opposed by labor unions. Government sponsored job programs, furthermore, tend to concentrate on finding work for higher functioning workers as unemployment mounts. All in all, it seems likely that, despite the best efforts and intentions of mental health professionals, it may not be possible completely to overcome the negative effects of the business slump on the course of schizophrenia.


## Labor Dynamics

Recovery from schizophrenia may worsen in the depression, it seems, because unemployment directly affects schizophrenics and because the reduced demand for labor results in a deterioration of rehabilitation and reintegration efforts. Economic hardship in the depression may also affect psychotic individuals. We can explore just how powerful is the effect of labor dynamics on the course of schizophrenia by looking beyond the effects of the business cycle to broader relationships between the utilization of labor and outcome in schizophrenia. Specifically, we may predict:

142

- If one sex is less severely affected by labor market forces, members of that sex will tend to achieve better outcome in schizophrenia.
- If one social class is more affected by the rigors of the labor market, that class should experience poorer outcome in schizophrenia.
- Schizophrenic outcome will be better in industrial nations with continuous full employment unaffected by cyclical changes.
- Outcome in schizophrenia will be better in non-industrial societies where wage labor and unemployment are uncommon.

These predictions allow us to discriminate, to a certain extent, between the effects of the labor market and of economic hardship—only in some of these instances can we expect economic hardship to produce the same direction of change in the course of schizophrenia. Let us see how accurate are these predictions.

## Sex Differences in Recovery from Schizophrenia

Despite the fact that the level of female unemployment is often higher than for males in the United States, for most of this century men have suffered more from the fluctuations of the labor market than have women. In general, substantially fewer women have been involved in wage work than men, and women are more likely to have a valued social role when not earning a wage. One could argue that patients who return to an assured role as a homemaker will experience less difficulty than those who must re-enter the competitive labor market. Furthermore, as Brenner[42] has pointed out, men are more adversely influenced by a recession than women. During the Great Depression and subsequent business downturns, male unemployment increased more than female unemployment and often surpassed it. From this, one might reasonably predict that the course of schizophrenia in women in Western industrial society will be milder than in men.

'That the probability of recovery is greater in women than in men ... may now be regarded as established,'[43] wrote Dr Thurnam in his *Observations and Essays on the Statistics of Insanity*, as early as 1845. His analysis showed that the proportion of patients discharged as recovered from the asylums of his day was consistently higher for female than for male admissions. In more recent times Professor Ödegard, in studying all first admissions to Norwegian psychiatric hospitals from 1936 to 1945, found a higher early discharge rate for female schizophrenics than for males.[44] Psychiatrist, James Beck, has noted that outcome studies often demonstrate that male schizophrenics do worse than females but that women are never found to fare worse than men.[45] Similarly, in the WHO international follow-up study of schizophrenia, proportionally fewer women patients were in the worst outcome group at follow-up, and more were in the best outcome category. In the industrial countries, in particular, women tended to have shorter episodes of schizophrenic

143

psychosis.[46] In addition, Brenner's data show that female patients with functional psychosis are less likely than men to be admitted or readmitted to psychiatric hospital when unemployment increases.[47] These sex differences confirm the impression that labor dynamics may influence outcome in schizophrenia. The gap may narrow, however, as the proportion of women in the labor force in Western industrial societies continues to increase and the proportion of men falls.

## Social Class

Some social scientists have argued that the social groups which suffer the most stress during the depression are those which suffer the greatest *relative* decline in status—the unemployed amongst the middle classes, for example.[48] On this basis Brenner has explained the particularly heavy impact of the depression on the mental hospital admission rate of more highly educated male patients.[49] This is as may be; but the business cycle aside,the social classes which come off worst in the competition for jobs are, clearly, the poorest. Black unemployment in the United States, for example, is regularly twice that of whites, in good times or bad. Unskilled workers in the secondary labor force have the least job security of any group, and the lowest status. Their work is often casual, menial, highly routine and, always, poorly paid. Alienation from the creative process is greatest, in general, in the working class. Clearly, if any group were to experience constant difficulty in gaining and holding wage work and in deriving self-esteem and gratification from their employment it would be those in the lowest social classes.

It comes as no surprise to find that recovery from psychosis is worst in the lower socio-economic groups. Admission rates were higher for pauper lunatics in Victorian Britain and, as we saw in Chapter 5, their recovery rates were lower. Similarly, in modern times, not only is the incidence of serious mental disorder greater in the lower classes (as we saw in Chapter 2), but the outcome from psychosis is distinctly worse. A study conducted in Bristol, England, of male schizophrenics first admitted in the early 1950s found that patients from the lower social classes had longer hospital stays, were much less likely to be improved or recovered at the time of discharge, were liable to be readmitted earlier and were very much more likely to become chronically institutionalized than were upper-class patients. The lower-class patients in the community, moreover, were less likely to be employed and showed worse overall social adjustment.[50] The author of this study, Dr B. Cooper, concludes:

> It seems most likely that clinical condition and economic status are mutually related and interacting, and that the patient who fails to return to useful work is more prone to schizophrenic relapses.[51]

Other investigations have produced similar results. Another British study

144

of male schizophrenics from the 1950s found that lower-class patients had longer admissions.[52] In New Haven, Connecticut, August Hollingshead and Frederick Redlich in the 1950s showed that lower-class patients spent longer in hospital and were more likely to be readmitted.[53] Repeating that study a decade later, Jerome Myers and L. L. Bean also found that lower-class patients were more likely to be kept in hospital and more likely to be readmitted. In the community, the patient of low social class had a worse work record (except for homemakers, where ex-patients performed as well as normals), and was more socially isolated and stigmatized.[54] A 1974 follow-up study of schizophrenic patients from the eastern United States demonstrated that social class was strongly related to symptomatic outcome. Lower-class patients had more psychotic symptoms when interviewed 2–3 years after discharge from hospital.[55] Finally, the WHO international follow-up study of schizophrenia found that having a higher-status occupation was one of the best predictors of good outcome for patients living in cities in the developed world (London, Moscow, Prague, Washington, DC and Aarhus, Denmark).[56]

Three studies do *not* show a significantly longer duration of hospital stay for lower-class schizophrenics. Two of these, however, were conducted in Britain during the early 1950s, when there was full employment.[57] Under such conditions, one might expect some improvement in schizophrenic outcome in the lower classes (although Cooper's contrary findings for schizophrenics in Bristol were also from this period). Ödegard's study of Norwegian hospital admissions from 1936 to 1945 failed to show a consistent pattern of longer hospital stay for patients from lower-status occupations. Ödegard recognized that his results did not conform to the usual pattern found in other countries, and he attributed the findings to the fact that some of the lower-status occupations in Norway, such as public service employment, carried better economic job security, which resulted in the unusually high discharge rates for patients from these groups.[58]

Overall, it is apparent that the majority of studies, and the more comprehensive among them, point to worse outcome in schizophrenia for the lower classes. A number of factors might explain this phenomenon—economic hardship, different levels of tolerance in the family or in the community, or even, as some American workers have argued, 'more limited and rigid concepts of social reality' and poorer 'drug compliance' in the lower-class patients.[59] In conjunction with the other material in this chapter, however, the finding may be taken as further support for a link between labor dynamics and the course of schizophrenia.

## Full Employment

Professor Luc Ciompi argues that the benign course of schizophrenia in

Switzerland may be a result of the 'exceptionally favorable socioeconomic conditions which prevail' in that country. He followed up more than 1,600 schizophrenics admitted throughout the century to the University Psychiatric Clinic in Lausanne until they passed the age of 65. Twenty-seven per cent had completely recovered and a further 22 per cent were only mildly disturbed. Thus, about half of the patients had a favorable ultimate course of their illness.[60] Such results are better than average for the Western nations. Are they a result of the full employment which has long existed in Switzerland? Unemployment, there, has rarely reached 1 per cent since the Second World War, and through the 1960s and early 1970s was generally around a tenth of that figure. Even during the Great Depression Swiss unemployment did not scale the heights common throughout the rest of Europe.[61] As Professor Ciompi remarks:

> If the socioeconomic conditions in Switzerland did indeed exert a favorable influence on outcome, that would certainly be a highly significant finding. It would suggest that under favorable circumstances schizophrenia may run a predominantly favorable course.[62]

It would be equally significant if it could be shown that a benign course to schizophrenia was a by-product of the full employment found in planned socialist economies. The job security and the lower-intensity, slower-paced labor process which are usual under socialist central planning[63] might both be considered particularly suitable for the rehabilitation of schizophrenics. In the USSR, continuous full employment has existed since 1930. A right to work is recognized, and workers can expect jobs to be found for them even if they are barely productive.[64] As the mayor of Moscow was not slow to point out on a recent visit to London, 'It might be difficult for you to understand, . . . but one of the main issues we face in Moscow is the lack of labor hands in the city.'[65] In Moscow, Leningrad and other large cities, vocational rehabilitation programs for the mentally disabled are highly developed and psychiatrists give a great deal of attention to patients' optimal work placement.[66]

Outcome from schizophrenia in Moscow has, in fact, been shown to be better than for patients admitted for treatment in Western industrial countries. The WHO International Pilot Study of Schizophrenia is a large-scale, cross-national, collaborative project which was conducted simultaneously in nine countries in the West, in the Eastern Bloc and in the Third World. (This study will be discussed in more detail in the next chapter.) Schizophrenic patients were selected from among those admitted to psychiatric centers in 1968 and 1969. On initial evaluation (as mentioned in Chapter 1) the groups of patients in most centers appeared to be comparable, but a standardized evaluation procedure showed that psychiatrists in Moscow and Washington, DC were using a broader, more inclusive

146

diagnostic concept of schizophrenia. At two-year follow-up, overall outcome for the schizophrenics in Moscow was found to be better than for those admitted to the Western centers in London, Washington, DC, and Aarhus (Denmark). Although relatively few of the Russian patients made a rapid and complete recovery (as can be seen in Table 7.2, on page 155 of the next chapter), nearly half of these patients had a favorable outcome—that is, they had been non-psychotic for less than a year or had, at least, shown no serious social impairment for longer than four months during the two-year follow-up period. by the same standardized follow-up criteria, only slightly more than a third of the patients in the centers in Britain, America and Denmark showed as great a degree of overall improvement. Substantially fewer of the Russian patients, furthermore, were in the worst outcome category at follow-up.[67] The superior recovery rates for schizophrenics in Moscow may have been an artefact of the broader diagnostic approach there: yet a similarly inclusive diagnostic concept in Washington, DC, does not seem to have led to better outcome for the American schizophrenic patients.

Recovery from schizophrenia in the WHO study was, however, no better in Prague (Czechoslovakia), despite a labor shortage in that city, than in the Western centers. This difference between outcome in Moscow and Prague is difficult to explain. It may be a result of the broader Russian diagnostic approach to schizophrenia. The year these patients were admitted to the study (1968) happened to be the same in which the Warsaw Pact countries occupied Czechoslovakia. It is not at all clear, however, if or how this might have had an impact on the rehabilitation of schizophrenics. Until this point is settled, we can only say that the data so far available from full-employment societies are ambiguous; but that there is some evidence that such societies benefit from a more benign course to schizophrenia than is found in industrial nations with significant levels of unemployment.

We have gone a long way towards demonstrating that socio-economic conditions shape the course of schizophrenia. Outcome data on schizophrenia in the Depression, in the two sexes, in different social classes and in different political-economic systems all tend to support the notion that the effects of the labor market and, possibly, economic hardship are critical. In all of these instances the observed differences in the course of schizophrenia may be explained by both a direct effect of unemployment on the psychotic individual or by the influence of the demand for labor on rehabilitative and reintegrative efforts. In all these instances except one—the difference in recovery patterns for men and women—economic hardship may also be an important stress leading to relapse or poor outcome.

One further prediction remains to be examined—that if labor-market conditions can adversely affect the course of schizophrenia, the illness should be more benign in non-wage-labor settings. In the next chapter we will examine this possibility and, also, use the opportunity to study how

147

major differences in political and domestic economy may affect the schizophrenic.

## Summary

- Spending on psychiatric hospital care increases during the depression.
- The effect of both economic stress and unemployment on patients in the community could account for the decreased recovery rate from schizophrenia during the twentieth-century Great Depression.
- Many of the negative features of chronic schizophrenia are identical with the psychological sequelae of long-term unemployment.
- Rehabilitative and reintegrative efforts for the mentally ill fluctuate with the business cycle and may contribute to changes in schizophrenic outcome.
- Female schizophrenics achieve better outcome in schizophrenia than men.
- Schizophrenics of lower social class achieve worse outcome than higher-class patients.
- Schizophrenic outcome in full-employment societies may be better than in other industrial nations.

# 7  Schizophrenia in the Third World

Up to four billion dollars was spent on the treatment of schizophrenia in the United States in 1971[1]—about 0.5 per cent of the gross national product. This figure excludes social security benefits for schizophrenic patients. Such a substantial investment should surely have yielded Americans significantly better rates of recovery than in less affluent parts of the world. By contrast, psychiatric care is very low on the list of priorities in developing countries. Despite this fact, the evidence points overwhelmingly to much better outcome from schizophrenia in the Third World. It is worth looking at this evidence in some detail.

## Brief Psychoses in the Third World

There are numerous reports that psychoses have a briefer duration in the Third World, and virtually none to indicate that such illnesses have a worse outcome anywhere outside the Western world. Transitory delusional states (*bouffées délirantes*) in Senegal, for example, with such typical schizophrenic features as 'derealization, hallucinations, and ideas of reference dominated by themes of persecution and megalomania'[2] occasionally develop the classic, chronic schizophrenic course, but generally recover spontaneously within a short period of time. Acute paranoid reactions with a favorable course and outcome are common in the Grande Kabylie of northern Algeria[3] and throughout East Africa.[4] Acute psychotic episodes with high rates of spontaneous remission are frequent in Nigeria,[5] and brief schizophrenia-like psychoses are reported to account for four-fifths of the admissions to one psychiatric hospital in Uganda.[6] Indistinguishable from schizophrenia, acute 'fear and guilt psychoses' in Ghana manifest hallucinations, inappropriate emotional reactions, grotesque delusions and bizarre behavior. Under treatment at local healing shrines, such illnesses are generally cured within a week or so, although they may occasionally progress to chronic schizophrenia.[7] Doris Mayer, a psychiatrist, also found typical schizophrenic states to be more readily reversible in the Tallensi of northern Ghana.[8] Many more examples could be given of the prevalence of such brief psychoses in Singapore, Papua and other developing countries.[9] 'Acute, short lasting

149

psychoses,' according to Dr H. B. M. Murphy, a Canadian psychiatrist with much research experience in cross-cultural psychiatry, 'form a major part of all recognized mental disorders . . .' in the Third World.[10]

## Not Really Schizophrenia

But are they schizophrenia? Some psychiatrists would argue that these acute psychoses are indeed schizophrenia in view of the typical schizophrenic features such as hallucinations, delusions, bizarre behavior and emotional disturbances. They would also point to the minority of cases, initially indistinguishable, which develop the chronic schizophrenic picture. Others would deny that any brief psychosis can be schizophrenia precisely because schizophrenia, by definition, is a chronic illness. According to the American Psychiatric Association *Diagnostic and Statistical Manual — III*,[11] a psychosis must last six months to be labeled schizophrenia. This is a terminological issue which must not be allowed to obscure the point of logic. If schizophrenia has a more benign course in the developing world (and there is considerable evidence to show that this is the case), then we might well find many schizophrenic episodes in these societies which are of a shorter duration than six months. To argue that these are not schizophrenia is to prejudge the issue.

Could these be cases of organic psychosis? Certainly, many could be. There is an extremely high prevalence in Third World countries of trypanosomiasis, pellagra and related parasitic, nutritional and infectious disorders which may develop into psychotic states. Malaria, in particular, is often associated with acute psychotic episodes.[12] It is unlikely, however, that all brief episodes in the Third World are organic in origin. In conducting their social psychiatric survey of four aboriginal tribes in Taiwan, two psychiatrists, Hsien Rin and Tsung-Yi Lin, were particularly concerned about the diagnosis of organic and functional psychoses. They carefully separated schizophrenia from malarial psychosis, drug-induced psychosis and unclassifiable cases. Athough skeptical at the outset of the study, after cross-checking their information and cross-validating their diagnoses they were forced to conclude that psychoses in general, and schizophrenia in particular, had a particularly benign course among these Formosan farmers and hunters. Of ten confirmed cases of schizophrenia, only two had been active for more than two years, and five had been ill for less than a year.[13]

## Conflicting Reports

Some reports fail to show better outcome for schizophrenia and other psychoses in the Third World. They are relatively few and deserve a closer analysis. Dr J. De Wet, the assistant physician superintendent of a South

African mental hospital, concludes that the recovery rate from schizophrenia is no greater in his Bantu patients than is reported for Europeans. His observations were made, however, on patients treated in what appears to have been a particularly traditional and restrictive Western-style hospital setting, which we now know can have a profoundly deteriorating effect on the course of schizophrenia. Only a handful of patients in his 1943 sample were ever discharged from hospital, and these only after several months confinement. Those who were discharged were the patients who 'completely recovered': ten years later they were still doing well at home. None of the patients who remained in hospital regained anything but an indifferent functioning level or worse. The patients in De Wet's 1953 sample all received 15–30 electro-convulsive treatments and none 'was discharged until two months after E.C.T. in order that sudden relapses did not take place at home.'[14] Again the results were not good. By contrast, others who are familiar with the Bantu have described excellent recovery from schizophrenia-like psychoses in their own communities.[15] Dr De Wet's report demonstrates what happens to the usually excellent course of schizophrenia in Africans when they are managed in a traditional European hospital setting. The report is not evidence, despite De Wet's claims, of generally poor outcome from psychosis among the Bantu.

Another study which finds poor outcome from schizophrenia in a Third World peasant society comes from psychiatrist Joseph Westermeyer. Dr Westermeyer has published an interesting series of articles on 35 psychotic subjects whom he located in twenty-seven villages of Ventiane province, Laos. The cases were selected by asking villagers if any of their neighbors were considered *baa* or insane. Nine of the subjects so identified were rated as suffering from organic psychoses and 24 as having functional psychoses, mostly schizophrenia. Only 2 teenagers were considered no longer psychotic. The group of subjects was clearly very actively disturbed; only 2 were working and only 5 were lucid enough to provide useful information about themselves. Dr Westermeyer compares the current functioning of these psychotics with their pre-illness state and concludes, not unreasonably, 'that severe social dysfunction was associated with psychosis in a peasant society.'[16] He goes on to argue, however:

> These findings are in contrast to the social functioning of psychotic patients who are receiving psychiatric care. Follow-up studies of psychotic persons receiving psychiatric care in North America and Europe have shown that many return to economic productivity (about half of schizophrenics do so) and make a fair to good social adjustment.[17]

The problem with this conclusion is not difficult to detect. Dr Westermeyer is comparing Lao cases who are, by virtue of the selection technique, currently highly disturbed, with Western psychotics who are

151

followed up some time after their acute episode. Later in this chapter we shall see that many psychotics in Third World societies are never labeled insane. Dr Westermeyer himself, in an earlier paper, emphasizes that 'folk criteria for mental illness are determined primarily by the persistence of social dysfunctional behavior rather than by disturbances in thought and affect.'[18] Cases which are psychotic but not disruptive are overlooked by this study, as well as those who were psychotic and who have recovered. Drs Rin and Lin, in their community survey, located subjects who had been psychotic previously and had become well. They found three times as many of these individuals as active cases. Rin and Lin's technique provides something close to lifetime-prevalence data: Westermeyer, whose method only detected those who had been psychotic in the past year, provides period-prevalence data. As Dr Westermeyer confirmed when questioned about this issue, his method has 'a built-in bias for prolonged cases.'[19] It gives us no indication of true recovery rates.

Follow-up studies can give us a more definitive picture of recovery from schizophrenia in the Third World. Five such reports are available, and only one, the first listed here, fails to reveal substantially better recovery rates for schizophrenics in the developing world. Table 7.1 shows how these outcome figures compare with those calculated in Chapter 3 from Western studies.

## Chandigarh, India

P. Kulhara and N. N. Wig, British-trained psychiatrists, report that the outcome for schizophrenic patients treated by the Department of Psychiatry in the Postgraduate Institute of Medical Education and Research of Chandigarh, India, is no better than for schizophrenics in a previous study in London.[20] Modern inpatient and outpatient services were offered to the Indian schizophrenics admitted in 1966 and 1967 and followed up 4½–6 years later. Chandigarh is a newly built city and perhaps unlike much of India in its character; almost half of the patient sample, however, came from the surrounding rural area, where conditions are more typical of Indian peasant life. A more serious criticism of this study is that of 174 cases admitted, only 100 could be found for follow-up. These included, of course, all the patients who remained in hospital but excluded those who had moved away and others who might have been expected to show a good outcome.[21] This problem may explain why Drs Kulhara and Wig report a much less impressive recovery rate for India than that found in the WHO study to be described later.

## Mauritius

A follow-up study of African and Indian schizophrenics twelve years after their first admission to hospital was carried out in Mauritius, an island in the

Table 7.1 Outcome from schizophrenia in developing-world and industrial countries, 1956 to the present

| LOCATION | MAURITIUS | HONG KONG | CHANDIGARH, INDIA | SRI LANKA | EUROPE & N. AMERICA |
|---|---|---|---|---|---|
| YEAR OF ADMISSION | 1956 | 1965 | 1966-7 | 1970 | 1956-PRESENT |
| FOLLOW-UP PERIOD | 12 YEARS | 10 YEARS | 4½-6 YEARS | 5 YEARS | VARIABLE |
| STAGE OF ILLNESS | FIRST ADMISSION | FIRST ADMISSION | FIRST ADMISSION | FIRST ADMISSION | FIRST ADMISSION |
| *Course of illness* | % | % | % | % | % |
| No relapses | 59 | 21 | 45 | 40 | — |
| Relapses | 9 | 66 | 23 | 24 | — |
| Chronic disturbance | 32 | 12 | 32 | 36 | — |
| *Social functioning at follow-up* | | | | | |
| Normal | 64 } 75 | 43 } 66 | — | 58 } 71 | } 45 |
| Mild impairment | 11 | 23 | — | 13 | — |
| Moderate impairment | 8 } 24 | 26 } 33 | — | 16 } 29 | } 55 |
| Severe impairment | 16 | 7 | — | 13 | — |
| *Symptomatology at follow-up* | | | | | |
| No symptoms | 64 | — } 65 | over 29 | 45 | 22 |
| Non-psychotic symptoms | 11 | — | over 16 | 24 | — } 78 |
| Psychotic | 24 | 34 | over 32 | 31 | — |

153

Indian Ocean, by the Canadian social psychiatrist Dr H. B. M. Murphy and the superintendent of the hospital, Dr A. C. Raman. They found that although the incidence of schizophrenia was close to the British rate, the recovery rate was outstandingly better. Sixty-four per cent of the patients had maintained a complete, symptom-free recovery, and over 70 per cent were functioning independently. The patients were initially treated in hospital without the use of antipsychotic drugs. Strenuous efforts were made to trace as many as possible for follow-up, with the result that all but 2 per cent were found.[22]

### Sri Lanka

Very similar results were obtained in Sri Lanka by anthropologist Nancy Waxler, who followed up patients five years after their first admission to hospital in 1970 with schizophrenic episodes. Some of these patients had been ill for as long as five or ten years before admission. Most of the sample came from rural areas, generally from families of farmers and laborers. All but one of the 44 schizophrenic patients were traced. At follow-up, 45 per cent of the patients complained of no symptoms at all and 69 per cent had no psychotic symptoms; half of the patients were rated by a psychiatrist as having made a normal adjustment and 58 per cent were considered normal by their families. Clearly, these people were well not merely by virtue of the tolerance of their family members, they were well by a number of standards.[23]

### Hong Kong

Psychiatrists W. H. Lo and T. Lo attempted to follow up, after an interval of ten years, all of the schizophrenic patients who lived on Hong Kong Island and had first attended the Hong Kong Psychiatric Centre in 1965. They were able to evaluate only 82 out of the original 133 patients. Their outcome results for this densely urbanized manufacturing center are intermediate between those for European patients and those for schizophrenics in Mauritius and Sri Lanka. A substantial number of their subjects had a relapsing course to their illness, but at follow-up 65 per cent were free of psychotic symptoms and a similar proportion had achieved good social recovery.[24] The outcome for these patients compares favorably with the estimated 45 per cent social recovery rate for Western schizophrenics (see Chapter 3).

## WHO Pilot Study of Schizophrenia

A problem with attempts to compare recovery rates in different parts of the world is that research studies vary in the way patients are selected and diagnosed and in the criteria used for measuring outcome. To clarify this picture the World Health Organization international, collaborative follow-up study of schizophrenia[25] has brought standardized methods of diagnosis and follow-up to the analysis of outcome for psychotic patients from nine countries in the industrial and non-industrial world. Patients admitted to psychiatric centers in Aarhus (Denmark), Agra (India), Cali (Colombia), Ibadan (Nigeria), London (England), Moscow (USSR), Prague (Czecho-slovakia), Taipei (Taiwan), and Washington, DC (USA) were evaluated according to a standardized procedure and categorized by a computerized diagnostic scheme—the CATEGO system. By this method, groups of very similar acute and chronic schizophrenics were selected in each of the nine centers from among those patients applying for treatment during 1968 and 1969. In seven of the centers (as mentioned in previous chapters) the patients labeled schizophrenic were found to be essentially similar, but in Moscow and Washington, DC, the diagnosis of schizophrenia was distinctly broader. At two year follow-up the researchers were taken by surprise at the marked variability in the course and outcome of schizophrenia in the different centers. Patients in the developing world showed strikingly better results.

Combining various factors, patients were categorized into five groups according to overall outcome. As may be seen from Table 7.2, the

**Table 7.2  Percentage of schizophrenic patients in different overall outcome groups in the WHO International Outcome Study**

| CENTERS | BEST-OUTCOME GROUP | TWO BEST-OUTCOME GROUPS COMBINED % | TWO WORST-OUTCOME GROUPS COMBINED % | WORST-OUTCOME GROUP % |
|---|---|---|---|---|
| Aarhus | 6 | 35 | 48 | 31 |
| Agra | 48 | 66 | 21 | 15 |
| Cali | 21 | 53 | 28 | 15 |
| Ibadan | 57 | 86 | 7 | 5 |
| London | 24 | 36 | 41 | 31 |
| Moscow | 9 | 48 | 20 | 11 |
| Taipei | 15 | 38 | 35 | 15 |
| Washington | 23 | 39 | 45 | 19 |
| Prague | 14 | 34 | 39 | 30 |
| Developed nations | 15 | 39 | 37 | 28 |
| Developing nations | 35 | 59 | 23 | 13 |

155

best-outcome category includes 35 per cent of patients from centers in the Third World by comparison with only 15 per cent from centers in the industrialized world. These patients were psychotic for less than four months of the two-year follow-up period and developed a full remission with no social impairment. The two best-outcome categories combined embrace 59 per cent of patients from the developing world but only 39 per cent of those from industrial nations. More than a quarter of patients from the developed world were in the worst outcome category at follow-up, twice the proportion of those from the developing nations. These patients were psychotic for more than eighteen months of the follow-up period and were severely socially impaired. Nigeria and India, where the catchment areas were largely rural and most of the population was engaged in agriculture, recorded the best overall outcome. Urbanized Cali, where unemployment was significant, showed somewhat less satisfactory outcome. In Taipei, the most industrially developed of the Third World centers and with serious levels of unemployment, the outcome was little better than in the industrial West and less good than in Moscow. Although few patients in Moscow were in the best-outcome group, a large proportion was in the best two groups combined, and few were in the worst categories; these results place Moscow in an intermediate position between centers in the developed and developing worlds.

Could patient selection have influenced these results? It is possible that the schizophrenics presenting for treatment at Third World centers, while appearing comparable with those in the Western samples, were in fact not representative of all the schizophrenics in the community. It seems unlikely, however, that those who were admitted to treatment would be predominantly people with *less* severe forms of the illness.

One simple symptom measure, the proportion of patients either (1) psychotic, (2) symptomatic but not psychotic, or (3) completely free of symptoms, allows us to compare the WHO results with two of the other Third World follow-up studies. Figure 7.1 shows that the results for Mauritius and Sri Lanka closely match other nations of the developing world and suggests that the findings of these earlier outcome studies may give a fairly accurate picture.

The general conclusion is unavoidable. Schizophrenia in the Third World has a course and prognosis quite unlike the condition as we recognize it in the West. The progressive deterioration which Kraepelin considered central to his definition of the disease is a rare event in non-industrial societies, except perhaps under the dehumanizing restrictions of a traditional asylum. The majority of Third World schizophrenics achieve a favorable outcome. The more urbanized and industrialized the setting, the more malignant becomes the illness. Why should this be so?

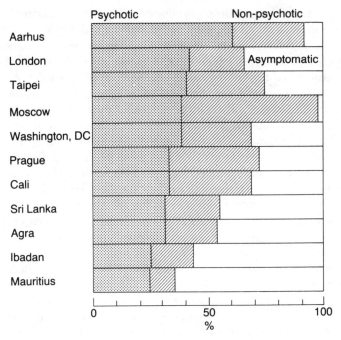

*Figure 7.1    Percentage of schizophrenics in the WHO Pilot Study and the Mauritius and Sri Lanka studies who were psychotic, non-psychotic and symptom-free at follow-up*

## Work

It was argued in earlier chapters that the dwindling cure rates for insanity during the growth of industrialism in Britain and America, and the low recovery rates in schizophrenia during the Great Depression, were possibly related to labor-force dynamics. The apparently superior outcome for schizophrenia in the USSR, if it is not a consequence of diagnostic bias, may be a result of full employment and an emphasis on work rehabilitation in that country. The picture which has now been drawn of schizophrenia in the Third World gives more support to the notion that the work role may be an important factor shaping the course of schizophrenia.

In non-industrial societies that are not based upon a wage economy, the term 'unemployment' is meaningless. Even where colonial wage systems have been developed, they frequently preserve the subsistence base of tribal or peasant communities, drawing workers for temporary labor only.[26] In these circumstances, underemployment and landlessness may become common but unemployment is rare. Unemployment, however, may reach high levels in the urbanized and industrial areas of the Third World.

157

The return of a psychotic to a productive role in a non-industrial setting is not contingent upon his actively seeking a job, impressing an employer with his worth or functioning at a consistently adequate level. In a non-wage, subsistence economy, psychotics may perform any of those available tasks which match their level of functioning at a given time. Whatever constructive contributions they can make are likely to be valued by the community and their level of disability will not be considered absolute. Dr Adeoye Lambo, a psychiatrist well known for developing a village-based treatment and rehabilitation program in Nigeria, reports that social attitudes in Nigerian rural communities permit the majority of those with mental disorders to find an appropriate level of functioning and thus to avoid disability and deterioration.[27] In India, research workers for the WHO follow-up study of schizophrenia encountered difficulty in interviewing their cases as the ex-patients were so busy—the men in the fields and the women in domestic work.[28] The more complete use of labor in pre-industrial societies may encourage high rates of recovery from psychosis.

But what of the nature of the work itself? John Wing, a British social psychiatrist who has done a great deal of research on schizophrenia, identifies two critical environmental factors which lead to optimal outcome from the illness. The first of these, which we will return to later, is freedom from emotional over-involvement—smothering or criticism—from others in the household. His second criterion, which is relevant here, is that there should be stable expectations precisely geared to the level of performance that the individual can actually achieve.[29] Industrial society gives relatively little leeway for adapting a job to the abilities of the worker. High productivity requirements and competitive performance ratings may be particularly unsuitable for a rehabilitating schizophrenic. In a peasant culture he or she is more likely to find an appropriate role among such tasks of subsistence farming as livestock management, food- and fuel-gathering or child-minding. As the authors of the WHO schizophrenia study comment about life in the countryside of India:

> work in the rural setting is mostly collective, agricultural, and often does not require particular skills. Many occupations are passed from father to son. Thus, competitive situations seldom exist. The occupational pursuits do not usually require fine skill and adaptability and often do not demand much effort or strain. . . . Employment conditions in the country usually do not have any untoward effects on most patients.[30]

Many clinicians in the West have noticed that the demands of a full 40-hour week are overly taxing for psychotic clients. In hunter-gatherer and peasant societies, the distinction between work and non-work may be hard to make (in some cultures it is not linguistically possible to differentiate 'work' from 'ritual' or from 'play'[31]), but the demands of subsistence are unlikely to be burdensome. !Kung Bushmen work no more than two to three (6-hour) days a week in hunting and food-gathering for themselves and their dependents, and about two hours further each day is spent on food preparation and 'housework.'[32] Slash-and-burn agriculture, for example among the Bemba of north Zimbabwe or the Toupouri of north Cameroon, calls for only three or four (5-hour) working days a week.[33] Plough agriculture commonly requires a 30–35 hour work week.[34] Estimates of labor requirements for irrigation agriculture vary. In Yunnan Province in pre-revolutionary China, the working day was seldom longer than 7–8 hours, including frequent rest periods, even at the busiest time of year; during the slack months, there was virtually no farm work to be done. Elsewhere a demanding 50- to 70-hour work week has been recorded, but both of these examples of irrigation agriculture involve market production, not just local subsistence needs.[35] Where production is for use and not for exchange, labor needs tend to be low.[36]

In each setting there is wide individual variation. In pre-revolutionary Russia, for example, peasant farmers in Volokolamsk were found to work between 79 days a year in the least industrious households and 216 in the most industrious.[37] This compares with an expectation of around 230–40 working days a year for employees in modern industrial society. Work demands in many cultures are particularly low for young, unmarried adults[38] (who may be at higher risk for developing schizophrenia), but whatever the usual pattern, work-load expectations are more readily adjusted to meet the capacities of the marginally functional individual in a village setting than in the industrial labor market. There can be little doubt that it is simpler for a schizophrenic to return to a productive role in a non-industrial community than in the industrial world. The merits of tribal and peasant labor systems are apparent: as in the West during a period of labor shortage, it is easier for family and community members to reintegrate the sick person into the society, and the psychotic is better able to retain his or her self-esteem. The result may well be not only better social functioning of the psychotic person but also more complete remission of the symptoms of the illness.

## Occupation and Outcome

In searching for predictors of good outcome in schizophrenia, the WHO Pilot Study examined a number of patient characteristics. We may look at these data for evidence of an association between occupation and outcome in schizophrenia but, in so doing, we encounter difficulties presented by the variety and complexity of work and subsistence patterns in the developing world. Poverty can be extreme in the urban slums of the Third World, where many eke out an existence by self-employment in street-vending and similar activities or with low and irregular earnings from work in the formal and

159

informal segments of the urban labor market. Outright unemployment, however, is often most severe in the upwardly-striving, urban middle classes. In rural areas, this reversal of the usual Western pattern is even more marked, with unemployment among the aspiring educated at times being severe, while those working the land are largely outside the labor market.[39]

In rural districts, therefore, we should look for a reversal of the usual Western pattern of outcome from schizophrenia and for superior outcome in the less educated—the subsistence farmers with limited exposure to Western acculturative forces. A mixed recovery picture might be expected to occur in those urban areas where economic development is incomplete and is creating stresses for the new managerial and professional classes. In the most highly-developed cities of the Third World we should expect a pattern of recovery similar to the West with the best outcome in the high-status occupations. In general, we might anticipate outcome to be better in villages, where more of the population is outside the wage-labor market, than in the cities.

In fact the WHO data show neither rural nor urban living to be strong predictors of good outcome.[40] The information on residence, however, was gathered at intake rather than at follow-up. The lack of association between residence and outcome, therefore, may merely reflect what several authors have noted—that migrant laborers who fall ill while working in the industrial areas return to the village to recuperate.[41] Urban psychotics may benefit from this return to traditional village roles.

Other WHO data more clearly document an association between occupation and outcome. Farmers were more likely than patients of any other occupation to experience the most benign pattern of illness—full remission with no relapses—and the unemployed were least likely to experience such a mild course to the psychosis. In urbanized Cali and Taipei patients from high-status professional and managerial occupations were found to achieve good overall outcome, while this was not the case in the largely rural catchment area around Agra, India.[42] This pattern confirms the impression that schizophrenia may be more benign in the successful upper classes in the industrialized setting, but more malignant among the better educated in India who are known to suffer rates of unemployment several times greater than the poorly educated and illiterate.[43] The data from Nigeria do not fit as neatly. Even though many patients in the sample appear to have come from rural districts, Nigerian schizophrenics in managerial jobs experienced good overall outcome.[44] This could be explained by a strong local demand for educated labor at that time or, again, the high mobility of the migrant labor force may confuse the picture: patients who were unable to continue in managerial positions could return to a less demanding role in their farming community.

Migrant-labor practices allow Third World schizophrenics to change occupation and residence after developing psychotic symptoms. Level of education, however, is less easily changed. It is therefore interesting to note that a high level of education is one of the few strong and consistent indicators of poor outcome in the Third World,[45] thus standing in contrast to Western patterns of recovery. This point, then, may be one of the most useful pieces of evidence in the WHO study, pointing to a link between good outcome for schizophrenia in the Third World and the maintenance of traditional occupational roles.

## Stress

Unemployment on the one hand and intensified work demands on the other are special stresses of modern industrial society. Are there other increased stresses of life in the fast-paced industrial world which might account for the poor prognosis for schizophrenia in the West? It depends what we mean by stress. Urban overcrowding, job insecurity, productivity pressure, and alienation from the creative process are all chronically stressful facets of industrial life. Those who live in peasant communities, however, must face equal levels of domestic discord and often suffer problems of poor health, high infant mortality and inadequate housing, clothing, food and water. With the development of state-level societies and colonialism come increasing difficulties with authority, status disparity, poverty and starvation. To passing tourists, the palm-studded fishing village near Mazatlan on the west coast of Mexico might seem a subtropical paradise; but when Russell McGoodwin, an anthropologist, asked the inhabitants what caused them most suffering they listed many complaints including poverty, family problems, the burden of work, inadequate water supplies and poor clothing. In response to the question, 'What do you enjoy?' nearly half answered, 'Nothing.'[46] Life in non-industrial societies is not low in stress. Rousseau's 'noble savage' leading a life of peace and perfect order in 'the state of nature' cannot be found. But some features of tribal and peasant life might well improve the social integration and the outlook for those who suffer from a psychotic episode.

## A Psychotic Episode in Guatemala

Maria, a young Indian woman living in a village on Lake Atitlan in Guatemala, alienates her close relatives and the people of the community by her irresponsible behavior before finally suffering a full-blown psychotic episode. She hallucinates, believing that spirits are surrounding her to take her to the realm of the dead, and she walks about the house arguing with ghosts. A local shaman perceives that she is *loca* (crazy) and diagnoses her as suffering the effect of supernatural forces unleashed by the improper

161

behavior of certain relatives. He prescribes a healing ritual which calls for the active participation of most of her extended family. Her condition requires her to move back to her father's house, where she recovers within a week. Benjamin Paul, the anthropologist who describes Maria's case, points out several features of interest. Maria is never blamed for her psychotic behavior or stigmatized by her illness, because her hallucinations of ghosts are credible supernatural events and she is innocently suffering the magical consequences of the wrong-doing of others. The communal healing activities lead to a dramatic reversal of Maria's course of alienation from family and community. In the West, a psychotic episode is likely to lead to increased alienation. In the case of Maria, conflict resolution and social reintegration are central to her recovery and result from the folk diagnosis and treatment of her symptoms.[47]

## The Folk Diagnosis of Psychosis

Throughout the non-industrial world, the features of psychosis are likely to be given a supernatural explanation. The Shona of southern Rhodesia, for example, believe visual and auditory hallucinations to be real and sent by spirits.[48] In Dakar, Senegal:

> one can have hallucinations without being thought to be sick. A magical explanation is usually resorted to and native specialists are consulted. There is no rejection or alienation by society. The patient remains integrated within his group. As a result, the level of anxiety is low . . .[49]

The psychiatrist who gives this report claims that 90 per cent of the acute psychoses in Dakar are cured because the patient's delusions and hallucinations have an obvious culturally relevant content, and he or she is not rejected by the group.

Similarly, in the slums of San Juan, Puerto Rico:

> If an individual reports hallucinations, it clearly indicates to the believer in spiritualism that he is being visited by spirits who manifest themselves visually and audibly. If he has delusions . . . his thoughts are being distorted by interfering bad spirits, or through development of his psychic faculties spirits have informed him of the true enemies in his environment. Incoherent ramblings, and cryptic verbalizations indicate that he is undergoing a test, an experiment engineered by the spirits. If he wanders aimlessly through the neighborhood, he is being pursued by ambulatory spirits who are tormenting him unmercifully.[50]

In many cases where a supernatural explanation for psychotic features is used, the label 'crazy' or 'insane' may never be applied. I once remarked to a Sioux mental health worker from the Pine Ridge Reservation in South

Dakota that most Americans who heard voices would be diagnosed as psychotic. Her response was simple. 'That's terrible.'

## Nigerian Attitudes to Mental Illness

Urban and rural Yoruba with no formal education, from the area of Abeokuta in southwestern Nigeria, were asked their opinions about descriptions of typical mentally ill people. Only 40 per cent of those questioned thought that the paranoid schizophrenic described was mentally ill.[51] (Some 90–100 per cent of Americans label the subject of this vignette as mentally ill.[52]) Only 21 per cent of the uneducated Yoruba considered the description of the simple schizophrenic to be a mentally ill person. (Some 70–80 per cent of American respondents call this hypothetical case mentally ill.[53])

What is perhaps even more impressive than the details about labeling psychosis in this Nigerian study is the very high level of tolerance revealed. More than 30 per cent of the uneducated Yoruba would have been willing to marry the paranoid schizophrenic person described and 55 per cent would have married the simple schizophrenic. In contrast, when skilled workers from the area of Benin in midwestern Nigeria were asked their opinions about someone specifically labeled a 'nervous or mad person,' 16 per cent thought that all such people should be shot and 31 per cent believed that they should be expelled from the country. These educated Nigerians conceived of mad people as 'senseless, unkempt, aggressive and irresponsible.'[54]

## Malaya

In Nigeria it appears that the label 'mad,' 'crazy' or 'mentally ill' is only applied to highly disruptive individuals and brings with it harsher treatment. The same pattern has been observed in a Malay village in Pahang state. Here the term for madness, *gila*, is only applied to violent people. 'Madmen' are always handed over to authorities outside the village for permanent banishment. Within the community of over 400 people, however, are many probable psychotics who have never been labeled mad—twelve who are 'eccentric,' including senile elderly people and marginally functional hermits; and one 'person with less than healthy brains' who spends a good deal of time praying and reading in solitude. Five people exhibiting *latah*—a so-called culture-bound psychosis—were also identified:[55] but this condition may not be a psychosis in the proper sense of the term.[56]

## Laos

Although Dr Westermeyer in some of his publications disputes that psychotics often escape being labeled *baa* (insane) in Laos, his own observations are very close to the findings in Nigeria and Malaya. Lao villagers are apparently slow to apply the term *baa*, and a person so labeled tends to have a chronic illness, usually of several years' duration, and to be highly disruptive, assaultive or bizarre. Hallucinations are never mentioned by the villagers as a feature of insanity. Unless there are local conditions restricting the development of brief psychoses so common elsewhere in the Third World, then one must assume that the reason there are so few acute cases in Dr Westermeyer's Lao sample is that they are not considered by the villagers to be *baa*. Interestingly, the severely psychotic *baa* individuals in Laos are not exiled or assassinated but continue to receive food, shelter, clothing and humane care and are restrained and incarcerated only as long as their violent behavior requires.[57] It is apparent that labeling is an important issue only insofar as it affects management. As we shall see in the next example, it is the concept of illness which lies behind the label which is also critical in determining care and treatment.

## Four East African Societies

Anthropologist Robert Edgerton, describing attitudes to psychosis among tribesmen of four East African pastoral and farming societies, confirms that violence and destructiveness are emphasized in descriptions of psychosis (*kichaa*) and hallucinations are virtually never mentioned.[58] Most commonly reported features of psychosis include murder, assault, arson, abuse, stealing and nakedness. The pastoralists whose homesteads are more widely dispersed and who are more free to move away from disagreeable circumstances are less concerned than the farmers about the social disruption of psychotics.[59] The intriguing conclusion of Edgerton's survey is that the tribal view of the cause of psychosis determines not only the manner of treatment but also the level of optimism about recovery.[60] The Pokot of northwest Kenya and the Sebei of southeast Uganda have a naturalistic conception of the cause of psychosis. They implicate a worm in the frontal portion of the brain and are very pessimistic about the possibilities of cure. The Kamba of south-central Kenya and the Hehe of southwest Tanzania, on the other hand, attribute the cause of psychosis to witchcraft or stress and are optimistic about curing such disorders. The two tribes which are most unsure about their respective theories of causation, the Pokot and the Hehe, also tend to be more ambivalent about the curability of the condition. The Kamba and the Hehe, holding a supernatural theory for the cause of psychosis, favor the use of tranquilizing herbs and ritual in treatment. The pessimistic Sebei and Pokot, with the naturalistic belief system, are much more inclined to treat psychotics harshly, as illustrated by the remarks of a Pokot shaman: 'I am able to cure mads. I order the patient tied and placed upon the ground. I then take a large rock and pound the patient on the head for a long time. This calms them and they are better.'[61] The Pokot and Sebei recommend that psychotics should be tied up forever, allowed to starve, driven away to die or killed outright.

## Stigma

Life for some psychotics in the Third World, according to a few of these reports, is not a bed of roses. But we should not allow reports of harsh treatment of the most severely disturbed psychotics in some areas to obscure the central facts. Many people who would be considered psychotic in the West are not so labeled in the Third World, especially if their condition is brief or not disruptive. Many more, though labeled 'crazy' like Maria the Guatemalan Indian woman, are treated vigorously and optimistically with every effort to reintegrate them rather than reject them.

Psychiatrists working in the Third World have repeatedly noted the low level of stigma which attaches to mental disorder. Among the Formosan tribesmen studied by Rin and Lin, mental illness is free of stigma.[62] Sinhalese families freely refer to their psychotic family members as *pissu* (crazy) and show no shame about it. Tuberculosis in Sri Lanka is more stigmatizing than mental illness.[63] The authors of the WHO follow-up study suggest that one of the factors contributing to the good outcome for schizophrenics in Cali, Colombia, is the 'high level of tolerance of relatives and friends for symptoms of mental disorder'—a factor which can help the 'readjustment to family life and work after discharge.'[64]

The possibility that the stigma attached to an illness may influence its course is illustrated by research on Navajo epileptics conducted by anthropologist Jerrold Levy in cooperation with the Indian Health Service. Sibling incest is regarded as the cause of generalized seizures, or Moth Sickness, in Navajo society, and those who suffer from the condition are highly stigmatized for supposed transgressions of a major taboo. It is interesting to learn that these individuals are often found to lead chaotic lives characterized by alcoholism, promiscuity, incest, rape, violence and early death. Levy and his co-workers attribute the career of the Navajo epileptic to the disdain and lack of social support which he or she is offered by the community.[65] To what extent, we may wonder, can features of schizophrenia in the West be attributed to similar treatment?

## High Status in Psychosis

It seems strange in retrospect that tuberculosis should have been such a romantic and genteel illness to eighteenth- and nineteenth-century society that people of fashion chose to copy the consumptive appearance.[66] Equally curious, the features of psychosis in the Third World can, at times, lead to considerable elevation in social status. In non-industrial cultures throughout the world, the hallucinations and altered states of consciousness produced by psychosis, fasting, sleep deprivation, social isolation and contemplation, and hallucinogenic drug use are often a prerequisite for gaining shamanic power.[67] The psychotic features are interpreted as an initiatory experience. For example, whereas poor Puerto Ricans who go to a psychiatric clinic or insane asylum are likely to be highly stigmatized as *locos* (madmen), schizophrenics who consult a spiritualist may rise in status. Sociologists Lloyd Rogler and August Hollingshead report: 'The spiritualist may announce to the sick person, his family, and friends that the afflicted person is endowed with *facultades* (psychic faculties), a matter of prestige at this level of the social structure . . .'[68]

The study indicates that Puerto Rican schizophrenics who consult spiritualists may not only lose their symptoms, they may also achieve the status of mediums themselves. So successful is the social reintegration of the male Puerto Rican schizophrenics studied that, after some readjustment of family roles, their wives found them *more* acceptable as husbands than did the wives of normal men.

Similar folk beliefs exist in Turkey. Dr Orhan Ozturk, a psychiatrist in Ankara, writes:

> A person may be hallucinated or delusional, but as long as he is not destructive or very unstable he may not be considered insane. . . . Such a person may sometimes be considered to have a supernatural capacity for communication with the spirit world and may therefore be regarded with reverence and awe.[69]

Ruth Benedict tells us that Siberian shamans who dominate the life of their communities

> are individuals who by submission to the will of the spirits have been cured of a grievous illness. . . . Some, during the period of the call, are violently insane for several years; others irresponsible to the point where they have to be constantly watched lest they wander off in the snow and freeze to death. . . . It is the shamanistic practice which constitutes their cure.[70]

Several other writers have suggested that indigenous healers who have suffered psychotic episodes may find their elevated status and well-defined curing role to be a valuable defense against relapse.[71] Psychiatrist Fuller Torrey argues, however, that few shamans can be psychotic. The role is too responsible and demanding, he claims, for a schizophrenic to manage.[72] While, no doubt, many healers are not psychotic, Dr Torrey underestimates the importance of features of psychosis as an initiatory experience. He is

166

neglecting on the one hand, the heightened possibility of complete remission for Third World psychotics and, on the other hand, the capacity of schizophrenic individuals to be completely functional in some areas of their lives despite islands of illogical thinking. One well-known North American Indian medicine man with whom I am familiar would doubtless be diagnosed schizophrenic by a Western psychiatrist by virtue of his extremely tangential and symbolic speech, which is often incomprehensible, his inappropriate emotional responses and his hallucinations. This man, however, is highly respected by his community and often travels the country on speaking engagements. The psychotic may be able to function well as a shaman, argues anthropologist Julian Silverman of the US National Institute of Mental Health, because 'the emotional supports . . . available to the shaman greatly alleviate the strain of an otherwise excruciatingly painful [schizophrenic] existence. Such supports are all too often completely unavailable to the schizophrenic in our culture.'[73]

## Healing Ceremonies

Being thought of as a spiritualist or healer is not the only way Third World psychotics may gain status. Curing rituals for those with mental disorders may also enable the individual to increase his or her social status and redefine his or her social role. Anthropologist Ralph Linton observes that low-status individuals among the Tanala of Madagascar, such as second sons and childless wives, may rise in status as a result of the elaborate healing rite for mental illness.[74] Patients who participate in the curing possession cults in Trinidad[75] among the Yoruba of Nigeria[76] and in the Zar cult of northern Ethiopia[77] have all been observed to achieve an elevation of social status as a consequence of their membership.

Initiation into these cults also provides new friends, ongoing group support and the opportunity for social involvement, and similar benefits appear to result from other healing rites. Robin Fox, a British anthropologist, gives a detailed account of a clan cure for a 40-year-old woman with a chronic mental disorder in the Pueblo Indian community of Cochiti in New Mexico. The woman is a member of the Oak clan by birth, but by undergoing a healing ritual which entails adoption also into the Water clan, she acquires additional supportive relatives, a new social role and a new home. She subsequently shows complete recovery.[78]

## Group Participation

The process of curing in pre-industrial societies, it is clear, is very much a communal phenomenon tending not only to reintegrate the deviant individual into the group but also to reaffirm the solidarity of the community.

Thus, the N'jayei secret society of the Mende tribe in Sierra Leone, which aims to treat mental illness by applying sanctions to those who are presumed to have committed a breach of social rules, provides members with a mechanism for social reintegration and, simultaneously, reinforces the integrity and standards of the culture.[79] Such a dual process of unification of the group and integration of the individual is seen to result from the great public healing ceremonies of the Zuni medicine societies[80] or from the intense communal involvement and dramatic grandeur of a Navajo healing ceremony. The Navajo patient, relatives and other participants alike take medicine and submit to ritual procedures in a symbolic recognition that illness is a problem for the community as a whole.[81]

Nancy Waxler, in her research on psychotics in Sri Lanka, was impressed with the way in which the intense community involvement in treating mental illness prevents the patient from developing secondary symptoms from alienation and stigma and results in the sick person being reintegrated into society. She writes:

> Mental illness is basically a problem of and for the family, not the sick person. Thus we find among the Sinhalese that almost all treatment of mental illness involves groups meeting with groups. When a mad person is believed to have been possessed by a demon the whole family, their relatives and neighbours, sometimes the whole village, join together to plan, carry out and pay for the appropriate exorcism ceremony. The sick person is usually the central focus, but often only as the vehicle for the demon, and during some parts of these ceremonies the patient is largely ignored.[82]

The importance of this process of social reintegration is confirmed by data from the WHO Pilot Study. In both the developed and developing worlds, social isolation was found to be one of the strongest predictors of poor outcome in schizophrenia.[83] Several other researchers have found this factor to be important in the genesis and outcome of schizophrenia.[84]

## Social Consensus

There is some anthropological evidence that broad group participation in healing not only aids the reintegration of the patient but is also a necessary and powerfully effective element in the treatment of emotional illness. The French anthropologist Claude Levi-Strauss, for example, analyzes the effectiveness of a highly respected Kwakiutl shaman from British Columbia who is skeptical of his own healing powers. Levi-Strauss concludes that the shaman is effective despite his cynicism because 'the attitude of the group' endorses his treatment. The social consensus is more important than the attitude of the healer or even of the patient.[85]

A related example of the importance of social consensus in the outcome of mental illness is provided by anthropologist Lloyd Warner's discussion of the role played in the voodoo death of an Australian aborigine by his own social group after he has been 'boned' by an enemy. First the victim's kin withdraw their support and he becomes an isolated and taboo person. Then the community conducts a mourning ritual to protect the group from the soul of the 'half dead' man. Unless the group attitude is reversed by the performance of a counter-ritual, the victim shortly dies.[86] These examples illustrate, on the one hand, the powerful effect of social rejection and stigma on the course of emotional illness and the importance of social acceptance and reintegration: on the other hand, they suggest that any form of treatment which does not receive full community endorsement (and much of institutional psychiatry in the West falls into this category) has a limited chance of success. This analysis, for example, would predict that the Kamba and the Hehe of East Africa who are optimistic about the treatment of mental illness would have better recovery rates from psychosis than the Pokot and Sebei who have no confidence in the ability of their doctors to effect a cure. Edgerton's study presents no evidence, unfortunately, to indicate whether or not this is the case.

Understanding the potential of social consensus to affect outcome allows us to explain why even those individuals who are treated in modern Western-style hospitals and clinics in the developing world rather than by indigenous therapists may experience a higher recovery rate from psychosis. It is not the specific treatment technique which is critical (as long as it is not too regressive) but the social expectations that are generated around the episode of illness. The treatment approaches of the psychiatric clinic may well be supplemented by community diagnosis, rediagnosis and indigenous healing ceremonies which facilitate social reintergration of the sick person. Even among relatively Westernized city-dwellers, according to a report from Senegal, traditional cultural beliefs persist which help to alleviate psychological distress and mental disorder.[87] The existence of a social consensus for recovery and the willingness and capacity of the community to reintegrate the psychotic person are, no doubt, strongly influenced by whether he or she can serve a useful social role. The benefits of traditional community life for the psychotic are less likely to persist in the face of changing patterns of labor use which increase the risks of unemployment and dependency.

## The Family

One of John Wing's criteria for good outcome in schizophrenia mentioned earlier in the chapter was freedom for the patient from excessive emotional demands or criticism within the family. His recommendation is backed up by a good deal of social psychiatric research from the Medical Research

Council in London, which was outlined in Chapter 1. The extended family structure, which is more common in the Third World, allows a diffusion of emotional over-involvement and interdependence among family members. In Qatar, on the Persian Gulf, for example, schizophrenic patients in extended families show better outcome at follow-up than those who return to nuclear family households.[88] The emphasis on community involvement in the treatment of mental illness in non-industrial societies similarly tends to reduce family tensions. Responsibility is shared broadly and the patient often escapes blame and criticism, allowing the family to be more supportive. According to recent research, for example, relatives of schizophrenics in Chandigarh, north India, are much less likely to be demanding or critical of their psychotic family member than are the relatives of schizophrenics in the industrial world. In London, nearly a half of schizophrenics have such emotionally stressful relatives; in Rochester, New York, the proportion is similar; but in north India, fewer than a fifth of schizophrenic patients were found to have critical and demanding relatives.[89] As mentioned in Chapter 1, this difference might be a consequence of the higher achievement expectations placed on Western psychotics or of the emotional isolation so common for families of schizophrenics in the West but so much rarer in the developing world.

In the Third World, it appears, the psychotic is more likely to retain his or her self-esteem, a feeling of value to the community and a sense of belonging. These are things which, as we shall see, four billion dollars does not buy the schizophrenic in the United States or elsewhere in the Western world.

## Summary

- Brief psychoses clinically indistinguishable from schizophrenia are a common occurrence in the Third World.
- Outcome from schizophrenia is better in the non-industrial world than in the West.
- Intermediate levels of outcome from schizophrenia are found in the more industrialized parts of the Third World and in the USSR.
- Third World schizophrenics are more readily returned to a useful working role.
- In the developing world, outcome from schizophrenia is worse among the better educated—a finding which may be explained by the greater labor-market stresses affecting the educated.
- The folk diagnosis of insanity stresses violence and disruption, and many psychotics from the developing world escape this label.
- Many psychotics in the Third World are not stigmatized and some may even rise in status.

- Although some psychotics in non-industrial societies may be brutally treated, in the majority of cases vigorous and optimistic efforts are made to achieve a cure.
- Curing rituals encourage broad community involvement and aid the social reintegration of psychotics.
- The optimistic social consensus mobilized by the curing ceremony may aid recovery from emotional disorders.
- Family patterns of support in the Third World are better suited to the rehabilitation of schizophrenics.

# 8  The Schizophrenic in Western Society

What is it like to be schizophrenic in Western industrial society? For Mary Byrd in New York City, according to a 1982 newspaper report, it is an unbelievably bitter experience.

> One night last week ... when the air felt like ice and half a foot of snow sent thousands of New Yorkers home early ... Charlie, Mary Byrd and Frank Jarnot went home to a cluster of IBM cartons, covered with mailing labels and stamped: 'Handle With Care.' ... By day, Mary huddles outside a subway entrance. There she stays until Frank comes to lead her the 50 paces to a choice spot alongside the bank building.... Taking care of Mary is almost a full-time job for the men, who call the 23-year-old 'just a baby,' and who take turns leaving hamburgers, coffee and cakes outside her box. ... 'She's living in a fantasy world,' Frank says.[1]

An extreme case? Not at all. According to one estimate, roughly half of New York City's 36,000 homeless are thought to be mentally disabled.[2] According to another, there are 25,000 chronically mentally ill in New York living on the street, in missions, public shelters, flophouses and cheap hotels.[3] Of 1,235 men sleeping at a public shelter on New York's Bowery on a night in 1976, 50 per cent showed signs of obvious mental illness, excluding alcoholism; many of these men were former state hospital residents. At the Women's Shelter in New York City more than three-quarters of the women admitted in 1971 were suffering from a psychosis.[4] The degree of mental disturbance amongst such down and out New Yorkers is by no means slight. Mental health professionals who interviewed 100 long-time residents at the same Men's Shelter on the Bowery in 1965 found 50 per cent of the men to be psychotic and diagnosed 36 per cent of the whole group as schizophrenic. They compared this group of 100 Bowery men with a large sample of recently admitted inpatients at five local psychiatric hospitals. Startlingly enough, the residents of the Men's Shelter were found to be *more* disturbed than the inpatients according to several measures in a standardized evaluation procedure.[5]

Researchers who conducted an ethnographic survey of New York City's homeless in 1981 concluded that the ranks of the destitute on Skid Row had

172

been greatly swollen over the prior fifteen years by large numbers of former state hospital patients. 'By a stroke of grim irony,' they report, 'some of these ex-patients had come full circle back to the institution that had originally discharged them—this time for shelter not treatment.'[6] As the result of a class action suit filed on behalf of the city's homeless, the municipal government had been forced to open an empty state hospital building on Ward's Island as an emergency shelter.

This time around, though, conditions were far worse than when the facility had been staffed as a hospital. Now the building was crammed full of cots and there was no type of treatment or recreational activity. Infestation, disease, violence and fear were pervasive. In consequence, staff pushed and prodded the residents with nightsticks to avoid contact and to maintain order. They dealt with the men in rough language and through barked orders. One feature had not changed since the days when the building was a hospital, however—the characteristics of the residents. Eighty-four per cent of the men seeking shelter there in May 1980 were mentally ill; 60 per cent were found to be moderately or severely disturbed—mostly psychotic.[7]

There can be little doubt that patients are ending up on the streets because of the deficient aftercare planning and services of the mental health system. Nearly a quarter of the patients discharged from New York state psychiatric centers were released to 'unknown' living arrangements. From one hospital, nearly 60 per cent of patients were released to an 'unknown' address.[8]

This state of affairs is not confined to New York. In a random sample of 50 men on Chicago's Skid Row in the late 1960s, Robert Priest, a British psychiatrist, found 25 per cent to be certainly or probably schizophrenic.[9] Only a decade earlier, however, in 1957 and 1958, before deinstitutionalization was far advanced, an American researcher, Donald Bogue, found a mere 9 per cent of men on Skid Row in the same city to have mental illness. At that time, Bogue reported, 'mentally unsound persons . . . are picked up rather promptly by the police, and . . . institutionalized.'[10] In Los Angeles at the present time, 50 per cent of 7,000–15,000 people living on Skid Row are incapacitated by chronic mental illness—40 per cent of the men amd 90 per cent of the women.[11] According to a recent report, 44 per cent of the Skid Row homeless in Philadelphia, and at least a quarter of the people living on the streets and in the shelters of Washington, DC, are schizophrenic.[12] In Denver in 1981, the judge who heard most of the cases related to the mental illness statute remarked that the primary residential care provider for mental patients was the city bus company. When they stopped offering free rides on the buses 'the mentally disabled people who had found a home on the Ride (the bus system) hit the streets again.'[13] If we assume that approximately 200,000–400,000 men and women are living on Skid Row in the major cities of the USA[14] and conservatively estimate that a quarter of this population are

173

schizophrenics, it becomes clear that lives such as Mary's are to be counted in the tens of thousands.

The dimensions of the problem are similar in other countries. Twenty-seven per cent of a sample of men sleeping in a Skid Row mission in Toronto in the 1970s were found to be psychotic; 20 per cent of all the men were suffering from schizophrenia or a paranoid state.[15] Twenty-four per cent of the men who booked into the Camberwell Reception Centre in London on a night in 1965 had previously been admitted to a psychiatric hospital for reasons other than drinking.[16] Another survey of the same shelter in the 1960s found 22 per cent of the longer-term residents to be mentally ill, mostly with schizophrenia. It was apparent that their destitution was a consequence of their illness—90 per cent had been living in settled homes before they fell ill.[17] In two Salvation Army hostels in Central London in the late 1960s, 15 per cent of a sample of residents were 'gross and unequivocal cases' of schizophrenia.[18] And Robert Priest found that 32 per cent of the men in his random sample of residents of Edinburgh doss houses in the late 1960s were definitely or probably schizophrenic.[19] At least a tenth of Britain's 30,000 homeless[20] were psychotic in the 1960s,[21] and it seems probable in the deepening economic gloom of recent times that these figures have become considerably greater. A tenth of all the schizophrenics seen at the emergency psychiatric clinic of the Maudsley Hospital in south London during six months in 1978 and 1979, for example, were homeless: few were offered any ongoing treatment.[22] British psychotics increasingly are leading lives of vagrancy and neglect.

## Jails and Prisons

To escape hunger many of the destitute and homeless psychotics steal or eat meals for which they cannot pay; to avoid cold, damp and the discomforts of homelessness many sleep in public buildings or empty houses and are arrested. As described in Chapter 4, around 6–8 per cent of the inmates of local jails in the United States are psychotic; but as they account for only 2–5 per cent of jail admissions,[23] it is clear that they are detained longer than other offenders. Being destitute, they cannot bail themselves out, and judges hesitate to release the unemployed, homeless and mentally disturbed on their own recognizance.

Some of the psychotics in jail are being held on serious charges, such as burglary, assault, sexual assault and arson—their crimes often a product of their mental illness. Substantial numbers of these inmates have proven too dangerous to be treated effectively in the community, but no long-term hospital care can be found for them.[24] Whatever the type of crime, in fact, many psychotics remain in US jails because hospital care or effective community care is not available. During twelve months of 1980–1, 150 misdemeanants in the city and county jail of Denver, Colorado, although found by mental health professionals to be in need of inpatient treatment, were obliged to remain in jail. A further 250 inmates of the treatment unit attached to the jail also failed to be transferred to needed psychiatric inpatient care.[25] Even non-criminal mental patients are housed in jail for the sake of mere convenience. Three-quarters of a random sample of admissions to Bryce Hospital in Alabama were confined in jail while awaiting admission.[26]

In US state and federal prisons a similarly large proportion of the inmates are psychotic.[27] In some states, psychotic patients are even sent from mental hospitals to prison for treatment; in Massachusetts, according to a 1979 report, approximately one patient every four days is transferred to prison because mental hospital staff consider the person unmanageable. Judges, furthermore, send severely mentally ill offenders to prison in preference to hospital because they find that mental health facilities frequently fail to provide adequate long-term hospital or community care for dangerous and highly disruptive patients.[28] The number of inmates of US prisons and local jails substantially exceeds 400,000, and a crude but modest estimate would allow that two or three out of every hundred of these prisoners is schizophrenic and more suffer from other psychoses. Thus, there may be as many as 10,000 schizophrenic prisoners in the US. But if only 1 per cent of the 6 million US jail *admissions* a year are schizophrenic (almost certainly an underestimate), then tens of thousands of such psychotic people spend some time behind bars annually (even allowing for the repeated admission of many).

What are conditions like for imprisoned psychotics? Large jails and prisons in the US generally have so many such inmates, often acutely disturbed, that they establish cell blocks as 'hospital' units. In one such unit in the Baltimore city jail, mental patients may be seen sitting on their beds in a large, bare, unpainted cell gazing blankly into space. In the old asylums, conditions as bankrupt and deadening as these were rare. When I visited this jail in 1978, in one part of the unit I saw a psychotic patient locked in a darkened linen closet which had been converted to a 'seclusion room' by affixing a wire mesh window to the door. This patient was being detained on a misdemeanor charge but was not released to the city psychiatric hospital because, argued the staff, care was no better at the hospital.

Similar conditions have been described on the 'mental ward' of a large midwestern city jail. There iron mesh had to be fixed over the inside of the barred doors 'because,' reported a deputy, 'inmates kept running headfirst into the bars trying to injure and kill themselves.'[29] In the same jail, one overtly psychotic woman who had been detained for four months was found lying in her own trash and excrement. Jail staff had not attempted to bathe her, but had instead sprayed her with disinfectant.[30] The disruptive behavior of

175

psychotics in jail is routinely regarded as a 'disciplinary problem;' such individuals are often held in bare cells of solitary confinement, shackled to the wall if necessary. Staff of an Illinois jail even reported 'calming down' psychotic inmates with a jet of cold water from a fire hose borrowed from the neighboring fire department.[31]

Psychiatrist Edward Kaufman criticizes the violation of standards of care in the psychiatric units of US prisons. One such unit in a western penitentiary

> consisted of 8 barred cells with no windows. This unit did not permit more than 1 patient out of his cell at a time. There was no television or recreational activity of any kind because the ward psychiatrist did not want a 'country club atmosphere' that would attract patients to make them want to stay.[32]

In another prison psychiatric unit, the ward psychiatrist ordered the use of a 'stun-gun firing rubber bullets to control threatening behavior.' In a third, 'inmates who were "suicidal" were strapped nude to the bars of their cells for 48 hours before they were given a psychiatric evaluation.'[33] 'Jails,' states an administrator of the U.S. Department of Justice, 'are without question, brutal, filthy cesspools of crime— institutions which serve to brutalize and embitter men to prevent them from returning to a useful role in society.'[34] Open toilets in overcrowded cells, vermin, filth, delapidation, brutality, homosexual rape and lack of medical care, of hygiene or constructive progams have all been documented as existing widely in US jails and prisons.[35] To attempt to treat psychotic patients in such settings by the mere addition of antipsychotic drugs is scarcely calculated to improve their chances of recovery.

What accounts for such treatment of the mentally ill in a civilized society? In a word, money. State governments have drastically cut back the funding for psychiatric hospitals and have failed to maintain community mental health services at an adequate level. Police and judges have responded as they feel they must to protect the community from the crime, disruption and violence which result from the lack of support and treatment of psychotics. State legislators do not counter this problem by boosting mental health funding because, in the first place, prison care is cheaper than hospital treatment (about four times cheaper in Colorado) and, in the second place, the expense of law enforcement and the upkeep of local jails is borne, not by the state government, but by the counties and municipalities.

In the broadest sense, however, the mentally ill are incarcerated in these degrading conditions because, where there exists a massive reserve army of unemployed, the concern to establish social control over the deviant takes precedence over the concern to provide effective rehabilitation. The same is true of sane offenders—incarceration rates rise during an economic

176

recession (but are unrelated to crime or conviction rates),[36] and jail and prison populations tend to be greater in those Western industrial nations with the highest rates of unemployment.[37] The larger the surplus population, the greater the extent of confinement and the worse the conditions of the poor—the mentally ill among them.

## Where Are American Schizophrenics?

The plight of the chronically mentally ill who lead a barren existence in America's boarding homes and nursing homes has been described in Chapter 4. Here we may attempt to estimate the number of these patients who suffer from schizophrenia. Some 300,000–400,000 chronic mental patients reside in board and care homes in the United States according to the 1981 report of a committee of the Department of Health and Human Services which investigated the conditions of the chronically mentally ill.[38] Based on observations that the large majority of these patients are chronic schizophrenics, one may reasonably assume that at least 60 per cent of this number could be so diagnosed.[39] The same government report indicates that there are 250,000 patients in nursing homes with a primary diagnosis of mental illness, excluding elderly patients with non-psychotic, senile mental disorder. One hundred thousand of these patients were transferred directly into nursing home care from state mental hospitals, but this number excludes former state hospital patients who spent an interim period in another nursing home or in hospital or in the community.[40] Only 38,000 of the mentally ill in nursing homes are under age 65. We might conservatively estimate that half of this number are schizophrenic. It is more difficult, unfortunately, to estimate the proportion of the elderly mentally ill in nursing homes who suffer from schizophrenia—a large proportion of these more than 200,000 patients are afflicted with organic psychoses of late life. At a guess the proportion of schizophrenics among them lies between 20 and 25 per cent. A crude estimate, therefore, of from 60,000 to 70,000 schizophrenics in US nursing homes may not be too inaccurate.

If we add to these numbers another quarter of a million schizophrenics resident in state, county, private and Veterans Administration hospitals,[41] and if we accept the estimate that there are fewer than 1.25 million schizophrenics in treatment in the United States,[42] we are forced to the discomforting conclusion that close to half of American schizophrenics are to be found in institutions, in inadequate community settings, in jail, prison or on the streets (see Table 8.1). Only 5 out of 10 schizophrenics in treatment in the United States are likely to be living in anything resembling a family home or domestic environment. These figures alone might be considered sufficient explanation for the poor outcome from schizophrenia in America.

**Table 8.1   Crude estimates of the location of schizophrenics in the USA in the late 1970s**

| LOCATION | TOTAL POPULATION | % SCHIZOPHRENIC | NUMBER SCHIZOPHRENIC | % OF ALL US SCHIZOPHRENICS |
|---|---|---|---|---|
| Skid Row homeless | 200,000–400,000 | 25 | 50,000–100,000 | 4–8 |
| Jails and prisons | 400,000–450,000 | 2½–3 | 10,000–13,500 | 1 |
| Boarding homes | 300,000–400,000 | 60 | 180,000–240,000 | 15–20 |
| Nursing homes | — | — | 60,000–70,000 | 5–6 |
| Hospitals | — | — | 200,000–250,000 | 17–21 |
| Total in non-domestic setting | | | 500,000–673,500 | 42–56 |

Note: See the text for an explanation of the derivation of these estimates.

## Restraints and Seclusion

We should not assume that the patients who are in hospital are necessarily in ideal therapeutic environments. Their conditions of confinement may be quite harsh. Although both restraints and seclusion, for example, have proved to be largely unnecessary in British practice, their use is still commonplace in hospitals in the United States. One report indicates that 44 per cent of patients on an acute admission unit in California are locked up in seclusion for varying periods of time.[43] The seclusion room experience often colors and dominates the psychotic's view of his or her illness. When 62 patients at a major US psychiatric hospital were asked to draw pictures of themselves and their psychosis, over a third spontaneously drew a picture of the seclusion room. Even a year after the hospital stay, the experience of seclusion, with its associated feelings of fear and bitterness, symbolized for many patients the entire psychiatric illness.[44]

It is also common for patients to be tied down to their beds with restraints in US hospitals. During one month in 1980, a quarter of all the patients evaluated in a psychiatric emergency room in Cincinnati, Ohio, were placed in restraints.[45] Mechanical restraints are frequently used on psychiatric wards,

178

the commonest reasons being not violence but 'nonconformity to community rules'[46] and 'behavior disruptive to the therapeutic environment.'[47] Understaffing and overcrowding may also force the use of such measures. The Colorado Foundation for Medical Care found that the overuse of both restraints and seclusion at Fort Logan Mental Health Center in Denver, Colorado, in 1981 was the result of a shortage of direct care staff. At the Colorado State Hospital in the same year, overcrowding on the forensic unit was so severe that patients were transferred to the surgical ward and shackled to their beds in order to accommodate the overflow.[48] Such are the human consequences of cost-cutting in public psychiatric services.

## Stigma

There is more to the degradation of being schizophrenic in Western society, however, than harsh treatment and inadequate living conditions. 'Let's just say I have a case of shame—I really do,' says an American schizophrenic woman. 'When I look at some of the things I've really gone through—some of the things I've done, some of the things I've said—my father's feeling of shame for me does not equal my own.'[49] Another patient writes,

> I have often been fraught with a profound guilt over my diagnosis of schizophrenia. . . . I had little idea how dehumanizing and humiliating the hospital would be for me. . . . I felt that I had partly lost my right to stand among humanity . . . and that for some people I would be forevermore something of a subhuman creature. . . . Mental health professionals often treated me . . . as if I were a stranger or alien of sorts, set apart from others by reason of my label.[50]

In contrast to Maria, the Guatamalian Indian woman whose episode of psychosis was described in the last chapter, these American schizophrenics must accept blame, and must blame themselves, for their condition. They feel estranged from others; the stigma of their illness obstructs their social reintegration.

With the growth of interest in community psychiatry, considerable attention was focused on the question of the stigma of mental illness in the 1950s and 1960s. Shirley Star, using a series of vignettes depicting people with psychiatric symptoms, conducted a nationwide survey of members of the American public in 1950 and found the general reaction to the mentally ill to be negative and poorly informed.[51] Elaine and John Cumming, using the same techniques, uncovered essentially similar attitudes among residents of a rural town (which they called Blackfoot) in Saskatchewan, Canada, in 1951, and found that the negative attitudes towards the mentally ill were untouched after a six-month psychiatric educational campaign.[52] After a six-year survey of residents of the Champaign-Urbana area of Illinois in the

179

1950s, J. C. Nunally concluded that the insane are viewed by the general public with 'fear, distrust, and dislike.'[53] 'Old people and young people,' reported Nunally, 'highly educated people and people with little formal training—all tend to regard the mentally ill as relatively dangerous, dirty, unpredictable and worthless.'[54] They are considered, in short, 'all things bad.'[55]

In more recent years a dispute has arisen over whether the initial impressions of high levels of stigma attached to mental illness continue to hold true. A number of researchers in the 1960s concluded that the public tolerance of the mentally ill had improved.[56] In the late 1970s, twenty years after Nunally's original survey, William Cockerham again analyzed public attitudes towards the mentally ill in Champaign-Urbana and found them to be somewhat more tolerant.[57] But other researchers have found no improvement in popular mental health attitudes between the 1960s and 1970s;[58] and a second survey of public tolerance of the mentally ill in Blackfoot, Saskatchewan, twenty-three years after the Cummings' original study, revealed that virtually no change had occurred.[59]

It is possible that gains were made in public acceptance of the mentally ill in the 1960s but that, as the consequences of the abandonment of the psychotics in the community have become apparent, no further progress has taken place. Whatever the truth of the matter, it is obvious that mental patients are still highly stigmatized. Branded as 'psychos' in popular parlance, they encounter great hardship in finding employment[60] and generate fear as to their dangerousness. Citizens fight to exclude psychiatric treatment facilities and living quarters for the mentally ill from residential neighborhoods.[61] The status afforded the mentally ill is the very lowest—lower than that of ex-convicts or the retarded.[62] Even after five years of normal living and good work, according to one survey, an ex-mental patient is rated as less acceptable than an ex-convict.[63] Usually indigent and unemployed, the chronic mental patient has no valued social role. He or she rarely possesses any of the indicators of mainstream social status: if working, the job is likely to be the most menial available; he or she generally has no decent housing, no yard, no family, and no car. Such patients rarely have social or sexual contacts with any but other mental patients. The chronic mental patient in our society truly has pariah status.

Even the agencies serving the mentally ill are tainted by association. Mental health professionals often disdain chronic psychotic patients, preferring to work with 'good therapy cases' closer to their own class and interests.[64] Psychiatrists may avoid such patients—in one sample, only 5 per cent of private psychiatric patients were schizophrenic[65]—and community mental health centers often fail to address their needs. Mental health professionals are likely to hold attitudes towards mental patients which are similar to those of the general public; they may even be *more* rejecting. In one study, mental hospital staff were considerably less likely than members of the public to take the trouble to mail a sealed, addressed letter which they believed to have been accidentally lost by a mental hospital patient.[66]

Professional conceptions of mental illness may reinforce the popular tendency to dehumanize mental patients. Do patients with schizophrenia experience human emotions? Most people who know some schizophrenics would say they do. Yet the *American Journal of Psychiatry* in 1981 published a study of schizophrenic functioning the central finding of which was: 'The chronic schizophrenic, in his attempt to cope with various demands placed on him, experiences anxiety, and when he perceives that his efforts are inadequate, he experiences depression.'[67] The author argues that it is 'an important clinical issue' that 'chronic schizophrenics do become depressed when they are aware of their marginal lifestyle in the community.'[68] How could the editors of the *Journal* possibly imagine that such findings were worth publishing? Only by assuming that a number of their readers would have doubts about the human qualities of their schizophrenic patients.

Most tragic of all, the mentally ill themselves accept the stereotype of their own condition. Young patients in rural Ireland viewed their 'spending time in the "madhouse" . . . as a permanent "fall from grace" similar to a loss of virginity.'[69] A number of studies have shown that mental patients are as negative in their opinions of mental illness as the general public.[70] Some reports, indeed, indicate that mental patients are *more* rejecting of the mentally ill than were their family members or the hospital staff.[71]

## Labeling Theory

Research on the stigma of mental illness has been fueled by interest in labeling theory. Once a deviant person has been labeled 'mentally ill,' argues sociologist Thomas Scheff, society responds in accordance with a pre-determined stereotype and the individual is launched on a career of chronic mental illness from which there is little opportunity for escape.[72] There is a good deal of evidence to support Scheff's position. A study of the attitudes of residents of a small New England town, published in 1963 by Derek Phillips, shows that a normal person of an 'ideal type' who is described as having been in a mental hospital is socially rejected to a much greater degree than is a simple schizophrenic who seeks no help or who instead consults a clergyman.[73]

In David Rosenhan's well-known study, normal volunteers presented themselves for voluntary admission to a dozen different psychiatric hospitals with complaints of auditory hallucinations. Every pseudo-patient was admitted, and although they reverted to normal behavior and denied psychotic symptoms immediately upon admission, each one was labeled schizophrenic at the time of discharge. Staff described the reasonable

181

actions of the pseudo-patients as if they were pathological. None was discharged in less than a week—one was detained for almost two months.[74] One might reasonably conclude from studies such as these that pressures to conform to stereotypic expectations may well influence hope of recovery and the features of schizophrenia.

Critics of labeling theory argue that the approach understates the importance of the initial deviance and of the inherent pathology of mental illness in causing a label to be attached, and that it minimizes the capacity of mental patients to shake off the harmful effects of stigma.[75] Such criticisms may be valid, but they fail to refute the possibility that labeling may have a significant effect on shaping the features of mental illness once established— an effect which may be substantial in many cases. John Strauss and William Carpenter, American psychiatrists who are authorities on the outcome of schizophrenic illness, conclude that

> Labeling is an important variable affecting the course, and perhaps the onset of schizophrenia. . . . Who can doubt the devastating impact on a fragile person of perceiving that the entire social milieu regards him (wittingly or not) as subhuman, incurable, unmotivated, or incompetent to pursue ordinary expectations. . . ? Can we doubt that a deteriorating course of disorder is fostered when fundamental roles are changed by social stigma and employment opportunities become limited?[76]

## How Stigma Influences the Course of Illness

Exactly how could the stigma and degradation of mental illness affect the symptoms of schizophrenia and shape the course of the illness? Cognitive dissonance theory helps explain this process. In outline this social psychological theory states that:
(a) pieces of knowledge or ideas (cognitions) are dissonant if one contradicts the other;
(b) dissonance is psychologically uncomfortable and motivates a person to resolve the contradiction; and
(c) the person will actively avoid situations which increase the dissonance.
For example, if a woman smokes two packs of cigarettes a day, believes herself to be reasonably strong-willed and sensible but knows that cigarettes cause lung cancer, she may reduce the level of dissonance between these ideas by quitting cigarettes, coming to see herself as weak-willed and foolish, or minimizing the evidence that links smoking with cancer.

Experiments have shown the following consequences of cognitive dissonance theory to hold true:
(a) After a change in opinion has been made with the aim of reducing dissonance, the person will select from available information evidence to confirm his or her decision, and will tend to overvalue such evidence.

182

(b) In the face of contradictory evidence which increases dissonance the individual will become *more* active in defense of his or her belief.

(c) If a person is obliged to state a public opinion which is contrary to his or or her privately held opinion (thus creating dissonance), there is a tendency for the opinion to change to conform more closely with the public statement: the smaller the external pressure to make the public statement, the greater is the opinion change.[77]

Faced with the need to accept a diagnosis of major mental illness (and its associated stigma and debased status), anyone with an internal sense of relative worth and competence will experience dissonance (see Figure 8.1). In fact, those who accept a diagnosis of mental illness tend to be people with a sense of ill-being (dysphoria) and a poor self-image: the grandiose and euphoric reject the illness label.[78] Cognitive dissonance theory predicts that those who choose to accept the diagnosis of mental illness will attempt to resolve their sense of dissonance by conforming to their new outcast status and to the stereotype of worthlessness; they will become more socially withdrawn and adopt a disabled role. In seeking to confirm the incurable and incapable features of their role, their psychotic symptoms will tend to persist and they are likely to become dependent on the treatment agency and others in their lives.

Such patterns will be even more exaggerated if the patient's stigmatized status is made evident by discernible physical traits; at worst these may be the shuffle, rigid facial expression and drooling secondary to the use of high doses of antipsychotic drugs; at the least they may include the slow gait of the unemployed, devalued individual with nowhere to go and nothing to do.

Under pressure to return to adequate functioning, symptoms of illness will tend to recur as a defense against mounting dissonance. However, gentle and gradual efforts which lead such individuals to demonstrate publicly that they can function at a more adequate level, may result in a change in their self-concept and a movement towards labeled but competent status. Cognitive dissonance theory thus helps explain the precarious balance of functioning which is found in rehabilitating the chronic mental patient. High expectations for his or her level of achievement can lead the patient to a higher level of functioning and decreased segregation and stigma, but they can also create an increased risk of psychotic decompensation and hospitalization.[79] We may now see why success is so often frightening and stressful to psychotic patients.

In contrast, those who initially reject the label and status of mental illness (and psychiatric treatment) will usually attempt to maintain their previous occupational and social status. Any social rejection they experience is likely to result in an increase in grandiosity and even more aggressive avoidance of treatment. Strong efforts to compel such individuals to accept a diagnosis of mental illness may result in superficial compliance but little genuine change

183

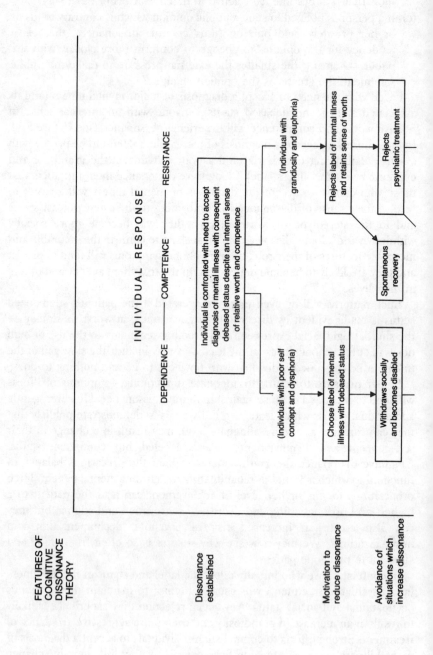

FEATURES OF
COGNITIVE
DISSONANCE
THEORY

INDIVIDUAL RESPONSE

DEPENDENCE ——— COMPETENCE ——— RESISTANCE

Dissonance
established

Individual is confronted with need to accept
diagnosis of mental illness with consequent
debased status despite an internal sense
of relative worth and competence

(Individual with poor self
concept and dysphoria)

(Individual with
grandiosity and euphoria)

Motivation to
reduce dissonance

Choose label of mental
illness with debased status

Rejects label of mental illness
and retains sense of worth

Spontaneous
recovery

Avoidance of
situations which
increase dissonance

Withdraws socially
and becomes disabled

Rejects
psychiatric treatment

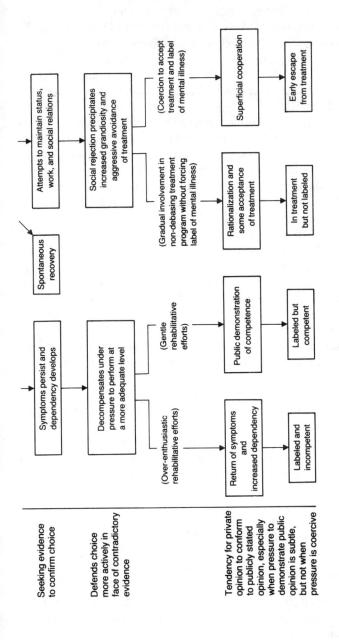

*Figure 8.1  Impact of labeling individual 'mentally ill' as predicted by cognitive dissonance theory*

in their privately held opinion; consequently they are likely to attempt to evade treatment at every opportunity. However, gradually increasing involvement in a non-debasing treatment program, coupled with a high degree of rationalization, may lead these people to a limited compliance with treatment, provided a dissonant label of mental illness is not forced upon them.

Thus, the patient with 'insight' will tend to function less well than expected and may become excessively dependent, while the patient who functions well will be inclined to reject treatment. Cognitive dissonance theory gives the mental health professional an explanation of the common observation that he often seems to be encouraging each patient to do the opposite of what the patient wants to do—a situation which can lead to 'burn-out' among staff and punitive attitudes towards patients. A reduction in stigma should reduce this conflict and, more directly, result in improved outcome in schizophrenia. If schizophrenia were a high-status illness (as it is in some cultures), it would be less debilitating.

If we were looking for experimental verification of this viewpoint, we would expect to find, counter-intuitively, that patients who accept that they are mentally ill will have the worst course to their illness, that those who reject the label from the outset might do better and that the patients who show the most improvement will be those who accept the label of mental illness but subsequently are able to shake it off. This is, in fact, precisely the finding of Edmund Doherty's study of self-labeling by 43 psychiatric inpatients. Patients who accepted throughout their hospital stay that they were mentally ill were rated as showing the least improvement: those who consistently denied that they were mentally ill did slightly better: and the patients who began by accepting that they were mentally ill but subsequently rejected that notion showed the greatest gains. All three groups were equally disturbed at admission.[80]

Similar, though less direct, confirmation of the importance of the patient's attitude to illness on the eventual outcome can be found in a study of 30 acute schizophrenics conducted by psychiatrists Thomas McGlashan and William Carpenter. One year after admission with severe psychosis, patients who held either strongly positive or negative attitudes about their illness had the worst outcome: those who treated the psychotic experience as neither positive nor negative were functioning at the best level.[81]

## Social Isolation

As might be expected from the humiliating living conditions of the majority of psychotics and from their pariah status, Western schizophrenics lead lives of social isolation. Many studies have shown that such patients have networks of social contacts which are much more restricted than is usual in our society. Schizophrenics are found to have close contacts with a third to a fifth of the number of people which is average for healthy members of the community. A third of the chronically mentally ill have no friends at all. Schizophrenics' relationships tend to be more one-sided, dependent and lacking in complexity of content and diversity of interconnections. Although family relationships deteriorate less than contacts with friends, a considerable disintegration of family ties does occur.[82] The collapse of the patient's social network appears to be a consequence of the illness, for it occurs after the first hospital admission.[83]

The social isolation of the Western schizophrenic stands in contrast to the effective social reintegration of the psychotic in the Third World. Although disruptive and violent individuals living in peasant villages who have been designated 'mad' do have restricted social networks,[84] the same problem does not apply, as we saw in Chapter 7, to less chronic and severely disturbed psychotics in the Third World. It was pointed out in that chapter, furthermore, that social isolation in both the developed and developing world has been repeatedly shown to be associated with poor outcome. The recent reports on the social networks of schizophrenics confirm this pattern. One study of schizophrenics housed in New York hotels demonstrated that, regardless of the severity of the patients' symptoms, those with broader and more complex social networks were less likely to be readmitted to hospital.[85]

## Families of Schizophrenics

The contrast between the social reintegration of psychotics in the developing world and the isolation of the mentally ill in Western society is highlighted by the plight of the families of Western schizophrenics. The stigma which attaches to mental illness also taints the relatives. Some react by talking to no one about the illness for years, not even to close friends. Those who do discuss the matter openly may find themselves snubbed by acquaintances. 'Some old friends quit talking to us,' described the mother of a schizophrenic client. 'They absolutely dropped us.' Other families respond by withdrawing socially. 'We haven't done much entertaining because of this,' commented the parent of another schizophrenic youth. 'I'm never quite sure . . . he's so up and down.' One-third of the wives in an American study followed a course of aggressive concealment including dropping and avoiding friends or even moving to a new residence. Another third of the wives discussed their husbands' illness with only a select few friends or relatives.[86] Although there is a marked tendency for family members to deny the stigma, their secrecy, concealment and withdrawal point to an underlying sense of shame and lead them into social isolation.[87]

In a survey of relatives of schizophrenics in Washington, DC, Agnes Hatfield observed 'a picture of unremittingly disturbed family life marked by

187

almost constant stress'[88] as the consequence of caring for a patient at home. She noted that marital disruption, blame, grief and helplessness were common results. In a study of British families in which a schizophrenic was living at home, half of the family members reported severe or very severe impairment of their own health as a consequence of their relative's psychiatric condition.[89]

All of the parents of the mentally ill in a discussion group at the Massachusetts Mental Health Center 'to a greater or lesser extent saw themselves and the others as ogres responsible for the misfortune that befell their children.'[90] The burden of guilt which such relatives carry is the result of the popular conception that mental illness is a product of faulty upbringing. Mental health professionals, adopting this same attitude, all too often see the family members as adversaries and add to their estrangement. Carried to its logical extreme the notion of the 'schizophrenogenic' family led to the bizarre occurrence in a Colorado court recently of a 24-year-old man, with the support of his psychiatrist, suing his parents for 'malpractice' which supposedly caused his schizophrenia.[91] Censured, isolated and guilt-ridden as they are, it is scarcely surprising that the families of schizophrenics in Western society are sometimes found to exhibit harmful over-involvement with their sick relatives.[92] Not only are they unable to seek support from neighbors and friends, they may also be rejected by the treatment agencies concerned. Seeing the destructive interactions between the schizophrenic and an over-involved family, mental health professionals will often strive to separate them, encouraging the patient to move away from home and minimize contact with his or her relatives. This final step completes the process of social disintegration. The patient is separated from almost everyone except other stigmatized patients; the family members are socially isolated and feel banished not only from the social mainstream but also from their affected relatives.

## Alienation

Where pre-industrial cultures offer social reintegration with maintenance of social status and provision of a valued social role for many psychotics, Western society maintains schizophrenics in poverty and creates for them social disintegration with pariah status and a disabled role. In the non-industrial world, communal healing processes operate within a social consensus which predicts recovery and minimizes blame, guilt and stigma; whereas in Western society schizophrenia is treated through marginal institutions with a social expectation that all concerned are to blame to a high degree and that the condition is incurable. These differences in the status, integration and role of the mentally ill may well account for the distinctly worse outcome for schizophrenia in industrial societies.

This constellation of problems has been described before, however: it is encompassed by the concept of alienation. As noted in Chapter 2, Marx listed a number of aspects of estranged or alienated labor. Men and women become estranged from:

- the product of their work (the Ford worker feels no creative pride in the cars rolling past him on the line);
- the process of working (the burned-out professional cannot face another day of it);
- their own human qualities (the key-punch operator is reduced to a cog whose human attributes are unnecessary); and
- other people (our work role determines which administrators we shall fight and which sections of society we shall look down on).[93]

These hardships, according to Marx's analysis, are less severe for the subsistence farmer in the non-industrial world who works for himself, uses his own creations, and establishes his own pace of working.

How does this apply to the schizophrenic? It is in the menial jobs which are the only ones psychotics are likely to find—dishwashing, envelope-stuffing, day-laboring—that work is most dehumanizing and alienation is most severe. But the more common fate of the schizophrenic—unemployment—is even worse. To stand idle, to be unable to provide for oneself, to fulfill no useful social function, to be of no value to oneself or others—these are the ultimate in alienation—a confrontation with the existential concern of meaninglessness. In the stigma of mental illness, the most debased status in our society, we see the utmost in painful estrangement of one human from another. And in the schizophrenic's own acceptance of this same dehumanized stereotype we witness the loss of his or her sense of fully belonging to humankind.

The schizophrenic, then, is amongst the most alienated of industrial society, and it is in this condition that one may perceive the causes of the malignancy of the illness. Looking beyond this, the origins of the schizophrenic's alienation are to be found in the political and economic structure of society—in the division of labor and development of wage work. For it is these aspects of production which have rendered the schizophrenic —with his or her limited ability to withstand stress, limited productive capacity and limited drive—marginal to the industrial work force, marginal members of (what anthropologist Jules Henry terms) 'the driven society.'[94]

Caste systems do not perpetuate themselves. Continued enforcement of discriminatory economic and physical sanctions is necessary to maintain the existence of a pariah group.[95] Similar political and economic pressures are necessary to restrict the interclass mobility of members of US ethnic minority groups.[96] The same is true of the low status of the mentally ill in the West. The postwar drive to influence public opinion and increase the community acceptance of mental patients was equivalent to earnest attempts to adjust the status of a caste. The political motivation in some areas, at that time, was to bring the mentally ill into the work force, in other areas, to transfer the responsibility for their care from the state to the community. These efforts have decreased as the political motivation recedes. Now public policy has created the poverty, unemployment and squalid conditions in which the mentally ill live in much of the Western world and, indirectly, has inflamed the pessimism and alienation which are to blame for the malignant course of schizophrenia in our society.

## Summary

- Five out of every ten American schizophrenics are living in boarding homes or nursing homes, in hospital, on Skid Row or in jail or prison.
- The stigma of mental illness in Western society continues to be great.
- A combination of labeling theory and cognitive dissonance theory allows us to explain how the stigma of mental illness can lead to poor outcome from psychosis.
- Schizophrenics in Western society have restricted social networks and they and their families become relatively estranged from society.
- The social plight of the Western schizophrenic is encompassed by the single concept of alienation, and has its roots in the division of labor and the development of wage work.

# 9 *The Prevalence of Schizophrenia*

Does political economy influence the prevalence of schizophrenia? Could labor conditions and unemployment trigger the onset of the disorder in previously healthy people? Up to this point we have concentrated upon the *course* of schizophrenia—recovery from the illness and the level of functioning achieved by chronic sufferers. The course of schizophrenia, it has been argued, is strongly influenced by the utilization of labor, a factor which affects the social role, status and integration of psychotics. At this juncture it may be valuable to make a diversion and to examine the *frequency of occurrence* of this illness and the extent to which it is affected by labor dynamics.

If the role and identity stresses associated with unemployment and the conditions of wage labor have an adverse effect upon schizophrenics, it is quite possible that these same tensions could precipitate a schizophrenic illness in predisposed individuals and increase the rate of occurrence of the disease. In this case we might predict that:

- First-time admissions to hospital for schizophrenia will increase in times of high unemployment.
- The incidence of schizophrenia will be lower in those parts of the world where patterns of wage labor have not developed.
- The incidence of schizophrenia in the industrial world will be greater in local pockets of high unemployment.
- Where wage labor exists, the occurrence of schizophrenia will be greater in the castes and classes most adversely affected by labor conditions and unemployment.
- The incidence of schizophrenia among immigrants will be higher than in the population of their countries of origin if they encounter harsher labor conditions in their new country.
- Schizophrenia will be more common in the sex most adversely affected by labor-market forces, and the age of onset of the illness will be influenced by the age at which each sex enters the labor market.
- The dramatic increase in wage labor during the eighteenth and nineteenth centuries will have been associated with an increase in the occurrence of schizophrenia in industrializing countries.

191

The first of these predictions has been shown to be true: the evidence was presented towards the end of Chapter 2. Let us take the remaining points in turn.

## Cross-Cultural Comparisons of Prevalence

Within the space of a few months in 1980 and 1981, two books appeared which gave diametrically opposed answers to the question 'Is schizophrenia less common in pre-industrial parts of the world?'. In *Schizophrenia and Civilization*, Fuller Torrey, a psychiatrist employed at the US National Institute of Mental Health, argues that schizophrenia is rarer in primitive settings and that it is essentially a disease which has become more widespread with the development of industrial civilization. (Dr Torrey ignores political-economic factors, dismisses social explanations and contends that this apparent association between schizophrenia and Western civilization is evidence for viral contagion as a cause for the illness.) He presents a mass of anthropological and epidemiological data to support his claim that schizophrenia is rare in less developed societies, and many of the examples which are discussed in this chapter are to be found in Dr Torrey's book.[1]

British social psychiatrist Julian Leff takes the opposite viewpoint in *Psychiatry Around the Globe*. Reviewing some of the available epidemiological studies of psychosis in detail, Leff concludes

> that the prevalence rates of schizophrenia and manic-depressive illnesses vary relatively little from one developing country to another, and in the case of schizophrenia are very similar to the corresponding rates in Western countries.[2]

Which view is correct?

Before exploring this issue it is necessary to address two points; we should first clarify the difference between the incidence and the prevalence of a disease and, second, explain the difficulties and pitfalls involved in using these kinds of data to make comparisons between one group of people and another.

The *incidence* of an illness is the rate at which new cases occur in a given period of time (usually a year). The *prevalence* of an illness is the total number of cases, new and old, known to exist. The number in existence at any one point in time is the *point prevalence*; the number observed in a given period (say a year) is the *period prevalence*; and the number of people in the population who have suffered from the illness at any time in their lives gives us the *lifetime prevalence*. Whereas the lifetime prevalence is unaffected by the rate at which people recover, the point prevalence for schizophrenia will tend to be lower in those areas, such as parts of the Third World, where outcome from the illness is better.

*Incidence* data are difficult to gather by any method other than by counting the number of referrals to treatment agencies. Such information on schizophrenia is therefore hard to obtain in much of the Third World, where health services are not comprehensively available. In US studies the annual incidence rate for treated schizophrenia is close to 0.5 per 1,000 of the general population; in Britain the figure is in the region of 0.2 per 1,000.[3] The rather wide difference between the incidence in the two countries is largely a reflection of the broader diagnosis of schizophrenia which, until recently, was applied in the United States.

True *prevalence* may be assessed by conducting a community survey of all the households in a given area and detecting all current cases, treated and untreated. In carrying out such a survey the researchers may plan to interview every person in the community or, to save time and expense, they may evaluate only those people who are identified by key informants (such as tribal chiefs or general practitioners) as possibly suffering from the illness. An approximation to prevalence can also be calculated from the number of cases in treatment at hospitals and clinics during a given period. Again this method, which assumes that virtually all cases of a disorder are in treatment, is inapplicable to the study of schizophrenia in most of the Third World. Prevalence data for schizophrenia vary more widely than incidence data—from 0.3 to 4.7 per 1,000 of the population in studies of the United States, from 1.8 to 17.0 per 1,000 in Europe, from 2.1 to 4.7 per 1,000 in Japan and from 0.4 to 7.0 per 1,000 in the developing world (see Table 9.1).

While we may use incidence data to draw conclusions about what causes the appearance of an illness, strictly speaking, we should not use prevalence data in the same way. Prevalence figures for schizophrenia are the product of three processes—the rate of appearance of the illness (the incidence), the death rate of schizophrenics (which may well be greater in the Third World), and (except in the case of lifetime prevalence) the rate of recovery. In practice, however, the only data we can gather in developing-world countries are prevalence estimates. We may use them as useful indicators only if we recognize these limitations.

A problem with comparing prevalence studies, especially for Third World peoples, is that to draw an accurate picture it is necessary to know the age distribution of each population. Where a large proportion of the population is below age 15, for example, and not at risk of developing schizophrenia, one should expect a spuriously low prevalence of the illness. This source of error would be particularly evident in the Third World, where birth rates tend to be higher and life expectancy shorter than in the West. In order to correct for this effect it is necessary to calculate a standardized, age-corrected prevalence figure, but this can only be done where a census is taken to establish the age structure of the population. The age correction brings its own problems. The age range chosen as the basis for the correction may vary from one study to another; in some studies it is not available at all; and in others a more complicated calculation is made of the cumulative risk of developing the illness through the susceptible period of an individual's life (Weinberg abridged method). The various computations are not comparable with one another.

The size of the population sample studied is another important factor. Schizophrenia is a relatively rare condition. Only a small handful of affected cases is likely to be found in a sample of fewer than, say, a thousand adults. Small-scale studies will, therefore, provide less accurate estimates of prevalence.

A serious hazard in comparing prevalence figures arises from the wide variability in the diagnosis of schizophrenia. A broad definition of the illness will yield prevalence data five times greater than a narrow definition.[4] Such wide differences render comparison of studies difficult unless they are rigorously standardized or unless they are conducted by the same research team.

The obstacles to comparing the rates of occurrence of schizophrenia in different parts of the world are obviously numerous—point prevalence versus lifetime prevalence, community survey versus treatment statistics, narrow versus broad diagnosis and sample size and age-correction differences. It is not surprising that the statistics vary substantially. Can any conclusions at all be drawn from them? Since other researchers have already looked at the data and drawn different conclusions, and since there already exists a mainstream opinion in psychiatry that the prevalence of schizophrenia varies little from one part of the world to another, we may be excused for attempting to check these views by conducting a cautious comparison.

## Epidemiological Studies

Table 9.1 is an attempt to compile a fairly comprehensive list of prevalence studies of schizophrenia.[5] Many of the studies upon which Julian Leff and Fuller Torrey base their opposite conclusions are included. Morbidity risk figures (which use Weinberg's method and are common in Scandinavian and Japanese studies) have been excluded since they are markedly different from the usual method of correcting for the age distribution of the population. A standard age correction has been listed wherever it is given in the original study or can be calculated from the available statistics. The range of the age-corrected prevalence figures is shown diagramatically in Figure 9.1. Studies with a sample size of fewer than 1,000 adults have been excluded. It should be recognized that even these selected studies are not comparable. The age corrections are not all for the same age group: some of the lower rates from the Third World—Dr Lin's reports from Taiwan and Dr Sethi's studies of Lucknow, India—appear artificially low as they are calculated for the

194

**Table 9.1 Prevalence of schizophrenia**

| LOCATION | CHARACTERISTICS OF POPULATION | PREVALENCE PER 1,000 POPULATION | AGE-CORRECTED PREVALENCE | AGE RANGE CORRECTED FOR | PREVALENCE PERIOD | AUTHOR(S) |
|---|---|---|---|---|---|---|
| *Europe* | | | | | | |
| Denmark | rural & small town | 3.3 | — | — | lifetime | Strömgren (1938) |
| Denmark | rural & small town | — | 8.2 | 51–6 | lifetime | Fremming (1951) |
| Denmark | rural | 2.2 | 2.7 | over 14 | lifetime | Nielsen & Nielsen (1977) |
| Finland | rural | 4.3 | — | — | lifetime | Kaila (1942) |
| Finland | rural | — | 15.1[a] | 15–64 | point | Väisänen (1975) |
| Germany | rural | 1.9 | — | — | lifetime | Brugger (1931) |
| Germany | rural | 2.6 | — | — | lifetime | Brugger (1937) |
| Iceland | urban & rural | — | 6.0 | 60–2 | lifetime | Helgason (1964) |
| Ireland | rural | 7.1 | 9.8 | over 14 | point | Walsh et al. (1979) |
| Norway | rural | 4.5 | 5.6 | over 9 | lifetime | Bremer (1951) |
| Norway | rural | 5.8 | 8.9 | over 19 | 2 years | Fugelli (1975) |
| Scotland | rural | 4.2 | — | — | lifetime | Mayer-Gross (1948) |
| Scotland | rural | 1.8 | 2.4 | over 14 | point | Primrose (1962) |
| Sweden | rural | 5.6 | 7.2 | over 15 | 45 years | Sjögren (1948) & Larsson & Sjögren (1954) |
| Sweden | rural | 9.5 | 15.8 | over 14 | 48 years | Böök (1953) |
| Sweden | rural | 6.7 | 9.4 | over 15 | lifetime | Essen-Moller (1956) |
| Sweden | rural | 4.5 | 5.1 | over 10 | lifetime | Hagnell (1966) |
| Sweden | rural | 17.0 | — | — | 77 years | Böök et al. (1978) |
| Yugoslavia | urban | — | 7.3 | 20–64 | 3 months | Crocetti et al. (1971) |
| Yugoslavia | urban | — | 4.2 | 20–64 | 3 months | Crocetti et al. (1971) |

**Table 9.1 continued**

| LOCATION | CHARACTERISTICS OF POPULATION | PREVALENCE PER 1,000 POPULATION | AGE-CORRECTED PREVALENCE | AGE RANGE CORRECTED FOR | PREVALENCE PERIOD | AUTHOR(S) |
|---|---|---|---|---|---|---|
| *North America* | | | | | | |
| Canada | rural | — | 5.0 | over 17 | point | Leighton et al. (1963) |
| Canada | 'old' French villages | — | 10.5 | over 14 | point | Murphy & Lemieux (1967) |
| Canada | 'new' French villages | — | 7.1 | over 14 | point | Murphy & Lemieux (1967) |
| Canada | Anglo-Protestant villages | — | 4.2 | over 14 | point | Murphy & Lemieux (1967) |
| Canada | Irish-Catholic villages | — | 7.1 | over 14 | point | Murphy & Lemieux (1967) |
| Canada | Polish villages | — | 7.2 | over 14 | point | Murphy & Lemieux (1967) |
| Canada | German villages | — | 5.8 | over 14 | point | Murphy & Lemieux (1967) |
| USA | urban | 2.9 | — | — | 1 year | Lemkau et al. (1942 & 1943) |
| USA | rural | 2.0 | — | — | lifetime | Roth & Luton (1943) |
| USA | urban | 3.6 | — | — | 6 months | Hollingshead & Redlich (1958) |
| USA | urban | 4.7 | 6.4 | over 14 | 1 year | Kramer (1978) |
| *Japan* | | | | | | |
| Japan | rural | 3.8 | — | — | point | Uchimura (1940) |
| Japan | urban | 2.2 | — | — | point | Tsugawa (1942) |
| Japan | small town | 2.1 | — | — | point | Akimoto et al. (1943) |
| Japan | urban & rural | 2.3 | — | — | point | Japanese Ministry of Health & Welfare (1955) |

196

| | | | | | | |
|---|---|---|---|---|---|---|
| Japan | urban & rural | 2.3 | — | — | point | Japanese Ministry of Health & Welfare (1965) |
| Japan | urban | 2.8 | — | — | 5 years | Sato (1966) |
| Japan | rural | 4.7 | — | — | point | Kato (1969) |
| *Special Populations in the Industrial World* | | | | | | |
| Australia (Western) | Aborigines | 4.7 | 9.3[a] | over 16 | point | Jones & Horne (1973) |
| Australia (Northern) | Aborigines | 5.0 | 9.9 | over 16 | point | Eastwell (1975) |
| Canada | Indians | 5.7 | 11.0 | over 14 | point | Roy et al. (1970) |
| Canada | Non-Indians | 1.6 | 2.4 | over 14 | point | Roy et al. (1970) |
| Canada | Hutterites | 1.1 | 2.1 | over 14 | lifetime | Eaton & Weil (1955) |
| USA | Amish | 0.3 | 0.5 | over 14 | 5 years | Egeland & Hostetter (1983) |
| *Third World* | | | | | | |
| India | urban | 1.5 | 2.6 | over 14 | point | Surya et al. (1964) |
| India | urban | 2.3 | 3.4 | over 10 | point | Sethi et al. (1967) |
| India | rural | 4.3 | 8.0[a] | over 14 | point | Elnagar et al. (1971) |
| India | urban & rural | 2.2 | 3.7 | over 14 | lifetime | Dube & Kumar (1972) |
| India | urban | 2.4 | — | — | point | Sethi et al. (1972a) |
| India | rural | 1.1 | 1.7 | over 10 | point | Sethi et al. (1972b) |
| India | urban | 1.7 | 2.6 | over 12 | point | Verghese et al. (1973) |
| India | urban | 2.5 | 2.9 | over 10 | point | Sethi et al. (1974) |
| India | rural | 2.8 | — | — | point | Nandi et al. (1975) |
| India | urban | 1.9 | 3.3 | over 15 | point | Thacore et al. (1975) |
| India | rural | — | 7.2 | over 14 | point | Carstairs & Kapur (1976) |
| India | rural | 7.0 | — | — | point | Murthy et al. (1978) |
| India | rural | 2.2 | — | — | point | Nandi et al. (1980) |

**Table 9.1 continued**

| LOCATION | CHARACTERISTIC OF POPULATION | PREVALENCE PER 1,000 POPULATION | AGE-CORRECTED PREVALENCE | AGE RANGE CORRECTED FOR | PREVALENCE PERIOD | AUTHOR(S) |
|---|---|---|---|---|---|---|
| *Third World* (contd) | | | | | | |
| Sri Lanka | semi-rural | 3.2 | — | — | point | Jayasundera (1969) |
| Sri Lanka | semi-rural | 2.3 | — | — | point | Jayasundera (1969) |
| Sri Lanka | rural | 5.2 | — | — | point | Jayasundera (1969) |
| Sri Lanka | traditional rural | 1.3 | — | — | point | Jayasundera (1969) |
| Sri Lanka | semi-urban | 3.7 | 5.5 | over 14 | 6 months | Wijesinghe et al. (1978) |
| Sudan | village | 7.0 | — | — | point | Baasher (1961) |
| Taiwan | Chinese | 2.2 | 3.1 | over 10 | lifetime | Lin (1953) |
| Taiwan | Aborigines | 0.9 | — | — | lifetime | Rin & Lin (1962) |
| Taiwan | Chinese | 1.4 | 2.0 | over 10 | lifetime | Lin et al. (1969) |
| Tonga | rural | 0.4 | 0.9 | over 14 | 1 year | Murphy & Taumoepeau (1980) |
| Tonga | rural | 0.7 | 1.3 | over 14 | 1 year | Murphy & Taumoepeau (1980) |

Sources: Listed in general bibliography.
Note: ª Size of adult population sample less than 1,000 but greater than 700.

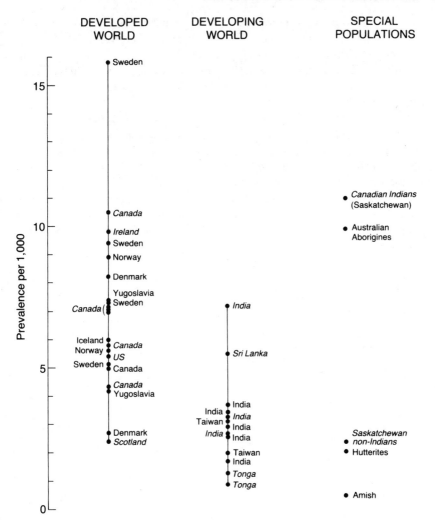

*Figure 9.1   Age-corrected prevalence of schizophrenia per 1,000 of the population in the developed and developing world and in special populations in the industrial world*

Sources: As for Table 9.1.
Notes: [a] Age corrections are not uniformly for the same age segments of the population.
    [b] Only studies in which the size of the adult population sample was 1,000 or more are included.
    [c] Studies marked in italics offer the most closely comparable prevalence figures.

population over age 10 (whereas for most of the studies the calculation is based on the population over age 14 or 15). Many studies included in Figure 9.1 estimate point-prevalence or period-prevalence rates and will tend to yield lower figures than the lifetime-prevalence studies. The studies labeled

199

in italic type in the figure are those which are most closely comparable with one another and which share the following characteristics: (a) the age correction is for the population aged over 14 or 15 years; and (b) point prevalence or prevalence for a period of up to one year is calculated. These studies are not necessarily uniform, however, in diagnostic approach or survey technique.

Figure 9.1 gives the impression that the range of prevalence values in the Third World is lower than in the West. A statistical analysis (using the t-test) confirms the impression given by the eye (see Table 9.2). Most importantly, a comparison which is restricted to the studies with comparable research characteristics shows a significant difference between the figures for the developed and the developing world. We cannot draw the definite conclusion from this analysis that schizophrenia is less common in the Third World—the data are not sound enough. We can say, however, that the evidence does *not* support the widely held belief that the prevalence of schizophrenia is similar all around the globe.

**Table 9.2  Statistical comparison of the age-corrected prevalence of schizophrenia in the developed and developing worlds**

All studies in Figure 9.1[a,b]
— sample size over 1,000 adults
$$t = 3.2584$$
$$df = 36$$
$$p < .005$$

Studies in Figure 9.1 with comparable characteristics[a,b]
— sample size over 1,000 adults
— age correction for population over age 14 or 15
— point prevalence or prevalence over a period of up to one year
$$t = 1.8495$$
$$df = 14$$
$$p < .05$$

Notes: [a] Calculations include studies included under the heading of special populations in the industrial world.
[b] Only one of the two prevalence figures for Tonga is used, since the statistics are for the same population on two occasions separated only by two years.

How did it come about that two researchers drew opposite conclusions from essentially similar data? Dr Leff was able to argue that the prevalence in the Third World was similar to that in the West because he chose only two European studies as his standards of comparison: one was Helgason's Icelandic survey; the other was the Camberwell Register in London, which yields a low prevalence figure and has not been included among the studies listed here as it is not a true community survey. Dr Torrey, at the other extreme, emphatically concluded from these studies that schizophrenia was less common in the developing world by repeatedly failing to take into account the importance of making age corrections to the Third World data and by emphasizing the comparison with European studies at the *high* end of the spectrum.

There is an alternative approach to the question of whether exposure to Western patterns of wage labor increases the risk of developing schizophrenia. We may look at studies where the same group of researchers conducts surveys of different populations, each of which is involved in wage-labor practices to a different extent. By this means we may avoid many of the pitfalls in the way of finding comparable data.

### Taiwan

An opportunity of this sort is provided by the series of studies conducted in Taiwan by psychiatrists Tsung-Yi Lin and Hsien Rin and their colleagues. In their first survey, between 1946 and 1948, the researchers studied the lifetime prevalence of mental disorder in three Chinese communities—7,546 people in Ampeng, a district of a modern city, 6,000 inhabitants of Simpo, a small market town, and 5,585 villagers in the rice and tea growing Baksa area, near Taipei. Using key informants, census data and interviews with suspected cases, 43 schizophrenics were identified, yielding an overall prevalence of 2.2 per 1,000 of the general population (3.2 per 1,000 of the population over age 10). The lowest prevalence of schizophrenia—1.8 per 1,000—was in the rural villages.[6]

Between 1949 and 1953 the researchers applied the same survey and diagnostic methods to the study of four aboriginal Formosan tribes, the Atayal, the Paiwan, the Saisat and the Ami. Although some of the more acculturated of these tribesmen were employed as laborers, clerks or teachers, the aborigines' principal livelihood came from subsistence farming. The least acculturated group, the Atayal, lived by hunting and crude farming in scattered hamlets in a rugged mountain area. Among the total group of 11,442 tribesmen surveyed, 10 schizophrenics were located, for a lifetime-prevalence rate of 0.9 per 1,000. No age correction was made. This is one of the lowest schizophrenia prevalence rates identified for any group by a formal epidemiological survey.

The prevalence of schizophrenia among the Formosan aborigines was less than half the rate found by the same research team for the more economically developed Chinese communities. Since the researchers were recording both active and recovered cases in order to calculate lifetime prevalence, the figures, if accurate, could reflect a lower incidence or rate of inception of the illness among the tribesmen. It is also possible, as the authors suggest, that schizophrenic tribesmen were more likely to die as a consequence of their inability to care for themselves. There was no evidence, however, that the tribesmen treated their psychotics less well than did the Chinese, and severely deteriorated psychotics found among the tribesmen were apparently having their daily needs met adequately.[7]

Julian Leff argues that the prevalence figure for the aboriginal tribesmen may have been low because of a shortened life expectancy in these communities and that an age correction was necessary.[8] He is correct in principle; however, we must question how different the age structure of the aboriginal population (which was unavailable information) would have been from the Chinese with whom they were being compared. Well over half of the Chinese population sample was under 20 years of age;[9] it is difficult to imagine that there was a distinctly smaller proportion of adults than that among the tribesmen.

Dr Leff also argues that too many of the aboriginal psychotics may have been labeled as having malarial psychosis rather than schizophrenia.[10] This is hard to determine in retrospect. The research team identified 12 such cases of malarial psychosis among the tribesmen; they had all suffered 'psychotic episodes concurrent with the attacks of malaria' and subsequently recovered.[11] The researchers also diagnosed 4 such cases among the Chinese.[12] Even if all of the cases labeled malarial psychosis had been better diagnosed schizophrenia (which is, of course, highly improbable—malarial psychosis is very common in the Third World), the prevalence of schizophrenia would still have been greater in the Chinese population. The prevalence of schizophrenia and malarial psychosis combined amount to 2.9 per 1,000 of the Chinese and 2.4 per 1,000 of the tribesmen.

Fuller Torrey argues the converse point—that too *many* of the aboriginal psychotics were diagnosed schizophrenic. He contends that several of these psychotic episodes were too acute and too brief to be cases of schizophrenia.[13] As we saw in Chapter 7, however, schizophrenia in the developing world does often have just such an acute, benign course.

Fifteen years after their original survey of the three Chinese communities in Taiwan, Dr Lin and his colleagues conducted another comprehensive survey of mental illness in these same areas. They determined that the prevalence rate for schizophrenia among this section of the Chinese population had fallen from 2.2 per 1,000 (3.2 per 1,000 over age 10) in 1946–8 to 1.4 per 1,000 (2.0 per 1,000 over age 10) in 1961–3.[14] This change had taken place during a period of industrialization when many peasant farmers, fishermen and small traders had turned to laboring and factory work, the educational level of the population had risen and farming villages had evolved into residential suburbs. The drop in prevalence clearly does not support a simple link between involvement in the industrial labor force and an elevated risk of schizophrenia. The finding may have been related, however, to the dramatic fall in unemployment in the Taiwanese sample from 7.0 per cent in 1946–8 to 2.2 per cent in 1961–3.[15] The study suggests, perhaps, that if labor-market forces are relevant to the onset of schizophrenia, it is unemployment which is critical rather than the conditions of employment. Alternatively, the early phase of industrialization may be more stressful than later stages. As we shall see towards the end of the chapter, this may be true, at least, for the upper classes in developing countries.

**The Pacific**
In the South Pacific, social psychiatrist H. B. M. Murphy and a local psychiatrist B. M. Taumoepeau conducted a community survey of the island of 'Eua in the archipelago of Tonga. The economy of this region is based on subsistence farming, the authors report, and every adult male Tongan is entitled to a portion of land for this purpose. There is consequently no landless plantation labor force in Tonga such as exists elsewhere in the Pacific. Virtually no industry has developed, and only a third of the adult population is involved in the cash economy. Overseas migration for work and training is still fairly uncommon and tourism is minor.

Using key informants, the psychiatrists surveyed the 4,486 inhabitants of 'Eua (2,250 over age 14) on two occasions—once in 1977 and once in 1979. They identified individuals who had been psychotic during the twelve months prior to each visit, applying the same survey techniques and diagnostic criteria that Dr Murphy had previously used in epidemiological research in Quebec. Only 4 active psychotics were identified in 'Eua in 1977, and 2 of these were diagnosed as suffering from schizophrenia (including schizo-affective forms of the disorder). The one-year period prevalence of schizophrenia in 1977 may be calculated as 0.4 per 1,000 (0.9 per 1,000 over age 14). In 1979, 5 psychotics were found, 3 of them schizophrenic. The prevalence of the illness on this occasion was, therefore, 0.7 per 1,000 (1.3 per 1,000 over age 14).

Dr Murphy points out that the prevalence of psychosis, including schizophrenia, was several times lower in Tonga than in the villages of Quebec which he had previously studied using the same methods. In similar but more superficial surveys of other Pacific territories—the Solomon Islands, Truk, the Cook Islands and Niue, areas where traditional lifestyles have undergone more drastic change—Dr Murphy found the prevalence of psychosis to be higher than in Tonga, but still well below the prevalence rates for Quebec. He argues that this prevalence gradient cannot readily be explained by genetic factors, but that it may be due to variations in recovery and inception rates for psychosis which result from differences in the economy and social ecology of the various populations.[16]

Another report from the Pacific reveals a similar picture. People from eight different cultural and language groups live on the more than 2,000

Micronesian islands of the US Trust Territory of the Pacific Islands. For several years a mental health program using local paraprofessionals has operated under the supervision of an American psychiatrist who makes regular and frequent visits to the islands.[17] At the Pacific Congress of Psychiatry in 1980, Dr P. W. Dale, the psychiatrist responsible for these services, presented information on the prevalence of schizophrenia detected by this treatment program in the Pacific. A gradient from high prevalence in the most economically developed islands to a low prevalence in the least developed was found. No age correction was made to the figures, however, no attempt at a comprehensive household survey was made, and the numbers of cases involved were low enough that small errors would have made large differences to the result.[18]

Dr Murphy's epidemiological survey revealing a low prevalence of major mental illness in Tonga in comparison with a Western nation is an impressive finding. Dr Dale's report, being based on treatment statistics for a thinly-staffed mental health program, however, cannot carry as much weight. A number of other authors have reported differences in the prevalence of treated schizophrenia between non-Westernized and Western populations, but these differences may well reflect only the distaste for modern psychiatric treatment among tribesmen and peasants or their limited access to such facilities.

### Fiji
Ernest Beaglehole, for example, reports that the treated prevalence for psychosis among different cultural groups in Fiji in 1936 varied dramatically. Among the tribal Fijians, the admission rate for psychosis was 0.16 per 1,000. For the Indian population—more upwardly mobile and Europeanized sugar-cane growers and small-town businessmen—the rate was 0.67 per 1,000. Admissions for psychosis among the economically developed Chinese population totaled 2.02 per 1,000.[19] Dr Beaglehole found it hard to believe that such dramatically different admission rates could be accounted for entirely by an increased willingness among the less acculturated peoples to care for their psychotics in their own communities. Nevertheless, such an explanation is possible and we cannot conclude from these figures that the true incidence of psychosis was necessarily lower in the tribal groups.

The same caveat applies to Dr Beaglehole's observation of a lower prevalence of hospitalized psychosis among the Maoris of New Zealand (0.42 per 1,000 over age 15) in 1926 compared with the European poulation (0.84 per 1,000 over age 15).[20] Fuller Torrey's study of Papuan psychotics deserves the same caution.

### Papua New Guinea
Using psychiatric records only, Fuller Torrey and his associates located

the district of birth of psychotics in Papua New Guinea admitted to treatment between 1970 and 1973. A greater proportion than expected was admitted from the westernized coastal districts and fewer from the highland districts, which had only established contact with Europeans in recent times. The inadequacy of the treatment statistics in representing the true prevalence of psychosis is revealed by the reports of officials from the highland districts. The *treated* prevalence of psychosis in the various districts, according to Dr Torrey, ranged from 0.03 per 1,000 to 0.77.[21] A patrol officer and an administrator from the highlands, however, each estimated that there were 2 schizophrenics per 1,000 living in their districts.[22] Clearly, only a tiny proportion of the psychotics from these areas were in treatment. Seen in this light, Dr Torrey's claim that 'Papua New Guinea provides another case study in which schizophrenia appears more common in areas with longer contact with Western civilization and rare in areas with little such contact'[23] appears somewhat excessive.

## Sri Lanka

Studies in which a single research team survey urban and agricultural areas of a developing country might allow us to analyze the effect of participation in the industrial work force. One such report is M. G. Jayasundera's survey of four areas of Sri Lanka. Between 1960 and 1964, medical students interviewed a member of every household in the study areas and psychiatrists subsequently diagnosed individuals with suspected mental illness. The prevalence of schizophrenia was found to be greatest in the areas closest to major cities. In Seeduwa, 20 miles from the capital city of Colombo, where many of the residents worked in business, industry or government, the prevalence of schizophrenia was 2.3 per 1,000 (5 cases among 2,212 people). In Uda Peradeniya and Urawela, two villages close to the country's second largest city of Kandy, where many of the villagers were employed as unskilled laborers, prevalence was 3.2 per 1,000 (8 cases among 2,497 inhabitants). In the two hamlets of Aluthgama and Brandaragama, although only 19 miles from Colombo, almost all the population was engaged in agriculture. Here the prevalence of schizophrenia was found to be highest at 5.2 per 1,000 (13 cases among 2,506). The prevalence was lowest in Vadukoddai, two hamlets 200 miles north of Colombo; in this distant and culturally traditional area the rate was 1.3 per 1,000 (2 cases among 1.519). The author of the report felt that this figure may have been artificially low as a result of the suspicion and conservatism of the inhabitants and the organizational difficulties of surveying the district. No age correction was made. The study appears to have assessed point prevalence (although this is not clear), and the figures may therefore be influenced by the recovery rate in each area. While suggesting that schizophrenia may be more prevalent close to urban-industrial centers (as in the Taiwanese studies), this study from Sri Lanka does not, on the surface, appear to point to wage work as a stress factor: the area with the highest prevalence was a region of subsistence agriculture.[24]

## India

A similar pattern of increased prevalence of schizophrenia in the rural area close to a major city is revealed by a 1972 study of the Agra region of Uttar Pradesh, India. Dr K. C. Dube and Dr Narendra Kumar conducted a thorough community survey of contiguous rural, semi-rural and urban areas. A team of psychiatrists determined the diagnoses of suspected cases. The prevalence of schizophrenia was highest in the rural district, though the differences between the areas were not statistically significant:[25]

| | PREVALENCE OF SCHIZOPHRENIA PER 1,000 GENERAL POPULATION |
| --- | --- |
| Rural | 2.58 |
| Semi-rural | 2.08 |
| Urban: non-industrial | 2.15 |
| Urban: industrial | 2.03 |

In another part of Uttar Pradesh, however, a survey team led by psychiatrist B. B. Sethi found a *lower* prevalence of schizophrenia in the rural area. In four villages within 12–20 miles of Lucknow they found 3 schizophrenics among 1,814 people over age 10— an age-corrected prevalence of 1.7 per 1,000. In the city of Lucknow itself the prevalence was twice as great at 3.4 per 1,000 (4 cases among 1,192 people over age 10).[26]

There appears to be no consistent rural–urban pattern of distribution of schizophrenia in these Third World samples. The observation in the Agra region and in Sri Lanka of a greater concentration of schizophrenics in the rural area close to a major city does not necessarily refute the possibility that wage work increases the risk of schizophrenia. The rural areas of the Third World provide a vast pool of reserve labor for the industrial and economically advanced areas. Workers commonly migrate from rural districts to the cities to take wage work. If they fall sick, they are likely to return home to their villages. The labor force is replenished by drawing new migrants from the peasant economy; the burden of providing for the disabled is thrown back on to the village.[27] The prevalence of schizophrenia might, thus, rise higher on the farm while the stresses are, in reality, in the urban workplace. This phenomenon could explain why the *course* of schizophrenia appears to be more benign in the Third World while the *prevalence* is not

206

markedly less than in the West. The village may be highly efficient at rehabilitating schizophrenics—the industrial areas at producing them.

## Anthropological Reports

### Ghana

The impression that the back country indirectly suffers the impact of economic development is confirmed in a report from anthropologist Meyer Fortes and his wife, a psychiatrist, Doris Mayer. Dr Fortes first worked among the Tallensi of Northern Ghana for two-and-a-half years in the mid-1930s. At that time it was a traditional, subsistence farming culture, little touched by the money economy, Western education or technological development. During his stay Dr Fortes encountered only one clearly psychotic person and one other possible psychotic in a population of 5,000. Dr Fortes, who was particularly interested in psychological issues, identified a few other eccentric people who appeared to be suffering from mental deficiency or senility but not from functional psychosis.

When he returned with his wife in 1963, however, the picture had changed dramatically. Psychosis had become common. In three months, among the Tallensi alone Dr Mayer identified 13 psychotic people, 10 of whom were schizophrenic. They were not the sort of cases which Dr Fortes would have been likely to miss if they had been there thirty years before. Most were floridly psychotic, several were aggressive and some were so disturbed they had been chained to logs outside the family dwelling. All of the new cases were from the cluster of clans with which Dr Fortes had been familiar; several were from families he knew well.

While the Tallensi population had grown during the intervening period, it had clearly not increased sufficiently to account for a six-to-thirteen-fold growth in the occurrence of psychosis. Dr Mayer and her husband believed that the roots of the phenomenon were to be found in the major changes which had taken place in Tallensi economy and social life. 'A money economy is now firmly fixed on top of the subsistence pattern,' writes Dr Fortes.

> This means that their economy now benefits substantially from money earned abroad and remitted home, to a degree that was not experienced thirty years ago. A large proportion of the younger men, . . . probably even the majority of them, now work periodically in Southern Ghana, and many spend many years there.[28]

How evident was it that participation in the wage-labor force was related to the onset of psychosis? Several of the Tallensi schizophrenics had worked in the south, and most of the psychotics had developed their illness while in

207

the south or shortly after returning from a trip there. Some women became psychotic shortly after their husbands died in Southern Ghana, the women then returning home to their families in the north for support.[29] The village was clearly functioning as a rehabilitation unit for the developed areas. Interestingly, Dr Mayer formed the impression that the neighboring Gorensi tribe, who were more Westernized than the Tallensi, had an even higher prevalence of psychosis.[30]

This report from Ghana is obviously not an epidemiological study. Its content, nevertheless, is striking. If we are to look at genuinely non-industrial cultures, it is necessary to use such anthropological field reports, and more of the relevant work of this type will be presented here.

Margaret Field, a British physician and anthropologist, for example, independently confirms the work of Dr Mayer and Dr Fortes in her 1968 report. She writes:

> Northern Ghana, till recently, was much isolated and it still has only primitive subsistance farms, but during the annual six months drought the men migrate South to work as labourers. ... In the North the elders declare that thirty years ago mental illness was almost unknown, but add—'Today it is the common sickness of our young men. They travel South and are brought back mad ...'. Everywhere there has been an explosive increase in schizophrenia in the last 20 years.[31]

## Indonesia

Another account of a dramatic increase in the prevalence of psychosis in a pre-industrial society as a possible consequence of economic change comes from northern Sumatra. (Both this example and the Tallensi case have been discussed at some length in an article by H. B. M. Murphy.[32]) In the 1890s, a Dutch doctor with an interest in anthropology visited the Atjehnese people of Sumatra and reported that mental disorder was rare among them, episodic and generally confined to the women. Twenty years later the local governor, struck by an increase in the prevalence of insanity, commissioned a Dutch psychiatrist, F. H. van Loon, to investigate the situation.

When Dr van Loon studied the Atjehnese in 1920 it was after they had been involved in fifty years of protracted warfare with the Dutch colonists of the Indies. The prevalence of mental illness among the Atjehnese was, indeed, high—in places as great as 20 cases per 1,000. In the neighboring, coastal Malays, who had not been involved in the war, the prevalence of psychosis was still low: only 5 cases were located in a population of 26,000.[33]

Had warfare and the shock of defeat led to the increase in the prevalence of schizophrenia among the Atjehnese as Dr von Loon suggested? Certainly men were now much more commonly affected than women. The writer points out that, in defeat, the Atjehnese warriors had lost status and role—women appeared to run most of the communal affairs. A further possibility, however, is that a change in the peasant economy had been the critical stress.

Atjehnese men were sitting around idle in their villages in these early years of the twentieth century, suffering the reproaches of their wives, argues anthropologist James Siegel, because of a decline in pepper production. The Atjehnese villagers had developed a division of labor under which women produced most of the household food, and men, for their part, were required to earn cash for the family. Women were given their own rice fields by their parents and did most of the rice cultivation. Men usually had no resources at the time of marriage and were expected to leave the village to work in the pepper-growing regions of Atjeh in order to meet their family obligations. In the course of time these workers would become part owners of an established pepper garden.

Diseases and pests devastated the pepper gardens in the years before 1920, however, and the Atjehnese men could find little other work. The cultivation of their other principal cash crop, areca-nut, was not sufficient to absorb much manpower, and the Atjehnese men refused to work on the foreign-owned coconut plantations. At the best of times, Atjehnese men were somewhat peripheral to village life, allowed no part in child-rearing, tolerated only as long as they paid their way and felt (they said) like guests in their wives' houses. Now that their principal occupation had failed, they became dependent on their wives, losing status and pride.[34] The sudden increase in the prevalence of schizophrenia among the Atjehnese men at this time was, perhaps, a reaction to these changes in the peasant economy and in the social role and status of the menfolk.

## Other Anthropological Reports

Fuller Torrey cites numerous early reports which suggest that insanity was rare among pre-literate peoples who had been little affected by Western culture. American physicians found no insanity among the Cherokee in the nineteenth century.[35] Schizophrenia was rare in the early twentieth century among Kalmuks and Kirghiz of the Central Asian Steppe, compared with Russians and Armenians, and the illness was practically unknown in pre-contact times.[36] C. G. Seligman, studying the people of Papua, writes in 1929, 'The psychoses do not occur except as the result of stresses set up by white influence.' He observed brief episodes of psychotic excitement occurring among the people of the villages, but the only extended cases of psychosis were in men employed in wage work for Europeans.[37]

Such anthropological reports as these are numerous and interesting, but they are certainly not conclusive. The epidemiological evidence, similarly, does not allow us to draw firm conclusions. The prevalence of schizophrenia, clearly, is not dramatically lower in much of the Third World than it is in some parts of the West. On the other hand, studies which have compared cultures where traditional lifestyles have been little touched by the cash economy with more developed areas have shown schizophrenia to be rarer in the less developed communities. Clearly, we cannot rule out the possibility that schizophrenia was a good deal more rare in the non-industrial world before European contact and economic development. It appears to be rare still in areas not involved in the industrial work force, but due to the widespread existence of migrant labor patterns such areas can scarcely be found any longer. Since sick and disabled workers tend to return to their village homes, we may well be seeing an increase in rural schizophrenia in the Third World secondary to economic and industrial development.

## Special Populations

If the extent of employment were a critical factor in determining the frequency of occurrence of schizophrenia, we should expect to find an increased prevalence of the illness among groups with chronically high unemployment and a low prevalence in areas where unemployment is never a serious problem. Epidemiological surveys of some special populations allow us to check this possibility.

### Canadian Indians and Eskimos

A high prevalence of schizophrenia has been revealed to exist among the Cree Indians and the Salteaux of northern Saskatchewan. Chunilal Roy and his colleagues located 27 schizophrenics among a population of 4,723. This prevalence rate of 5.7 per 1,000 of the general population, age corrected to 11.0 per 1,000 over 14 years, is one of the highest figures determined for any group in the world. It stands in sharp contrast to the low prevalence of schizophrenia found among the non-Indian population of the region. The same researchers identified 45 schizophrenics among the 28,096 non-Indians, yielding a prevalence of 1.6 per 1,000 (2.4 per 1,000 over age 14)—one of the *lowest* rates for any group in the industrial world[38] (see Figure 9.1).

Canadian Eskimos also appear to carry the burden of a very high prevalence of schizophrenia. In a village of 236 people on Hudson Bay, a researcher found 3 schizophrenics,[39] and among about 550 people (214 were over age 14) in another village on South Baffin Island, 7 cases of schizophrenia were identified.[40] While these samples of the population are too small to calculate accurate prevalence statistics, if they are representative of the larger population they suggest a dramatically elevated frequency of the disease—among the highest known rates for any group of people.

The stresses of life among these inhabitants of northern Canada are

210

numerous, and economic and labor-market stresses figure prominently among them. Most of the Indians in Dr Roy's study of northern Saskatchewan were unemployed, living on welfare and treaty money, whereas the whites in the area were in stable employment as farmers, shopkeepers and skilled workers. Only a third of the Indian and Eskimo males in the northern towns of eastern Canada are in steady or fairly steady work.[41] Recent years have seen a decline in hunting and trapping, which used to be the mainstay of life for these people. Wage labor in construction, mining or domestic service, although of growing importance, is usually irregular. By 1950, Eskimo villages in some areas around Hudson Bay derived as much as half of their income from government relief.[42] Soapstone carving became a major source of income for the Eskimos of the eastern Canadian arctic in the 1950s. Virtually all of the men interviewed by anthropologist Nelson Graburn, however, 'said that they loathed the activity as an occupation and that they only carved for the money it brought them. ... Most of the men would rather go hunting.'[43] Welfare existence, the irregularity of employment and the loss of traditionally-valued roles may be significant stresses precipitating schizophrenia in predisposed members of these communities.

## Australian Aborigines

The same situation exists for ther majority of Australian Aborigines. Throughout the country these people are caught in the lowest socio-economic level of society, generally disadvantaged in education, health, employment and housing.[44] In New South Wales, for example, unemployment among Aboriginal males exceeded 20 per cent around 1970; those in work were largely employed as general laborers.[45] Even in the remote parts of the country nearly all of the Aborigines are in contact with Europeans, many living in squalid camps on the fringes of settlements. Some live around government-sustained missions in tumbledown houses, dependent upon welfare and the easy food supply, grudgingly accepting of mission authority and no longer reliant upon hunting and gathering subsistence practices.[46] These Aborigines on the reserves provide a source of cheap, menial labor to employers in the area. Such work is very irregular, however. Among over 500 adults settled around one mission in Eastern Australia in the 1960s employment fluctuated between a mere 6 per cent and 43 per cent of the men, and 6 per cent and 20 per cent of the women. Employment patterns were similar at other missions in the area.[47]

Not surprisingly, schizophrenia is found to be common among these people, and close to the rate for Canadian Indians. Fuller Torrey cites data from an unpublished survey conducted by H. Eastwell of 3,400 Aborigines in Eastern Arnhem Land in the Northern Territory of Australia. Dr Eastwell found 15 chronic schizophrenics and calculated a prevalence rate of 4.4 per

1,000 (8.7 per 1,000 over age 16). He excluded, however, cases of acute psychosis and two cases of chronic schizophrenia who also suffered from mental retardation.[48] The true prevalence is likely to be a good deal higher than Dr Eastwell calculated; just correcting for the two cases known to have been excluded increases the prevalence rate to 5.0 per 1,000 (9.9 per 1,000 over age 16).

Similarly high prevalence figures for schizophrenia have been reported for other Aboriginal groups. Malcolm Kidson, Ivor Jones and others surveyed seven settlements in Western Australia. Among 1,701 people they found 8 schizophrenics. These figures yield a prevalence rate of 4.7 per 1,000, and an age correction for the population over 16 increases this figure to 9.3 per 1,000.[49] At Walbiri in Central Australia, where unemployment was severe and dependence on government rations more or less complete, Dr Kidson found 4 schizophrenics in a group of 650 Aborigines.[50] Dr John Cawte located 5 schizophrenics in a small, socially disorganized settlement of 120 Aborigines in the Eastern Aranda area of Central Australia;[51] and he found 1 schizophrenic and 2 people with transitory schizophrenia-like conditions among the 276 adult inhabitants of Mornington Island off the coast of the Northern Territory.[52] Overall, these studies suggest an exceptionally high prevalence for schizophrenia among people who are leading marginal and dependent lives on the fringes of industrial society—an existence degraded in status and stripped of the social roles which accompanied their prior self-sufficiency.

### Ireland

In July 1911, the Inspector of Lunatic Asylums in Ireland, Dr W. R. Dawson, delivered the presidential address to the annual meeting of the Medico-Psychological Association. His topic was the 'Relation between the Geographical Distribution of Insanity and that of Certain Social and Other Conditions in Ireland.' Dr Dawson was searching for factors which were correlated with the occupancy rate of the public asylums. His conclusion:

> If we now lastly compare the pauperism with the insanity rate, a high degree of correspondence becomes evident. Thus Waterford, which gives the highest rate of insane in institutions, gives also the highest but one of pauperism. . . . The same general correspondence is found at the other end of the scale.[53]

The counties with high rates of pauperism and insanity tended to be agricultural areas. None of the other factors which Dr Dawson chose to study, such as emigration rates, population density, mortality rates, drunkenness or the proportion of elderly people in the population, was significantly associated with the number of hospitalized insane.

Modern Eire is afflicted with an unemployment rate and an incidence of schizophrenia both of which have for decades been among the very highest in the Western world. Irish unemployment rates in recent times have generally been three times as great as those of England and Wales; and the prevalence of treated schizophrenia in Ireland is three times that found in Camberwell in south London.[54] Is it possible, as Dr Dawson's unsophisticated data from the early years of the century suggest, that the two are linked? A comparison of the distribution of unemployment and the first-admission rate for schizophrenia (an approximation to true incidence) for Ireland in 1969 indicates that the two may be related (see Table 9.3), but only if data for the three counties of Ulster which are in Eire are excluded. It is not clear, however, why these small parts of Ulster should be different from the pattern for the rest of Eire; one possibility might be that some patients from these counties are being treated over the border in Northern Ireland. Another, more likely explanation is that the official unemployment rate in the 1960s in the three Republican border counties of Ulster was artificially boosted by Irish citizens working in Londonderry and other industrial districts of the North while simultaneously claiming unemployment compensation in Eire. Until this point is clarified we should use caution before accepting that a direct link exists between labor dynamics and the incidence of Irish schizophrenia.

Further evidence, nevertheless, points to a connection between Irish rural poverty and high rates of the illness. As the distribution of poverty and unemployment in Ireland has changed in the twentieth century, so has the prevalence of insanity. In Dr Dawson's day, before the First World War, the high rates of pauperism and insanity were in central and southern Ireland. These areas have since become more developed, and at the present time the high levels of unemployment and the greatest incidence of schizophrenia are to be found in the west of Eire. A shifting prevalence of this type argues against a genetic explanation for the concentration of the illness in the Irish countryside. Northern Ireland, furthermore, which has long been the most industrially developed part of the island, had the lowest rates of pauperism and insanity in Dr Dawson's survey. Now politically part of the United Kingdom, Northern Ireland still has a comparatively low unemployment rate and incidence of schizophrenia.[55] Research on the diagnostic practices of psychiatrists in London and in different parts of Ireland confirms that there are no major differences between the two countries in the labeling of schizophrenia which could account for these variations in the prevalence of the illness.[56] The Irish lower classes, which are most affected by unemployment, suffer a strikingly greater prevalence of schizophrenia than do professional groups. Farm laborers, among whom unemployment is very great, show the highest prevalence of schizophrenia.[57]

It may be that migrant-labor practices add to the build-up of schizophrenics in the poorer parts of Eire, as may happen in rural areas of the Third World.

213

## Table 9.3 First admissions for schizophrenia by county, and unemployment by province, for Ireland in 1969

| REGION | FIRST ADMISSIONS FOR SCHIZOPHRENIA | | UNEMPLOYMENT | |
|---|---|---|---|---|
| | RATE/1,000 POPULA-TION | RANKING | % | RANKING |
| Ulster (parts of) | | low | 10.1 | high |
| Monaghan/Cavan | 0.3 | | | |
| Donegal | 0.4 | | | |
| North Leinster | | low | 5.7 | low |
| Louth | 0.4 | | | |
| Westmeath/Longford/Meath | 0.3 | | | |
| Dublin | 0.4 | low | 4.5 | low |
| South Munster | | intermediate | 4.7 | low |
| Kerry | 0.6 | | | |
| Cork | 0.3 | | | |
| Waterford | 0.5 | | | |
| South Leinster | | intermediate | 5.9 | intermediate |
| Offaly/Laois | 0.6 | | | |
| Kildare/Carlow | 0.4 | | | |
| Wicklow | 0.3 | | | |
| Kilkenny | 0.5 | | | |
| Wexford | 0.3 | | | |
| North Munster | | high | 6.0 | intermediate |
| Tipperary | 1.0 | | | |
| Clare | 0.7 | | | |
| Limerick | 0.4 | | | |
| South Connaught | | high | 6.4 | high |
| Galway | 0.6 | | | |
| North Connaught | | high | 9.4 | high |
| Sligo/Leitrim | 0.5 | | | |
| Mayo | 0.5 | | | |
| Roscommon | 0.6 | | | |

Sources: First admissions for schizophrenia; O'Hare, A. and Walsh, D., 'Further data on activities of Irish psychiatric hospitals and units, 1965–1969,' *Journal of the Irish Medical Association*, 67: 57–63, 1974. Unemployment: Central Statistics Office, *Irish Trade Journal and Statistical Bulletin*, Dublin: 1969.

Migration to urban areas and emigration to the United Kingdom and elsewhere are particularly common in the west of Ireland. Some of those who become mentally ill while away from home may possibly return to their families of origin. High levels of unemployment and the disappearance of the subsistence economy, though, would tend to limit the chances of the psychotic's successful rehabilitation when he or she reaches home.

Any attempt to explain the Irish distribution of schizophrenia, however, must tackle something of a puzzle. Why should rural poverty in Ireland spawn large numbers of schizophrenics while the backward rural provinces of Southern Italy are characterized (as we shall see later in the chapter) by a low incidence of treated schizophrenia? The answer may conceivably lie in the patterns of agriculture in the two countries and in the history of Irish land tenure.

Ireland was regarded as conquered territory by the people of Cromwell's Britain. In the seventeenth century Irish land was parceled out among the soldiers and creditors of the Commonwealth. By the next century less than 10 per cent of the land was held by Catholics. Ireland became a country of great estates in the hands of alien landlords. Tenants were burdened with unfair rents and lacked security of land tenure. In the nineteenth century the peasants of Ireland, to an even greater degree than the rural British, felt the disastrous impact of the Agricultural and Industrial Revolutions. Evictions, due to the tenant's nonpayment of rent or the landlord's desire to create large grazing farms, were common.[58] The Poor Enquiry of 1835 found that three-quarters of the laborers in Ireland were without regular employment—nearly 2.5 million out of a total population of 8 million.[59] Even before the Famine, evicted families wandered the lanes and slums, begging, living and dying in the ditches by the roadside. So general was the switch to cash-crop farming from subsistence husbandry that during the Great Famine of the 1840s huge exports of wheat, barley and livestock left the country, under military escort, while millions died of starvation.[60]

In these desperate years of the early nineteenth century, insanity was first recognized as being prevalent in rural Ireland—a segment of the growing mass of beggars and vagrants who could no longer expect charity at cottagers' doors. The population of the new lunatic asylums and workhouses as in Britain, grew dramatically.[61]

Ireland's rural economic problems have continued into modern times. The cottier system of subsistence farming faded away in the late eighteenth century and small subsistence holdings were consolidated into larger, market-orientated farms. Land-tenure reform was not complete until the 1930s, and Irish agriculture has remained essentially static throughout the better part of the twentieth century. The lack of agricultural growth is seen as a consequence of both residual conservatism from the time of the landlord system and of a present shortage of capital investment. Agricultural unemployment remains high and land scarce. Rural men routinely delay marriage until age 35 or older, waiting to obtain a farm. Fishing has also been generally unproductive, the Irish economy essentially stagnant until well into the postwar period, and emigration has continued at a high level.[62]

Anthropologist Nancy Scheper-Hughes finds that the traditional patterns of agriculture, sheep-grazing and fishing are quite insufficient to sustain the rural community which she has studied in the west of Ireland. Grants, subsidies, welfare, unemployment, forced early retirement of farmers and prevalent bachelorhood arising from economic scarcity have led to widespread anomie. Dr Scheper-Hughes sees this form of alienation as the source of the high rates of schizophrenia in the region.[63] Her impression is supported by the work of epidemiologists Dermot and Brendan Walsh. They have shown that the regional variations in the age-corrected first-admission rates for schizophrenia to Irish hospitals in 1964 were very closely correlated with marriage rates. In those parts of the country, like Connaught and Munster, where large numbers of males remained unmarried for economic reasons, the incidence of schizophrenia was also found to be particularly high.[64]

Enforced bachelorhood linked to high rates of schizophrenia may be traced back to post-Famine Ireland. In 1864 the *American Journal of Insanity* reported that 'in the asylums the unmarried are three times as numerous as the married in Ireland, while in England the reverse is the case.'[65] Then as now, the cause may well have been economic. 'By the 1840s,' writes H. B. M. Murphy,

> control of land on which to grow food had become crucial, and brother was set against brother in rivalry for inheritance. Marital attachments were weakened by reluctance to breed more mouths to feed . . .; elders withheld land from their sons, thereby delaying the age of marriage in an indirect method of population control.[66]

Like Nancy Scheper-Hughes, psychiatrist H. B. M. Murphy sees these distorted marriage patterns leading ultimately to high rates of schizophrenia. For over a century, land-tenure arrangements, subsistence hardships, bachelorhood and unemployment appear to have fostered schizophrenia among the rural Irish.

## Italy

In southern Italy, by way of contrast, reforms redistributed land to the peasants as early as the 1840s. Even today, 80 per cent of such farms are run by the owners without wage labor. The holdings are small and, unlike most Irish farms, geared more to subsistence than to the modern market economy.[67] Official statistics have indicated high levels of postwar unemployment in the rural provinces of southern Italy, but these figures have more recently been recognized as spurious—artificially inflated by the 'submerged economy.' Such unlicensed operations as artisans' shops and cottage industries are now thought to equal 10 per cent of Italy's gross national product. In the south, many of those employed in such activities are also drawing unemployment insurance, boosting the official count. Some Italian economists claim that an unemployment-office figure of 8 per cent in fact represents true unemployment in the region of only 2 per cent.[68] Certainly, in the northern provinces a distinct labor shortage has existed for much of the time since Italy's 'second industrial revolution' exploded in the 1950s (with a rate of postwar economic growth exceeded only by Japan).

The pull of this labor market largely accounts for the flight from the land which became most dramatically evident in the 1950s.[69] While those who have remained in the rural districts of the south clearly have a lower income than the industrial workers of the north, it is likely that they are not as poor as was once thought. It seems probable, at least, with the preservation of subsistence agriculture and widespread involvement in cottage industries, that traditional roles and marriage and family patterns have not been as seriously disrupted as in the west of Ireland. From this one might conclude that anomie among the Italian rural poor is not as great as in the west of Ireland.

Treated schizophrenia appears to be unusually rare in southern Italy. In such a region, however, one must expect that treatment statistics will seriously underestimate the true incidence and prevalence of the illness. In the southern provinces in 1947–9 (when farming preserved its traditional character to an even greater extent than at present) the incidence of treated schizophrenia ranged between 0.03 and 0.06 per 1,000—a tenth of the Irish rates; such a large difference is probably more than would be expected from variations in diagnosis or in the rate of detection alone. In the northern industrial areas the incidence exceeded 0.1 per 1,000.[70] If the Italian rural-urban gradient can be accepted as roughly correct, it is the reverse of the Irish pattern. (In the United States the rural-urban gradient for schizophrenia is the same as in Italy, but the overall incidence is substantially greater.[71])

Sylvano Arieti, an American psychoanalyst who is considered an authority on schizophrenia, argues that the maintenance of occupational roles and family solidarity in rural environments and the loss of these integrating characteristics in urban-industrial living accounts for the relative scarcity of schizophrenia in both rural Italy and rural America.[72] Viewed from this perspective, Nancy Scheper-Hughes's conclusion appears distinctly possible —that the high rates of schizophrenia in rural Ireland are a consequence of economically-driven family and role disintegration and the accompanying alienation.

Constancy in social roles and relations may protect against the appearance of schizophrenia, and breakdown in these patterns can occur in rural or urban environments. We may speculate that in Ireland such problems have had their roots in exploitative land-tenure arrangements, the failure of traditional subsistence modes and the effects of migrant-labor practices; and that they are perpetuated by the weakness of the economy. Canadian Indians, Australian Aborigines and the rural Irish—these are instances where the loss of valued roles may be a stress contributing to a high prevalence of schizophrenia. In southern Italy the maintenance of traditional roles may protect against the development of schizophrenia. Can we identify other societies in the industrial world which, like rural Italy, breed a low incidence of the disease?

## The Hutterites

If one aimed to set up a community which would minimize the risks of members developing schizophrenia and limit the severity of the course of the illness, one might hope to establish stable role expectations precisely geared to each individual's capacity. Unemployment would be avoided and rehabilitation of the mentally disabled assured. Such communities may be found in Hutterite society.

The Hutterite Brethren, Anabaptist by tradition, live in collective agricultural colonies across the northwestern United States and the Canadian prairies. Sharing of goods and property is central to their existence; all are assured food, shelter, clothing and care in old age. 'Problems of alienation,' writes sociologist John Hostetler, 'are virtually nonexistent.'[73]

Every capable person in a Hutterite colony is expected to work. Expectations are clearly set by the leaders of the colony and tasks are assigned weekly. 'The leaders plan ahead and provide enough work for all males during the entire year,' writes Dr Hostetler. 'Lack of work would mean the breakdown of harmony.'[74] Although the tempo varies with the seasons, 'the work pattern is predictable, regular and satisfying.'[75]

The mentally ill are routinely cared for by their families and are encouraged to participate as fully as they are able in community life. 'The patient is not stigmatized for life,' reports Dr Hostetler, 'and persons who recover from mental disorders can achieve any position available to a normal person in the colony.'[76]

In Hutterite society schizophrenia is exceptionally rare. In a thorough survey of the whole Hutterite population of 8,542 people in 1951, Joseph Eaton and Robert Weil identified only 9 schizophrenic individuals. The findings suggest a prevalence rate of 1.1 per 1,000 (2.1 per 1,000 over age 14). This prevalence is one of the lowest recorded in the industrial world (see Figure 9.1). (Although the prevalence rate for non-Indians in Saskatchewan, one of the regions where Hutterites live, is only a little higher, the prevalence of schizophrenia among whites and Indians combined is substantially greater.) In contrast to the low prevalence of schizophrenia, manic-depressive illness was found to be particularly common among the Hutterites. Thirty-nine cases of this affective psychosis were diagnosed, more than four times the number of schizophrenics.[77] This is a striking reversal of the usual prevalence pattern in which schizophrenia is the more common psychotic disorder.

The low rate of schizophrenia among these people and the high incidence of manic-depressive illness might merely be the result of a diagnostic bias on the part of the psychiatrist who performed the evaluations. A frequently cited alternate explanation for this and other pockets of unusually high or low prevalence of psychosis in discrete populations is that inbreeding may lead to a genetic predisposition to the various illnesses. To these explanations must be added the possibility that socio-cultural factors among the Hutterites have a specific protective effect against schizophrenia but exacerbate affective disorder. None of these alternatives is mutually exclusive and a more recent study of another self-sufficient, North American, agrarian sect, the Amish of Pennsylvania, allows us a further opportunity to weigh these possible explanations.

## The Amish

The Old Order Amish are a highly conservative Protestant sect. Living in more than seventy communities across North America, members maintain a separation between themselves and the modern world. Amishmen dress distinctively, speak Pennsylvania-German in the home, travel by horse and buggy and avoid the domestic use of such modern conveniences as electricity and telephones. There is virtually no migration in or out of the Amish community. Insisting on self-sufficiency, they refuse government farm subsidies and pensions. Although property is not communally owned, as it is among the Hutterites, mutual aid, economic sharing and intense social concern for community members are core qualities of Amish life. Fulfillment is found in one's relations with others and in work. The Old Order Amish are highly successful farmers, despite their rejection of some modern agricultural implements and practices, and their ownership of land is expanding. Many young Amishmen spend some years working in wage labor in agriculture or associated trades while saving money to rent or buy farmland. Mutual support ensures security for each individual, however, the aged and disabled included, and the mentally ill are encouraged to work whenever possible.[78]

A six-year epidemiological survey of mental illness among the Amish of Lancaster County and surrounding districts of Pennsylvania, completed in 1982 by Janice Egeland and Abram Hostetter, reveals that the prevalence patterns of psychosis are similar to those of the Hutterite Brethren. Schizophrenia was found to be rare and manic-depressive illness more common. Cases of mental illness which were active during a five-year period were located through hospital records and a community survey. The emphasis on diagnostic accuracy in this study, however, points up the critical importance of this variable and the dangers inherent in comparing one study with another. Standardized clinical descriptions of the cases identified by community survey were submitted to a panel of psychiatrists for diagnosis according to the recently developed third edition of the American Psychiatric Association *Diagnostic and Statistical Manual.* Embodied in the manual, published in 1980, is an extremely narrow definition of schizophrenia. The psychiatrists diagnosed the psychotic and severely ill individuals as follows:

| DSM-III DIAGNOSIS | NUMBER OF CASES |
| --- | --- |
| Bipolar disorder (formerly included in the category of manic-depressive illness) | 38 |
| Unipolar depressions (without episodes of mania and including non-psychotic patients) | 41 |
| Schizoaffective disorder (formerly known as schizoaffective schizophrenia) | 7 |
| Schizophrenia | 4 |
| Atypical psychosis | 2 |
| Paranoid disorder | 2 |

The researchers point out, however, that 22 of the patients with bipolar disorder (manic-depressive illness) had previously been labeled schizophrenic during periods of hospital treatment.

The size of the Amish population studied was around 12,500 people—8,186 were over age 14.[79] We may calculate, then, that the five-year period prevalence for schizophrenia among these people is only 0.3 per 1,000 (0.5 per 1,000 over age 14) when the narrow DSM III diagnostic definition is used. A very broad definition, however, such as has commonly been applied in the United States prior to the 1970s, might include also those labeled in this study atypical psychosis, schizoaffective disorder, paranoid disorder, and the 22 bipolar patients who were diagnosed schizophrenic in hospital. This definition would give a prevalence figure of 3.0 per 1,000 (4.5 per 1,000 over age 14) for schizophrenia, and would make the prevalence of schizophrenia and affective illness more closely similar.

It is clear that diagnostic variation can render comparison of prevalence statistics meaningless, and that a diagnostic bias could certainly have contributed to the unusual pattern of psychosis among the Hutterites and the Amish. We should recognize, however, that the diagnostic extremes revealed by the Amish study represent the worst possible case; American psychiatry has switched very suddenly from one of the broadest definitions of schizophrenia in the world to one of the narrowest. A middle-of-the-road diagnostic approach, such as British psychiatrists apply, might well exclude all of the clear-cut cases of affective disorder but include most of the other psychotics under the label schizophrenia. Such an approach would yield an age-corrected prevalence for schizophrenia among the Amish in the region of 1.5–2.0 per 1,000—still a strikingly low figure.

Another approach to the question of whether the prevalence of schizophrenia among these two Anabaptist sects appears artificially low as a result of diagnostic variation is to examine the prevalence of manic-depressive illness. If it were the same as usual, or lower,the likelihood that schizophrenics were being misdiagnosed as manic-depressive would be decreased. The authors of the Amish study, in fact, conclude that: 'The rates for both mental illness in general and affective disorders specifically appear to be below average.'[80] Their conclusion, however, is based upon a comparison of psychotic *and non-psychotic* affective illness among the Amish and in the United States population. If we restrict ourselves to manic-depressive *psychosis*, a different picture emerges. The usual age-corrected prevalence for this disorder around the world seldom exceeds 3 or 4 per 1,000 adults.[81] Among the more than 8,000 Amish adults we should expect no more than 24–32 manic depressives; in fact, the study located 38 bipolar cases alone. Among the more than 4,000 Hutterite adults we should expect only 12 manic depressives; Eaton and Weil, however, identified 39 such cases.

In both Anabaptist sects, therefore, we find an increased prevalence of manic-depressive illness and a paucity of schizophrenia. The findings might be the result of diagnostic bias, but in both studies the clinical data provided suggest that a majority of the psychotics were suffering from a clear-cut affective illness and that schizophrenia was, in fact, rare. Genetic factors may be relevant; finding the same prevalence pattern, however, in two populations which are presumably genetically quite distinct but which are culturally similar suggests that socio-cultural forces are more important in forming the overall design.

## USSR

Alienation is certainly not low in the USSR, and life in Moscow is not like that of a Hutterite colony. One might predict, however, that the sustained full employment in that city could lead to a diminished incidence of schizophrenia. Comprehensive community surveys are not available for Eastern Bloc countries (except Yugoslavia which has a market economy and significant unemployment), and the political overtones of the topic are such that we should use caution in evaluating any information which is released. Professor A. V. Sneznevskij has published data which suggest a low prevalence of schizophrenia in Moscow and possibly a decreasing postwar

221

incidence. The total number of schizophrenics (diagnosed by broad Russian standards and including forms similar to the neuroses) registered in the various Moscow neuropsychiatric dispensaries in the mid-1950s ranged between 1.3 and 2.0 per 1,000 (1.5 per 1,000 overall for the population of Moscow). This figure is very low by Western standards but, being a prevalence figure for patients in treatment only, may be quite incomplete.

Table 9.4, which lists the number of first admissions to the neuropsychiatric dispensaries in Moscow for certain conditions, shows a low *incidence* of schizophrenia in the 1950s by US standards. Again, the data may be incomplete. The apparent decline in the incidence of schizophrenia after the Second World War, argues Dr Sneznevskij, may be an artifact of the expansion of psychiatric services in Moscow in the 1940s, leading to the enrollment of previously untreated patients at that time. The evidence given for an increasing incidence of alcoholism suggests that these figures have, perhaps, not been adjusted for the purposes of political propaganda.[82]

**Table 9.4  First admissions for mental disorder to Moscow neuropsychiatric dispensaries per 1,000 of the population**

|      | SCHIZOPHRENIA (INCLUDING NEUROTIC AND LATENT) | MANIC-DEPRESSIVE ILLNESS | ALCOHOLIC PSYCHOSES AND CHRONIC ALCOHOLISM |
|------|------|------|------|
| 1940 | 0.55 | 0.07 | 0.81 |
| 1945 | 0.55 | 0.04 | 0.20 |
| 1946 | 0.47 | 0.05 | 0.31 |
| 1947 | 0.39 | 0.03 | 0.30 |
| 1948 | 0.38 | 0.02 | 0.20 |
| 1949 | 0.34 | 0.02 | 0.30 |
| 1950 | 0.30 | 0.02 | 0.55 |
| 1953 | 0.25 | 0.013 | 0.59 |
| 1954 | 0.24 | 0.007 | 0.56 |
| 1955 | 0.29 | 0.014 | 0.60 |
| 1956 | 0.24 | 0.011 | 0.50 |

Source: Sneznevskij, A. V., 'Dispensary method of registering psychiatric morbidity and the Soviet system of psychiatric service,' *Living Conditions and Health,* 1: 236–41, 1959.

## Yugoslavia and Scandinavia
Political-economic factors and labor-market stresses do not necessarily account for all of the geographic variations in the incidence of schizophrenia. A variety of stresses or constitutional factors could increase the risk of developing the illness. The prevalence of schizophrenia is higher in the Istrian region of Yugoslavia than in the remainder of Croatia;[83] the illness is

also more prevalent in a district of Sweden inside the Arctic Circle than in the rest of the country.[84] Genetic predisposition or special local stress factors could be important in these cases. There are some indications, however, that the material conditions of existence and political and economic factors may be significant among the local causes of stress.

H. B. M. Murphy, for example, has pointed to demographic and economic similarities between Ireland and Istria which might contribute to the high rates of schizophrenia in each of these areas.

> The Irish and the Istrians have experienced centuries of resented domination by some neighboring power, both have experienced massive overseas emigration ... and anthropological descriptions from each describe much intergenerational tension.[85]

In both areas the age of marriage is frequently delayed, and behind this and some of the other similarities is the problem of land shortage. Until recent decades, the poor karstic soil of the Istrian peninsula maintained a population always on the edge of hunger—at times of crisis suffering outright starvation. Those who were not driven to emigrate or who did not choose to become sailors delayed marriage, like the rural Irish, while awaiting their share of family land. Opportunities for employment have increased substantially in modern times but, as before, many villagers have had to move to other areas to find the good jobs. The people who remain are, to a great extent, those whose lives have been shaped by economic hardship.[86]

Environmental factors could possibly play a part in creating the high prevalence of schizophrenia (15.8 per 1,000 over age 14) identified by J. A. Böök in an isolated area of Norrbotten in the north of Sweden inside the Arctic Circle. Although inbreeding has been thought to be important in producing this heavy concentration of the illness, such a possibility becomes less likely when we recognize that other genetically distinct populations in the same area show similarly elevated rates of schizophrenia. In neighboring Finland an epidemiological survey revealed the prevalence of schizophrenia to be 15.1 per 1,000 aged 15–64—close to that observed in Norrbotten.[87] Not far away, in arctic Norway, the prevalence of psychosis is also high—twice as high among the Lapp minority population as among the non-Lappish north Norwegians. The prevalence of psychosis is highest among the Lapps who have most recently quit the nomadic existence for a residential lifestyle with its attendant high rate of unemployment and dependency.[88]

Dr Böök describes the population in the study area of Norrbotten, at the time of his first survey in 1949, as leading a hard life in primitive conditions, working small farms which provided insufficient subsistence for a family. Death rates were elevated, in part because of widespread poverty. In recent times conditions have substantially improved but, as in the cases of Istria and

Western Ireland, emigration has been great.[89] We cannot rule out the possibility that the harsh conditions of subsistence in these various arctic regions have somehow increased the risk in the population of developing schizophrenia.

There is not enough information available here to tell us whether labor dynamics have played an important role in boosting the occurrence of schizophrenia in Istria or in arctic Scandinavia. There are several indications, however, that we need to look beyond genetic explanations.

## Caste and Class

If wage-labor practices and unemployment are critical stresses influencing the onset of schizophrenia, then we should expect a greater incidence in those sections of society most adversely affected by the labor market. The wealth of evidence indicating a greater incidence and prevalence of schizophrenia in the lower classes in cities of the industrial world was set out in Chapter 2. At that juncture it was pointed out that the social-class gradient for schizophrenia was rarely found in rural areas, a fact which eliminates the likelihood of a selective, genetic cause. The drift of schizophrenics or pre-psychotic individuals into lower-status occupations might partly explain the concentration of schizophrenia in the poorer classes, but there is an important observation which forces the conclusion that some class-specific stress must additionally be at work—the social-class gradient for schizophrenia appears to slope in the reverse direction in peasant cultures and in non-industrialized parts of the world.

The province of Lazio in Italy in the early 1950s, for example, although it included the city of Rome, sustained a largely rural population many of whom were peasant farmers. An analysis of all reported cases of mental illness in the province between 1951 and 1955 revealed that schizophrenia was most commonly reported in the better educated, clerical workers and professionals. As in the Third World, those who had migrated to the city from rural areas appeared to be most at risk for schizophrenia. The author of this study, American sociologist Arnold Rose, suggests 'that those rising in social status—as indicated by both education and migration to the nation's capital—have a tendency to become paranoid schizophrenics.'[90] One must expect, however, significant under-reporting of psychosis in peasant communities, especially when contrasted with a major city such as Rome, and this factor may account for the observed findings in Lazio. A similar pattern, though, has been noted in other economically underdeveloped areas.

Several studies from India have made the observation that schizophrenia is more common among high-caste members than among the lower castes. First admissions for schizophrenia to the only public mental hospital in Bihar state in 1959 and 1960, according to psychologist Sharadamba Rao, were much higher among the rich Bania merchant caste, the urbanized and upwardly mobile Kayasthas (many of whom are in managerial and government jobs) and the educated Brahmin and Rajput landowners than among the lower-caste peasants who work the land themselves—the Kurmis, Goalas and Koiris—or among the low-caste Telis and the untouchable scheduled castes. The incidence of treated schizophrenia was nearly fifty times greater among the Banias in this study and more than ten times greater among the Kayasthas than in the lowest castes.[91]

These differences might be explained by a greater tendency for the more educated castes to refer their relatives for Western-style psychiatric treatment. That this explanation is not sufficient is shown by three door-to-door psychiatric surveys which confirm the greater prevalence of schizophrenia among the higher castes in India. The field survey of villages in West Bengal conducted by D. N. Nandi and his colleagues found the prevalence of schizophrenia among Brahmins (at 7.2 per 1,000) to be four times greater than among the untouchable scheduled castes (1.8 per 1,000) or the non-stratified Munda and Lodha tribesmen (1.3 per 1,000).[92] In a house-to-house survey of rural, semi-rural and urban inhabitants of the Agra region of Uttar Pradesh, conducted by K. C. Dube and Narendra Kumar, schizophrenia was shown to be three or four times more prevalent among the high-caste Brahmins and Vaishes than among the lowest castes. This study also demonstrated that the unemployed were most at risk for schizophrenia.[93] The field survey of M. N. Elnagar and his co-workers in rural West Bengal revealed that schizophrenia was more common in the high-caste *paras* (neighborhoods) of the village. The *para* occupied by high-caste Singha Roys, where a large proportion of the residents were well educated and worked in business and professional occupations, had the highest prevalence of schizophrenia. In the *para* for low-caste Mahisyas, where the proportion of people working in agriculture was highest, no schizophrenics could be found.[94]

Why should the relationship between social status and schizophrenia be turned upside-down in these Third World peasant cultures? One reason could be that, in such settings, the lowest-status groups are largely outside the wage-labor force and are occupied in subsistence agriculture. Educated high-caste individuals, by contrast, are more likely to be trained for paid employment. In India, this situation is exacerbated by a severe national problem of high levels of unemployment among the educated.[95] Hence the finding in the study of the Agra region that the high prevalence rates of schizophrenia are concentrated, at the same time, in the higher castes and among the unemployed.

The authors of these studies from India confirm that changes in status and patterns of labor may be critical in establishing the inverse social-class

225

gradient. Dr Rao notes that: 'The Brahmin is losing the traditional respect he commanded, and has to eke out a living in a competitive world. . . . So he attempts to get higher education and compete with other castes for supremacy.'[96] But as Dr Nandi and associates remark:

> The gap between the aspiration and the achievement remains wide. The resulting stress has affected the upper classes in many parts of India. . . . The higher prevalence of mental disorders in the upper classes . . . may be a result of the greater stress caused by this sudden change in their way of life.[97]

The social-drift hypothesis clearly fails to explain the Indian patterns of occurrence of schizophrenia—one could scarcely argue that the low-caste psychotics drift into the upper castes or migrate to upper-caste *paras*. It might be argued that inbreeding leads to a genetic loading for schizophrenia in certain castes, but that these high schizophrenia castes should all be ordered according to status rather than having a random distribution is highly unlikely. It would be somewhat arbitrary, furthermore, to argue that genes predisposing to schizophrenia cluster in the high socio-economic sections of Indian society, but in the lower classes in the West. The mirror-image social-class gradients in the developed and developing worlds are likely to be caused by stresses which are greater on opposite ends of the class spectrum in the two parts of the world. The stresses of participation in the urban-industrial work force meet this criterion.

The extent of involvement in the industrial work force and the associated stresses vary considerably from one area of the Third World to another, and between rural and urban areas of single countries; and they change significantly with time. Early in the industrializing process we might expect the greatest impact to fall upon the most educated classes; at a late stage of industrialization we would look for patterns of labor-market involvement and stress to be similar to those in the West. An equivalent pattern of change in the prevalence of schizophrenia may be seen to have occurred in Taiwan during the postwar period of rapid industrial development. In studies of the Taiwanese Chinese conducted between 1946 and 1948 by Dr Lin and his associates the prevalence of schizophrenia was high in the upper classes, highest in merchants and the unemployed and increasingly prevalent with higher levels of education. By 1961–3, however, after a period of dramatic growth in urbanization, industrialization and education and during a spell of economic prosperity, the patterns of illness had switched to mirror those of the West.[98] These changes are detailed in Table 9.5.

Overall, this evidence from the non-industrial worlds suggests that those engaged in peasant farming, fishing and subsistence activities usually have a low prevalence of schizophrenia and the unemployed routinely have a high rate of the illness. (The unemployment, of course, will often be a

Table 9.5  Prevalence of schizophrenia per 1,000 of the Taiwanese Chinese population in 1946–8 and in 1961–3

|  | 1946–8 | 1961–3 |
|---|---|---|
| Social class |  |  |
| Upper | 3.5 | 0.8 |
| Middle | 1.2 | 1.1 |
| Lower | 4.5 | 2.1 |
| Occupation |  |  |
| Professional | 0 | 0 |
| Merchant | 3.6 | 0.9 |
| Salaried worker | 0.9 | 0.4 |
| Laborer | 1.7 | 1.9 |
| Farmer and fisherman | 1.7 | 1.1 |
| Unemployed | 3.8 | 5.5 |
| Education |  |  |
| College | 18.2 | 0.0 |
| Senior high school | 13.0 | 1.9 |
| Junior high school | 5.7 | 0.0 |
| Elementary education | 1.1 | 1.2 |
| No formal education | 3.8 | 3.7 |

Source: Lin, T., Rin, H., Yeh, E. et al., 'Mental disorders in Taiwan, fifteen years later: A preliminary report,' in W. Caudill and T. Lin (eds), *Mental Health Research in Asia and the Pacific*, Honolulu: East-West Center Press, 1969, pp. 66–91.

consequence of schizophrenia or of pre-schizophrenic traits, but this circumstance will only affect wage-workers.) During the transition to industrialism, in some instances, the most educated and high-class individuals may initially come under greater stress in adapting to the new urban-industrial work force and be at a considerable risk of developing schizophrenia. In other cases, for example in nineteenth-century England and Ireland, the shock of agricultural and industrial changes may strike the displaced rural poor most heavily and among these people will be found the high rates of insanity. The critical factor may be whether or not the rural poor in each instance retain land holdings and can maintain a subsistence base. As a healthy industrial economy develops, nevertheless, it is the educated middle- and upper-class citizens who are most likely to be secure in employment and to lead lives of relative comfort and low stress. In these circumstances it is generally the urban poor who have the highest prevalence of schizophrenia. Seen from this perspective, it is not industrialization or urbanization themselves which might promote the occurrence of schizophrenia;

227

it is the role change, the status loss and the occupational uncertainty affecting certain groups within the work force—here the educated unemployed, there the urban poor—which could lead to an increased risk of developing the illness.

## Immigrants

It has frequently been noted that immigrants to the industrial world from less developed parts of the globe have a higher incidence of schizophrenia than native-born citizens. Some studies demonstrate that the high rates of the illness are also greater than in the immigrants' countries of origin. The common explanations for these observations are that (a) there is a selective tendency for individuals to emigrate who are constitutionally predisposed to develop schizophrenia and (b) the stress of migration or living in an alien culture increases the risk of developing the illness.[99]

A third explanation is equally probable but less commonly considered. Immigrants frequently enter the lowest ranks of society and encounter the hardships of urban poverty, menial employment and unemployment; these lower-class pressures, and not factors specific to their immigrant status, may account for their high incidence of schizophrenia. If this last explanation is correct, then we would expect immigrants to show rates of schizophrenia similar to those found in members of the same socio-economic class in their new country. Studies of schizophrenia among immigrants, however, rarely control for the effects of class status. To study this point we must examine whether immigrants who enter the middle classes (or at least avoid the lowest socio-economic levels) escape the increased risk of developing schizophrenia.

There is no shortage of evidence to demonstrate that low-class immigrants show high rates of schizophrenia; the data on this point are clear. In the United States and Canada, numerous studies have shown that successive waves of poor immigrants in the first half of the twentieth century—Greeks, Poles, Irish, Russians and Swedes—exhibited first-admission rates for schizophrenia considerably higher than those of the general population.[100] Refugees entering Norway were ten times more likely than the native population to suffer from psychosis.[101] West Indian immigrants living in the London boroughs of Lambeth and Camberwell in 1961 were three times more likely (after a correction for the age distribution of the population) than native-born residents to be admitted to hospital with schizophrenia.[102] Hospital statistics for England and Wales show that West Indians and (to a lesser degree) Asian immigrants from India and Pakistan had higher rates of admission for schizophrenia than the general population.[103]

Reports of higher-status immigrant groups stand in contrast. British immigrants to Victoria, Australia, in 1959 and 1960, for example,

228

demonstrated an incidence of treated schizophrenia which was similar to the native-born rate but only a quarter of the incidence among immigrants from southern and eastern Europe.[104] European Jews settling in Israel in the 1950s had a lower incidence of schizophrenia than Jewish immigrants from the Middle East or the minority population of native-born Jews.[105] American-born residents of England and Wales experienced rates of hospitalization for schizophrenia in 1971 which were lower than those for most other immigrants and close to those for native-born residents.[106] Finally, English-born immigrants to New York State between 1949 and 1951 exhibited a strikingly lower first-admission rate for schizophrenia than immigrants from other nations or even native-born, white Americans.[107]

Many of these studies may be faulted for their use of hospital statistics as the measure of incidence. More low-class immigrants might be admitted to public health facilities than affluent native-born citizens, leading to a statistical bias. Community surveys which distinguish immigrants from non-immigrants would theoretically be more accurate, but such studies are rare.

One report is of particular interest, not only because it was a community survey but also because it compared an immigrant group with native-born citizens of *similar class* from the same urban neighborhood. When Raymond Cochrane and Mary Stopes-Roe evaluated a hundred Indian and Pakistani immigrants to Birmingham in the West Midlands of Britain, they found *less* psychopathology among them than among the native-born Britons of the same inner-city area. The better emotional health of these immigrants in comparison to their local-born neighbors may reflect the fact that the Asian residents had more stable employment and less disrupted lives than the British-born group, who had been left behind in the urban slum.[108] The study, which unfortunately does not specifically measure the prevalence of schizophrenia, confirms the possibility that high rates of psychopathology may be a consequence not of immigrant status but of class status.

When Irish-born patients admitted to treatment from Camberwell in 1966–7 and in 1970 were compared with a class-matched group of English-born patients the prevalence of schizophrenia was found to be no greater in the Irish.[109] This observation confirms the impression that the prevalence of schizophrenia among immigrants is close to that of natives of a similar socio-economic status.

Another piece of research yields more direct information about the effect of socio-economic status on immigrants. British sociologist Christopher Bagley, seeking an explanation for the high prevalence of schizophrenia among West Indians in Camberwell, South London, demonstrated that the stresses of poverty existence—low income, slum living, overcrowding and long working hours—were more common in healthy West Indians and West Indian schizophrenics than in a matched group of English schizophrenics. The West Indian schizophrenics, moreover, were significantly more likely than the healthy Caribbean group or the native-born patients to have aspiration to improve their status. The striving to rise out of poverty appeared to be associated with the development of schizophrenia in these immigrants.[110]

Most researchers have emphasized that the elevated incidence of schizophrenia among low-status immigrants is greater than among the population of their countries of origin. Psychiatrist Silvano Arieti points out that in the non-industrial regions of southern Italy in 1949 (as mentioned earlier in this chapter) the first-admission rate for schizophrenia was around 0.03–0.06 per 1,000, in the northern industrial areas of Italy the treated incidence rate was 0.10–0.12 per 1,000, but among Italian immigrants to New York the rate was 0.30 per 1,000—three times greater than the highest incidence in Italy.[111] (Diagnostic variations may account for part of this difference.) Örnulv Ödegard found that treated schizophrenia among Norwegian immigrants to Minnesota was twice as common as among native-born Americans or among the general population of Norway.[112] The Irish-born residents of Camberwell in London, however, have a prevalence of schizophrenia which is only a quarter of the rate among the Irish who remain in Eire.[113] Some Irish schizophrenics may return to their home country, partially accounting for the low rate among the London Irish, but so substantial is the prevalence difference between Ireland and London that we must assume there is a real difference in the occurrence rates among the Irish in the two areas.

The rate of schizophrenia *improves* among people leaving Eire for London and probably *worsens* among those leaving Italy for New York. Neither social selection nor the stresses of migration could produce such a pattern. Nor could these factors account for finding elevated rates of schizophrenia among low-status immigrants but not among higher-class immigrants. It seems likely that the prevalence of schizophrenia is strongly influenced by environmental factors—both in the country of origin and in the area of settlement. The risks of developing the illness are greatest for those who enter the lowest ranks of society where economic and employment hazards are most severe.

## Sex Differences

In Chapter 6 it was argued that the more benign course of schizophrenia in women when compared with men may be a result of the fact that fewer women participate in the labor force and that, overall, women are less severely affected by labor-market forces. If we were to look for differences in the *occurrence* of schizophrenia in the two sexes as a consequence of the influence of labor-market stresses, we might expect to find a lower incidence in women. The incidence of schizophrenia in adult men and women in the industrial world, in fact, is so similar that it is generally regarded as being equal. As the age-specific incidence rates for schizophrenia in Monroe County, New York, indicate (see Figure 9.2), however, this overall similarity in the rates masks the fact that there are wide differences between the sexes in the incidence of the illness at different ages.

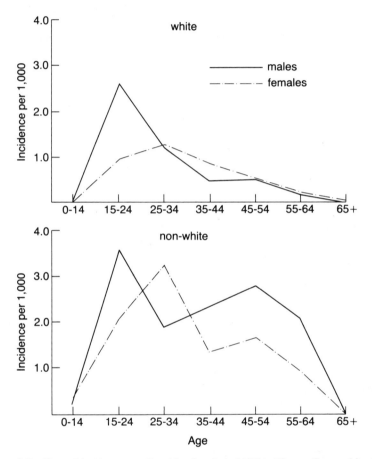

*Figure 9.2    Treated incidence rates for schizophrenia in 1970 in Monroe County, New York*

Source of statistics:   Barbigian, H. M., 'Schizophrenia: Epidemiology,' in H. I. Kaplan, A. M. Freedman, and B. J. Sadock (eds.), *Comprehensive Textbook of Psychiatry - III*, Baltimore: Williams & Wilkins, 1980, pp. 1113–21.

The incidence of schizophrenia is roughly twice as great for men aged 15–24 years than for women of the same age. As psychiatrist John Strauss argues, this peak may reflect the intense career and work-related stress upon

231

men at this stage of their lives.[114] Unemployment among adolescents is generally three times the rate for adults[115] and more severely affects males, whose participation in the labor force is substantially greater than females at all ages.[116]

In the next decade of life, from ages 25 to 34 years, the incidence of schizophrenia in women peaks. For black women the rate substantially exceeds that of black men. While labor-market stresses may play a part in shaping this pattern (the rank ordering of the incidence of schizophrenia at this age, with black women highest and white males lowest, precisely matches the unemployment rates for these groups), it is likely that other life stresses are important. These are years of child-bearing and child-rearing, when women are called upon to make stressful role adjustments equivalent to the occupational demands placed upon men. They are also years when many women are required to make major career changes, to enter the labor force for the first time or to re-enter after a long absence.

Although the incidence of schizophrenia is similar in men and women in the West, in the Third World this is not the case. A greater prevalence of schizophrenia in males has been reported for numerous developing countries. In the early years of the century the preponderance of detected schizophrenia in males was particularly high—6:1 in Malaysia in 1920 and in East Africa in 1936, for example, and 9:1 in early studies from West Africa. More recent reports show a male excess of schizophrenia which is more moderate—2:1 in Malaysia in a 1973 study, 1.5:1 in India in 1970 and 2.5:1 in Bangaladesh in 1972.[117]

It is possible that more female schizophrenics go undetected in the Third World, but this picture is also what one would expect if the acculturative stress of wage working were a major precipitant of schizophrenia. In the developing world, migrant-labor patterns early in the century called much more heavily on males. With increasing urbanization and industrialization Third World women have increasingly entered the work force but usually not to the extent that is common in the industrial world. In the rural areas women are more likely to remain in the villages and their traditional roles are less prone to disruption than are those of the men.

As might be expected from this analysis, a review of early hospital records suggests that it is only in recent decades that the prevalence of psychosis has become roughly equal in the two sexes in the West. In the early nineteenth century admissions to the York Lunatic Asylum in England showed a 25 per cent excess of males over females.[118] First admissions to asylums in Massachusetts in the 1850s were more common among males at every age.[119] These crude admission figures for undefined illness are at best only suggestive evidence. A similar preponderance of males in twentieth-century US hospital admissions for psychosis and for schizophrenia, however, held true until the Second World War.[120] The subsequent change in the treated

232

incidence rates may reflect a change in the true incidence of schizophrenia or merely in the referral rate. One of the major developments affecting women in modern industrial society has been the dramatic postwar increase in the enrollment of married women in the labor force. It is reasonable to suppose that this factor may have influenced the emergence of the current picture in which the treated incidence of schizophrenia in women in the industrial world is close to that of men, but with a substantially later onset.

## The Industrial Revolution

From the evidence presented in this chapter, it is plain that we cannot rule out the possibility that the incidence and prevalence of schizophrenia vary substantially between populations with different economic and ecological characteristics; that the concentration of the illness in the lower classes in the industrial world is not solely a result of social drift; and that the dynamics of labor, changes in traditional roles and the growth of alienation are significant triggers to the development of schizophrenia.

An implication of this view is that the growth of insanity which so concerned the Victorians—the crowding of eighteenth-century rural work-houses with insane paupers, the tenfold expansion of the proportion of population occupying nineteenth-century British asylums, the twentieth-century increase in the rate of institutionalized psychosis which continued until the postwar era—that this phenomenon was not just a product of the increasing recognition and treatment of mental disorder. It may be that the class structure, the work-related stress, the poverty, unemployment, anomie and status loss which accompanied the Agricultural Revolution and industrial development in the West disabled an increasing number of predisposed persons.

In a recent article, psychiatric historian Edward Hare argues that there was, indeed, a real increase in the occurrence of insanity during the nineteenth century. He points out that not only were the numbers of insane occupying the asylums increasing throughout the Victorian era, but so also were the rates of admission and first admission. First admissions to asylums (as a proportion of the population) more than tripled between 1869 (when such figures began to be kept) and 1900. While some of this increase could have been accounted for, Dr Hare agrees, by increased recognition of insanity, this one factor cannot persuasively explain a sustained growth in the appearance of insanity which continued over many decades. If increasing numbers of mild cases were being admitted to the asylums, one would have expected progressive improvements in recovery and falling death rates. In fact, the mortality rate remained unchanged and the recovery rate declined through the late Victorian period.

Which disorder or disorders were growing in frequency? Dr Hare tells us that the evidence points to an increase in what nineteenth-century psychiatrists called melancholia—a condition which included our modern category of schizophrenia. According to contemporary accounts, schizophrenia as we know it today may have been relatively rare in the early nineteenth century.[121]

Dr Hare theorizes that the increasing occurrence of schizophrenia-like disorders in the last century points to an infectious or dietary cause. Dr Torrey implicates a slow virus in the production of higher rates of schizophrenia which, he argues, occur in the developed world. Such infectious or dietary factors, however, cannot explain all of the data. We need to turn to political-economic causes—to subsistence patterns, class status and labor dynamics—if we wish to explain why schizophrenia is so common in Eskimos, Aborigines and the western Irish but so rare in the Hutterites and the Amish; why the class gradient for schizophrenia is turned upside-down in the Third World; why only some immigrants are at a heightened risk for the illness; and why the occurrence pattern is different in men and women.

## Summary

- The prevalence figures for schizophrenia in the Third World appear to fall within the lower end of the spectrum of results for Western countries.
- Studies which contrast different cultures find a lower incidence of schizophrenia in the less economically developed societies.
- Rural parts of the Third World may experience an elevated risk of schizophrenia as a consequence of participating in migrant-labor practices.
- Alienated and dependent subpopulations on the fringes of the industrial world (Canadian Indians, Eskimos and Australian Aborigines) suffer from a high prevalence of schizophrenia.
- The elevated incidence of schizophrenia in western Ireland may be related to the longstanding rural unemployment in that country and to an economically-driven breakdown in family and marriage patterns.
- The assured employment in Moscow, and the stable role expectations among the Hutterite Brethren and the Amish of North America may contribute to the low prevalence of schizophrenia in these societies.
- The greater prevalence of schizophrenia in lower-class Westerners and in the high castes and classes in non-industrial areas of the world may be a consequence of labor-force hardships.
- Immigrants who enter the lower classes experience a high prevalence of schizophrenia; those who enter at a higher level of status do not.
- Women in industrial society show a peak incidence of schizophrenia a decade later in life then men, and women in the Third World show a lower

234

prevalence of the illness than males. Those sex differences may be related to labor-market pressures.

- The Industrial Revolution may have been accompanied by an increase in the occurrence of schizophrenia.

*Part 3*
*Treatment*

# 10 Antipsychotic Drugs: Use, Abuse and Non-Use

Hundreds of double-blind studies of the efficacy of the antipsychotic (or neuroleptic) drugs have now been conducted. The large majority of these studies suggests that these drugs are significantly more effective than inactive placebos in improving the condition of acute and chronic schizophrenics.[1] Time after time, in many thousands of treatment settings, clinical experience has shown that the antipsychotic drugs can bring dramatic relief from psychotic symptoms in most schizophrenic patients. Long-term use of these medications appears to help forestall relapse. Twice as many schizophrenic patients will relapse if placebos are substituted for their active medication than if they continue to take a neuroleptic drug.[2] Yet the overall outcome in schizophrenia, as shown by the analysis of dozens of follow-up studies in Chapter 3, has not improved since the introduction of the antipsychotic drugs in 1954. How can this be?

The issue is a complex one, and we may begin to tackle it by first addressing another related question.

## Which Schizophrenics Should Not Be Treated with Antipsychotic Drugs?

The antipsychotic drugs have emerged as a routine, almost automatic, remedy in psychosis and relatively little effort has been made in psychiatry to use these medicines selectively. One might search a long time to find a diagnosed schizophrenic who has never been treated with a neuroleptic drug. It may be better, however, to avoid the use of antipsychotic drugs in the care of substantial numbers of these patients, but the existence of such subgroups of schizophrenics has not been well recognized.

### Misdiagnosed patients
Among any large group of patients labeled schizophrenic there will be several for whom an alternate diagnosis is more appropriate. This is particularly true for chronic patients in the United States who received their diagnosis before the mid-1970s, when American psychiatrists began to distinguish manic-depressive illness from schizophrenia according to

European criteria. The history of some patients diagnosed schizophrenic may reveal clear evidence of the mood swings characteristic of manic-depressive psychosis. Others, who may have been taking antipsychotic drugs for years, perhaps suffered only one or two late-onset psychotic episodes with depressive features. Others may be in treatment for schizophrenia although their hallucinations and other symptoms are more suggestive of hysteria. In all such cases a regular review of the history and diagnosis is warranted with a view to changing or discontinuing the medicine for a trial period.

## Drug refusers

Many schizophrenics prefer not to take drugs. Some have grandiose delusions and fail to recognize that they have an illness. Others dislike the unpleasant effects of the antipsychotic drugs and would rather suffer their psychotic symptoms. US courts have recognized the right of psychiatric patients to refuse medication even while they are detained involuntarily under the state's mental illness statute. Such rulings have established that the patient's lack of competence to make a decision about his or her own treatment must be demonstrated (over and above the grounds for involuntary detention) before he or she may be medicated unwillingly.[3]

Seen initially by psychiatrists as 'the profession's dark hour'[4] and leading to patients 'rotting with their rights on,'[5] the legal constraints placed upon physicians in the use of involuntary medication have not proved as harmful as feared. Psychiatrists and patients alike have been forced to weigh more carefully the benefits and disadvantages of drug treatment in psychosis. While there are occasions when the local court must be asked to rule whether a client is competent to refuse drug treatment, in the majority of cases the patient and physician come to an agreement. The psychiatrist may accept that the patient's refusal is appropriate, or the patient may be persuaded to accept his or her doctor's advice. There is now clear recognition that, for some patients, the course of the schizophrenic illness is not so severe as to require the involuntary use of antipsychotic drugs.

## Tardive dyskinesia

The same necessity to weigh the costs and benefits of drug treatment has resulted from the appearance of delayed neurological side effects from the use of the neuroleptic drugs. Tardive dyskinesia comprises disfiguring, involuntary movements of the lips, tongue, jaw and other parts of the body, which may appear after a patient has been taking antipsychotic drugs for several months or years. If the medicines are not discontinued promptly, the condition may become irreversible. As many as one-third of outpatients taking antipsychotic drugs have been found to suffer from these symptoms.[6] Patients taking high doses of medication are at greater risk. In some cases in which tardive dyskinesia has developed the patient and the doctor are likely to conclude that the disability from the psychosis is less severe than the possible disfiguration due to the drug-induced neurological disorder. In these cases neuroleptics are to be avoided.

## Non-responders

Ironically, amongst the patients who are most likely to develop tardive dyskinesia are those for whom the antipsychotic drugs have proven *least* beneficial.[7] This may well be a result of the understandable tendency for psychiatrists to give ever-increasing doses of medicine to patients who are functioning poorly and who are not responding adequately to the usual drug dosages. Each new crisis or relapse may lead to another dosage increase. Unfortunately, many such patients may find themselves taking very substantial—even incapacitating—amounts of medication to no real benefit.

Interestingly enough, it may be possible to predict which schizophrenics will respond poorly to treatment with the neuroleptics. Different groups of researchers have independently shown that patients who find the first dose of these drugs particularly unpleasant are most likely to show little benefit from their use and to relapse early. Such 'dysphoric responders' react to a small amount of the drug with depression, anxiety, suspiciousness and immobilization—symptoms which are not alleviated (in one study, at least) by the usual antidotes to the extrapyramidal side effects of the neuroleptics.[8] (Extrapyramidal side effects—rigidity, tremor and restlessness—mimic the symptoms of Parkinson's Disease and may be relieved by the drugs used to treat that condition.)

What proportion of schizophrenics are unresponsive to antipsychotic drug treatment? In one British study 7 per cent of a large group of schizophrenics showed no improvement with drug treatment and a further 24 per cent relapsed within a year despite such therapy.[9] In a large study conducted by the US National Institute of Mental Health, 5 per cent of the acutely-ill schizophrenic patients failed to show improvement with drug therapy,[10] and a number of American studies have found that 10–20 per cent of schizophrenic patients relapse within six months while in treatment with antipsychotic drugs.[11] All those patients who show no short-term benefit from drug treatment, and many of those who relapse despite taking them, might reasonably be treated without medication. This is seldom done, however.

## Good-prognosis schizophrenics

There remains a further subgroup of schizophrenics as large as all of the categories above combined, for which there are grounds to believe that the usual drug treatment is unnecessary or even harmful in the long run. These are the good-prognosis schizophrenics—the patients who show some

241

indication that the course of their illness will be benign. Generally speaking, these are psychotics whose illness began with sudden onset later in life than is usual in schizophrenia, whose previous work history and social functioning have been good and whose illness has not yet become long-lasting. To understand why the antipsychotic drugs may be contraindicated for such patients, however, we must review some of what is known of the neurochemistry of schizophrenia and of the action of the antipsychotic drugs.

## The Dopamine Hypothesis

Messages flow through the central nervous system as impulses in the nerve cells, or neurons. Where neurons link up, at the synapse, a chemical mediator is released from one cell which transmits the impulse to the next cell by its influence on a specific receptor. A number of these neurotransmitters have been identified: some, because of their particular importance in areas of the brain concerned with the emotions, have been quite intensively studied and have been implicated in the origin of various neurological and psychiatric disorders. Deficiencies of norepinephrine (noradrenalin) and serotonin at brain synapses, for example, are thought to underlie the development of different types of depressive illness. The predominant theory for a neurochemical deficit in schizophrenia is that the illness is a result of a relative overactivity of certain tracts of neurons in which the chemical mediator is dopamine (dopaminergic tracts).

The dopamine hypothesis of schizophrenia[12] is based upon two main pieces of evidence:

(1) The antipsychotic drugs block the ability of dopamine receptors in the synapse to respond to dopamine and thus reduce the activity in dopaminergic tracts. The relative antipsychotic potency of the different drugs, furthermore, appears to be directly proportional to the capacity of each drug to block dopamine receptors.

(2) The stimulant drug, amphetamine, which increases the release of dopamine and other catecholamines in the brain, will produce in humans an acute psychosis which is very similar to schizophrenia if it is taken in sufficient amounts. The drug will also bring about an exacerbation of psychotic symptoms in schizophrenic patients.

Dopaminergic fibers are to be found in a number of major tracts in the central nervous system. Two of these pathways, the mesolimbic and the mesocortical tracts, are considered to be possible sites of defective dopamine activity in schizophrenia. A disturbance in the mesolimbic system, in particular, can result in an inability to filter out multiple environmental stimuli—a characteristic disorder in schizophrenia.[13] Damage to the limbic system, or electrical stimulation of this pathway, can result in a number of

242

other schizophrenic-like symptoms, including hallucinations, disturbances in thinking and emotion, paranoia, depersonalization and perceptual distortion.[14]

## Dopamine Supersensitivity

The dopamine hypothesis must accommodate itself to the repeated finding that the amounts of the breakdown products of dopamine (homovanillic acid and 5-hydroxyindolacetic acid) leaving the brain in the cerebrospinal fluid are no higher in schizophrenics than in normals.[15] In fact, one well-designed study demonstrated that the release of dopamine products was *reduced* in schizophrenics with the worst prognostic indicators. This observation is the reverse of what might be expected from the hypothesis that dopamine activity is elevated in schizophrenia.

Malcolm Bowers, a researcher in neurochemistry, has neatly explained this paradox by arguing that the elevated dopamine activity in schizophrenia is a result, not of an excess of dopamine at the synapse, but of a supersensitivity of dopamine receptors to the effects of the neurotransmitter. Consequently, the dopaminergic neurons are more readily stimulated but, through a negative feedback process, the neuronal system attempts to minimize the defect through a reduction in dopamine turnover.[16] Bowers' hypothesis gains support from the observation, made by several groups of researchers, that dopamine receptor binding capacity is increased post-mortem in the mesolimbic tract of schizophrenics. (Although some of these reports indicate that this finding is restricted to schizophrenics who were taking neuroleptics, a larger number of studies has shown that it holds true also for drug-free patients.)[17]

If the basic neurochemical deficit in schizophrenia is a dopamine receptor supersensitivity, it would still be possible for sudden increases in dopamine turnover to lead to an acute exacerbation of the psychosis. Recurrent exposure to stress in mice leads to an increase in dopamine turnover.[18] If humans respond similarly, then stress-induced episodes of psychosis in schizophrenics could result from the effect of an acute increase in dopamine turnover on the chronic receptor supersensitivity.

How do the antipsychotic drugs fit into this scheme? Clearly, by blocking the hypersensitive dopamine receptors they diminish the activity of the neurons and reduce the symptoms of psychosis. The dopamine-blocking action, however, eliminates the feedback process which has been keeping dopamine turnover at a low level. With the administration of these drugs dopamine turnover promptly increases.[19] This is not an immediate problem, as the receptors are blocked by the neuroleptic drugs and the increase in neurotransmitter can have little effect. There is a potential, however, for serious long-term effects.

Chronic dopamine receptor blockade by the administration of the neuro-leptic drugs, and the consequent elevation in dopamine turnover, have been found to produce a substantial increase in the number of binding sites for dopamine in the brains of rats.[20] That is, the drugs create an artificial dopamine supersensitivity. There is strong evidence that the same process occurs in humans. It is believed, for example, that tardive dyskinesia—the delayed neurological side effect of chronic neuroleptic drug use which occurs in a large proportion of patients—is a dopamine supersensitivity phenomenon. Dopamine receptors in the nigrostriatal tract overcompensate for the chronic blockade by becoming hypersensitive. The symptoms of tardive dyskinesia (involuntary muscle movements) usually appear after a reduction in the dose of the neuroleptic drug, as this change exposes some of the previously blocked, supersensitive receptors to the action of the neurotransmitter. An increase in drug dosage, on the other hand, will block the receptors and mask the symptoms of the disorder.

An important potential hazard of the neuroleptic drugs should now be apparent. The basic neurochemical deficit in schizophrenia may well be a supersensitivity of dopamine receptors. The immediate action of the neuroleptic drugs is to minimize the effects of that deficit; on this basis rests the great value of these drugs in psychiatry. The long-term effect of the neuroleptics, however, may be *a worsening of the basic neurochemical defect in schizophrenia.* As in tardive dyskinesia the supersensitivity effect may be temporary, gradually disappearing over the course of weeks or months after drug withdrawal, or—if drug treatment continues long enough—it may become permanent. Herein may lie one reason for the failure of the antipsychotic drugs to produce improvements in the long-term outlook for schizophrenics.

For the neuroleptics to present a risk of worsening the schizophrenic defect they would need to produce a dopamine supersensitivity not just in the nigrostriatal tract (where they cause tardive dyskinesia) but also in the mesolimbic pathway. Several studies now indicate that they accomplish just this. There is an increase in dopamine binding sites in the mesolimbic region of the brains of schizophrenic patients which is related to the extent of their prior treatment with neuroleptic drugs.[21] Clearly, this formulation, if correct, has serious implications for drug treatment in schizophrenia.

## Implications of Drug-induced Dopamine Supersensitivity

We may predict that certain consequences will flow from the tendency of the neuroleptic drugs to produce dopamine supersensitivity if they are, in fact, worsening an underlying defect in schizophrenia. These include:

• The antipsychotic effect of the drugs will decrease with time. That is,

244

tolerance to the drugs will develop and greater doses will be required to achieve the same effect.

- Psychotic symptoms will rebound after the withdrawal of antipsychotic drug treatment to a higher level than would have been the case without treatment. Drug-withdrawal studies which evaluate the efficacy of neuroleptic drugs by substituting a placebo for the active drug will therefore give an over-optimistic impression of the value of the drugs.
- The adverse long-term effects of the antipsychotic drugs will be most evident in the case of schizophrenics who would otherwise have had a good prognosis. As illustrated in Figure 10.1, the outcome for poor-prognosis schizophrenics is likely to be so serious that a worsening due to

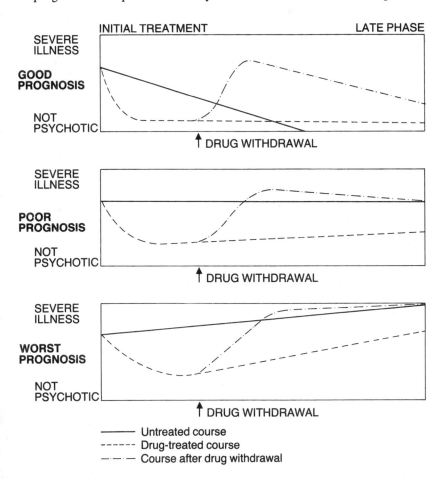

*Figure 10.1   Postulated course of illness in good- poor- and worst-prognosis schizophrenics with and without neuroleptic drug treatment and after drug withdrawal*

drug withdrawal would be difficult to detect and the continuous use of drugs will still offer distinct advantages for these patients. In the case of good-prognosis schizophrenics, on the other hand, drug withdrawal may worsen the course of an otherwise benign condition and drug maintenance therapy may increase the risk of psychosis, cause side effects or, at best, prove worthless.

We may examine the evidence relating to these predictions in turn.

## Tolerance to the Antipsychotic Drugs

Most psychiatrists would argue that tolerance does not commonly develop to the neuroleptic drugs. All could cite numbers of patients who have taken the same dose of medication for years without needing an increase but whose condition worsens when the drug is decreased or discontinued. There is, nevertheless, evidence that tolerance to these drugs does develop in a substantial proportion of schizophrenic patients. According to a number of follow-up studies, for example, anywhere from a fifth to a half of schizophrenic patients on maintenance drug therapy relapse within the first two years.[22] Gerard Hogarty and Richard Ulrich have calculated that the risk of relapse for schizophrenic outpatients in the second and third years of such treatment runs at an average rate of about 2 per cent a month.[23] The implication is that the efficacy of the drugs steadily declines over time.

It might be argued that many of these relapses are due not to the development of tolerance to the antipsychotic effects of the drug but to the patients' failure to take the medicine reliably. This view is contradicted, however, by studies which compare the relapse rate of schizophrenic patients taking a neuroleptic drug, fluphenazine (prolixin or modecate) as a daily oral medication with those who receive the same type of medication as a long-acting intramuscular injection. In the second instance there could be no question of the patients failing to receive the medication regularly. No significant difference, nevertheless, has been found between the relapse rates of the two groups. However the drug is administered, a substantial proportion of the patients relapse in the first year.[24]

Confirmation of the development of tolerance in neuroleptic drug treatment has been offered by Guy Chouinard and Barry Jones—two psychiatrists at McGill University in Montreal, who have been most active in arguing that drug-induced supersensitivity psychoses are a real phenomenon. They report that schizophrenics who are treated over a period of years with injections of long-acting fluphenazine at regular intervals consistently require an increase in their dosage of medication in order to maintain the same therapeutic effect. At the end of three years of treatment the dosage for many of their patients had doubled or tripled and in some cases the dosage had increased 30- or 100-fold. These researchers also report that, as might be expected, psychotic deterioration in patients withdrawn from neuroleptic drugs is commonly associated with the appearance of symptoms of tardive dyskinesia—a finding which suggests that dopamine supersensitivity has developed in both the nigrostriatal and mesolimbic tracts as a result of the drug treatment.[25]

## Immediate Assignment Studies

Drug-withdrawal (placebo substitution) studies may exaggerate the long-term benefits of the antipsychotic drugs on the course of schizophrenia. In particular, they may give a spurious impression of the value of drug treatment for good-prognosis patients which is the reverse of their real long-term effect (see Figure 10.1). Accordingly, the only drug studies which would be expected to give an accurate reflection of the efficacy of the neuroleptic drugs in schizophrenia are those which:

(a) assign patients to drug or placebo treatment at the beginning of the study (immediate assignment studies) and do not withdraw neuroleptic treatment part-way through the study; and which also

(b) distinguish between good-prognosis and poor-prognosis patients.

Such studies are few.

### Rosen et al.

Psychopharmacology researchers Bernard Rosen and David Engelhardt and their co-workers followed a group of over 400 schizophrenic outpatients of a New York clinic for between four and eight years. They divided the group into good- and poor-prognosis categories on the basis of their own 'Hospital Proneness Scale' which measured the patients' prior social attainment, the extent of their previous treatment and their performance in psychological tests. The patients were randomly assigned at the very outset of the study to treatment with either a placebo or one of two antipsychotic drugs, chlorpromazine or promazine. The subsequent hospital admission rate indicated that the neuroleptic drugs were effective in keeping the poor-prognosis schizophrenics out of hospital:

|  | HOSPITAL ADMISSION RATE OF POOR-PROGNOSIS PATIENTS |
| --- | --- |
| Patients taking chlorpromazine | 35.7% |
| Patients taking promazine | 29.4% |
| Patients taking placebo | 61.5% |

For good-prognosis patients, however, drug treatment appeared to be unhelpful or even harmful:[26]

|  | HOSPITAL ADMISSION RATE OF GOOD-PROGNOSIS PATIENTS |
| --- | --- |
| Patients taking chlorpromazine | 12.2% |
| Patients taking promazine | 28.4% |
| Patients taking placebo | 7.7% |

Subsequently these researchers followed up the 129 patients who had been hospitalized to see which schizophrenics were hospitalized for a second time. The results were even more striking. Drug treatment proved effective in keeping poor-prognosis patients out of hospital longer:

|  | AVERAGE TIME BEFORE REHOSPITALIZATION OF POOR-PROGNOSIS PATIENTS |
| --- | --- |
| Patients on chlorpromazine | 14 months |
| Patients on promazine | 16 months |
| Patients on placebo | 6 months |

But good-prognosis patients treated with chlorpromazine were hospitalized significantly sooner:[27]

|  | AVERAGE TIME BEFORE REHOSPITALIZATION OF GOOD-PROGNOSIS PATIENTS |
| --- | --- |
| Patients on chlorpromazine | 6 months |
| Patients on promazine | 14 months |
| Patients on placebo | 30 months |

## University of California Group
In a study at Camarillo State Hospital, California, psychologist Michael Goldstein and his associates divided a group of 54 newly hospitalized, male schizophrenic patients into good- and poor-prognosis cases (using a scale devised by Leslie Phillips). The patients were randomly assigned to treatment with a placebo or an antipsychotic drug soon after admission. After three weeks of treatment the poor-prognosis patients appeared to benefit from taking active medication. The good-prognosis patients, however, did better if they were taking placebo—they improved more rapidly

248

and were discharged sooner. This finding was particularly true for nonparanoid, good-prognosis patients.[28] The researchers uncovered a similar pattern of response when they repeated their study with a new sample of 24 good-prognosis, male schizophrenics—neuroleptic drugs failed to benefit the nonparanoid, good-prognosis patients in three weeks of treatment.[29] Unfortunately, no long-term follow-up of the patients in either of these studies was done.

Interestingly enough, this research group obtained analogous findings when they compared the effect of high versus low doses of antipsychotic drugs treatment on a group of 104 young, acute schizophrenics. The good-prognosis patients—particularly males—showed a negligible rate of relapse and had fewer symptoms at the end of six months on the *lower* dose of medication. (Female good-prognosis patients in this study only did well on a low dose of medication when they were also receiving adequate family-oriented psychosocial treatment.)[30]

### Rappaport et al.

Eighty young, male, acute schizophrenics admitted to Agnews State Hospital in California were randomly assigned on admission to chlorpromazine or placebo treatment by Maurice Rappaport and his co-workers. After discharge from the hospital the patients were treated with or without active medication depending, presumably, on their clinical condition and their compliance with the psychiatrist's recommendation. Patients who did well on placebo treatment in hospital tended to be treated without medication after leaving hospital and to be good-prognosis schizophrenics with a history of good functioning before admission. Placebo treatment failures were likely to be given active medication after discharge. At three-year follow-up the patients who took a placebo in hospital and were off medication as outpatients showed the greatest clinical improvement and the lowest levels of pathology and functional disturbance. They also had the lowest rate of rehospitalization:

| HOSPITAL/OUTPATIENT TREATMENT | REHOSPITALIZATION RATE |
| --- | --- |
| Placebo/no medication (N=24) | 8% |
| Chlorpromazine/no medication (N=17) | 47% |
| Placebo/neuroleptic (N=17) | 53% |
| Chlorpromazine/neuroleptic (N=22) | 73% |

The superiority of the placebo/no-medication group to the chlorpromazine/no-medication category is particularly worth noting, although part of this

249

difference in outcome may be due to there being a greater proportion of good-prognosis patients in the former group. The authors of the study conclude: 'Antipsychotic medication is not the treatment of choice, at least for certain patients, if one is interested in long-term clinical improvement.'[31]

## Carpenter et al.

Good-prognosis schizophrenics with adequate records of prior work and social functioning and a short history of illness were selected for a study conducted at the US National Institute of Health by William Carpenter and his associates. The 49 patients were treated with or without neuroleptic medication at the discretion of their psychiatrists—the assignment to drug treatment was fairly arbitrary but not random. The two groups were equivalent in their prognostic ratings and had similar initial clinical characteristics. At one-year follow-up the patients in the drug-free treatment group demonstrated a more benign course in a number of ways:

|  | DRUG-FREE | DRUG-TREATED |
| --- | --- | --- |
| Average length of hospital stay | 108 days | 126 days |
| Rehospitalization rate | 35% | 45% |
| Outpatient neuroleptic drug treatment | 44% | 67% |

Patients receiving drug treatment in hospital were also significantly more likely to suffer a postpsychotic depression.

The research team who conducted this study

> raise the possibility that antipsychotic medication may make some schizophrenic patients more vulnerable to future relapse than would be the case in the natural course of their illness. Thus, as with tardive dyskinesia, we may have a situation where neuroleptics increase the risk of subsequent illness but must be maintained to prevent this risk from becoming manifest.[32]

## Klein and Rosen

One study alone which fits the criteria of (a) immediately assigning patients to a drug-free or drug-treatment category and (b) distinguishing good-prognosis patients fails to support the picture drawn by the research cited so far. Donald Klein and Bernard Rosen randomly assigned 88 schizophrenic inpatients of the Hillside Hospital, New York, to chlorpromazine or placebo treatment. The researchers differentiated good- and poor-prognosis patients by means of the Premorbid Asocial Adjustment Scale. On rating the patients after six weeks of treatment the investigators found that chlorpromazine was more beneficial for the *good*-prognosis than for the poor-prognosis patients.

From the standpoint of this analysis, however, the Klein and Rosen study has two flaws. In the first place, it is not a follow-up study. It gives only the outcome of six weeks of treatment and has no bearing on whether drug-induced dopamine supersensitivity has a detrimental effect on the long-term course of schizophrenia. It therefore stands in contradiction to Goldstein's short-term studies only, and is unrelated to the findings of the research teams of Rosen and Engelhardt, Rappaport and Carpenter. Secondly, the research design itself was biased against recovery in the good-prognosis patients. The research sample was composed of patients who were referred to the drug study after they had failed to improve in milieu (drug-free) treatment and psychotherapy. This selection procedure would automatically weed out the patients who could be expected to do well in drug-free treatment.[33]

## Goldberg et al.

The authors of another study of the effect of drug treatment in schizophrenia—Solomon Goldberg and his associates—have also claimed to refute many of the findings presented above. 'We find no evidence,' they argue, 'that patients with good signs are not in need of drugs; instead they profit most from drug treatment.'[34] Goldberg's research, however, is a drug-*withdrawal* study; as such, it may be expected to demonstrate a benefit for drug treatment in good-prognosis patients—but, according to the super-sensitivity psychosis hypothesis, the benefit is spurious.

## May et al.

A number of studies may be found in the literature which, while not precisely fitting the criteria established for this analysis, nevertheless yield useful information. Philip May and his colleagues, for example, in a four-year follow-up of over 200 first-admission schizophrenics showed that 59–79 per cent of patients recovered in various drug-free treatments (including electroconvulsive therapy and psychotherapy) and that the successes from such treatment (presumably good-prognosis patients) did as well in the long term as patients who were initially treated with neuroleptics.[35]

## Schooler et al.

Nina Schooler and her co-workers made a similar finding in another immediate assignment drug study of a large sample of schizophrenics conducted through the US National Institute of Mental Health. In a follow-up of the discharged patients one year after leaving hospital the researchers were surprised to find that 'patients who received placebo treatment in the drug study were *less* likely to be rehospitalized than those who received any of the three active phenothiazines.'[36]

## Pasamanick et al.

We should recognize, however, that there is another immediate assignment study which does not discriminate good- and poor-prognosis patients—Benjamin Pasamanick's comparison of outcome of drug-treated and placebo-treated patients in home care—and that this report does *not* show a long-term benefit to placebo treatment.[37] Why should the placebo-users in Schooler's NIMH study have had a superior outcome? One possibility is that there were more good-prognosis patients admitted to that study than to Pasamanick's. The subjects in the NIMH study typically had a number of good prognostic features—the illness was at an early stage, the onset had been acute and later in life, and many of the patients were currently or previously married.[38]

## The Soteria Project

One further immediate assignment study of treatment in schizophrenia is well worth examining—the Soteria Project. Under the direction of psychiatrist Loren Mosher (at that time Chief of the Center for Studies of Schizophrenia at NIMH) and social worker Alma Menn, this project set out to compare the effectiveness of a nonmedical, psychosocial treatment program for first-break schizophrenics with the drug-oriented treatment of a community mental health center. Acutely ill patients who had previously had no more than two weeks of inpatient psychiatric treatment were arbitrarily assigned to treatment in a short-stay inpatient unit followed by outpatient aftercare or to Soteria House, a home for up to six patients in the community staffed by nonprofessionals. Patients in the standard community mental health center program spent a much shorter time in their initial period of residential (hospital) care—one month compared with five-and-a-half months of residential care for Soteria patients. Whereas all the mental health center patients were initially treated with neuroleptic drugs only 8 per cent of Soteria patients received such therapy.

Follow-up, two years after admission, showed that the outcome for Soteria patients compared quite favorably with that of the schizophrenics treated by the community mental health center. (see *table opposite*) The overall levels of psychopathology in the two groups of patients were not significantly different at follow-up.

'Our data,' suggest Mosher and Menn, 'indicate that antipsychotic drugs need not be used routinely with newly admitted schizophrenics if a nurturant, supportive psychosocial environment can be supplied in their stead.'[39] The authors point out that their sample of patients was not composed of particularly good prognosis cases—they selected individuals

252

**Two-year follow-up**

| TREATMENT AFTER DISCHARGE | SOTERIA | MENTAL HEALTH CENTER |
|---|---|---|
| Readmitted to hospital or Soteria House | 53% | 67% |
| Taking neuroleptic drugs continuously or intermittently | 34% | 95% |
| Receiving psychiatric treatment | 59% | 100% |

**Circumstances at follow-up**

| | | |
|---|---|---|
| Working (full-time or part-time) | 76% | 79% |
| Living independently | 58% | 33% |

who were young and single, generally considered indicators of poor outlook. All patients, however, were at a very early stage of their illness. Patients with the fewest relapses in both treatment programs tended to have good prognostic features (better prior social competence and a later age of onset), but there is no indication as to whether or not good-prognosis patients did better in drug-free care.[40]

The weight of evidence in these immediate assignment studies suggests that the neuroleptic drugs are, indeed, either unnecessary or harmful, in the long run, for good-prognosis schizophrenics. Taken together with the well-established fact that drug-*withdrawal* studies have consistently shown the neuroleptics to be superior to placebos in preventing psychotic relapse,[41] we now have a strong indication that the antipsychotic drugs produce a heightened risk of relapse for drug-withdrawn patients. They may do this by worsening an underlying dopamine receptor supersensitivity in schizophrenia. On the one hand, then, we have sound reasons to offer good-prognosis and early schizophrenics an adequate trial of drug-free treatment (and in the Soteria Project we have a suggested model for doing this cost effectively). On the other hand, we have at least one possible explanation for the failure of the antipsychotic drugs to have a measurable impact on overall outcome in schizophrenia.

If we now look at the interactions between environmental stress and antipsychotic drug treatment in schizophrenia we may find further reasons for the poor showing of the antipsychotics and, in addition, useful indications as to how we can help make drug-free treatment effective.

## Stress, Schizophrenia and Drug Treatment

Stress, as noted in Chapter 1, may precipitate a psychotic episode in a predisposed individual.[42] The antipsychotic drugs, furthermore, may be minimally necessary for preventing relapse of schizophrenics living under conditions of low social stress, and of maximal utility to those in a more harsh and demanding environment. As British social psychiatrist John Wing writes:

> Drug treatment and social treatments are not alternatives but must be used to complement each other. The better the environmental conditions, the less the need for medication: the poorer the social milieu, the greater the need (or at least the use) of drugs.[43]

A number of pieces of research support this point of view.

A series of projects conducted through the Medical Research Council Social Psychiatry Unit in London has shown that the relapse rate is higher in schizophrenics who return home to live with critical or over-involved relatives than in those (the majority) whose relatives are more supportive and less smothering. The relapse rate in the patients living in the more stressful households is reduced by two factors: (a) restricting the contact between patient and relatives to less than 35 hours a week and (b) using neuroleptic drugs. For patients living in the low-stress families, however, the relapse rate was found to be low regardless of whether the patients were taking medicine or not. Figure 10.2 illustrates the nine-month relapse rates for 128 schizophrenics (71 from low-stress homes and 57 from high-stress families)—the combined subject groups from the two studies.[44] The rate of relapse among patients living in low-stress households and taking no medication can be seen to be several times lower than the rate for those schizophrenics who are exposed to a high-stress environment for much of the time even when these patients are protected by medication.

In a later (two-year) follow-up of one of these groups of schizophrenics, psychiatrist Julian Leff and psychologist Christine Vaughn found that neuroleptics did eventually appear to be of some benefit to the patients in low-stress homes. The researchers speculated that the drugs were of value in protecting these patients against additional sources of life-event stress (e.g., job loss) to which they were exposed independent of the fact that their home environments were warm and supportive.[45] Dr Leff and Dr Vaughn had demonstrated in an earlier piece of research that relapse was unavoidably common in schizophrenics living in high-stress homes but that relapse in patients in low-stress homes was only likely to occur if they were subjected to additional independent stressful events.[46] One may conclude from these findings that neuroleptic drugs are less necessary for schizophrenics living in environments which are both supportive and also somewhat protective in warding off unpredictable stresses.

The therapeutic effect of a warm and non-critical relative has been demonstrated in two further studies carried out by the same group of

254

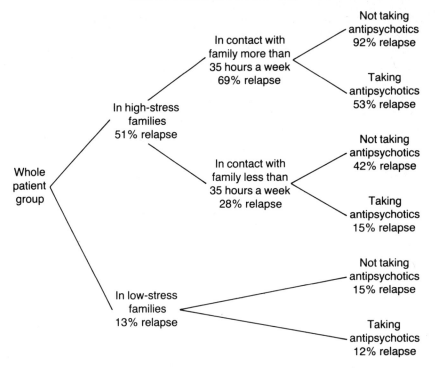

*Figure 10.2    Relapse rates of schizophrenics in high- and low-stress families*

Source: Vaughn, C. E. and Leff, J. P., 'The influence of family and social factors on the course of psychiatric illness: A comparison of schizophrenic and depressed neurotic patients,' *British Journal of Psychiatry*, 129: 125–37, 1976.

researchers. Heart rate and skin conductance tests showed that schizophrenics had a higher level of arousal than normal individuals, irrespective of whether the patients were living in high-stress or low-stress households. This heightened level of arousal dropped to normal in a schizophrenic when in the company of a non-stressful relative but continued at an elevated rate when in the company of a critical, over-involved relative. The finding held true for both acutely psychotic patients[47] and those in remission.[48] The neuroleptic drugs similarly are known to decrease the level of arousal in schizophrenics—a property which is thought to contribute to their anti-psychotic effect. This evidence, then, also implies that the neuroleptic drugs may be less necessary where the social environment is therapeutic and non-stressful.

The level of arousal in schizophrenics in hospital or residential treatment can be controlled by creating an environment which is optimally stimulating and supportive. In such a setting drug treatment is minimally necessary. Long-stay hospital patients withdrawn from low-dosage maintenance drugs, according to psychologist Gordon Paul's review of the published research, rarely show any harmful effects, and a majority of the relevant studies indicates that drug treatment is unnecessary for such patients when they are in a progressive psychosocial treatment program.[49]

One such study is Gordon Paul's own report on a drug-withdrawal project involving 52 severely incapacitated, long-stay schizophrenics from an Illinois state hospital. The patients were transferred to two active psychosocial treatment programs and matched groups were assigned to either continuation of their usual drugs or to placebo substitution. Staff and patients were not even aware that a drug study was in process. After four months the drug-withdrawn patients were doing equally as well as those on drugs (initially, in fact, the drug-withdrawn patients had responded *more* rapidly to the treatment programs).[50] By the end of the six-year experimental program, 85 per cent of the schizophrenics in psychosocial treatment were still off drugs.[51] Why was drug-withdrawal supersensitivity psychosis not a problem with these patients? Perhaps because, in this instance, they were generally taking only moderate to low doses of medication before withdrawal.

Research cited earlier in this chapter—William Carpenter's study at the National Institute of Health and Loren Mosher's Soteria House—has demonstrated that the same observation holds true for young acute schizophrenics. Active, individualized, psychosocial treatment programs render antipsychotic drug therapy unnecessary for a substantial number of patients.

One prominent, recent study might be seen as conflicting with the general trend of this research. The study, by Solomon Goldberg with his associates in the NIMH Collaborative Study Group, was discussed earlier in the chapter when it was mentioned as showing that the relapse rate of schizophrenics withdrawn from antipsychotic drugs was greater than that of patients who continued the drug treatment. Another aspect of the research report is relevant here. At the time of discharge from hospital these patients were randomly allocated to either routine outpatient care or to a more intensive program of sociotherapy—major role therapy, a combination of social casework and vocational counseling. The researchers found that, overall, the intensive sociotherapy was ineffective. This was because the therapy helped some patients and hindered others. Mildly ill patients benefited and more severely ill patients relapsed *sooner* if they were receiving intensive sociotherapy.[52] Patients taking antipsychotic drugs responded well, but those taking placebos had a *worse* community adjustment if they were in major role therapy.[53]

At first glance it appears that these results contradict the evidence for the benefits of psychosocial treatment in schizophrenia, but on closer examination this does not prove to be the case. The psychosocial treatment programs in Gordon Paul's study or on William Carpenter's research ward or at Soteria

House were comprehensive attempts to shape a total therapeutic residential environment in such a way as to maximize the psychotic patients' chances of recovery. Major role therapy, on the other hand, consisted of outpatient treatment delivered to schizophrenics living in any one of a number of community locations. The patients in this 'intensive' therapy program were seen, on average, only twice a month.[54] The main thrust of the therapy was to urge 'the patient to become more responsible and to expand his horizons.'[55] The authors appropriately conclude that the major role therapy was probably too intrusive and stressful for the marginally functioning patients and that its toxic effect was similar to the influence of the critical and over-involved relatives in the British studies of the family environment of schizophrenics cited above.

By way of contrast, some forms of outpatient therapy which do aim to reduce the stresses in the patients' environment have proved successful. Julian Leff and his co-workers were able to minimize the impact of critical and over-involved relatives on schizophrenic patients through family therapy and thus to reduce the relapse rate in these patients.[56] British psychiatrist Ian Falloon in association with a team of researchers in California achieved a similar result working with the families of schizophrenics in their homes—family-treated patients showed fewer psychotic symptoms and fewer relapses.[57]

We may conclude that when schizophrenics are in an environment which is protective but not regressive, stimulating but not stressful, and warm but not intrusive (whether it be their own family home or a residential treatment unit) many of these patients will not need antipsychotic drug treatment. On the other hand, schizophrenics who are exposed to significant stress (whether it be status loss, intrusive relatives, over-enthusiastic psychotherapy or hunger, cold and poverty)—such patients will have a high relapse rate and will require substantial doses of neuroleptic drugs to achieve minimal functioning levels.

In Western society in recent decades, too few schizophrenics have been placed in the more therapeutic settings identified here. With the advent of antipsychotic drugs and the advance of radical deinstitutionalization policies, too many have been thrust into environments in which they can only survive with the aid of drugs. As we saw in Chapter 8, around a third of all schizophrenics in the United States exist in settings which scarely pretend to be therapeutic—in jail, on Skid Row, in nursing homes or boarding homes. A study of the mentally ill in Utah nursing homes, for example, showed that their use of medication increased with time but that their levels of activity decreased.[58]

Here we find another explanation of the failure of the drug-treatment era in psychiatry to usher in improved outcome in schizophrenia. In the rush to transfer patients to the community—to cut institutional costs regardless of the social costs—the antipsychotics have been used not as an *adjunct* to psychosocial treatment, as John Wing recommends, but as an *alternative* to such care. Too often the psychiatrist is called upon to wedge the schizophrenic into an ill-fitting slot because an appropriately therapeutic setting is not available, affordable or even considered feasible. In these circumstances the prescription becomes a document in a political process.

## The Revolving-Door Patient

The ascendency of psychopharmacology over psychosocial treatment is epitomized by the revolving-door patient. This creation of the neuroleptic era, referred to frequently in this book, has become a focus of public concern—the central character, for example, in a seres of *New Yorker* articles and the subject of a ground-breaking court decision. Sylvia Frumkin's ten admissions to Creedmoor Hospital, New York City, by age 31, her multiple hospital admissions elsewhere, and her family's consequent suffering, all documented in the *New Yorker*,[59] represent nothing unusual. Not uncommonly, several times in one year the same patient will be medicated back to sanity in an American public hospital and discharged to an inadequate environment, placed in an unworkable setting or simply released to live on the street with the full knowledge that readmission will shortly be necessary.

Such a case was Kathy Edmiston. In a hearing concerning her circumstances in the Probate Court of Denver, Colorado, in 1980, Judge Wade commented:

> On virtually innumerable occasions respondent has been certified and institutionalized for short periods of time (during which periods her condition has been stablized by use of medication in a structured setting). She has then been placed either on out-patient status or in a nursing home. She then becomes sufficiently ill that she is picked up or delivered to the emergency room at Denver General Hospital, placed under certification, and the process begins again. Without even a minimally adequate treatment program, respondent and others like her will continue to be victims of their own inadequacies (often including their delusional systems) and will be targets for the influence and exploitation of others. For example, the behavior of this respondent in the community, which is related to the nature of her mental illness, has made her the victim of physical, sexual, and financial exploitation.[60]

The judge ruled that the next time this patient was certified the mental health agency must establish a suitable program for her treatment.

## Side Effects

There are further reasons why we should not continue to emphasize drug

258

treatment at the expense of environmental considerations—why we should use comprehensive psychosocial approaches to minimize the use of the neuroleptics. Many patients distinctly dislike taking these drugs. One cause of their distaste is the side effects of the medication. Immediate reactions to these medications may include stiffness, shakiness, restlessness or acute muscle spasms. These symptoms may often be controlled by taking anti-Parkinsonian medication. Other adverse reactions to some or all of the antipsychotic drugs are blurred vision, oversedation, blunting of spontaneity, sexual impotence and failure of ejaculation, epileptic seizures and disorders of the eyes, liver, blood and skin.

The long-term risk of developing tardive dyskinesia, a neurological consequence of using neuroleptic drugs, has already been mentioned. Another potential long-term hazard of these medicines has also caused concern—the theoretical possibility that they may promote the development of breast cancer. By blocking transmission in the dopaminergic nerves to the pituitary gland, the neuroleptic drugs cause an elevation in the blood level of prolactin. High levels of this hormone, in turn, are known to induce the growth of breast tumors in mice and rats. Some breast cancers in women appear to respond to prolactin in a similar way. The epidemiological data are not yet sufficient to tell us with any degree of certainty whether women taking antipsychotic drugs are at greater risk of developing breast cancer or not.[61]

Other possible adverse reactions to the antipsychotic drugs—and these are also effects which could help to explain the disappointing influence of these drugs on the long-term outlook in schizophrenia—are an increase in post-psychotic depression and an adverse effect on learning ability. A number of researchers have reported that schizophrenics treated with neuroleptics may become more depressed after their acute psychosis subsides, possibly as a result of their drug treatment. Some authors have observed that post-psychotic depression is associated with the slowing (akinesia) induced by some antipsychotic drugs.[62] More recent reports have disputed that these drugs increase post-psychotic depression:[63] the evidence is not strong either way. (It is quite possible that much of the observed post-psychotic depression is, in fact, the depressive phase of manic-depressive illness misdiagnosed as schizophrenia.)

The evidence is better, however, that the neuroleptic drugs diminish learning capacity in animals, normal subjects and psychiatric patients.[64] The implication of this side effect is that drug treatment may possibly reduce the capacity of schizophrenics to benefit from programs of social and vocational retraining and add to their employment difficulties.

There are good reasons, it is clear, to limit the use of the neuroleptic drugs, and there is sound evidence indicating that drug-free treatment can result in good outcome for a substantial number of schizophrenics. Two

259

questions remain: 'How should we select schizophrenics for treatment without neuroleptics?' and 'How is such treatment to be done?'

## Prognostic Indicators

In the course of treatment it should become obvious that some patients are appropriate for drug-free management—those with mild psychoses who refuse drugs or who have developed tardive dyskinesia, and those who fail to respond significantly to adequate doses of the neuroleptic drugs. If we wish to refrain, however, from using drugs on those schizophrenics who have not been ill long and whose disorder will be benign without treatment, we have a tricky task on our hands—the task of predicting the future course of the illness. As many as half of all schizophrenics, according to a review of drug-withdrawal studies, can survive for a reasonable time in the community without relapse:[65] and, as we saw in Chapter 3, a similar proportion of schizophrenics achieved good social functioning in the years preceding the introduction of the antipsychotic drugs. How can we predict, though, *which* half will do well?

Efforts to pinpoint indicators of good prognosis have revealed that schizophrenics whose illness is more sudden in onset and is a response to a clear life stress, those whose psychosis developed late in life and those who have functioned well before their illness developed (including having good social relationships and getting married)—these patients are more likely to improve and recover.[66] The degree of accuracy in using these criteria to predict outcome is not high, however; at best we can correctly sort three out of four patients into good- or poor-outcome groups, but we would be wrong the other quarter of the time.[67]

One point emerges clearly from the research—the symptoms and clinical features of the psychotic episode are of very little value in predicting outcome.[68] Indeed, the diagnosis of schizophrenia itself does not predict an outcome which is necessarily much worse than the prognosis in other psychoses.[69] The best indicator of future functioning, according to two pieces of research, is the patient's functioning before he or she fell ill. The measure of previous competence in any one area, furthermore, is the best predictor of functioning in that same area. Thus, a good work record predicts good vocational functioning, good social relations in the past point to good future social functioning and multiple prior hospital admissions indicate the likely extent of future hospital use.[70]

In practice it is reasonable to assume that a patient who is (a) early in the course of a schizophrenia-like illness and (b) has previously achieved a reasonable level of functioning deserves a trial of treatment without antipsychotic drugs. Most of these patients will eventually improve and do well.

260

## Good-Prognosis Schizophrenia versus Manic-depressive Illness

The objection has been raised that many or all so-called 'good-prognosis schizophrenics' are really misdiagnosed patients with manic-depressive illness. The implication of this view is that we might be better advised to treat such patients with lithium carbonate (a substance which does not cause the same severe side effects as the neuroleptics and which is often highly effective in manic-depressive psychosis) rather than to pursue drug-free treatment. It is possible that some of these good-prognosis patients are, in fact, suffering from manic-depressive illness. This affective psychosis characteristically begins later in life than schizophrenia and allows patients the opportunity to develop a higher level of social and vocational functioning. It is often difficult to distinguish between episodes of affective illness and schizophrenia, as they share many common features (see Chapter 1).

A number of studies have shown that good-prognosis schizophrenics have a high incidence of manic-depressive illness among their relatives—a finding which suggests that they may themselves suffer from an affective illness.[71] Some of these studies are handicapped, however, by using an exceptionally broad concept of schizophrenia, which magnifies the problem of inappropriately incorporating manic-depressives under the label 'schizophrenia.' Richard Fowler and associates, who claim that 'most good prognosis cases are variants of affective disorder,'[72] appear to have classified all psychotics with good premorbid histories who were not classical examples of manic-depressive illness as 'good prognosis schizophrenia.' All of these patients had several symptoms of affective illness and some had even suffered prior episodes of clearly defined manic-depressive illness.[73] Michael Taylor and Richard Abrams, who argue that 'good prognosis schizophrenia is frequently indistinguishable from manic-depressive illness'[74] also admit that not one of their so-called 'good prognosis schizophrenics' earned a diagnosis of schizophrenia according to formal research criteria but half of them satisfied criteria for a diagnosis of mania. It seems probable, therefore, that many of these patients with good prognostic indicators would have been readily labeled as manic-depressive by an astute diagnostician and never categorized as schizophrenic. It is important to recognize, furthermore, that these good-prognosis cases, while they have many relatives with manic-depressive illness, also have a greater incidence of schizophrenia among their family members than is usual in the general population—a finding which suggests that some of the patients suffer from a schizophrenic illness.[75]

A more telling piece of research has been carried out by Jack Hirschowitz and his colleagues. They selected ten good-prognosis patients who did meet research criteria for schizophrenia and found that eight of these patients improved during a two-week trial with lithium carbonate. They did not, however, report whether these patients deteriorated again after withdrawal from lithium.[76] Since good-prognosis schizophrenics may also improve during two weeks of drug-free treatment, it is not possible to say whether or not the patients' gains were attributable to the medication.

The plainest evidence that there is, indeed, such an individual as a good-prognosis schizophrenic (according to standard diagnostic practices) is the mass of research material which forms the basis of this book. Since the turn of the century in all the developed countries, scores of outcome studies of schizophrenia (often rigorously defined) have shown that there is always a proportion of patients with schizophrenia who recover. The myth that these patients are not really schizophrenic goes back to Kraepelin's original mistake—that dementia praecox was inevitably a deteriorating disorder. As we have seen, Kraepelin's error was forced upon him by the economic and institutional conditions of his place and time.

We may conclude that it is certainly appropriate for the psychiatrist to screen his or her good-prognosis patients closely for evidence of manic-depressive illness. A history of distinct, prior, extended episodes of pathologically elevated or depressed mood is most helpful in this respect. In some instances a clear diagnosis is not possible until the passage of time has revealed a characteristic course of the illness. For some patients a trial of lithium may be in order. In many more cases a trial of drug-free treatment is most appropriate.

## Neuroleptic-Free Treatment

In modern times, the deliberate treatment of schizophrenia without neuroleptic drugs is seldom practiced outside long-stay, private hospitals which offer psychoanalytic therapy and can only serve the relatively wealthy or well-insured. Can such care be offered routinely in community mental health where cost considerations are paramount? The answer is a qualified 'yes.' Does drug-free treatment necessarily call for intensive dynamic psychotherapy by highly trained therapists? The answer is 'no.' What must be provided is an opportunity for the acutely ill schizophrenic to be cared for in a non-stressful environment which maximizes the chance for a spontaneous remission to occur.

### The setting
The characteristics of a therapeutic environment for schizophrenics have already been set down—warm, protective and enlivening without being smothering, overstimulating or intrusive. In addition, as earlier chapters of this book have indicated, the patients should be allowed to maintain a valued social role, together with their status, dignity and a sense of belonging to the community at large. Patients must be able to stay in residential treatment long enough for their condition to improve and to be free of urgency to move

on. With a week's stay in a private psychiatric hospital ward in the United States costing roughly the same as a round-the-world trip, it is clear that extended, drug-free care must be provided in a low-cost, alternative community setting.

Soteria House, mentioned earlier, provides a model for such community treatment. A large house in a San Francisco Bay neighborhood, Soteria provides accommodation for six schizophrenic people and two staff. 'Recently admitted, very psychotic residents receive a great deal of special one-to-one, or two-to-one attention,' write Loren Mosher and his associates, 'and performance expectations are minimal.'[77] As residents become less psychotic they participate more actively in the therapeutic community—planning and performing household tasks and working out interpersonal differences. Each pursues recreational activities of his or her own choice. When compared with the local community mental health center's inpatient ward, Soteria was found to be less orderly and controlling and the staff were more involved, supportive and spontaneous.[78]

Despite the much greater length of residential treatment for the Soteria patients (five-and-a-half months) than for the control group of patients in mental health center care (one month), the average costs of treatment at the end of the first year were almost exactly the same. One reason for this surprising finding may be the Soteria patients' more limited use of outpatient care after discharge. Another reason is that the nonprofessional Soteria staff were paid distinctly less than the standard salary for mental health professionals. A further explanation is that the average period of in-hospital care for the control group of patients—at one month—was considerably longer than is now usual in cost-efficient, drug-oriented, community mental health center inpatient programs.

It is not clear whether the Soteria model can be adopted by community mental health programs and prove cost-effective in comparison with drug-orientated programs—the answer will depend partly on the size of the catchment area and the number of early, good-prognosis patients needing treatment at any time. With some loss of therapeutic aptness, however, drug-free treatment can be performed in a facility which is cost-efficient—a large (around 16 beds), well-staffed, community-based, intensive treatment unit. Essentially a low-cost, acute hospital ward in the community, such a facility is described in a later chapter. While the central purpose for an intensive treatment house of this type is to treat all types of seriously disturbed psychiatric patients in an affordable, non-coercive community setting, it can readily be used for the drug-free treatment of those appropriate, good-prognosis schizophrenics who are admitted. Unfortunately, the high turnover of patients in such a unit, the moderate degree of urgency to discharge patients, the large number of residents and the fairly high level of stimulation all detract from the value of this type of facility for treating

263

schizophrenics without drugs. It may, however, be the only affordable way that such care can be offered by community-based agencies.

## The treatment

How long should attempts to treat a schizophrenic episode without neuroleptics persist before calling a halt? Patients in the Soteria Project were generally started on an antipsychotic drug if they showed no change after six weeks. Fewer than a tenth of their patients came to require such drug treatment.[79] In other programs the decision as to whether or not to begin neuroleptic treatment will partly depend upon the pressure for quick results in order to make room for new admissions and partly upon the patient's level of agitation and distress. Two or three weeks of drug-free trial, however, may be sufficient for a large proportion of good-prognosis schizophrenics to show considerable improvement.

Acutely disturbed schizophrenics who are overactive and excited or at risk of hurting others, attempting suicide or running away from treatment—such patients may often be helped in the short run by the use of moderate doses of the minor tranquilizers instead of the neuroleptic medication. The belief is widespread in psychiatry that the minor tranquilizers, including the benzodiazepine drugs, diazepam (Valium) and chlordiazepoxide (Librium), are harmful or at best worthless in psychosis. Such is not the case. These drugs are often effective in calming agitated psychotic patients—more immediately so, in fact, than the antipsychotic drugs. In some cases they even have a prompt antipsychotic action, as the following actual case illustrates.

A woman in her mid-twenties has experienced a number of brief schizophrenic-like psychotic episodes in her life, often in association with the stress of returning to visit her parents in another state of the union. Between these episodes she leads a full social life, performs with a group of musicians and holds a responsible job. She is admitted to a residential intensive treatment facility in a severely disorganized psychotic state. Apparently overwhelmed by auditory hallucinations and environmental stimuli competing for her attention, she stands in one spot all day, immobilized. She is unable to answer simple questions, each hesitant phrase trailing off unfinished. She appears frightened, highly aroused and her pupils are widely dilated. Within one hour of taking a moderate dose (5 to 10 milligrams) of diazepam (Valium) she has completely returned to her normal self—capable, outgoing and calm. After a few hours the effect of the drug wears off and the patient is again extremely psychotic. Taking the drug regularly, the patient's psychosis is well controlled but, after a week, tolerance to the antipsychotic effect of the drug develops and higher doses are required to achieve the same benefit.

The effectiveness of the benzodiazepines in this case and in other psychotics maybe due to a reduction in the patient's level of arousal. It is also

264

likely that the benzodiazepines exert an antipsychotic effect by their action in blocking dopamine release. They may achieve this effect by stimulating a feedback loop (in which the neurotransmitter is gamma-aminobutyric acid) which damps down the release of dopamine.[80] Several reports have shown that the benzodiazepines in moderate or high doses, alone or in combination with neuroleptic drugs, are effective in controlling psychotic symptoms.[81] Somewhat fewer studies have found them to be ineffective or to produce equivocal results.[82] It seems likely that the benzodiazepines are effective in schizophrenia but only in some cases. They are most useful, perhaps, in those schizophrenics who are paranoid or who have a high internal level of arousal and, as a result, are particularly withdrawn and under-active.[83]

A potential advantage of the minor tranquilizers over the neuroleptics is that, by blocking dopamine *release* rather than dopamine *receptors*, the benzodiazepines should not lead to dopamine supersensitivity, tardive dyskinesia or a prolonged withdrawal psychosis. Another advantage is that the minor tranquilizers are much more pleasant to take then the antipsychotic drugs and are generally free from serious side effects. A possible disadvantage is that tolerance may develop to the antipsychotic action of the drugs, rendering them suitable only for short-term use. Whether or not this is the case is not yet known.

The minor tranquilizers may be a useful tool in reducing arousal in acutely psychotic patients. Other techniques of stress reduction are equally as important. Quiet areas of the treatment facility should be available to allow patients to withdraw from an environment which may be perceived as over-stimulating. Close personal contact with staff and other residents, reassurance, and the provision of an absorbing activity may also be valuable. Dynamic, 'uncovering' psychotherapy is likely to be too stressful and intrusive for many patients and more toxic than beneficial. Along the same lines, expectations for the patient's functioning must be precisely geared to his or his current capability—over-enthusiastic exhortations to become more active or sociable may lead to an increase in psychotic symptoms.

Much of the patient's treatment will involve making appropriate plans for his or her life after discharge—finding a place to live and an occupation, neither of which should be too stressful. Some form of supportive but independent living arrangement and supervised or sheltered employment (as described in later chapters) may be appropriate. For all but the most resilient patients a gradual transition into the new living and occupational arrangements will be required. It is useful to minimize the number of changes at any one time and to continue 'drop-in' attendance at the residential treatment facility for some time after discharge.

Especially where there is a likelihood that the schizophrenic patient will return to live with his or her family, some meetings with the family members should take place. Where the home environment is accepting, and not stressful, the relatives will learn to be even more helpful if given the advantage of accurate information about the patient's illness and guidance as to reasonable expectations for his or her performance. If the patient's household is found to be highly stressful, family therapy should aim to reduce the relatives' intrusiveness or hostility, and plans may be made to reduce contact between patient and family or to devise alternate living arrangements.

Therapists' respect for the patient's individuality will help meet his or her need for status and independence. Using an unlocked community facility encourages staff to find non-coercive ways to protect the patient and others from hazards arising from psychotic thinking and behavior and poor judgment. These measures may include increased personal contact rather than restraint and distracting recreational activity instead of seclusion. Such methods maintain the patient's own reliance on self-control. Increasing levels of responsibility and involvement in the management of the household and concern for the welfare of other residents gives the patient a useful social role and a sense of personal value to others.

In short, aside from a lessened emphasis on stern paternalism and an increased emphasis on family relations, these treatment approaches attempt to recreate the principles of moral management as practiced in the York Retreat.

## Summary

- Antipsychotic drugs may be unnecessary or harmful in the treatment of a substantial proportion of schizophrenics: such patients include drug non-responders and good-prognosis cases.
- Long-term treatment with antipsychotic drugs creates dopamine receptor supersensitivity, worsening the underlying biochemical deficit of schizophrenia.
- Withdrawal of antipsychotic drugs may cause a rebound of schizophrenic symptoms to a higher level than would have been the case without treatment.
- Drug-withdrawal studies, consequently, may give an over-optimistic impression of the benefits of the neuroleptic drugs in schizophrenia.
- The majority of non-withdrawal studies indicate that good-prognosis schizophrenics do as well or better without antipsychotic drug treatment.
- Stress precipitates psychotic relapse in schizophrenics and drug treatment is less necessary for patients in low-stress settings.
- The revolving-door patient has been created by the use of drug treatment coupled with a neglect of the psychosocial needs of the psychotic.
- The best prognostic measures give a rather crude indication of which patients will recover without drug treatment.

- Some, and only some, 'good-prognosis schizophrenics' in fact suffer from manic-depressive illness.
- Neuroleptic-free treatment is indicated for a number of schizophrenics, is practical, and can be carried out cost-efficiently by community mental health agencies.

# 11 Work

'Of all the modes by which the patients may be induced to restrain themselves,' wrote Samuel Tuke in his *Description of the Retreat*, 'regular employment is perhaps the most generally efficacious.'[1] To the moral-treatment advocates, in fact, work was not merely a means to occupy and control their charges: it was a central pillar of the moral-treatment edifice. William Ellis, superintendent of the Hanwell Asylum, believed that proper employment 'has frequently been the means of the patient's complete recovery.'[2] In 1830, Eli Todd wrote to the family of a patient about to leave the Hartford Retreat in Connecticut: 'I cannot too strenuously urge the advantage and even the necessity of his being engaged in some regular employment which shall hold out the promise of some moderate but fair compensation to his industry and prudence.'[3] W. A. F. Browne, superintendent of the Montrose Royal Asylum had this vision, in 1837, of the perfect asylum of the future:

> The house and all around appears to be a hive of industry. When you pass the lodge, it is as if you had entered the precincts of some vast emporium of manufacture: labour is divided, so that it may be easy and well performed, and so apportioned, that it may suit the tastes and powers of each labourer. You meet the gardener, the common agriculturalist, the mower, the weeder, all intent on their several occupations, and loud their merriment. .... The curious thing is, that all are anxious to be engaged, toil incessantly, and in general without any recompense other than being kept from disagreeable thoughts and the pains of illness. They literally work in order to please themselves.[4]

Looking back upon such typically Victorian beliefs and dreams we may be excused for doubting the extent to which they were grounded upon accurate observation of the insane and for wondering how far they merely reflected the prominent, middle-class work ethic of the day. Scottish philosopher Thomas Carlyle, for example, made the extravagant claim that 'Work is the grand cure of all the maladies and miseries that ever beset mankind.'[5] Nonetheless, we have seen evidence to support the moral-treatment advocates in their emphasis on the importance of work (Browne's fantasies aside). As previous chapters have indicated, unemployment and material circumstances may well be significant in the genesis of insanity, and employment important for recovery. Work may often be crucial for the development of self-esteem and in shaping the social role of the psychotic.

## Research on Work and Schizophrenia

Up to this point the evidence presented in support of this position has been largely macrostatistical in scale. Such observations have included:

- increasing hospital admissions for schizophrenia during economic slumps (Chapter 2);
- the worsening outcome for schizophrenia during the Great Depression (Chapter 3);
- improved rehabilitative efforts under full-employment conditions (Chapter 4);
- high cure rates for insanity during the labor shortage of industrializing America (Chapter 5);
- better outcome for higher-class and female schizophrenics (Chapter 6); and
- superior outcome from schizophrenia in the Third World (Chapter 7).

At this juncture it would be valuable to change the level of magnification and to look for evidence on a smaller scale of the effect of employment and unemployment on the *individual* schizophrenic. Such evidence, unfortunately, is sparse. Why should this be so?

A clear reason is the difficulty in devising adequate controls for such research. If schizophrenics who are working do well and those who are unemployed relapse frequently, how can we tell if the unemployment causes a deterioration in the patient's condition or if the patient's severity of illness leads to job loss? When work is scarce and few schizophrenics are employed, it is difficult to set up an experiment where a group of patients is maintained in employment, and it would not be ethical to keep a control group of patients out of employment if they were able to work.

Such problems are not insuperable, but they are compounded by the general lack of interest within the psychiatric profession in vocational rehabilitation. In the index to the three large volumes of the latest edition of the American *Comprehensive Textbook of Psychiatry*, for example, there are only nineteen references to 'Work,' 'Working,' 'Vocational,' etc., but ten times as many references to 'Sex,' 'Sexual' and related items. Psychiatrists appear to have taken seriously only half of Freud's well-known dictum that the ability to love and to work are central issues in the lives of men and women.[6] That this lack of interest in work is, in large part, a response to the fact that there *is* little work available for schizophrenics becomes clear when we note that the few pieces of research which are in the literature were almost all conducted two or three decades ago during the postwar years of labor scarcity.

In reviewing these studies, rehabilitation experts have generally concluded that work has a proven benefit on the course of mental illness.[7] To draw this conclusion, however, requires a certain amount of wishful thinking. Working patients *do* fare better, this much is clear. What is less obvious is whether employment leads to clinical improvement or if higher functioning makes employment possible.

An American psychiatrist, James Stringham, for example, reviewing the progress of 33 older male patients discharged from a large psychiatric hospital in 1947 and 1948, found that 24 were still out of hospital at follow-up; he concluded that having a job had contributed to the successful rehabilitation in half of these cases.[8]

More persuasive evidence for the benefit of work in schizophrenia may be found in a 1955 report by psychologist Leon Cohen of 114 chronic schizophrenics discharged from a Veterans Administration hospital. He found that patients who had a job to go to or a definite vocational plan at discharge and those who found employment after discharge were able to stay out of hospital longer. That work was the important element leading to the patients' success is suggested by his additional finding that the severity of the patient's psychosis at discharge was in no way related to the likelihood of rehospitalization.[9]

A British study published in 1958 reports very similar findings. Psychologist George Brown and his colleagues followed for a year 229 male patients (mostly schizophrenics) discharged from seven London area mental hospitals. Over 40 per cent of these patients worked for six months or more and of these nearly all (97 per cent) succeeded in staying out of hospital. Another 43 per cent of the patients never worked at all, and of these fewer than half (46 per cent) succeeded in avoiding rehospitalization. Again there is a suggestion that work was more important than clinical status in determining success, for a full third of the patients who worked for most of the year were rated as moderately or severely disturbed and many more had residual symptoms.[10]

In 1963 Howard Freeman and Ozzie Simmons published *The Mental Patient Comes Home*, a comprehensive report on the fate of 649 psychotic patients discharged in 1959 from nine US state hospitals and three Veterans Administration hospitals. Like the researchers before them, they found that patients who were successful in staying out of hospital were substantially more likely to have been employed than those who were rehospitalized. They also found only a moderate degree of correlation between the patient's working ability and his or her level of psychotic symptoms.[11]

Psychologist George Fairweather has become well known for devising a model community program in which psychiatric patients live together in

270

community lodges and work together in teams as independent businesses providing various needed services to the community. These programs will be discussed in more detail later in the chapter. At this point it is sufficient to note that a follow-up study of patients in the lodge program showed that they realized substantial benefits when compared with a matched control group of patients who entered typical psychiatric aftercare programs. Patients in the lodge program had assured employment and those in routine aftercare, almost to the last person, were unable to find full-time work. Residents of the lodge spent five or six times as much time out of hospital as patients in the control group. Lodge patients were more satisfied with their lives in the community, but very little difference was found between the level of symptoms manifested by the two groups of patients.[12] We cannot conclude from this study that employment alone led to the patients' success, for the lodge program offered, in addition, assured accommodation and a relatively sheltered environment coupled to opportunities for autonomy, an important role within the lodge society and enhanced self-esteem.

One study might be cited as *failing* to support the notion that employment improves outcome in psychosis. Psychologist Robert Walker and his co-workers developed a program of assured employment in industry for Veterans Administration clients—both inpatient and outpatient. They compared the progress over six months of a group of 14 of these patients with 14 similar patients who were placed in the hospital workshop and who were left to find regular employment on leaving hospital. Half of the patients in each group were schizophrenic. The researchers found no difference between the two groups in the amount of inpatient care required during the six-month period. The failure to find a difference in outcome, however, may have been a consequence of the fact that the control-group patients received the benefit of in-hospital work therapy and had surprisingly high rates of success in finding employment after discharge. The employment records of the two groups, in fact, were comparable.[13]

As much research appears to have been done on the effects of work therapy as on the benefits of work itself. Some writers, foremost among them rehabilitation psychologist William Anthony, have painted a dismal picture of the efficacy of inpatient work therapy programs.[14] Such pessimism, however, is not justified by a thorough examination of the available research. True, one study conducted at Fort Logan Mental Health Center in Denver found that patients placed in the hospital sheltered workshop stayed in hospital longer than a similar group who were not given work therapy; rehospitalization rates for the two groups were similar.[15] Other pieces of research on the effects of work therapy, nevertheless, are more positive.

Numerous early postwar studies revealed that institutionalized patients who were given routine work around the hospital improved dramatically.[16] We know, however, that more or less any activating experience improves the

271

condition of neglected, regressed, long-stay hospital patients. A more recent study of a state hospital rehabilitation program, published in 1965, compared patients in work therapy with a matched group in routine ward care. The patients who received work therapy stayed out of hospital for longer periods after discharge, or if they remained in hospital they showed greater clinical improvement. The condition of the patients in the control group actually worsened.[17]

A study of patients treated in a Veterans Administration hospital showed that schizophrenics placed in the work therapy Member Employee Program were half as likely to be rehospitalized as a control group. Neurotic patients placed in the same program, however, showed no benefit.[18]

A British study aiming to compare the outcome for schizophrenics in work therapy and in occupational therapy (arts and crafts activities) placed 50 patients randomly in the two types of treatment. After six months the patients in work therapy showed greater willingness and ability to work and greater skills in forming relationships.[19]

Finally, a recent uncontrolled study conducted by the Colorado Division of Mental Health compared treatment requirements of patients who attended a sheltered workshop for any period of time from 1980 to 1983 with similar psychotic patients who were on the waiting list to enter the same workshop. The amount of treatment required was dramatically lower for the clients in sheltered employment—inpatient care was seven times less frequent and acute residential care proved four times less common.[20] These results must be viewed with considerable caution, however, in view of the non-random way in which the comparison groups were selected.

Overall, these studies show that working psychotic patients are more likely to stay out of hospital than unemployed patients and they *suggest* that employment may contribute to the patients' success. Work therapy also appears to offer some benefit to psychotic patients. The studies do not show, however, that working patients have fewer symptoms. The provision of work may improve the social functioning of psychotics, but it is not clear that it leads to symptomatic improvement. The definitive research on the latter point remains to be done. There is a good deal of evidence of an impressionistic or anecdotal nature, however, suggesting that patients' symptoms improve if they are working regularly. The following report provides an interesting example.

---

HELP WANTED: Ten factory workers wanted for private employment. Must have a history of mental illness to qualify.

---

The production work force of a toy company was recruited by this advertisement when it was run in a California newspaper in 1960. Eleven mentally ill applicants were hired; over half of them were schizophrenic, and all had been unemployed for a year or more. The work force proved to be efficient and, as the company expanded, more mentally ill people were hired. The company's personnel director, physician Ray Poindexter, reported

> that the type, severity, and duration of the mental illness was not related to job performance. Disappearance of symptoms accompanied the opportunity to perform for an employer who had confidence in his employees and whose success in business depended on their work.[21]

This illustration allows us to see that there is no contradiction between the repeated finding, on the one hand, that successfully employed patients may be highly disturbed[22] and the possibility, on the other hand, that the patient's condition may improve substantially with employment.

We may conclude, then, that the limited volume of clinical research provides moderate support for the central thesis of this book, which is based on macrostatistical data, that the availability of employment influences outcome in schizophrenia. If this thesis is correct, we must accept that improvement in the course of schizophrenia requires a change in the relationship between the psychotic and the labor force—a point which has been little recognized in psychiatry. How may such a change be achieved? The possibilities appear to be:

- the development of programs to improve the employment of the mentally ill in our current partial-employment society; or
- a return to a full-employment economy.

To what extent is either of these options possible?

## Vocational Rehabilitation Programs

At least a quarter of a million schizophrenics in the United States, we can estimate, are unemployed but potentially productive members of society. Sheltered work and other vocational placements are available for fewer than a tenth of these individuals.[23] While the situation in Britain is more satisfactory, sheltered work provisions for the mentally ill are also inadequate in that country.[24] The declining economy and the labor glut on both sides of the Atlantic stand in the way of improvement in these services.

### Sheltered Workshops
It has become clear that industrial therapy programs cannot exist without financial subsidies from government or other sources. Such programs use marginally productive workers and they cannot successfully compete for work on the open market against more efficient enterprises. This observation is

well accepted in Europe, but in the United States the hope persists that industrial therapy services can be profit-making or may, at least, break even.[25] Sheltered workshops ordinarily obtain work from industry by bidding for contracts. The work obtained is often a series of boring, repetitive tasks which would lead to high staff turnover under usual economic conditions if performed in-house by the private company's own employees. When business is in decline, however, such sources of work begin to dry up. Companies may cut back production, perform more work in-house, or go out of business. Competition for the remaining available contracts can become severe. Under these conditions sheltered workshops may go out of business, lower their bidding rates so far that they lose money, or cut back operations and lay off patient employees. In the sheltered workshop of the Mental Health Center of Boulder County, Colorado, for example, the number of clients employed fluctuates, with economic conditions, between 35 and 50; in hard times the waiting list for placement may be several months long.

Pressures against subsidizing sheltered work come from several directions. Labor unions complain about unfair competition; government agencies argue that state funds should not be used to subsidize private business (which is getting work done for well below cost) but only to provide rehabilitation services to the clients; and local mental health agencies, often not at all sure that they want to be offering sheltered work in the first instance, are quite unlikely to want to pay extra to keep it going. The result of these pressures is a tendency to screen out the lower-functioning clients, who require a greater subsidy, and to keep the more productive patients on the rolls.

There is a limit, moreover, to the extent that such workshops can subsidize their activities, for subsidized workshops end up competing with one another. 'In Wales, for instance,' report British rehabilitation specialists Nancy Wansbrough and Philip Cooper,

> Remploy [a subsidized company employing the disabled] and Blind Workshops were at one time fighting each other quite hard for contracts. Hospital Industrial Therapy Units were also thought to be accepting work at unrealistic prices and undercutting sheltered workshops of every sort.[26]

Under cut-throat conditions such as these it is not surprising that many sheltered workshops in Britain and the United States become financially insolvent and close down.

The working philosophy of most sheltered workshops for the mentally ill is borrowed from the field of rehabilitation of the physically disabled—clients should be evaluated, retrained and placed in appropriate employment within a limited period of time. For many psychotic clients this may be an appropriate approach; for others it is too optimistic. Unlike those with physical disabilities, some mentally ill clients can never function well enough to move into more demanding employment. Services in workshops for the mentally disabled, therefore, may need to be offered long-term or on repeated occasions depending on the client's current level of functioning.

Unfortunately, the employment available in such workshops is commonly the most boring and low-status work to be found. This is true, in part, because such is the kind of work which business makes available for contract, and partly because many clients prefer repetitive jobs—for those with concentration difficulties or interfering hallucinations this type of work may be a relief; but other patients, particularly those with higher levels of self-esteem, will not accept such work, or the low pay which they might earn. It is ironic that the most alienated members of our society, and those whose level of motivation to participate in any activity is often extremely low, should be required to perform the most alienating work—tasks so boring that no one else will do them.

## Client-Operated Businesses

Given the limitations of sheltered work, we might well expect that independent businesses operated by disabled clients would be a more satisfactory rehabilitation model. Such employment would hopefully be of higher status and more rewarding than a workshop, offer a greater variety of jobs, and be more adaptable to the clients' needs than competitive employment. A number of effective models, in fact, have been established along these lines.

Remploy is a company, established in Britian in 1945, which employs severely disabled people to produce a variety of goods. Among the products the company manufactures are furniture, knitwear, leather goods and textiles. In 1977, at eighty-seven factories distributed across the country, nearly 8,000 disabled people were employed. Of these, a fifth suffered from some kind of a mental disability, but most of these employees were neurotic or intellectually subnormal. Fewer than 5 per cent of all employees suffered from a psychosis. Twenty-two of the factories at that time employed no mentally disabled people at all.[27]

Some independent businesses have been established which employ only the mentally ill. George Fairweather and his colleagues, for example, created an innovative program of this type in the San Francisco Bay area of northern California. The positive results of their program were described earlier in this chapter. In 1963 a group of 15 chronic mental patients moved from hospital into a set of former motel buildings—the lodge. Initially under the direction of a psychologist, they organized themselves into work teams and contracted with area residents and businesses to provide janitorial and gardening services. Residents of the lodge assumed such tasks as business

275

manager and cook and, as professional supervision and financial support were progressively withdrawn, the lodge developed within a few years into an autonomous and self-sufficient business enterprise.[28] Several similar programs have since been established, from Anchorage, Alaska to Concord, New Hampshire, usually affiliated with state mental hospitals. They have achieved varying degrees of success. Few have developed to the same level of autonomy as Fairweather's original model, and some have closed down.[29]

Although not exclusively for the mentally ill, a similar residential work program has been developed in North London. The Peter Bedford Trust offers accommodation to unemployed and homeless single people who demonstrate an interest in working. The employment arm of the trust, John Bellars Ltd, hires the participants for cleaning, decorating and gardening activities. A substantial proportion of their work force is comprised of psychiatric patients.[30]

Small, non-residential, client-operated businesses have also been success-fully established. The community rehabilitation program, Fountain House, in Manhattan, New York, for example, has for many years operated a thrift shop (secondhand goods store) manned by community volunteers and by the clients.[31] Fast-food restaurants, laundries and shoe-repair stores have also been run along similar lines. In the London borough of Croydon, the industrial therapy unit operates an out-working scheme under which mobile work groups of clients fulfill a variety of contracts. The work includes tending the gardens of elderly residents of borough housing projects, concrete-laying and so on.[32] The Croydon program demonstrates that there may be little practical difference between some types of sheltered work and the less autonomous of the client-run business ventures.

Ultimately, in fact, client-operated businesses confront the same problems as sheltered workshops. The available work is often the most menial going—for a mobile work crew, in this instance, instead of a factory-based work force. True self-sufficiency, moreover, appears to be more or less unattainable. Fairweather's California lodge program almost collapsed when research funds were pulled out, and the project only survived because residents' earnings were supplemented by Veterans Administration pensions. Replica-tion projects of the lodge model have required substantial subsidies to survive.[33] Each year Remploy has to subsidize substantial business losses: in 1977 the difference between expenditure and income amounted to £16 million (around $38 million at that time). It would be cheaper, in fact, to put Remploy's disabled employees on social security than to keep them at work.[34]

We should not be misled into thinking that such businesses for the disabled are not cost-effective merely because they require financial subsidies. We must also take into account the likelihood of increased treatment expenses (including hospital care) and increased social costs (such

276

as involvement of the criminal justice system) if psychotic patients are left drifting idle and unsupported. We must recognize, however, that client-run ventures need money to operate—without it they cannot be established or maintained.

As economic conditions worsen, client-run businesses, like many small operations, are increasingly likely to fail. Fairweather recognized that his demonstration model lodge, begun in 1963, operated during a period of continuous expansion in the American economy and within range of a prosperous trading area. As such, it had unusual opportunities to flourish.[35] Later replication projects of his model have encountered trouble in finding contracts as times have become harder. In Britain, organizations which would like to follow the lead of the Peter Bedford Trust and John Bellars Ltd protest that suitable work cannot be found. Many of the successful British projects, in fact, have relied rather heavily on government sources of work. The core of the John Bellars program is office-cleaning contracts won from the Department of Health and Social Security and the London borough of Islington.[36] In Britain, government departments and nationalized industries, such as the Post Office and the Ministry of Defence, are required to give priority in the placement of contracts to institutions like Remploy which are supported by government funds.[37] In the United States, government contracts appear to be less commonly awarded to rehabilitation programs; the contract which the Denver lodge program has earned to clean houses repossessed by a government agency seems to be one of the few.[38] A scheme designed to award government contracts to sheltered workshops does exist in the United States, but it is burdened with red tape and initial investment requirements and is widely considered to be unworkable for the majority of small programs.

## Sheltered Employment in Industry

Higher-functioning, productive patients often make headway when they are placed in a job in a private business under close professional supervision. In the Transitional Employment Program of the Mental Health Center in Boulder, Colorado, up to ten clients occupy such slots. Some of these jobs are on the production line of a furniture factory, another involves office work and blueprint copying. The client receives close supervision from a Mental Health Center employee during the early stages of the job. For psychotic clients, such close attention may be essential for success. Under the stress of learning a new job and meeting new people psychotic symptoms often appear. The patient may feel co-workers are talking about him or her, for example, or plotting some harm; naturally, the patient is likely to quit. Help in adjusting to the job can avert such problems, and the professional supervision can also be reassuring to the employer and to other employees.

Such supervision becomes less necessary as the patient and everyone else involved become more comfortable. The placement is ordinarily for three months. At the end of that period the employee may be hired permanently by the company or he or she may move on to other competitive employment.

Supervised job openings, such as these, are not hard to develop, even during hard times. The program has several attractions for employers. Job-hiring costs and turnover are reduced. Job-training is done by the Mental Health Center employee. If the client-employee is unable to work one day, the Mental Health Center insures that someone else does the work, even if the Center staff member has to do it himself or herself. These jobs are often low-paid but essential to the production process, and the promise of reliability is of considerable benefit to the employer. The problem, indeed, is not so much in creating such job openings, but in finding clients who are productive and dependable enough to fill them.[39]

Similar programs have been successfully developed by many rehabilitation agencies. Fountain House in New York has around 150 transitional jobs in a variety of small businesses and large firms and banks. Most of these jobs are unskilled positions such as messenger, mail clerk and kitchen helper.[40] Sometimes groups of clients are placed in the same employment setting; when they work together as a permanent team, such sheltered working groups may be termed enclaves. These groups proved particularly successful for the rehabilitation of hospitalized chronic mental patients in the early stages of deinstitutionalization. At that time they were pioneered by the Bristol Industrial Therapy Organization in England[41] and the Veterans Administration Hospital in Brockton, Massachusetts.[42] These days group placements may be found in a number of businesses including a car-accessory company in Croydon, London,[43] a cafeteria in Chicago, and a department store in New York City.[44] In Britain, placements of this type have been declining due, in part, to the depressed economy and, in part, to difficulty in finding suitably high-functioning patients.[45]

## Patients as Volunteers

Patients who are not productive enough for a supervised placement in industry or for open employment can get job-training and build self-esteem by working as unpaid volunteers. This alternative may particularly appeal to those who find workshop employment too demeaning. In the community support system in Madison, Wisconsin, mental health staff find volunteer jobs for psychotic patients with local non-profit agencies. The mental health staff supervise the patient as he or she adjusts to the work in the same way that clients are followed in transitional employment programs.[46] A similar project has been developed at the Mental Health Center in Boulder. It is modeled after the Madison program but has reduced costs by using volunteers instead of paid staff to supervise the client in the volunteer placement.

The advantages of this type of program are numerous. The patient may choose employment which closely matches his or her interests—for example, library work, delivering meals to the elderly or helping to maintain public parks and forests—opportunites which might otherwise be unavailable. Working hours may be short and flexible and productivity pressure low. The patient, furthermore, does not run the risk of losing his or her disability income by earning too much money—a very real fear for many of the mentally ill.

Similar training programs which aim to place patients with voluntary and social agencies are offered by such rehabilitation centers as Council House in Pittsburgh and Thresholds in Chicago. Small amounts of incentive pay are awarded to the clients in these programs by the rehabilitation agency.[47]

Volunteer work is, perhaps, the only kind of vocational rehabilitation available to those mentally disabled who are less than fully productive which is not sharply limited by high levels of general unemployment. As the economy sickens and declines, government becomes more concerned with finding employment for the healthy and fully productive than for the disabled and marginal workers. If we wish to see just how comprehensive rehabilitation efforts for the mentally ill can become, we must look at a society with permanent full employment.

## Soviet Work Therapy

The Soviet emphasis on work therapy in psychiatry is not only a product of the Marxist ideology which fixes work as a central element in social life and individual development, but is also an understandable response to long-standing labor shortage. The aim of Soviet work therapy is not so much to keep the patient occupied as to train him or her to become productive.[48] 'For the worker who is hospitalized,' writes Mike Gorman, an American observer of Soviet psychiatry, 'the plan for his eventual return to a productive role in society is begun almost on the day of his admission.'[49]

Early in treatment the patient will be jointly assessed by the psychiatrist and industrial therapist and assigned to an appropriate task in the workshop. Sheltered workshops attached to neuropsychiatric dispensaries are available to inpatients and outpatients alike and are said to exist in all large cities in the Soviet Union. They constitute a major and integral component of the psychiatric treatment services. Patients are paid on a piece-rate scale comparable to that of private industry. The work available includes metal-manufacturing jobs, assembly work, shoemaking, sewing and weaving. Many work at home, deliver their finished product to the workshop and collect more raw materials. For those in the workshop, the working day is usually six hours or less. Soviet psychiatrists report that they encounter difficulties in motivating schizophrenics to work, but that focused efforts can be successful. Work therapy, the physicians believe, can lead to increased periods of remission from the illness and reduced need for medication.

In addition to the urban clinics and sheltered workshops, there are rural psychiatric colonies or work villages for severely disturbed patients. Here the work is largely agricultural, but residents may be employed at times by nearby industries or collective farms.

A patient may continue to work in a sheltered workshop for months or years, but the ultimate objective is to place him or her in permanent employment. Many progress to join invalid cooperatives. These special cooperatives are for both physically and mentally handicapped people. They generally produce small consumer goods and share earnings among the workers on a piece-rate basis. Earnings are in addition to a disability income. Each worker must meet a specified production norm.

Other patients return to work in the ordinary industrial workplace. Special district committees evaluate patients' working capacities and recommend placement. The factory manager usually accepts such recommendations. By law, a factory is obliged to rehire a person who worked there before falling ill, offering work suited to the person's current ability.

The psychiatrist and staff of the neuropsychiatric clinic visit the factory floor to follow their client's progress. Working through the labor union, they may attempt to adapt the patient's job to fit his condition. The worker may be switched, for example, to a different shift or type of work within the plant. Psychiatrists have unusual freedom to intervene in the workplace. 'For example,' writes American psychiatrist Simon Auster,

> when a psychiatrist notices a disproportionate number of patients coming from a single plant or office, he will visit the setting and evaluate it. When he feels that a change is needed, his recommendation is binding on the plant or office manager.[50]

While we may admire the Soviet system of psychiatric rehabilitation and the extent to which psychotic patients are reintegrated into mainstream society, we cannot hope to copy it. Their psychiatry is a reflection of their political economy, their ideology and their labor needs. In rehabilitating Western schizophrenics, we must set our sights lower. We must do so, that is, if we cannot establish full employment in our society.

## Can We Get Back to Full Employment?

Peacetime unemployment is a malaise peculiar to capitalism—a chronic condition afflicting many of the advanced market economies, with remissions of full employment being rare. It may well be that permanent full employment is incompatible with the capitalist mode of production: it may undermine labor discipline, decrease productivity, threaten profits, generate inflation and hinder the manning of new plants to an unacceptable degree.[51]

Why is it that in the centrally-planned economies of the Eastern Bloc, by way of contrast, full employment is the rule and urban unemployment rare? Socialist planning achieves this end by a series of measures many of which are not currently feasible under capitalism. By government control, for example, wages are kept well below the growth of labor productivity. This policy requires the strict limitation of independent labor organization—labor unions merely transmit government dictates to workers. In addition, administrative measures restrict the migration of rural workers to the cities. Right-to-work policies prevent the dismissal of even marginal workers, and huge state investment programs create industrial employment. As a consequence of these policies, the centrally-planned societies obtain full employment but incur the very costs which capitalists seek to avoid—poor labor discipline and productivity and disabling labor shortages.[52] On the other hand, they avoid the extremes of social inequality which are the product of a free market in labor.[53]

Can we create permanent full employment under capitalism? Economists of various political persuasions have called for measures, often similar to those applied in planned socialist societies, which might reduce unemployment, but in so doing they are often pessimistic about their proposals being adopted in the foreseeable future.

In *The Zero-Sum Society*, for example, liberal economist Lester Thurow argues that Americans *must* eliminate unemployment if they are to reduce the serious inequities and the relative deprivation of groups within their society. He proposes a permanent guaranteed jobs program which would assure adequate work and reasonable income for everyone who wants to work. The cost, he argues, would be balanced by savings in welfare payments, by the benefits from the completed public work projects and by new incentives for the creation of private sector employment.[54] In essence, Thurow's suggestion is equivalent to the socialist right-to-work policy. To institute such a policy, he agrees, would require a major restructuring of the economy, and he is not optimistic about his plan being adopted in the near future.

Other economists, moreover, argue that such a plan would not work. Subsidizing jobs and expanding public sector employment, they argue, would be costly and inefficient; it would increase taxes and inflation, reduce private sector growth and ultimately might backfire by creating more unemployment.[55] Conservative Harvard economist Martin Feldstein, for example, holds that modern high rates of unemployment coexist with wage and price inflation because government aid programs have divorced incomes from work effort. In consequence, argues Feldstein, workers will not accept available jobs.[56]

In a similar vein, supply-side economists such as Milton Friedman and his colleagues of the Chicago School contend that policies which promote low unemployment *now* can only lead to high unemployment *later*. They argue that there is a 'natural' rate of unemployment to the economy; to force unemployment below this level is to create inflation and to push the actual rate of unemployment higher. The natural unemployment rate, they suggest, can only be reduced by removing obstacles to the free market in labor through such measures as repealing minimum-wage laws and by getting rid of restrictive union practices.[57]

Mainstream economist Paul Samuelson suggests that before the strategies proposed by Friedman and his associates could achieve a new, low-unemployment equilibrium, 'the system may well have been torn apart by voter revolt, urban riots, and unemployment-induced hardships and dissatisfactions.'[58] Nevertheless, Samuelson himself sees that 'larger and larger amounts of unemployment are now needed to have the same wage and price restraining effect as in the past.'[59] The root cause, as he sees it, 'lies in the fact that we no longer run the cruel economy that was taken for granted in the days of unbridled laissez-faire.'[60] Samuelson refuses to accept that we must turn to a more cruel exploitation of the worker. Instead he calls for structural reforms which are humane but allow more flexibility in wage-setting. Precisely what form a successful incomes policy of this type should take, however, he is unable to say.[61]

Many mainstream economists argue that the only sound strategy for reducing unemployment is to encourage the market sector of the economy to generate more employment. To achieve this end, British economist Kevin Hawkins calls for an incomes policy, cutbacks in government subsidies and increased incentives to investors and businessmen with the ultimate goal being an increase in industrial productivity. He does not foresee the economy expanding fast enough, however, for the demand for labor ever to catch up with the supply, particularly in view of the progressive decline in the use of labor in manufacturing industry in the advanced countries.[62]

Like others, British economists Maurice Scott and Robert Laslett see the cause for pessimism over the possibility of reducing unemployment in the failure to control wage increases. In *Can We Get Back to Full Employment?* they reason that full employment requires not only a reflation of demand, increasing profits and an increase in labor-using types of investment, but also wage increases would need to be kept down to the same level as the growth in labor productivity. Here they are proposing something similar to the 'rational low wage policy' which is central to state socialist methods of maintaining full employment. Such a policy, Scott and Laslett point out, would require major changes in trade union approaches to wage negotiation.[63]

Ultimately, as in the Eastern Bloc, trade unions would lose autonomy and would be required to act in concert with government policy. Such a possibility seems distant.

Peter Jay, economics editor of *The Times*, agrees that trade union bargaining has the effect of creating a monopoly price for labor and leads ultimately to inflation and unemployment. Pointing out that incomes policies never work for long, he proposes a more radical solution—to replace private enterprise by worker cooperatives. Ownership and control of businesses should be transferred to the people who work in them, he suggests, and such ventures would then have to sink or swim in the market economy. On the scale envisioned by Jay—so universal that corporate state, trade union and economic bureaucracy would 'wither away'— such a radical development is not close upon the horizon.[64]

A socialist prescription for economic recovery put forward by American economists Barry Bluestone and Bennett Harrison also calls for increased worker ownership of industry. In addition, they stress the need for government planning for emerging and declining industries and much greater public control over production and investment decisions. Bluestone and Harrison concede, however, that their proposals leave unanswered the great questions of how to control inflation, how to gain the cooperation of private capital and how to finance the called-for improvements in social security for workers. They assume, moreover, the development of broad political support for such a plan in the 1980s and 1990s in reaction to current, conservative, *laissez-faire* policies—a move further to the left than the American public has ever before ventured.[65]

We should not rule out any potential solution to the problem of unemployment purely on the basis that it would require major changes in the economic system. As economist Robert Heilbroner points out, capitalism has changed dramatically during this century. Government intervention, for example, has become essential to the workings of the system and central planning will almost certainly become a more prominent aspect of the economy. Through the coming decades exhaustion of basic resources and the constraints of the environment must lead to fundamental changes in a system which requires exponential growth as a precondition for health.[66]

As changes occur, however, and as trade-offs of one benefit for another take place, as they must, it is not at all clear that the loudest call will be for full employment rather than, say, price stability or lower taxes. Nor can we be sure that we will ever return again to a simple definition of full employment as work for everyone who wants to work. Economists now variously define full employment as the rate of unemployment which is high enough to provoke government to reflate the economy or, again, the level at which real wages fall sufficiently to induce employers to expand recruitment. By such measures the definition of full employment rose from around 1½

283

per cent unemployment in the postwar years to close to 4 or even 6 per cent in the late 1970s.[67] In the future the number of people considered unemployable by virtue of age, physical and mental handicap, lack of training or interest in working may expand a great deal.

Whichever set of solutions we might consider the most likely to be adopted, it is apparent that full employment is not just around the corner. Nor, it seems, are comprehensive employment opportunities for schizophrenics.

## Summary

- Clinical research indicates that psychotic patients who are working stay out of hospital longer than unemployed patients.
- The research suggests (but does not prove) that employment may be the cause of the patient's better functioning.
- There is no evidence in the clinical research that working leads to an improvement in the symptoms of psychosis.
- Work therapy appears to benefit psychotic patients.
- Long-term sheltered work is necessary for many of the mentally ill.
- Both sheltered work and client-run businesses become less viable as the economy declines.
- Volunteer work may be the only secure occupation for marginally functional psychotics during hard times.
- Labor shortages in the USSR are a spur to the development of comprehensive psychiatric rehabilitation services.
- None of the potential methods for creating full employment in Western society seems likely to be effective in the near future.

284

# 12 Desegregating Schizophrenia

It is easy to tell horror stories, and there are plenty in this book. It is harder to come up with ways to alleviate the plight of the mentally ill in the Western world. How can we help schizophrenics re-enter society as it is presently structured and achieve a genuine degree of social integration? In this chapter we will look at practical answers to this question.

## Community Support Systems

The treatment programs of the Mental Health Center of Boulder County, Colorado, will frequently be used as examples. They illustrate what is possible given the usual level of community mental health funding[1] and a commitment to providing decent care for the most seriously ill patients. This center, like a number of others across the United States, has been designated as a model community support system for severely disturbed patients by the US National Institute of Mental Health.

The range of services and programs which may be offered by a community support system is illustrated in Figure 12.1. The functions of such a system may be succinctly expressed by the following commandments. The treatment agency shall:

- adopt total responsibility for the severely disabled client's welfare, including helping the patient acquire such material resources as food, shelter, clothing and medical care;
- aggressively pursue the client's interests—insuring that other social agencies fulfill their obligations, for example, or actively searching for patients who drop out of treatment;
- provide a range of supportive services which can be tailored to fit each patient's needs and which will continue as long as they are needed;
- educate the patient to live and work in the community; and
- offer support to family, friends and community members.[2]

Community support, then, comprises everything the old, long-stay institutions used to furnish and a host of additional services besides, which are essential for community tenure. By these means, if they are all supplied, we may virtually eliminate the revolving-door phenomenon.

285

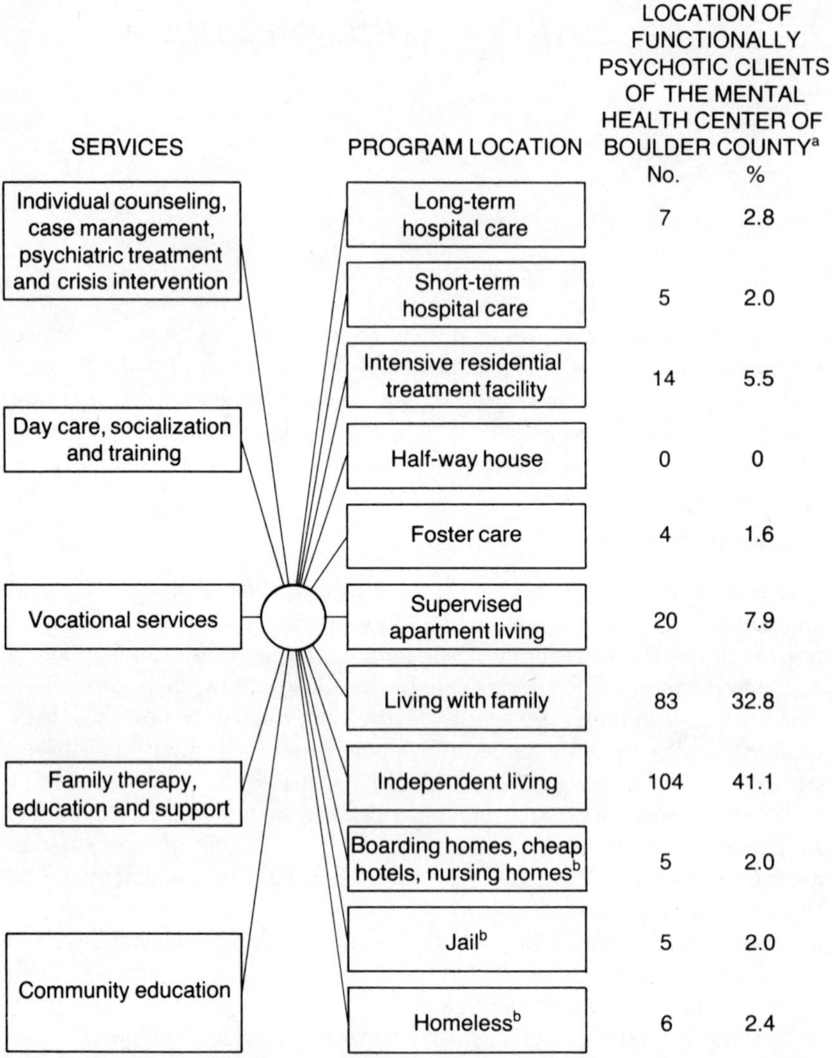

| SERVICES | PROGRAM LOCATION | LOCATION OF FUNCTIONALLY PSYCHOTIC CLIENTS OF THE MENTAL HEALTH CENTER OF BOULDER COUNTY[a] | |
|---|---|---|---|
| | | No. | % |
| Individual counseling, case management, psychiatric treatment and crisis intervention | Long-term hospital care | 7 | 2.8 |
| | Short-term hospital care | 5 | 2.0 |
| | Intensive residential treatment facility | 14 | 5.5 |
| Day care, socialization and training | Half-way house | 0 | 0 |
| | Foster care | 4 | 1.6 |
| Vocational services | Supervised apartment living | 20 | 7.9 |
| | Living with family | 83 | 32.8 |
| Family therapy, education and support | Independent living | 104 | 41.1 |
| | Boarding homes, cheap hotels, nursing homes[b] | 5 | 2.0 |
| | Jail[b] | 5 | 2.0 |
| Community education | Homeless[b] | 6 | 2.4 |

*Figure 12.1 Components of a community support system*

Note: [a] On September 30, 1983.
    [b] These are living situations to be avoided: the principal goal of the treatment service should be to arrange for the patient's transfer to a more therapeutic setting.

Keeping the patient in the community, however, does not necessarily mean that he or she, in any real sense, is recovered (though it may well help in that recovery). Required in addition, as the earlier chapters have argued, are efforts to raise the degraded social status of the schizophrenic, to offer him or her a meaningful role in life leading to a sense of worth and a reduction of alienation. Given these criteria, treatment becomes more than just a matter of providing services to patients and their relatives—it becomes social action, political lobbying and community education directed towards the desegregation of a minority group.

## Escaping the Ghetto

The ghettoes of the long-term mentally ill are the nursing homes, the inner-city boarding homes and the Skid Row missions. How do we help patients escape? In Boulder County the mental health center places no physically healthy schizophrenics in nursing homes. (In 1983, the center's staff treated four functionally psychotic patients who were living in nursing homes because of ill health or who were placed there by other agencies.) In fact, the administrators of the center have actively discouraged local nursing home operators from opening wards for chronically ill psychiatric patients, arguing that nursing homes cannot provide an adequate quality of care and environment for such patients. Elsewhere mental health center personnel have welcomed nursing homes as valuable 'community resources' and cost-saving alternatives to hospital care. Even Richard Lamb, a well-known community psychiatrist working in California, noted for his criticism of board and care homes, has espoused the value of 'L facilities'—locked, private establishments with up to a hundred residents, essentially similar to locked nursing homes.[3] If we are concerned to achieve better social integration, status and outcome for schizophrenic patients, however, such establishments are to be avoided.

In Boulder County there are no boarding homes housing the mentally ill (though there is a cheap hotel which clients have used on occasion), and when patients are located living on the streets or in a reception center, efforts are made to accommodate them in one of the residential facilities described below.

## Intensive Residential Treatment

Cedar House is a large house for sixteen psychiatric patients in a residential and business district of the city of Boulder. It functions as both an alternative to a psychiatric hospital and as a half-way house. Like a psychiatric hospital it offers all the usual diagnostic and treatment services but, costing less than a third of private hospital treatment, it is feasible for patients to remain in residence for quite long periods of time if necessary. Usually admitted with some kind of an acute psychiatric problem (most often an acute psychotic relapse), a client may stay anywhere from a day to a year; the average period is around three weeks.

Unlike a psychiatric hospital, Cedar House is non-coercive. No patient can be strapped down, locked in or medicated unwillingly. Staff must encourage patients to comply voluntarily with treatment requirements and house rules. The people who cannot be managed are those who repeatedly walk away or run away and those who are violent. Since the alternative for patients who are unable to stay at Cedar House is hospital treatment, which none prefers, the large majority of residents accept the necessary restrictions. Very few patients, as we shall see, need to be transferred to hospital. In practice, virtually all clients with schizophrenia or psychotic depression can be treated at Cedar House through all phases of their illness, and many patients with acute mania can also be managed successfully. There is no doubt that a large number of the people treated in this residential facility would be subject to coercive measures, such as restraints or seclusion, if they were admitted to a hospital where such approaches are available and routinely used. The avoidance of coercion is the first step in maintaining the psychotic patient's status and self-esteem. As the moral-treatment advocates recognized, to cultivate the patient's self-control is to elicit his or her collaboration in treatment.

Like the York Retreat, also, the environment is similar to that of a middle-class home, not a hospital. The floors are carpeted, a fire burns in the hearth, two cats curl up in the most comfortable chairs, shelves of books are available, residents and visitors come and go fairly freely, staff and patients interact casually, eat together and are encouraged to treat one another with mutual respect. As in Tuke's establishment, the goal is to allow therapists and clients alike to retain their dignity and humanity and to foster cooperation.

In line with this emphasis, each resident is intimately involved in running the household. He or she is responsible for specific tasks which are assigned and supervised by one of the residents. These cooperative living arangements reduce treatment costs, increase the resident's sense of belonging and can be useful training for marginally functional people. A full-scale, therapeutic community style of patient government has not been established. In view of the relatively brief length of patient stay and the necessity for staff and administration to exercise close control over patient admission and discharge (in order to make room for new acute admissions at all times) patient government is not considered workable. The ethos of the community, however, calls for residents routinely to assist in the care of others.

Residential treatment of this intensity requires a staffing pattern similar to that of a hospital. A mental health worker and a nurse are on duty at all times. At night, one of the two is awake and the other sleeps. On weekdays, three experienced therapists (one of them half-time) work with the patients. A psychiatrist is present for three hours a day, a psychologist directs the program and a secretarial assistant manages the office work and the purchasing of household supplies. The treatment setting calls for staff who are tolerant and empathic and it brings out their capacity independently to find inventive solutions to difficult problems.

There is no commonly used form of psychiatric treatment (except for electro-convulsive therapy) and no diagnostic measure which cannot be provided for residents of this treatment facility. Patients with acute or chronic organic brain disorders, for example, can be evaluated using the laboratories and diagnostic equipment of local hospitals. Consulting physicians provide treatment for medical problems.

An essential step in the treatment of people entering Cedar House is the evaluation of the patient's social system. What has happened to bring the patient in for treatment at this particular time? What are his or her financial circumstances, living arrangements and work situation? Have there been recent changes? Are there family tensions? From the answers to such questions as these, a plan may be made which will hopefully diminish the chances of relapse after the patient leaves residential treatment.

In some cases the solution may be straightforward. The patient has been living on the street, sleeping in doorways on cold nights, and eating out of garbage cans. Floridly psychotic at the time of admission, he (or, more rarely, she) may show few positive features of illness after a day or two of warmth and good food. This person needs help in applying for welfare entitlements, finding a place to live and, probably, a lot of supervision while settling into a new pattern of living. Another patient may relapse into acute psychosis after starting a job or losing one. He or she needs vocational assistance.

Other situations can be more difficult to ameliorate. A patient and his or her family members may be at loggerheads, periodically inflaming one another to psychotic outbursts, on the one hand, or angry rejection on the other; yet none of the parties wishes to separate. Although the patient is calm and well while in residential treatment, meticulous family negotiations may be necessary before the patient can be discharged.

A substantial majority of such seriously disturbed psychotic patients will benefit from taking some kind of psychoactive medication. The period of residential treatment allows the opportunity to spend time observing the patient's illness and selecting the most suitable drug (an antipsychotic may not be the best choice), monitoring and adjusting the dosage to minimize side effects and evaluating the benefits. An added advantage of the more leisurely pace of residential treatment (compared with brief hospitalization), as outlined in Chapter 10, is that it allows an opportunity for selected psychotic patients to be treated without drugs.

What has been described so far is just one approach to the community treatment of the acutely ill psychotic patients—an intensive residential treatment program. Various mental health agencies have developed other excellent methods for treating such clients during the acute phase of their illness. Two of these will be described next.

## Foster Care for the Acutely Ill

As part of Southwest Denver Community Mental Health Services in Colorado, Canadian community psychiatrist Paul Polak and his team have developed an innovative method of caring for the acutely psychotic patient. They have found several families in the neighborhood who are willing to take one or two acutely disturbed patients into their homes. Nurses, a psychiatrist and other staff from the mental health agency work with the foster family to provide care and treatment for the disturbed person. The patient's own family may also participate. Medications are used freely and are closely monitored by the medical staff. The average length of stay for such patients is ten days, after which some patients move on to a less intensively supervised apartment for a longer stay.

Foster families are chosen for their warmth and acceptance. Each client is given his or her own room and is treated as a guest. When able, the patient helps with shopping, cooking and household tasks. Often he or she will become friendly with the foster family and may remain in touch through telephone calls, letters or visits.

This program, which does everything possible to maintain the client's status and connection with the community, has proved to be workable and effective. In operation for over a decade, it is a viable alternative to hospital care for all but a handful of patients. A two-year study using random assignment of patients showed that the community homes were more effective in some respects than a psychiatric hospital in providing intensive treatment, one important advantage being that clients treated in the family homes felt better about themselves and their treatment.[4]

## Intensive Community Support

Another approach to the problem of caring for the most severely disturbed psychotic patients is to follow them so closely in the community—providing support at every step—that psychotic relapse is more or less eliminated. Leonard Stein, an American community psychiatrist, May Ann Test, a social worker, and their colleagues in Madison, Wisconsin, have put such a program into effect. Available twenty-four hours a day, seven days a week, mental health staff visit patients in their own homes and workplaces. They help their chronically mentally ill clients learn to do laundry, shopping, cooking, grooming and budgeting. They assist them in finding work and in settling disputes with their supervisors. If a patient does not show up for work or treatment one day, the staff member goes to his or her home to

290

discover the reason. Staff help patients to expand their social lives and to make good use of their leisure time and they also provide support to the patients' families. Early signs of the return of psychosis are immediately detected and lead to active treatment measures. In essence, the patient is watched and helped as closely as he or she would be on many hospital wards, but the treatment is provided instead in the patient's own neighborhood.

When these measures fail, the patient may be admitted briefly to hospital; such a move is rarely necessary, however. In a study of the course of illness in patients referred for admission to hospital with a severe psychiatric problem, it was found that nearly all of those randomly assigned to the Madison intensive community treatment program could be treated without hospital care; of the patients assigned to standard community mental health center care, on the other hand, nearly all were initially treated in hospital. At the end of a year the rate of readmission to hospital was 6 per cent for clients of the intensive community treatment team, in contrast to 58 per cent for patients in routine mental health center care. Mobile and intensive community treatment had put a stop to the revolving door.

The clients in this program reaped other benefits. Compared with the patients in standard community care, they had fewer symptoms, greater self-esteem and were more satisfied with their lives after one year of treatment. They were more likely to be living independently and had spent less time in jail.[5] This was accomplished, furthermore, with no increase in social cost to the patient's family or the community; there was no increased burden of social disruption or suicidal gestures.[6]

There is a popular school of thought in mental health which holds that treatment progams providing the comprehensive level of support to be found in Dr Stein's program are harmful to the patient; they supposedly discourage self-sufficiency. Such a view is similar to the prevalent American fear of the 'welfare mentality,' and has its roots in the Protestant ethic and the reverence for individualism which flourishes under capitalism. It overlooks the plain fact that many chronically psychotic patients are very severely handicapped. Without constant support they cannot maintain a bearable existence. The study of Dr Stein's program demonstrates this point. Given intensive support, these patients functioned better, but when they were transferred back to routine mental health center care at the end of 14 months of intensive support, their clinical condition and social functioning again deteriorated. After a few months they were faring as poorly as those who had been receiving standard care all along, *but no worse.* Their capacity for independent functioning had not been undermined, it had merely returned to baseline.

## Which Program?

We have now examined three programs aimed at boosting both the social functioning and self-esteem of the most severely disabled psychotic patients. All three rely upon the cost savings from reduced use of expensive psychiatric hospital beds to make the programs viable, but no mental health center with the usual current level of funding could afford to establish all of these programs; nor would such a plan be advisable since these are alternative approaches for treating the same group of clients. Each program has its merits and deficits. Which one should be used in which circumstances?

Cedar House is a relatively expensive program. The required level of staffing imposes high fixed costs which cannot be reduced without seriously altering the nature of the program. Such costs would not be justifiable for an agency with a small catchment area (much below 200,000 persons). For small agencies and scattered populations, either the family care program or the mobile treatment team would be more suitable. With the fixed costs of Cedar House, as available funding decreases, cuts have to be made instead in outpatient services and other parts of the community support system with consequent deterioration in continuity of care. In these circumstances the result could be the creation of a new type of revolving-door patient—one who repeatedly re-enters the residential community facility. By comparison with the foster care and intensive community treatment programs, further-more, it is more institutional. By treating patients a stage further removed from their usual surroundings it may be somewhat more like a hospital in stigmatizing and dehumanizing its clientele.

On the other hand, the two programs which are more deeply immersed in the community rely more heavily upon drug treatment for their success. Each of the programs instituted by Dr Stein and Dr Polak and their respective co-workers uses rapid tranquilization—a technique of administering substantial, incremental does of antipsychotic medication—in the treatment of acute episodes of illness. Periods of hospitalization have to be brief; psychotic behavior must be efficiently brought under control if the patient is to remain in the community. As mentioned previously, the intensive residential program allows treatment decisions, including decisions on the use of medications, to be taken at a more measured pace and it offers the possibility of drug-free treatment in selected cases. These features, in and of themselves, some would consider to be humanizing forces.

## Do We Need Psychiatric Hospitals?

In the 1960s politicians and mental health professionals alike were heralding the death of the psychiatric hospital—but it is still with us. Does it serve a useful purpose? Even using one of the intensive community treatment programs described above, there remains a handful of patients who cannot be adequately cared for outside a hospital. A few patients, for example, consistently refuse any type of treatment and will always walk away from an open-door establishment; a few become violent at times and, if they fail to improve with treatment, they represent a danger to mental health staff and members of the public. Some psychotics routinely exacerbate their condition by the constant abuse of hallucinogenic drugs, by heavy drinking or by sniffing glue and volatile solvents.

Attempts to treat such patients in the community are quite likely to fail. These psychotics will be found in jail, held for minor offenses; they will be committed by the criminal courts to forensic psychiatric hospitals for more serious offenses; or they will end up living on the streets, leading lives of degradation and becoming physically debilitated. The effort to help such patients, nevertheless, will have put an immense strain on the community support system. Many hours of work will have been put into makeshift treatment plans which have little hope of success. Some treatment agencies solve the problem by housing such clients in locked nursing homes, but this alternative can never be considered satisfactory.

The number of patients that cannot be treated in the community is extremely small, however. During 1983, around half a dozen psychotic patients from Boulder County were in long-term, public hospital care, placed there by the mental health center. Another half a dozen psychotic mental health center patients, at any time, are likely to be receiving medium- or short-term hospital treatment (lasting from a few days to six months) before returning to community care. These patients are drawn from a county population of close to 200,000 persons and a caseload of over 1,200 mental health center patients. The number of patients in long-term hospital care emerges as less than 3 per cent of all the functionally psychotic patients in treatment at the mental health center.[7]

It is important to identify these few clients and arrange for them to receive hospital care as the humane course of treatment. This may be easier said than done. Long-term hospital care in the United States is virtually a thing of the past. State budget cuts have so reduced hospital capacity that the ward staff feel obliged to discharge any patient who loses his or her psychotic symptoms regardless of what the patient's trajectory is likely to be after release. Those who are not well enough to be discharged are often transferred to a locked nursing home. Community mental health administrators must first fight to see a bare sufficiency of hospital beds funded; and then they must stand firm against the pressure to discharge from the hospital patients who cannot be properly treated once they leave.

If community support services were provided on a truly comprehensive basis, we would only need small hospitals but they would serve a highly specialized function. Based on the experience in Boulder and elsewhere, only two or three hospital beds for adults (aged 18–60) would be needed for each 10,000 of the general population. (Mental health staff working with the population of large cities might arrive at a higher estimate for the number of

293

required hospital beds.) The large majority of the patients, however, would be long-term and highly resistant or unresponsive to treatment. Locked doors would be necessary for many of these clients, but their hopes for improvement would depend upon their being provided with work therapy; a range of varied but low-stress recreational activities; skilled, humane care in small attractive units; and access to a pleasant, open-air environment. In other words, they would be as unlike nursing homes as it is possible for such places to be.

## Supervised Apartments

Like one's job, a powerful indicator of status is one's living environment. The unemployed schizophrenic, unless living with his or her family, is likely to occupy seedy, low-rent rooms, a boarding house or a nursing home. Many, having fallen ill early in life, have little experience of independent living. Some have poor judgement and lack the capacity to manage a household. For such people, supervised and subsidized housing is a necessity.

Several mental health agencies have demonstrated that cooperative apartments (or group homes, as they are often called) work well for chronically ill patients who are leaving mental hospital after several years of residence. Replicating a system established by the Littlemore Hospital in Oxford, England, British community psychiatrist Hilary Sandall set up Places for People—supervised apartments for patients leaving St Louis State Hospital in Missouri—in the early 1970s. Hospital staff would locate a suitable apartment in a lower- to middle-class area of the city and a small group of men or women who knew one another in the hospital would move in. The staff members visited the home regularly and were available at all hours to the residents, their families and to the landlords. The staff members helped the patients with every aspect of household management, gradually decreasing their involvement as the residents developed autonomy.[8]

The same system has been shown to be viable also for young adult psychotic patients who have not spent years in mental hospitals. Apartment programs for such clients exist in Fareham, England,[9] for example, in Madison, Wisconsin, and in Boulder, Colorado. For these patients, however, often more volatile, disruptive and subject to relapse, a more intensive level of supervision is required. In the Boulder supervised living program, staff members hold house meetings for the residents at least once weekly in their apartments and provide individual outpatient counseling in addition. The therapist may have to give a great deal of assistance with budgeting and, in some cases, actually manage the patient's money. Help with household management often includes sorting out problems with 'crashers'—initially welcome guests who end up exploiting the residents or stealing from them. The advantage of such group living is that it offers a substitute family to clients who may have difficulties in setting up a stable family of their own or in living with their parents. Achieving amiable domestic relations, however, may require the therapist to arbitrate a considerable number of disputes.

For many schizophrenics, living alone is the best arrangement—the stresses of cooperative living may provoke relapse; others find loneliness to be a major problem. Supervised apartments in Boulder range in size from one- to eight-person households. At some of the larger houses a university student is hired to live-in (rent free) and to provide a little supervision in the evenings. These larger houses can accommodate clients who have more limited capacity for independent living. By supplying increasing amounts of staff support on the premises it is possible to develop a range of community living arrangements up to the level of the traditional, staffed half-way house, for clients with progressively lower levels of functioning.

In high-rent Boulder, some form of rent subsidy is necessary for clients who must often exist on limited Social Security income. Such financial assistance is available through the federal Department of Housing and Urban Development, either as direct rent subsidies or as grants to mental health agencies to build or buy new accommodation. Interested members of the public have also provided houses at reduced rental for mental health center clients. In most instances, the center operates as a tenant, subleasing the house or apartment to the patients.

## Long-term Foster Care

Many patients who have not yet developed the ability to live independently may do well in long-term foster care. Dr Polak's short-term foster care program was established to treat acutely ill patients. In other mental health programs, however, a client moves in to live with a foster family when his or her condition is stable and may stay as long as he or she wishes. Fort Logan Mental Health Center in Denver, Colorado, has successfully operated such a system of family care for many years. Their clients often graduate to independent living. The boarding-out schemes in operation in Salisbury and in Hampshire, England, are similar.[10]

## Small Is Beautiful

There is an important common quality to each of the model treatment programs discussed so far—the setting is small. This factor can have a powerful influence upon the patient's social role and sense of worth. Where there are relatively few members of a group the contribution of each is seen as correspondingly more important. Students in small high schools, for example, have been found to have a better developed sense of responsibility and usefulness than students of large schools. In the small schools each student is more likely to be relied upon to contribute to sporting events, the band, dramatic productions and similar activities. Studies have shown that people in small settings such as these are more active and that they tackle more varied, difficult and useful tasks. In consequence, they feel challenged, valued and better satisfied with themselves.[11]

A patient living in a small community setting, therefore, where he or she is called upon to contribute to the operation of the household, will be more valued for any special abilities and will develop greater self-esteem and practical skills. More than this, he or she will be better accepted and socially integrated. As in the Third World village, where there is no labor surplus, it is necessary to accept those who are available to do the job. Where there are more people than are strictly required, the research of psychologist Roger Barker reveals, deviance and individual differences are not tolerated nearly as well.[12] This is one reason why boarding homes and nursing homes containing scores or hundreds of patients have such a pernicious influence on the course of schizophrenia.

## Cars

In a similar vein to improving the housing for the mentally ill, one might conceivably aim to improve the status of patients by helping them obtain cars. Very few chronically ill patients in the United States own any means of transportation—an unusual and disabling phenomenon in American society, restricting the disadvantaged person's residential options and employment prospects. Would substantial changes in self-concept and functioning occur if patients were given cars or given incentives to buy them?

For those with some hope of finding a job, such a measure might facilitate re-employment. In Poland, after rehabilitation a worker is provided with a car adapted to his needs. An employment demonstration project at a US rehabilitation hospital used wage supplements to encourage the purchase of private cars and achieved a high employment placement and better functioning amongst those clients who bought cars.[13] There is every reason to suppose that equally good results would emerge from a similar program for the mentally disabled.

On the practical side, nevertheless, such a program is scarcely feasible for a community mental health agency in hard times. In the first instance, the cost could not be justified while there are still patients with inadequate living arrangements and community support (and there are many). Secondly, in the depression few enough psychotic patients have any employment prospects to improve. Finally, most patients live in poverty and would sell a car if they had one in order to buy more basic necessities. A private hospital with rich clients or a mental health agency in a full-employment economy, however, might consider putting this idea into effect.

## Income Maintenance

A more straightforward way to improve the status of the mentally ill might be to raise them out of poverty. Participation in the mainstream of society is scarcely possible on a meager disability allowance (around $320 a month in the United States in 1984). The poverty of schizophrenics, however, is merely one example of the marked inequity of American society. If we were to respond to economist Lester Thurow's call for a minimum income which would never fall below half that of the average citizen,[14] the lives of many would be less degrading. The income of US schizophrenics receiving disability payments would double.[15] Able to live more like the rest of society, many of the mentally ill might have a greater interest in living independently. Until then the hospital (or acute treatment facility), with its promise of adequate food and shelter, human society and escape from the stresses of urban poverty, will be distinctly attractive, and many patients will pass through its revolving doors.

## Jail

Harmful and degrading though it is, increasing numbers pf psychotics are ending up in US local jails (as described in Chapter 8). To mitigate this problem it is important that mental health agencies supply outreach services to jails in their catchment areas. The object of such programs should be to arrange the transfer of all psychotic inmates to an appropriate treatment setting. This goal requires the development of working relationships with criminal court judges. Only in those rare instances when a judge will not release a mentally ill person because the crime is too serious, or when a psychotic inmate refuses to be transferred to a treatment setting and is too mildly disturbed for involuntary measures, should we resort to treating psychotics behind bars.

It has, in fact, become routine in most areas of the United States for psychotics to be treated in jail with antipsychotic drugs and to be detained for extended periods—largely because the public mental hospitals are filled to capacity and offer only brief care. Often the psychotics who spend most time in jail are those who have proved particularly difficult to treat in community programs. An important task of community mental health administrators, therefore, after insuring that they have done as much as they can to provide effective community support, is to put pressure on their legislators to maintain the adequacy and capacity of the public psychiatric hospitals.

Commonly embraced by mental health professionals is the notion that jail is good for certain psychotic patients. The 'structure' of the correctional institution is reassuring to the patient, they argue, and he (rarely she) will 'learn the consequences of his actions.' Needless to say, this is not a point of view which is given much credence by jail staff. Correctional workers (despite their title) are often justifiably pessimistic about the benefits of imprisonment for many of their charges. Such doubt is nowhere more appropriate than in the case of psychotic jail inmates whose crimes are so often a product of the poor judgment or poverty which flow from their illnesses. Correctional staff know, for example, that many of the psychotics who enter their jail do *not* learn from experience: they cycle through repeatedly for the same offenses, sometimes merely to gain shelter which they cannot obtain in any other way. Correctional staff also know that most psychotic inmates do *not* respond to the institutional structure; they are so resistant, in fact, to the usual controls that they spend their entire period of incarceration locked into solitary cells in order that they may be restrained from provoking violence among the inmates or protected from abuse and exploitation.

## Day Care

In the United States and Britain day care is one of the most widespread forms of community treatment for the mentally ill. If we are concerned with improving the community standing and integration of these patients, however, many of these programs will be found wanting. Writing of British practice, psychiatrist Mounir Ekdawi concludes,

> Severely disabled people attending a day unit have often led dependent, institutional lives for many years; nevertheless, it often seems that their past hospital experience was, if anything, richer and more socially stimulating.[16]

For many patients, day care offers a welcome release from an otherwise aimless existence. In a society where many of the mentally ill serve no useful function, the daily program of activities gives them somewhere to go and something to do which is more worth while than sitting at home watching daytime television or wandering the streets. Increasingly, day programs come to fill the void left by the lack of open employment opportunities or the shortage of sheltered work placements.

On a more positive note, day care can provide social activities for patients who would be unemployed at the best of times and otherwise isolated and friendless. Such programs can provide training in basic domestic and social skills, but this type of training, in fact, is often more effective when provided to the patient in his or her own home and neighborhood. To the mental

298

health agency, day care is a cost-efficient way of monitoring patients' progress and spotting the appearance of symptoms. Comprehensive vocational programs, however, can serve this function equally well.

A day program is most likely to be effective in building clients' self-esteem and in improving their social functioning and community integration when it is small in size and when it makes full use of facilities for the general public such as recreation centers and cinemas. Richard Lamb describes a program, for example, in which a number of patients enrolled in a local adult education department and participated in developing their own educational curriculum.[17] An emphasis on productive and goal-orientated activities is valuable (talent shows or community services), and events scheduled for the evening hours offer the advantage of being available to those clients who are working during the day.

## Psychotherapy

Serious questions have been raised as to the efficacy of psychotherapy in general and as to its value in schizophrenia in particular. Certainly most therapists would agree that insight-oriented, uncovering psychotherapy has a restricted application in psychosis and that environmental considerations and various types of drug treatment are usually of more immediate relevance. None of the treatment approaches discussed so far would be possible, however, without some of the basic ingredients of psychotherapy. The schizophrenic and the therapist must be able to form a relationship of mutual trust and to work through disagreements which arise between them in the course of treatment. The therapist should also be able to help the patient resolve conflicts with other people which may surface. The patient should feel free to discuss concerns about his or her life, illness and treatment. Where denial is preventing the patient from recognizing problems, the therapist must be able to approach the issues sensitively; and where resistance holds the patient back from a useful course of action, the therapist must attempt to uncover the reasons.

In other words, while social considerations and drug therapy are important, they must be humanized if the schizophrenic is to re-enter society. As psychiatrists John Strauss and William Carpenter argue,

> Therapeutic goals must extend far beyond achievement of symptom relief and prevention of relapse and rehospitalization. The most devastating aspect of much of schizophrenia is the defect state with its incapacities in social, work and psychological function.[18]

It has been argued in the foregoing pages, however, that much of this 'defect state' may be attributed to the purposeless lifestyle and second-class citizenship of the schizophrenic. As with any other disadvantaged group, to combat alienation therapy must in part be consciousness-raising. The patient should come to see his or her low self-concept as a product of the larger society. Depression and withdrawal may be merely the characteristic response of the unemployed person. Diminished spontaneity and enthusiasm can be the outgrowths of an aimless existence. Negativism may be little more than the recognition of the unequal power and status of patient and therapist—a reaction to the social control function of psychiatry.

The impotent and impoverished nature of the mental patient's life may explain the desire of so many to drop out of treatment and to escape into the richness of the psychotic experience. In the words of John Strauss and William Carpenter, they seek

> the sense of power from impulsivity, the enthrallment with perplexity, the smugness of the grandiose, the comforting organization of delusions, the companionship provided by hallucinations, the excitement of suspiciousness, and the importance of the self-referential.[19]

If reality is to appear more inviting than psychosis, the patient and therapist must examine not only those aspects of psychosis which the client finds positive but also the true poverty of the schizophrenic's existence.

To achieve desegregation, the mentally ill must first confront their debased status. As in any process of consciousness-raising they should expose, though sharing of experiences, the hidden social indicators of power and status—to discuss openly the subtle influences of stigma. They should be encouraged to join professionals in coordinated action to improve the social conditions and treatment of the mentally ill. Some years ago, for example, psychiatrist Hilary Sandall joined her patients at St Louis State Hospital, Missouri, in a demonstration against the transfer of some of their number to a psychosurgery ward of the institution. This is political action as psychotherapy.

Mental health professionals, however, are handicapped in their capacity to help raise the group consciousness of the mentally ill, for the professionals themselves are an integral part of the system which can breed oppression. The therapist's job security, for example, may depend upon the ability of the mental health agency to cut treatment costs for the indigent but severely ill. The lawyers who join with patients in class-action suits against the involuntary administration of medication, or against cuts in services for the mentally disabled are, in their way, providing an effective form of psychotherapy which is not available to mental health professionals.

The frustration of failure inherent in working in an inadequate system of care can lead staff to feel a degree of contempt for their clients. Such an attitude can be expressed in jokes which attribute animal characteristics to their psychotic patients or as more subtle forms of denigration. Sociologist David Rosenhan, for example, revealed that hospital staff often fail to respond to a patient's question, passing by as if the inquirer were not present.[20] Therapy which hopes to increase the schizophrenic person's sense of worth must begin with respect; and professionals with the greatest authority within a treatment agency are under the heaviest obligation to demonstrate respect for the clientele on all occasions. In a similar vein, therapy should aspire to identify and emphasize the patient's special strengths and individuality and not merely aim to control pathology.

An important element in avoiding frustration in therapy for the patient, relatives and therapist alike is to set suitable expectations. Like the moral-treatment pioneers, we should look for a certain level of self-control and performance from the psychotic patient, but goals must be achievable. The client should not be encouraged to apply for work which is beyond his or her current capacity; the family should be warned that the ambitions for their relative may need to be restricted in every sphere; and the therapist should not see the patient's occasional relapse as a failure. The therapist who leads his or her client to believe that a sufficient degree of insight through counseling will result in a removal of the illness is being over-optimistic.

Similarly, while the patient may be given the hope that one day medication will be unneccessary, such an option should not be seen as an end in itself. The patient's goals should be to do well and to feel good—the medication is a tool towards that end. The patient, however, may identify the medicine with the illness and see it as a stigmatizing and controlling force (which it often is, of course). To get around this problem one may do a number of things—help the patient identify certain goals and the extent to which medication can assist in reaching them; discuss the patient's reaction to the illness, to the medication, to control and to stigma as separate but related issues; and delegate to the patient authority over his or her own medications at the earliest workable opportunity so that he or she can set the dosage to achieve the desired benefit.

The schizophrenic patient does not respond well to ambiguity in therapy or to a neutral and distant therapist. Communication should be straight-forward, expectations clear-cut and the therapist should not hesitate to act as a role-model for the patient. Psychotic experiences may be discussed frankly, not necessarily to uncover dynamic origins, but more to alleviate the client's fears and perplexity about them and to identify stresses which provoke their appearance. The emphasis in therapy, though, needs to be on problems in daily living—work, personal and family relationships, finances and accommodation—and a major goal of treatment should be the reduction of stress in these areas.

Paradoxically, the therapist for psychotic clients will find that he or she is encouraging many patients that they can overcome their disability and accomplish more, while he or she must persuade the others that they suffer from an illness and should accept restrictions and limit their horizons. As

301

argued in Chapter 8, this phenomenon is exacerbated by the stigma of mental illness. To consider oneself both mentally ill and capable creates cognitive dissonance: patients tend either to accept the label of mental illness and adopt the associated stereotype of incompetence or they reject the notion that they are ill or disabled. The solution is to proceed slowly and to avoid confronting the receptive patient too harshly with success and to avoid vigorously attacking the denial of the patient who rejects the illness label.

Herein lies one of the potential advantages of group therapy for psychotic patients. Cognitive-dissonance research demonstrates that people are more likely to change their attitudes if they can be encouraged to express in public an opinion different from their usual belief. By bringing together in a therapy group psychotic patients who variously accept or reject the illness label and who have a variety of levels of functioning, one may hope that the less competent patients will accept the possibility of becoming more capable and that those who deny their illness will change their opinion. The danger, of course, is that all the patients will become equally stigmatized and incapable, but this is where the therapy comes in. A group focus on practical accomplishments and the development of social skills is indicated. A review of the research on the effectiveness of group psychotherapy for outpatient psychotics suggests, in fact, that such treatment is particularly valuable in boosting both the clients' levels of social functioning and their morale.[21]

## Family Therapy

While individual and group psychotherapy are universally applied in the treatment of schizophrenia—useful integrating forces which are sometimes overrated and sometimes undervalued—family therapy is an often neglected approach. This neglect is the more indefensible in light of the evidence that family therapy can be as effective in the treatment of schizophrenia as the antipsychotic drugs. From the outset, however, it should be clear that family therapy, here, does not mean efforts to uncover the root cause of the psychosis in family dynamics. As indicated in Chapter 1, there is little evidence to suggest that family pathology contributes to the *development* of schizophrenia. The successful family therapy programs, rather, have concentrated upon the influence of the family environment on the *course* of the condition, and have relied heavily upon practical support and education as the essential ingredients.

In Chapter 10, the research conducted by Julian Leff and his associates in London on the family environment of schizophrenics was reviewed in some detail. These researchers have shown that schizophrenic patients who return to a home in which their relatives are critical and overinvolved have a higher relapse rate than those who return to a low-stress home. The greater the proportion of time the patient spends with high-stress relatives, the greater the risk of relapse. Dr Leff and his co-workers have since conducted a study to evaluate whether the relapse rate of schizophrenics in high-stress households can be reduced by (a) helping the relatives become less hostile and intrusive or (b) decreasing the amount of contact between the patient and his relatives.

The research workers randomly divided into two groups a number of schizophrenics whose relatives had been identified as being critical and overinvolved. One group received routine follow-up care; the other, experimental group joined a family therapy program. The patients in both groups, all of whom were at high risk of relapse, were taking antipsychotic medication. The family treatment comprised (a) a series of sessions of education about mental illness, (b) participation in a relatives' group, and (c) individual family therapy conducted in the patient's home. The relatives' group, which was the central component of the program, offered support for the relatives, who often felt isolated and lonely; practical strategizing for those who were having trouble coping with difficult behavior; and role-playing to assist in the development of new attitudes.

With these forms of assistance, about half of the high-stress families had switched to expressing low levels of criticism or overinvolvement within nine months. In several families, also, contact between patients and high-stress relatives had been markedly reduced so that, overall, only about a quarter of the families in the experimental group remained high-stress households where the patient was still in contact for substantial amounts of time. Such beneficial changes had only rarely taken place in the control group.

In the experiental families where the desired changes had occurred, no patient relapsed within the first nine months. In the remaining families one patient relapsed. By contrast, half of the patients in the control group had relapsed—a high rate of relapse which was predictable from the researchers' earlier work. If we look back to Figure 10.2, we may see that antipsychotic drugs reduce the rate of relapse in schizophrenics spending large amounts of time in high-stress households from a virtual certainty to a 50–50 chance. Now we see that family intervention can change the stress pattern of such a household and almost eliminate the remaining risk (at least over a nine-month period).[22]

Confirmation of these results comes from California where New Zealand psychiatrist Ian Falloon and colleagues conducted a similar study. As in the London study, the researchers gathered a group of schizophrenic patients who were in close daily contact with relatives who had been rated (using the same technique as Dr Leff's group) as high in criticism and overinvolvement. The patients were randomly assigned to family therapy or individual psychotherapy. All patients received drug treatment. Again, as in the British study, the family therapy was conducted in the home and began with a series of educational sessions. At the end of nine months well over half of the patients in family therapy were free of symptoms whereas fewer than a quarter of those in individual psychotherapy had improved to this level. Only 11 per cent of the patients in family therapy had been readmitted to hospital, but half of the patients in individual treatment had been readmitted.[23]

The similarity between the results in the two studies is striking. In each case a roughly 50 per cent chance of relapse for schizophrenics in a high-risk family setting has been almost eliminated. A broad review of the research on family therapy in psychosis, in fact, suggests that it has repeatedly been found to be of value.[24] We should conclude that to withhold family assistance where we can identify high levels of stress is equivalent to withholding drug treatment from patients who we know will do poorly without it.

## Family Education and Support

We have seen, however, that the critical and intrusive family which has a detrimental effect on the lives of Western schizophrenics is far less common in the Third World city where similar research has been done than it is in the West.[25] Such family responses may indeed be a product of nuclear-family living, of the isolation of the Western family due to stigma, and of the high performance expectations and parental ambitions for schizophrenics which are generated in an industrial economy. If the domestic environment of schizophrenics can be influenced in this way by political economy, our patterns of intervention should, perhaps, begin to take the form of social change rather than therapy. 'Therapy' implies pathology and, hence, blame. Other approaches can be less stigmatizing and can enhance the desegregation of the schizophrenic's family.

Education for the relatives of the mentally ill, for example, and for psychotic patients themselves, can be provided as an evening class. Such courses, initially devised and organized by mental health professionals Pamela Hiner and Konnie Kindle, have been run regularly at the Mental Health Center of Boulder County. An outline of the topics for one series of classes is set out in Table 12.1 Such a course can be run at low cost, for the speakers may be drawn from volunteers among professionals in both the public and private sectors. For the teacher, the class is an agreeable experience; rarely does one encounter students so hungry for knowledge and so interested in the subject matter.

For the students, the class is more than an educational program. On each occasion the course has been run, the participants have gained great support from the informal sharing of experiences—the recognition that they are not alone, that other people have found strategies for the problems with which they have been struggling in isolation. With no specific direction from the

304

**Table 12.1  A course on major mental illness for family members of the mentally ill**

| CLASS* | TOPIC |
|---|---|
| 1 | The diagnosis of schizophrenia and manic-depressive illness |
| 2 | The causes of major mental illness |
| 3 | The prognosis of major mental illness |
| 4 | Medications |
| 5 | Community treatment of mental illness |
| 6 | Mental illness and the law |
| 7 | Treatment in the private sector |
| 8 | Recent research in mental illness |
| 9 | Psychotherapy for psychotics |
| 10 | Family support and treatment |
| 11 | Work and the mentally ill |
| 12 | Social services and housing |
| 13 | Public policy, funding and political action |

* Each class runs for 90 minutes.

mental health professionals, the relatives form themselves into a self-help group.

## Alliances for the Mentally Ill

Such groups move directly into social activism. An initial step is 'coming out of the closet,' for in solidarity lies the strength to combat stigma and exploitation. The first educational course for relatives taught in Boulder led to the formation of a formal organization of relatives of the mentally ill. This association, like many similar groups around the nation, has since grown in size and influence, and is now a local chapter of the National Alliance for the Mentally Ill. The parent organization is similar in character to the National Schizophrenia Fellowship in Britain.

The accomplishments of the Boulder Alliance for the Mentally Ill are impressive and serve as an illustration of the potential power of such interest groups. The organization has promoted media coverage on major mental illness including newspaper features on psychotic patients living in the community. It has suggested program needs to the mental health agency and helped to fund a supervised living project for psychotic patients. Through its meetings and a newsletter it has given support and education to many families, and by placing members on community boards it has influenced agency policies. The state-level organization has lobbied the legislature to increase mental health funding and has given backing to a class-action suit on behalf of a number of patients whose community treatment programs were being eliminated. At the national level the Alliance for the Mentally Ill has successfully fought the Reagan administration's efforts to cut back Social Security disability payments—a policy which was resulting in large numbers of the chronically mentally ill losing their only means of support.

In Britain the National Schizophrenia Fellowship, established a few years earlier than its American counterpart, has been similarly active in providing emotional support for its members, lobbying for needed services, fostering public education and sponsoring research. Its publications have covered such topics as inadequate services, mental health law and the importance of work for the mentally disabled.[26]

The mentally ill have never had a powerful lobby. Until recently only mental health professionals, who can be accused of self-interest, have argued for their needs. Now that their relatives are uniting, we have grounds for optimism that the conditions for seriously disturbed patients will improve, or at least be protected from the gathering economic storm. However successful their political efforts, the fight is worth it; for the struggle itself will educate the public, decrease stigma and bring the schizophrenic and his or her family further into the mainstream of society.

## Community Education

Although the mentally ill have been in the community for nearly three decades, we have scarcely begun to educate the public about the nature of major mental illness. Some community mental health professionals, it is true, have taken this task seriously. Leonard Stein in Madison, Wisconsin, for example, talked to downtown shopkeepers about their concerns that the eccentric behavior of discharged mental patients would affect business. (Dr Stein defended the patients' right to be different.) Our use of the media, however, has been very restricted.

Newspaper coverage of mental illness is generally limited to reports of crimes committed by 'former mental patients' or, more rarely, shocking disclosures of the degraded conditions of the deinstitutionalized mentally ill. Organizations such as the Alliance for the Mentally Ill and the National Schizophrenia Fellowship have appreciated that a more sensitive portrayal of mental illness is required if the associated stigma is to be lifted.

To this end, a series of radio programs were produced with the support of the Boulder Alliance for the Mentally Ill, which attempted to reveal the human side of psychosis. Parents of a schizophrenic man talk about their son's illness, in one program, describing both his disturbed behavior and his talents—revealing their love for him and their sense of tragic loss. In other programs, patients describe the inner world of psychosis and the frustrations of trying to be understood, of trying to get help and of mere survival.[27] Such first-hand accounts are moving—for those who hear them. Most radio stations, unfortunately, are not interested; the material does not fit with the usual programming.

We have far to go before the schizophrenic is welcome in Western society and before he or she can view himself or herself as an equal and useful member of society. Until that time schizophrenia is likely to continue to be a malignant condition.

We have the knowledge, nevertheless, to render the illness benign. We would need to:

- provide guaranteed jobs and training for the mentally disabled—work which is neither too demeaning nor too stressful;
- treat the acute phase of the illness in small, non-coercive settings which reflect the humane principles of moral treatment;
- insure adequate psychological and clinical support in the community, including a full range of independent and supervised, non-institutional accommodation;
- provide adequate material support, including an income which allows a decent status and standard of living;
- give recognition and support for the care offered by the schizophrenic's family, and provide family education and counseling;
- fight for the rights of schizophrenics and their families to participate as fully integrated members of society, taking the issue before the public through the media;
- use the antipsychotic drugs as a supplement to these measures, not as a substitute for them.

Such an effort might cost little more than our current, vast expenditure on the treatment and support of schizophrenics and on the associated disruption, crime and imprisonment which result from inadequate care. Our society is inherently unequal, however, and to provide such a quality of life for the schizophrenic is not feasible since such a large proportion of the population—including an army of unemployed—would be left in worse circumstances. To render schizophrenia benign we may, in essence, have to restructure Western society.

## Appendix: Psychiatric hospital beds and social indicators for nine Western industrial nations and seven centrally-planned economies

| | PSYCHIATRIC HOSPITAL BEDS (PER 10,000 POPULATION) | | | | UNEMPLOYMENT FIVE-YEAR AVERAGE[b] (%) | | | | PER CAPITA GNP (1979 US $) | | | | INFANT MORTALITY PER 1,000 LIVE BIRTHS | | | | POPULATION OVER AGE 65 (%) | | |
|---|---|---|---|---|---|---|---|---|---|---|---|---|---|---|---|---|---|---|---|
| | 1965 | 1968 | 1971 | 1974 | 1961–5 | 1964–8 | 1967–71 | 1970–4 | 1965 | 1967–8[c] | 1970 | 1974 | 1965 | 1968 | 1971 | 1974 | 1964–6 | 1969–71[d] | 1974–7 |
| *Western Industrial Nations* | | | | | | | | | | | | | | | | | | | |
| Australia | 27.1 | 24.3 | 21.6 | 20.7 | 2.1 | 1.5 | 1.6 | 2.2 | 5801 | 6398 | 6995 | 7874 | 18.5 | 17.8 | 17.3 | 16.1 | 8.4 | 8.3 | 9.0 |
| Canada | 35.9 | 30.2 | 26.2 | 21.8 | 5.4 | 4.1 | 4.9 | 5.8 | 6070 | 6538 | 7006 | 8497 | 23.6 | 20.8 | 17.5 | 15.0 | 7.6 | 7.9 | 8.0 |
| France | 20.5 | 21.9 | 23.0 | — | 1.5 | 1.9 | 2.5 | 2.8 | 6304 | 7173 | 8042 | 9508 | 21.9 | 20.4 | 17.1 | 14.7 | 12.2 | 12.9 | 13.0 |
| Germany, West | 17.7 | 18.2 | 18.7 | 17.8 | 0.5 | 0.7 | 1.0 | 1.0 | 7908 | 8719 | 9531 | 10681 | 23.9 | 22.8 | 23.3 | 21.1 | 12.0 | 13.2 | 14.0 |
| Italy | 22.4 | 21.8 | 20.9 | 20.9 | 2.9 | 3.3 | 3.3 | 3.2 | 3568 | 4086 | 4604 | 5243 | 35.6 | 32.7 | 28.5 | 22.6 | 9.9 | 10.6 | 12.0 |
| Japan | 13.3 | 16.8 | 18.0 | 18.4 | 1.3 | 1.3 | 1.2 | 1.3 | 3633 | 4908 | 6154 | 7425 | 18.5 | 15.3 | 12.4 | 10.8 | 6.4 | 7.1 | 8.0 |
| Sweden | 35.4 | 43.2 | 42.2 | 40.5 | 1.5 | 1.7 | 2.1 | 2.3 | 9374 | 10170 | 10966 | 11835 | 13.3 | 13.0 | 11.1 | 9.2 | 12.8 | 13.7 | 15.0 |
| UK | 28.5[a] | 26.2[a] | 23.8[a] | 31.9[a] | 2.6 | 2.7 | 3.3 | 3.3 | 5348 | 5595 | 5852 | 6529 | 19.0[a] | 18.3[a] | 17.5[a] | 16.3[a] | 12.3 | 13.0 | 14.0 |
| USA | 31.1 | 32.0 | 24.1 | 14.2 | 5.7 | 4.2 | 4.3 | 5.4 | 7873 | 8280 | 8688 | 9577 | 24.7 | 21.8 | 19.1 | 16.7 | 9.5 | 9.8 | 11.0 |

*Centrally-Planned Economies*

| | | | | | | | | | | | | | | | | | | | | | |
|---|---|---|---|---|---|---|---|---|---|---|---|---|---|---|---|---|---|---|---|---|---|
| Bulgaria | 4.2 | 5.3 | — | — | — | — | — | — | — | — | 1866 | 2093 | 2320 | 2645 | 30.8 | 28.3 | 24.9 | 25.5 | 8.5 | 9.6 | 11.0 |
| Czechoslovakia | 11.7 | 11.7 | 11.3 | 11.3 | — | — | — | — | — | — | 3567 | 3866 | 4165 | 4692 | 25.5 | 22.2 | 21.7 | 20.4 | 9.9 | 11.3 | 12.0 |
| Germany, East | 18.2 | — | — | 18.9 | — | — | — | — | — | — | 3412 | 3693 | 3974 | 4558 | 24.8 | 20.2 | 18.0 | 15.9 | 14.6 | 15.5 | 16.0 |
| Hungary | 2.4 | — | — | — | — | — | — | — | — | — | 2335 | 2449 | 2664 | 3039 | 38.8 | 35.8 | 35.1 | 34.3 | 10.2 | 11.5 | 13.0 |
| Poland | — | 11.9 | 12.2 | 12.1 | — | — | — | — | — | — | 2042 | 2226 | 2441 | 3069 | 41.7 | 33.4 | 29.5 | 23.7 | 7.0 | 8.3 | 10.0 |
| Romania | 3.1 | 3.7 | 5.0 | 7.0 | — | — | — | — | — | — | 1824 | 2000 | 2177 | 2804 | 44.1 | 59.5 | 42.4 | 35.0 | 7.6 | 8.6 | 9.0 |
| USSR | 9.9 | 9.8 | — | — | — | — | — | — | — | — | 3354 | 3713 | 4072 | 4913 | 27.6 | 26.4 | 22.6 | 27.7 | 7.3 | 7.8 | 9.0 |

Sources: Psychiatric hospital beds (except USSR) and infant mortality: World Health Organization, *World Health Statistics Annuals, 1964–77*, vol. I, III, Geneva: 1967–77; USSR psychiatric hospital beds (1962 figure): Field M. G. and Aronson, J., 'Soviet community mental health services and work therapy,' *Community Mental Health Journal*, 1: 81–90, 1965; (1968 figure): Gorman, M., 'Soviet psychiatry and the Russian citizen,' *International Journal of Psychiatry*, 8: 841–57, 1969; Unemployment: Sorrentino, C., 'Unemployment in international perspective,' in B. Showler and A. Sinfield (eds), *The Workless State*, Oxford: Martin Robertson, 1980; Per capita GNP: CIA National Foreign Assessment Center, *Handbook of Economic Statistics 1980*, Washington, DC: US Government Printing Office, 1980; Population over age 65: World Bank, *World Tables: The Second Edition*, Baltimore: Johns Hopkins University Press, 1980.

Notes: [a] Figure for England and Wales.
[b] Unemployment statistics are adjusted to US concepts to render them comparable.
[c] Per capita GNP for 1967–8 is an estimate derived from the mean of the figures for 1965 and 1970.
[d] Population over age 65 for 1969–71 has been used as the closest available data for both 1968 and 1971.

# *Notes*

## Introduction
1 See the preface to Marx, K., *A Contribution to the Critique of Political Economy*, New York: International Publishers, 1970; first published in 1859. Also Harris, M., *Cultural Materialism: The Struggle for a Science of Culture*, New York: Random House, 1979.

## 1 What is Schizophrenia?
1 Lee, R.B., '!Kung bushman subsistence: An input-output analysis,' in A.P. Vayda, (ed.), *Environment and Cultural Behavior: Ecological Studies in Cultural Anthropology*, Garden City, New York: Natural History Press, 1969, pp. 47–9.
2 This is a broad definition of political economy as is commonly used in anthropology. It is drawn from Harris, M., *Culture, Man, and Nature*, New York: Thomas Y. Crowell, 1971, p. 145. Similarly broad definitions may be found in Lange, O., *Political Economy*, vol. 1, New York: Macmillan, 1959 ('Political economy is concerned with the social laws of production and distribution'); and in Marshall, A., *Principles of Economics*, 8th edn, London: Macmillan, 1920, p. 1 ('Economics is a study of mankind in the ordinary business of life: it examines that part of individual and social action which is most closely connected with the attainment and with the use of material requisites of well being').
3 Szasz, T.S., *The Myth of Mental Illness: Foundations of a Theory of Personal Conduct*, revised edn, New York: Harper & Row, 1974.
4 American Psychiatric Association, *Diagnostic and Statistical Manual of Mental Disorders*, 3rd edn (DSM-III), Washington, DC, 1980.
5 Kraepelin, E., *Dementia Praecox and Paraphrenia*, Edinburgh: Livingstone, 1919, pp. 38–43.
6 Leff, J., *Psychiatry Around the Globe: A Transcultural View*, New York: Marcel Dekker, 1981, ch. 5.
7 Bleuler, E., *Dementia Praecox, or the Group of Schizophrenias*, translated by J. Zinkin, New York: International Universities Press, 1950. The German language edition first appeared in 1911.
8 Ibid., pp. 246–7.
9 Ibid., p. 248.
10 Ibid., pp. 258–9.
11 Ibid., p. 471.
12 Ibid., p. 475.
13 Ibid., p. 476.

14 Ibid., p. 471.
15 Ibid., p. 472.
16 Ibid., p. 480.
17 Ibid., p. 478.
18 Ibid., p. 479.
19 Langfeldt, G., 'The prognosis in schizophrenia and the factors influencing the course of the disease,' *Acta Psychiatrica et Neurologica Scandinavica*, supplement 13, 1937.
20 Leff, op. cit., pp. 37–40; Wing, J.K., *Reasoning About Madness*, New York: Oxford University Press, 1978.
21 Cooper, J.E., Kendell, J.E., Gurland, B.J. et al., *Psychiatric Diagnosis in New York and London*, Maudsley Monograph Number 20, London: Oxford University Press, 1972.
22 World Health Organization, *The International Pilot Study of Schizophrenia*, vol. 1, Geneva, 1973.
23 Cade, J.F.J., 'Lithium salts in the treatment of psychotic excitement,' *Medical Journal of Australia*, 36: 349 et seq., 1949.
24 Schou, M., Juel-Nielsen, N., Stromgren, E. and Voldby, H., 'The treatment of manic psychoses by the administration of lithium salts,' *Journal of Neurology, Neurosurgery and Psychiatry*, 17: 250 et seq., 1954.
25 Fieve, R.R., 'Lithium therapy,' in H.I. Kaplan, A.M. Freedman and B.J. Sadock (eds), *Comprehensive Textbook of Psychiatry-III*, vol. 3, Baltimore: Williams & Wilkins, 1980, pp. 2348–52. The reference is to p. 2348.
26 American Psychiatric Association, *DSM-III*, pp. 181–203.
27 Taylor, M.A. and Abrams, R., 'The prevalence of schizophrenia: A reassessment using modern diagnostic criteria,' *American Journal of Psychiatry*, 135: 945–8, 1978; Helzer, J., 'Prevalence studies in schizophrenia,' presented at the World Psychiatric Association Regional Meeting, New York, October 30–November 3, 1981; Endicott, J., Nee, J., Fleiss, J. et al., 'Diagnostic criteria for schizophrenia: Reliabilities and agreement between systems,' *Archives of General Psychiatry*, 39: 884–9, 1982.
28 Ciompi, L., 'Catamnestic long-term study on the course of life and aging of schizophrenics,' *Schizophrenia Bulletin*, 6: 606–18, 1980.
29 Kiev, A., *Transcultural Psychiatry*, New York: Free Press, 1972, p. 45.
30 Strauss, J.S. and Carpenter, W.T., *Schizophrenia*, New York: Plenum, 1981, ch. 2.
31 Weiner, H., 'Schizophrenia: Etiology,' in Kaplan, Freedman and Sadock (eds), *Comprehensive Textbook of Psychiatry-III*, vol. 2, pp. 1121–52. The reference is to p. 1124.
32 Heston, L.L., 'Psychiatric disorders in foster-home-reared children of schizophrenic mothers,' *British Journal of Psychiatry*, 112: 819 et seq., 1966; Kety, S.S., Rosenthal, D., Wender, P.H. and Shulsinger, F., 'The types and prevalence of mental illness in the biological and adoptive families of adopted schizophrenics,' in D. Rosenthal and S.S. Kety (eds), *The Transmission of Schizophrenia*, Oxford: Pergamon, 1968, pp. 345 et seq.; Kety, S.S., Rosenthal, D., Wender, P.H. et al., 'Mental illness in the biological and adoptive families of adopted individuals who have become schizophrenic,' in R.R. Fieve, D. Rosenthal and H. Brill (eds),

311

*Genetic Research in Psychiatry*, Baltimore: Johns Hopkins University Press, 1975, pp. 147 et seq.

33 Twin studies of the inheritance of schizophrenia are summarized in Rainer, J.D., 'Genetics and psychiatry,' in Kaplan, Freedman and Sadock (eds), *Comprehensive Textbook of Psychiatry-III*, vol. 1, pp. 135–54. The reference is to pp. 147–8.

34 Kallman, F.J., 'The genetic theory of schizophrenia,' *American Journal of Psychiatry*, 103: 309 et seq., 1946.

35 Kringlen, E., 'An epidemiological-clinical twin study of schizophrenia,' in Rosenthal and Kety (eds), *The Transmission of Schizophrenia*, pp. 49 et seq.

36 Meltzer, H.Y. and Stahl, S.M., 'The dopamine hypothesis of schizophrenia: A review,' *Schizophrenia Bulletin*, 2: 19–76, 1976; Haracz, J.L., 'The dopamine hypothesis: An overview of studies with schizophrenic patients,' *Schizophrenia Bulletin*, 8: 438–69, 1982.

37 Rosengarten, H. and Friedhoff, A.J., 'A review of recent studies of the biosynthesis and excretion of hallucinogens formed by methylation of neuro-transmitters or related substances,' *Schizophrenia Bulletin*, 2: 90–105, 1976.

38 Strauss and Carpenter, *Schizophrenia*, ch. 7.

39 Stevens, J.R., 'Neuropathology of schizophrenia,' *Archives of General Psychiatry*, 39: 1131–9, 1982.

40 For a list of references to this topic see Weinburger, D.R., DeLisi, L.E., Perman, G.P. et al., 'Computer tomography in schizophreniform disorder and other acute psychiatric disorders,' *Archives of General Psychiatry*, 39: 778–83, 1982.

41 Ibid.

42 Nasrallah, H.A., Jacoby, C.G., McCalley-Whitters, M. and Kuperman, S., 'Cerebral ventricular enlargement in subtypes of chronic schizophrenia,' *Archives of General Psychiatry*, 39: 774–7, 1982.

43 Weinburger et al., 'Computed tomography in schizophreniform disorder,' p. 782.

44 Joseph, M.H., Frith, C.D., and Waddington, J.L., 'Dopaminergic mechanisms and cognitive deficit in schizophrenia: A neurobiological model,' *Psychophar-macology*, 63: 273–80, 1979; Strauss and Carpenter, *Schizophrenia*, ch. 7; Weiner, 'Schizophrenia: Etiology,' pp. 1134–5.

45 Lawrence, D.H., *Apocalypse and the Writings on Revelation*, Cambridge: Cambridge University Press, 1980, p. 149. *Apocalypse* was first published in 1931.

46 Cooper, D., *The Death of the Family*, New York: Vintage Books, 1971.

47 Fromm-Reichmann, F., 'Notes on the development of treatment of schizophrenia by psychoanalytic psychotherapy,' *Psychiatry*, 11: 263–73, 1948.

48 Lidz, T., Fleck, S. and Cornelison, A., *Schizophrenia and the Family*, New York: International Universities Press, 1965.

49 Bateson, G., Jackson, D., Haley, J. and Weakland, J., 'Towards a theory of schizophrenia,' *Behavioral Science*, 1: 251–64, 1956.

50 Laing, R.D. and Esterton, A., *Sanity, Madness and the Family: Families of Schizophrenics*, Baltimore: Penguin Books, 1970.

51 Wynne, L.C. and Singer, M., 'Thought disorder and family relations,' *Archives*

*of General Psychiatry*, 9: 199–206, 1963.
52 Hirsch, S. and Leff, J., *Abnormality in Parents of Schizophrenics*, London: Oxford University Press, 1975.
53 Woodward, J. and Goldstein, M., 'Communication deviance in the families of schizophrenics: A comment on the misuse of analysis of covariance,' *Science*, 197: 1096–7, 1977.
54 Brown, G.W., Birley, J.L.T. and Wing, J.K., 'Influence of family life on the course of schizophrenic disorders: A replication,' *British Journal of Psychiatry*, 121: 241–58, 1972; Vaughn, C.E. and Leff, J.P., 'The influence of family and social factors on the course of psychiatric illness: A comparison of schizophrenic and depressed neurotic patients,' *British Journal of Psychiatry*, 129: 125–37, 1976.
55 Tarrier, N., Vaughn, C.E., Lader, M.H. and Leff, J.P., 'Bodily reaction to people and events in schizophrenics,' *Archives of General Psychiatry*, 36: 311–15, 1979; Sturgeon, D., Kuipers, L., Berkowitz, R. et al., 'Psychophysiological responses of schizophrenic patients to high and low expressed emotion relatives,' *British Journal of Psychiatry*, 138: 40–5, 1981.
56 Cheek, F.E., 'Family interaction patterns and convalescent adjustment of the schizophrenic,' *Archives of General Psychiatry*, 13: 138–47, 1965; Angermeyer, M.C., ' "Normal deviance": Changing norms under abnormal circumstances,' presented at the Seventh World Congress of Psychiatry, Vienna, July 11–16, 1983.
57 Wig, N.N., Menon, D.K. and Bedi, H., 'Coping with schizophrenic patients in developing countries,' presented at the Seventh World Congress of Psychiatry, Vienna, July 11–16, 1983.
58 Brown, G.W. and Birley, J.L.T., 'Crises and life changes and the onset of schizophrenia,' *Journal of Health and Social Behavior*, 9: 203–14, 1968.
59 Jacobs, S. and Myers, J., 'Recent life events and acute schizophrenic psychosis: A controlled study,' *Journal of Nervous and Mental Disease*, 162: 75–87, 1976.
60 Dohrenwend, B. and Egri, G., 'Recent stressful life events and episodes of schizophrenia,' *Schizophrenia Bulletin*, 7: 12–23, 1981; Andrews, G. and Tennant, C., 'Life event stress and psychiatric illness,' *Psychological Medicine*, 8: 545–9, 1978.

## 2 Health, Illness and the Economy

1 Thompson, E.P., *The Making of the English Working Class*, New York: Vintage, 1966, pp. 330–1.
2 Ibid., p. 325.
3 Doyal, L., *The Political Economy of Health*, Boston: South End Press, 1981.
4 Antonovsky, A., 'Social class, life expectancy and overall mortality,' in E.G. Jaco, *Patients, Physicians and Illness: A Sourcebook in Behavioral Science and Health*, 2nd edn, New York: Free Press, 1972, pp. 5–30; Lerner, M., 'Social differences in physical health,' in J. Kosa, A. Antonovsky and I.K. Zola, *Poverty and Health: A Sociological Analysis*, Cambridge, Massachusetts: Harvard University Press, 1969, pp. 69–167.
5 Comstock, G.W., 'Fatal arteriosclerotic heart disease, water hardness at home and socioeconomic characteristics,' *American Journal of Epidemiology*, 94: 1–8,

1971; Kitagawa, F.M. and Hauser, P.M., *Differential Mortality in the United States: A Study in Socioeconomic Epidemiology*, Cambridge, Massachusetts: Harvard University Press, 1973, pp. 11–33, 78–9; Weinblatt, E., Ruberman, W., Goldberg, J.D. et al., 'Relation of education to sudden death after myocardial infarction,' *New England Journal of Medicine*, 299: 60–5, 1978; Lown, B., Desilva, R.A., Reich, P. and Murawski, B.J., 'Psychophysiological factors in sudden cardiac death,' *American Journal of Psychiatry*, 137: 1325–35, 1980.

6  Doyal, *Political Economy of Health*, p. 65.

7  Lerner, 'Social differences in physical health,' p. 107.

8  McDonough, J.R., Garrison, G.E. and Hames, C.G., 'Blood pressure and hypertensive disease among negroes and whites in Evans County, Georgia,' in J. Stamler, R. Stamler and T.N. Pullman (eds), *The Epidemiology of Hypertension*, New York: Grune & Stratton, 1967; Dawber, T.R., Kannel, S.B., Kagan, A. et al., 'Environmental factors in hypertension,' in Stamler, Stamler and Pullman, *Epidemiology of Hypertension;* Borhani, N.O. and Borkman, T.S., *Alameda County Blood Pressure Study*, Berkeley: California State Department of Public Health, 1968; Shekelle, R.B., Ostfeld, A.M. and Paul, O., 'Social status and incidence of coronary heart disease,' *Journal of Chronic Disability*, 22: 381–94, 1969; Syme, S.L., Oakes, T.W., Friedman, G.D. et al., 'Social class and differences in blood pressure,' *American Journal of Public Health*, 64: 619–20, 1974; Hypertension Detection and Follow-up Program Cooperative Group, 'Race, education and prevalence of hypertension,' *American Journal of Epidemiology*, 106: 351–61, 1977.

9  Schwab, J.J. and Traven, N.D., 'Factors related to the incidence of psychosomatic illness,' *Psychosomatics*, 20: 307–15, 1979.

10  Eyer, J. and Sterling, P., 'Stress-related mortality and social organization,' *Review of Radical Political Economics*, 9: 1–44, 1977.

11  Coates, D., Moyer, S. and Wellman, B., 'The Yorklea Study of urban mental health: Symptoms, problems and life events,' *Canadian Journal of Public Health*, 60: 471–81, 1969.

12  Myers, J.K., Lindenthal, J.J. and Pepper, M.P., 'Social class, life events and psychiatric symptoms: A longitudinal study,' in B.S. Dohrenwend and B.P. Dohrenwend (eds), *Stressful Life Events: Their Nature and Effects*, New York: Wiley, 1974; Dohrenwend, B.S., 'Social status and stressful life events,' *Journal of Personal and Social Psychology*, 28: 225–35, 1973.

13  Pearlin, L.I. and Radabaugh, C.W., 'Economic strains and coping functions of alcohol,' *American Journal of Sociology*, 82: 652–63, 1976.

14  Faris, R.E.L. and Dunham, H.W., *Mental Disorders in Urban Areas: An Ecological Study of Schizophrenia and Other Psychoses*, Chicago: University of Chicago Press, 1939.

15  Schroeder, C.W., 'Mental disorders in cities,' *American Journal of Sociology*, 48: 40–8, 1942.

16  Gerard, D.L. and Houston, L.G., 'Family setting and the social ecology of schizophrenia,' *Psychiatric Quarterly*, 27: 90–101, 1953.

17  Gardner, E.A. and Babigian, H.M., 'A longitudinal comparison of psychiatric service to selected socioeconomic areas of Monroe County, New York,' *American Journal of Orthopsychiatry*, 36: 818–28, 1966.

18 Klee, G.D., Spiro, E., Bahn, A.K. and Gorwitz, K., 'An ecological analysis of diagnosed mental illness in Baltimore,' in R.R. Monroe, G.D. Klee and E.B. Brody (eds), *Psychiatric Epidemiology and Mental Health Planning*, Washington, DC: American Psychiatric Association, 1967, pp. 107–48.

19 Sundby, P. and Nyhus, P., 'Major and minor psychiatric disorders in males in Oslo: An epidemiological study,' *Acta Psychiatrica Scandinavica*, 39: 519–47, 1963.

20 Hare, E.H., 'Mental illness and social conditions in Bristol,' *Journal of Mental Science*, 102: 349–57, 1956.

21 Clark, R.E., 'Psychoses, income and occupational prestige,' *American Journal of Sociology*, 54: 433–40, 1949.

22 Hollingshead, A.B. and Redlich, F.C., *Social Class and Mental Illness*, New York: Wiley, 1958.

23 Srole, L., Langner, T.S., Michael, S.T. et al, *Mental Health in the Metropolis: The Midtown Manhattan Study*, (2 vols), New York: McGraw-Hill, 1962.

24 Leighton, D.C., Harding, J.S., Macklin, D.B. et al., *The Character of Danger: Psychiatric Symptoms in Selected Communities*. New York: Basic Books, 1963, pp. 279–94.

25 Ödegard, Ö., 'The incidence of psychoses in various occupations,' *International Journal of Social Psychiatry*, 2: 85–104, 1956.

26 Stein, L., ' "Social class" gradient in schizophrenia,' *British Journal of Preventive and Social Medicine*, 11: 181–95, 1957.

27 Kohn, M.L., 'Social class and schizophrenia: A critical review and a reformulation,' *Schizophrenia Bulletin*, issue 7: 60–79, 1973, p. 64.

28 Cancro, R., 'Overview of schizophrenia,' in H.I. Kaplan, A.M. Freedman and B.J. Sadock (eds), *Comprehensive Textbook of Psychiatry-III*, Baltimore: Williams & Wilkins, 1980, pp. 1093–1104. The reference is to p. 1097.

29 Weiner, H., 'Schizophrenia: Etiology,' in Kaplan, Freedman and Sadock, *Comprehensive Textbook of Psychiatry-III*, pp. 1121–52. The quotation is on p. 1139.

30 Strauss, J.S. and Carpenter, W.T., *Schizophrenia*, New York: Plenum, 1981, p. 131.

31 Turner, R.J. and Wagenfeld, M.O., 'Occupational mobility and schizophrenia: An assessment of the social causation and social selection hypotheses,' *American Sociological Review*, 32: 104–13, 1967.

32 Kohn, 'Social class and schizophrenia,' p. 62.

33 Leighton, D.C., Hagnell, O., Leighton, A.H. et al., 'Psychiatric disorder in a Swedish and a Canadian community: An exploratory study,' *Social Science and Medicine*, 5: 189–209, 1971.

34 Brown, G.W., Davidson, S., Harris, T. et al., 'Psychiatric disorder in London and North Uist,' *Social Science and Medicine*, 11: 367–77, 1977; Rutter, M., Yule, B., Quinton, D. et al., 'Attainment and adjustment in two geographical areas: III. Some factors accounting for area differences,' *British Journal of Psychiatry*, 126: 520–9, 1975.

35 Nielsen, J. and Nielsen, J.A., 'A census study of mental illness in Samsö,' *Psychological Medicine*, 7: 491–503, 1977.

36 Mandel, E., *Long Waves of Capitalist Development: The Marxist Interpretation*,

Cambridge: Cambridge University Press, 1980; Saul, S.B., *The Myth of the Great Depression, 1873–1896*, London: Macmillan, 1969; Church, R.A., *The Great Victorian Boom, 1850–1873*, London: Macmillan, 1975.

37 Willcox, W.F., 'A study in vital statistics,' *Political Science Quarterly*, 8(1), 1893.

38 Hooker, R.H., 'On the correlation of the marriage rate with foreign trade,' *Journal of the Royal Statistical Society*, 64: 485, 1901.

39 Ogburn, W.F. and Thomas, D.S., 'The influence of the business cycle on certain social conditions,' *Journal of the American Statistical Association*, 18: 324–40, 1922.

40 Thomas, D.S., *Social Aspects of the Business Cycle*, New York: Gordon & Breach, 1968. First published by Knopf in 1927.

41 Catalano, R. and Dooley, C.D., 'Economic predictors of depressed mood and stressful life events in a metropolitan community,' *Journal of Health and Social Behavior*, 18: 292–307, 1977; Dooley, D. and Catalano, R., 'Economic, life, and disorder changes: Time-series analyses,' *American Journal of Community Psychology*, 7: 381–96, 1979.

42 Dooley and Catalano, op. cit., p. 393.

43 Dooley, D., Catalano, R., Jackson, R. and Brownell, A., 'Economic, life, and symptom changes in a nonmetropolitan community,' *Journal of Health and Social Behavior*, 22: 144–54, 1981.

44 Ibid.

45 Gore, S., 'The effect of social support in moderating the health consequences of unemployment,' *Journal of Health and Social Behavior*, 19: 157–65, 1978.

46 Brenner, M.H., *Estimating the Social Costs of National Economic Policy: Implications for Mental and Physical Health, and Criminal Aggression*, prepared for the Joint Economic Committee of the Congress of the United States, Washington, DC: US Government Printing Office, 1976.

47 Ibid., p. 41.

48 Ibid., p. 39.

49 Kasl, S.V.' 'Mortality and the business cycle: Some questions about research strategies when utilizing macro-social and ecological data,' *American Journal of Public Health*, 69: 784–8, 1979, p. 786.

50 Mandel, E., *Marxist Economic Theory*, vol. 1, translated by B. Pearce, New York: Monthly Review Press, 1968, ch. 11.

51 Samuelson, P.A., *Economics*, 11th edn, New York: McGraw-Hill, 1980, ch. 14.

52 Eyer and Sterling, 'Stress-related mortality;' Eyer, J., 'Prosperity as a cause of death,' *International Journal of Health Services*, 7: 125–50, 1977; Eyer, J., 'Does unemployment cause the death rate peak in each business cycle? A multifactor model of death rate change,' *International Journal of Health Services*, 7: 625–62, 1977.

53 Eyer and Sterling, 'Stress-related mortality.'

54 Bunn, A. R., 'Ischaemic heart disease mortality and the business cycle in Australia,' *American Journal of Public Health*, 69: 772–81, 1979.

55 Ibid., p. 773.

56 Kasl, 'Mortality and the business cycle.'

57 Bunn, 'Ischaemic heart disease mortality,' p. 780.

58 Brenner, M.H., 'Influence of the social environment on psychopathology: The

historic perspective,' in J.E. Barrett, R.M. Rose and G.L. Klerman, (eds), *Stress and Mental Disorder*, New York: Raven Press, 1979, pp. 161–77.

59 Brenner, M.H., 'Fetal, infant, and maternal mortality during periods of economic instability,' *International Journal of Health Services*, 3: 145–59, 1973.

60 Hewitt, M., *Wives and Mothers in Victorian Industry*, Westport, Connecticut: Greenwood Press, 1958, pp. 115–16.

61 Ibid., ch 2, 3, 8, 9, 10.

62 Thomas, *Social Aspects of the Business Cycle*, footnote on p. 111.

63 Brenner, 'Fetal, infant, and maternal mortality,' p. 154.

64 Kinnersly, P., *The Hazards of Work: How to Fight Them*, London: Pluto Press, 1973, cited in Doyal, *Political Economy of Health*, p. 67.

65 Doyal, *Political Economy of Health*, p. 74.

66 Lown et al., 'Sudden cardiac death;' Rahe, R.H., Bennett, L. Rorio, M. et al., 'Subjects' recent life changes and coronary heart disease in Finland,' *American Journal of Psychiatry*, 130: 1222–6, 1973.

67 Rabkin, S.W., Mathewson, F.A.L. and Tate, R.B., 'Chronobiology of cardiac sudden death in men,' *Journal of the American Medical Association*, 244: 1357–8, 1980, p. 1358.

68 Rogot, E., Fabsitz, R. and Feinleib, M., 'Daily variation in USA mortality,' *Amerian Journal of Epidemiology*, 103: 198–211, 1976.

69 Russek, H.I. and Zohman, B.L., 'Relative significance of heredity, diet and occupational stress in coronary heart disease of young adults,' *American Journal of Medical Science*, 235: 266–77, 1958.

70 Liljefors, I. and Rahe, R.H., 'An identical twin study of psychosocial factors in coronary heart disease in Sweden,' *Psychosomatic Medicine*, 32: 523 et seq., 1970; Theorell, T. and Rahe, R.H., 'Behavior and life satisfaction characteristics of Swedish subjects with myocardial infarction,' *Journal of Chronic Disability*, 25: 139 et seq., 1972; Floderus, B., 'Psycho-social factors in relation to coronary heart disease and associated risk factors,' *Nordisk Hygienisk Tidskrift*, Supplement 6, 1974.

71 Friedman, M., Rosenman, R.H. and Carroll, V., 'Changes in the serum cholesterol and blood clotting time in men subjected to cyclic variation of occupational stress,' *Circulation*, 17: 852–61, 1958.

72 Theorell, T., 'Life events before and after the onset of a premature myocardial infarction,' in Dohrenwend and Dohrenwend, *Stressful Life Events*, pp. 101–17.

73 Theorell, T., Lind, E. and Flodérus, B., 'The relationship of disturbing life-changes and emotions to the early development of myocardial infarction and other serious illnesses,' *International Journal of Epidemiology*, 4: 281–93, 1975.

74 Haynes, S.G., Feinleib, M., Levine, S. et al., 'The relationship of psychosocial factors to coronary heart disease in the Framingham Study: II. Prevalence of coronary heart disease,' *American Journal of Epidemiology*, 107: 384–402, 1978.

75 Senate Bill 3916 (1972) sought

> to provide for research for solutions to the problems of alienation among American workers in all occupations and industries and technical assistance to those companies, unions, State and local governments seeking to find ways to deal with the problem.

317

Quoted in Rubin, L.B., *Worlds of Pain: Life in the Working Class Family*, New York: Basic Books, 1976, footnote on p. 233.

76 Marx, K., *The Economic and Philosophic Manuscripts of 1844*, New York: International Publishers, 1964; Novack, G., 'The problem of alienation,' in E. Mandel and G. Novack, *The Marxist Theory of Alienation*, New York: Pathfinder Press, 1973, pp. 53-94; Ollman, B., *'Alienation: Marx's Conception of Man in Capitalist Society,'* Cambridge: Cambridge University Press, 1971.

77 Garson, B., *All the Livelong Day: The Meaning and Demeaning of Routine Work*, New York: Penguin, 1977, p. 95.

78 Ibid., p. 88.

79 Ibid., p. 204.

80 Terkel, S., *Working*, New York: Avon, 1975, p. 2.

81 Ibid., p. 3.

82 Rubin, *Worlds of Pain*, p. 169.

83 Ibid., p. 183.

84 Jahoda, M. and Rush, H., *Work, Employment and Unemployment*, University of Sussex Science Policy Research Unit Occasional Paper, no. 12, Brighton: University of Sussex, 1980, pp. 15-16.

85 Kornhauser, A., *Mental Health of the Industrial Worker: A Detroit Study*, New York: Wiley, 1965, p. 270.

86 Jahoda and Rush, *Work, Employment and Unemployment*, pp. 16-17.

87 Kornhauser, *Mental Health of the Industrial Worker*, pp. 260-2.

88 Kohn, M.L. and Schooler, C., 'Occupational experience and psychological functioning: An assessment of reciprocal effects,' *American Sociological Review*, 38: 97-118, 1973.

89 Dalgard, O.S., 'Occupational experience and mental health, with special reference to closeness of supervision,' *Psychiatry and Social Science*, 1: 29-42, 1981.

90 Kasl, S.V., 'Changes in mental health status associated with job loss and retirement,' in Barrett, Rose and Klerman, *Stress and Mental Disorder*, pp. 179-200. The reference is to pp. 182-3.

91 Ibid.; Kasl, S.V. and Cobb, S., 'Blood pressure changes in men undergoing job loss: A preliminary report,' *Psychosomatic Medicine*, 22: 19-38, 1970.

92 Liem, R. and Rayman, P., 'Health and social costs of unemployment: Research and policy considerations,' *American Psychologist*, 37: 1116-23, 1982.

93 Little, C., 'Technical-professional unemployment: Middle-class adaptability to personal crisis,' *Sociological Quarterly*, 17: 262-74, 1976.

94 Eisenberg, P. and Lazarsfeld, P.F., 'The psychological effects of unemployment,' *Psychological Bulletin*, 35: 358-90, 1938.

95 Liem and Rayman, 'Health and social costs of unemployment,' p. 1120.

96 Strange, W.G., 'Job loss: A psychosocial study of worker reactions to a plant closing in a company town in Southern Appalachia', Doctoral dissertation, School of Industrial and Labor Relations, Cornell University, Ithaca, New York, 1977.

97 Warr, P., 'Studies of psychological well-being,' presented at the British Psychological Society Symposium on Unemployment, London, 1980.

98 Parnes, H.S. and King, R., 'Middle-aged job losers,' *Industrial Gerontology*, 4:

77–95, 1977.

99  Theorell, Lind and Flodérus. 'Disturbing life changes.'

100  Coates, Moyer and Wellman, 'The Yorklea Study.'

101  Eyer and Sterling, 'Stress-related mortality,' Brenner, *Social Costs of National Economic Policy;* Henry, A.F. and Short, J.F., *Suicide and Homicide,* Glencoe, Illinois: Free Press, 1954; Vigderhous, G. and Fishman, G., 'The impact of unemployment and familial integration on changing suicide rates in the U.S.A., 1920–1969,' *Social Psychiatry,* 13: 239–48, 1978; Hamermesh, D.S. and Soss, N.M., 'An economic theory of suicide,' *Journal of Political Economy,* 82: 83–98, 1974; Ahlburg, D.A. and Shapiro, M.O., 'The darker side of unemployment,' *Hospital and Community Psychiatry,* 34: 389, 1983.

102  Vigderhous and Fishman, 'Impact of unemployment;' Ahlburg and Shapiro, 'The darker side of unemployment.'

103  Pierce, A., 'The economic cycle and the social suicide rate,' *American Sociological Review,* 32: 457–62, 1967.

104  Personal communication from J.P. Marshall to D. Dooley and R. Catalano. Cited in Dooley, D., and Catalano, R., 'Economic change as a cause of behavioral disorder,' *Psychological Bulletin,* 87: 450–68, 1980, p. 455.

105  Durkheim, E., *Suicide,* Glencoe, Illinois: Free Press, 1951, p. 243.

106  Hamermesh and Soss, 'An economic theory of suicide.'

107  Powell, E., 'Occupation, status and suicide: Towards a redefinition of anomie,' *American Social Review,* 22: 131–9, 1958.

108  Resnik, N.L.P. and Dizmang, L.H., 'Observations on suicidal behavior among American Indians,' *American Journal of Psychiatry,* 127: 58–63, 1971.

109  Dublin, L.I., *Suicide: A Sociologial and Statistical Study,'* New York: Ronald Press, 1963, ch. 8; Hamermesh and Soss, 'An economic theory of suicide.'

110  Yap, P.M., 'Aging and mental health in Hong Kong,' in R.H. Williams (ed.), *Processes of Aging: Social and Psychological Perspectives,* vol. 2, New York: Atherton, 1963, pp. 176–91.

111  Lendrum, F.C., 'A thousand cases of attempted suicide,' *American Journal of Psychiatry,* 13: 479–500, 1933; Sainsbury, P., *Suicide in London: An Ecological Study,* London: Chapman & Hall, 1955; Morris, J.B., Kovacs, M., Beck, A. and Wolffe, A., 'Notes towards an epidemiology of urban suicide,' *Comprehensive Psychiatry,* 15: 537–47, 1974; Sanborn, D.E., Sanborn, C.J. and Cimbolic, P. 'Occupation and suicide,' *Diseases of the Nervous Sysem,* 35: 7–12, 1974; Shepherd, D.M. and Barraclough, B.M., 'Work and suicide: An empirical investigation,' *British Journal of Psychiatry,* 136: 469–78, 1980.

112  Breed, W., 'Occupational mobility and suicide among white males,' *American Sociological Review,* 28: 179–88, 1963; Portersfield, A.L. and Gibbs, J.P., 'Occupational prestige and social mobility of suicides in New Zealand,' *American Journal of Sociology,* 66: 147–52, 1960; Sanborn, Sanborn and Cimbolic, 'Occupation and suicide,'; Shepherd and Barraclough, 'Work and suicide.'

113  Tuckman, J. and Lavell, M., 'Study of suicide in Philadelphia,' *Public Health Reports,* 73: 547–53, 1958; Shepherd and Baraclough, 'Work and suicide.'

114  Rogot, Fabsitz and Feinleib, 'Daily variation in USA mortality;' Baldamus, W., *The Structure of Sociological Inference,* New York: Barnes & Noble, 1976, p. 94. Curiously, Baldamus presents the data on the daily frequency of suicide

declining from Monday to Sunday as an example of a phenomenon which defies explanation. This is because, he argues, of 'the difficulty of visualizing a characteristic quality inherent in each day of the week.' His experience of the work week is clearly different from that of the average working person.

115 Brenner, M.H., *Mental Illness and the Economy*, Cambridge, Massachusetts: Harvard University Press, 1973.

116 Pollock, H.M., 'The Depression and mental disease in New York State,' *American Journal of Psychiatry*, 91: 736–71, 1935; Mowrer, E.R., 'A Study of personal disorganization,' *American Sociological Review*, 4: 475–87, 1939; Dayton, N.A., *New Facts on Mental Disorders: Study of 89,190 Cases*, Springfield, Illinois: Charles C. Thomas, 1940; Dunham, H.W., *Sociological Theory and Mental Disorder*, Detroit, Michigan: Wayne State University Press, 1959; Pugh, T.F. and MacMahon, B., *Epidemiologic Findings in the United States Mental Hospital Data*, Boston: Little, Brown, 1962.

117 Brenner, *Mental Illness and the Economy*, p. 45.

118 Marshall, J.R. and Funch, D.P., 'Mental illness and the economy: A critique and partial replication,' *Journal of Health and Social Behavior*, 20: 282–9, 1979.

119 Dear, M., Clark, G. and Clark S., 'Economic cycles and mental health care policy: An examination of the macro-context for social service planning,' *Social Science and Medicine*, 136: 43–53, 1979.

120 Ahr, P.R., Gorodezky, M.J. and Cho, D.W., 'Measuring the relationship of public psychiatric admissions to rising unemployment,' *Hospital and Community Psychiatry*, 32: 398–401, 1981.

121 Parker, J.J., Community mental health center admissions and the business cycle: A longitudinal study, Doctoral dissertation, Department of Sociology, University of Colorado, Boulder, 1979.

122 Brenner, *Mental Illness and the Economy*, ch. 9.

123 Ahr, Gorodezky and Cho, 'Public psychiatric admissions;' Draughon, M., 'Relationship between economic decline and mental hospital admissions continues to be significant,' *Psychological Reports*, 36: 882, 1975.

## 3  Recovery from Schizophrenia

1 Strecker, H.P., 'Insulin treatment of schizophrenia,' *Journal of Mental Science*, 84: 146–55, 1938; Freyhan, F.A., 'Course and outcome of schizophrenia,' *Amerian Journal of Psychiatry*, 112: 161–7, 1955; Leiberman, D.M. Hoenig, J. and Auerbach, I., 'The effect of insulin coma and E.C.T. on the three year prognosis of schizophrenia,' *Journal of Neurology, Neurosurgery and Psychiatry*, 20: 108–13, 1957; and Ödegard, Ö., 'Changes in the prognosis of functional psychoses since the days of Kraepelin,' *British Journal of Psychiatry*, 113: 813–22, 1967.

2 Kelly, D.H.W. and Sargant, W., 'Present treatment of schizophrenia: A controlled follow-up study,' *British Medical Journal*, 1: 147–50, 1965; Holmboe, R. Noreik, K. and Astrup, C., 'Follow-up of functional psychoses at two Norwegian mental hospitals,' *Acta Psychiatrica Scandinavica*, 44: 298–310, 1968; Gross, G. and Huber, G., 'Zur Prognose der Schizophrenien,' *Psychiatrica Clinica* (Basel), 6: 1–16, 1973; Cottman, S.B. and Mezey, A.G., 'Community care and the prognosis of schizophrenia,' *Acta Psychiatrica Scandinavica*, 53:

95–104, 1976; and Bland, R.C., Parker, J.H. and Orn, H., 'Prognosis in schizophrenia; Prognostic predictors and outcome,' *Archives of General Psychiatry,* 35: 72–7, 1978.

3 Lehmann, H.E., 'Schizophrenia: Clinical features,' in H.I. Kaplan, A.M. Freedman and B.J. Sadock (eds), *Comprehensive Textbook of Psychiatry-III,* Baltimore: Williams & Wilkins, 1981, p. 1187.

4 Horwitz, W.A. and Kleiman, C., 'Survey of cases discharged from the Psychiatric Institute and Hospital,' *Psychiatric Quarterly,* 10: 72–85, 1936; Henisz, J., 'A follow-up study of schizophrenic patients,' *Comprehensive Psychiatry,* 7: 524–8, 1966; Bockoven, J.S. and Solomon, H.C., 'Comparison of two five-year follow-up studies: 1947 to 1952 and 1967 to 1972,' *American Journal of Psychiatry,* 132: 796–801, 1975; and Harrow, M., Grinker, R.R., Silverstein, M.L. and Holzman, P., 'Is modern-day schizophrenic outcome still negative?' *American Journal of Psychiatry,* 135: 1156–62, 1978.

5 Stephens, J.H., 'Long-term prognosis and follow-up in schizophrenia,' *Schizophrenia Bulletin,* 4: 25–47, 1978.

6 Bleuler, M., 'A 23-year longitudinal study of 208 schizophrenics and impressions in regard to the nature of schizophrenia,' in D. Rosenthal, and S.S. Kety, *The Transmission of Schizophrenia,* Oxford: Pergamon, 1968, p. 3.

7 Ibid., p. 5.

8 Ibid., p. 6.

9 The studies included in Table 3.1 are listed in the general bibliography. The results of this survey have previously been published in Warner, R. 'The influence of economic factors on outcome in schizophrenia,' *Psychiatry and Social Science,* 1: 79–106, 1981.

10 Kirchhof, T., *Geschichte der Psychiatrie,* Leipzig: Franz Deuticke, 1912.

11 Source of unemployment statistics: US, 1881–9, Eyer, J. and Sterling, P., 'Stress-related mortality and social organization, *Review of Radical Political Economics,* 9: 1–44, 1977; 1890–1970, US Bureau of the Census, *Historical Statistics of the United States: Colonial Times to 1970: Part I,* Washington, DC, 1975; UK, 1881–7, Mitchell, B.R. and Deane, P., *Abstract of British Historical Statistics,* Cambridge: Cambridge University Press, 1962; 1888–1970, Mitchell, B.R., *European Historical Statistics, 1750–1970,* New York: Columbia University Press, 1978; US and UK, 1971–8, International Labour Office, *Year Book of Labour Statistics,* Geneva, 1978.

12 Lehmann, 'Schizophrenia: Clinical features,' p. 1178.

13 American Psychiatric Association, *Diagnostic and Statistical Manual of Mental Disorders,* 3rd edn, (DSM-III), Washington, DC, 1980.

## 4 Deinstitutionalization

1 Davis, J.M., 'Organic therapies,' in H.I. Kaplan, A.M. Freedman and B.J. Sadock (eds) *Comprehensive Textbook of Psychiatry-III,* Baltimore: Williams & Wilkins, 1981, pp. 2257–89. The quotation is on p. 2257.

2 Ödegard, Ö., 'Pattern of discharge from Norwegian psychiatric hospitals before and after the introduction of the psychotropic drugs,' *American Journal of Psychiatry,* 120: 772–8, 1964.

3 Norton, A., 'Mental hospital ins and outs: A survey of patients admitted to a mental hospital in the past 30 years,' *British Medical Journal*, i: 528–36, 1961.

4 Shepherd, M., Goodman, N. and Watt, D.C., 'The application of hospital statistics in the evaluation of pharmacotherapy in a psychiatric population,' *Comprehensive Psychiatry*, 2: 11–19, 1961.

5 Lewis, A., untitled paper, in R.B. Bradley, P. Deniker and C. Radouco-Thomas (eds) *Neuropsychopharmacology*, vol. 1, Amsterdam: Elsevier, 1959, pp. 207–12, cited in Scull, A., *Decarceration: Community treatment and the Deviant—A Radical View*, Englewood Cliffs, New Jersey: Prentice-Hall, 1977, p. 82.

6 Pugh, T.F. and MacMahon, B., *Epidemiologic Findings in United States Mental Hospital Data*, Boston: Little, Brown, 1962.

7 Chittick, R.A., Brooks, G.W. and Deane, W.N., *Vermont Project for the Rehabilitation of Chronic Schizophrenic Patients: Progress Report*, Vermont State Hospital, 1959, cited in Scull, *Decarceration*, p. 82.

8 Epstein, L.J., Morgan, R.D. and Reynolds, L., 'An approach to the effect of ataraxic drugs on hospital release rates,' *American Journal of Psychiatry*, 119: 36–45, 1962.

9 Linn, E.L., 'Drug therapy, milieu change, and release from a mental hospital,' *Archives of Neurology and Psychiatry*, 81: 785–94, 1959.

10 Brill, H. and Patton, R.E., 'Analysis of population reduction in New York State mental hospitals during the first four years of large-scale therapy with psychotropic drugs,' *American Journal of Psychiatry*, 116: 495–509, 1959, p. 495.

11 Scull, *Decarceration*, p. 83.

12 Davis, 'Organic therapies,' p. 2257.

13 Freudenberg, R.K., Bennet, D.H. and May, A.R., 'The relative importance of physical and community methods in the treatment of schizophrenia,' in *International Congress of Psychiatry, Zurich, 1957*, Fussli, 1959, pp. 157–78. Quotation is from p. 159.

14 All of the information in this paragraph is from Clark, D.H., *Social Therapy in Psychiatry*, Baltimore: Penguin, 1974, pp. 22–5; and Langsley, D.G., 'Community psychiatry,' in Kaplan, Freedman and Sadock *Comprehensive Textbook of Psychiatry*, pp. 2836–53. The reference is to pp. 2839–40.

15 Jones, M., *Social Psychiatry in Practice*, Baltimore: Penguin, 1968, p. 17; Clark, *Social Therapy in Psychiatry*, p. 29.

16 Clark, *Social Therapy in Psychiatry*, pp. 25–6.

17 Ödegard, 'Pattern of discharge,' p. 776.

18 Rathod, N.H., 'Tranquillisers and patients' environment,' *Lancet*, i: 611–13, 1958.

19 The statistics in this paragraph are from Scull, *Decarceration*, p. 149.

20 Bassuk, E.L. and Gerson, S., 'Deinstitutionalization and mental health services,' *Scientific American*, 238(2): 46–53, February 1978, p. 50.

21 These examples are from Langsley, 'Community psychiatry,' p. 2847; and Lamb, H.R. and Goertzel, V., 'The demise of the state hospital: A premature obituary?' *Archives of General Psychiatry*, 26: 489–95, 1972.

22 Lehman, A.F., Ward, N.C. and Linn, L.S., 'Chronic mental patients: The quality of life issue,' *American Journal of Psychiatry*, 139: 1271–6, 1982.

23 Lamb, H.R., 'The new asylums in the community,' *Archives of General*

*Psychiatry*, 36: 129–34, 1979.

24 Van Putten, T. and Spar, J.E., 'The board and care home: Does it deserve a bad press?' *Hospital and Community Psychiatry*, 30: 461–4, 1979, pp. 461–2.

25 Bassuk and Gerson, 'Deinstitutionalization,' p. 49.

26 Morgan, C.H., 'Service delivery models.' Prepared for the Special National Workshop on Mental Health Services in Local Jails, Baltimore, Maryland, September 27–9, 1978; Gibbs, J.J., 'Psychological and behavioral pathology in jails: A review of the literature,' presented at the Special National Workshop on Mental Health Services in Local Jails, 1978; Olds, E., *A Study of the Homeless, Sick and Alcoholic Persons in the Baltimore City Jail*, Baltimore: Baltimore Council of Social Agencies, 1956; Arthur Bolton Associates, Report to the California State Legislature, October 1976; Swank, G.E. and Winer, D., 'Occurrence of psychiatric disorder in a county jail population,' *American Journal of Psychiatry*, 133: 1331–6, 1976; unidentified author, 'Mental ill inmates untreated, says GAO,' *Psychiatric News*, February 6, 1981, p. 1.

27 Roth, L.H. and Ervin, F.R., 'Psychiatric care of federal prisoners,' *American Journal of Psychiatry*, 128: 424–30, 1971.

28 Rollin, H., 'From patients into vagrants,' *New Society*, January 15, 1970, pp. 90–3.

29 Tidmarsh, D. and Wood, S., 'Psychiatric aspects of destitution: A study of the Camberwell Reception Centre,' in J.K. Wing and A.M. Haily (eds), *Evaluating a Community Psychiatric Service: The Camberwell Register 1964–1971*, London: Oxford University Press, 1972, pp. 327–40.

30 Rollin, 'From patients into vagrants,' p. 92; National Schizophrenia Fellowship, *Home Sweet Nothing: The Plight of Sufferers from Chronic Schizophrenia*, Surbiton: 1971.

31 Morris, B., 'Recent developments in the care, treatment, and rehabilitation of the chronic mentally ill in Britain,' *Hospital and Community Psychiatry*, 34: 159–63, 1983.

32 Korer, J., *Not the Same as You: The Social Situation of 190 Schizophrenics Living in the Community*, Dalston, London: Psychiatric Rehabilitation Association, 1978; Ebringer, L. and Christie-Brown, J.R.W., 'Social deprivation amongst short stay psychiatric patients,' *British Journal of Psychiatry*, 136: 46–52, 1980.

33 Hencke, D., 'Squalor in mental homes kept secret,' *Guardian*, July 20, 1983, p. 1; Hencke, D., 'Hospital report reveals faults,' *Guardian*, July 22, 1983, p. 3.

34 Scull, *Decarceration*, p. 152.

35 Fraser, D., *The Evolution of the British Welfare State: A History of Social Policy Since the Industrial Revolution*, New York: Harper & Row, 1973, pp. 212–16; Leiby, J., *A History of Social Welfare and Social Work in the United States*, New York: Columbia University Press, 1978, p. 289.

36 Ödegard, Ö., 'Changes in the prognosis of functional psychoses since the days of Kraepelin,' *British Journal of Psychiatry*, 113: 813–22, 1967, p. 819.

37 Foucault, M., *Madness and Civilization: A History of Insanity in the Age of Reason*, New York: Vintage Books, 1965, p. 49.

38 Parry-Jones, W.L., *The Trade in Lunacy: A Study of Private Madhouses in England in the Eighteenth and Nineteenth Centuries*, London: Routledge & Kegan Paul, 1972, p. 72.

39 All of the material in this paragraph is taken from Sinfield, A., *What Unemployment Means*, Oxford: Martin Robertson, 1981, pp. 130–1.
40 Clark, *Social Therapy in Psychiatry*, p. 23.
41 Ödegard, 'Prognosis of functional psychoses,' p. 819.
42 Pugh and MacMahon, *Epidemiologic Findings*.
43 Camberwell group prevalence study, 1965, cited in Torrey, E.F., *Schizophrenia and Civilization*, New York: Jason Aronson, 1980, p. 89.
44 McGowan, J.F. and Porter, T.L., *An Introduction to the Vocational Rehabilitation Process*, Washington, DC: US Department of Health, Education and Welfare, Vocational Rehabilitation Administration, 1967.
45 Tizard, J. and O'Connor, N., 'The employment of high-grade mental defectives. I,' *American Journal of Mental Deficiency*, 54: 563–76, 1950.
46 Field, M.G. and Aronson, J., 'The institutional framework of Soviet psychiatry,' *Journal of Nervous and Mental Disease*, 138: 305–22, 1964; Field, M.G. and Aronson, J. 'Soviet community mental health services and work therapy: A report of two visits,' *Community Mental Health Journal*, 1: 81–90, 1965; Hein, G., 'Social psychiatric treatment of schizophrenia in the Soviet Union,' *International Journal of Psychiatry*, 6: 346–62, 1968; Gorman, M., 'Soviet psychiatry and the Russian citizen,' *International Journal of Psychiatry*, 8: 841–57, 1969.
47 Maxwell Jones, personal communication.
48 Maddison, A., *Economic Growth in the West*, New York: Twentieth Century Fund, 1964, p. 220.
49 de Plato, G. and Minguzzi, G.F., 'A short history of psychiatric renewal in Italy,' *Psychiatry and Social Science*, 1: 71–7, 1981.
50 For a fuller discussion of this analysis see Warner, R., 'Mental hospital and prison use: An international comparison,' *Mental Health Administration*, 10: 239–58, 1983.
51 World Health Organization, *World Health Statistics Annual 1977*, vol. III, Geneva: 1977; Maxwell Jones and Loren Mosher, personal communications.
52 Field and Aronson, 'Institutional framework of Soviet psychiatry;' Field and Aronson, 'Soviet community mental health;' Hein, 'Soviet psychiatric treatment;' Gorman, 'Soviet psychiatry;' Wing, J.R., *Reasoning About Madness*, New York: Oxford University Press, 1978.

## 5 Madness and the Industrial Revolution

1 Charles-Gaspard de la Rive, a Swiss doctor. Quoted in Foucault, M., *Madness and Civilization: A History of Insanity in the Age of Reason*, New York: Vintage Books, 1973, p. 242. Also quoted in Jones, K., *A History of the Mental Health Services*, London: Routledge & Kegan Paul, 1972, p. 47. According to Foucault the passage appeared in a letter to the editors of the *Bibliothèque britannique;* according to Jones it was written in the visitors' book of the Retreat. One assumes both are correct, and that Dr de la Rive used the same material twice.
2 Daniel Hack Tuke stated that the name Retreat was suggested by his grandmother, William Tuke's daughter-in-law, to convey the idea of a haven. Quoted by Jones, *History of Mental Health Services*, p. 47.
3 These details of moral treatment at the York Retreat are drawn from the

following sources: Mora, G., 'Historical and theoretical trends in psychiatry,' in H.I. Kaplan, A.M. Freedman and B.J. Sadock (eds), *Comprehensive Textbook of Psychiatry-III*, Baltimore: Williams & Wilkins, 1980, pp. 4–98. The reference is to pp. 55–7; Jones, *History of Mental Health Services*, pp. 45–54; Foucault, *Madness and Civilization*, pp. 241–55.

4 Thurnam, J., *Observations and Essays on the Statistics of Insanity*, London: Simpkin, Marshall, 1845, reprint edition New York: Arno Press, 1976. Quoted in Jones, *History of Mental Health Services*, p. 66.

5 Both passages are from Godfrey Higgins' letter to the *York Herald*, 10 January 1814. Quoted in Jones, *History of Mental Health Services*, p. 70.

6 Both quotations are from Dickens, C. and Wills, W.H., 'A curious dance around a curious tree,' in H. Stone (ed.), *Charles Dickens' Uncollected Writings from Household Words 1850–1859*, Bloomington: Indiana University Press, 1968, pp. 381–91. The passages quoted are on pp. 382–3.

7 Parry-Jones, W.L., *The Trade in Lunacy: A Study of Private Madhouses in England in the Eighteenth and Nineteenth Centuries*, London: Routledge & Kegan Paul, 1972, p. 289.

8 Scull, A., 'Moral treatment reconsidered: Some sociological comments on an episode in the history of British psychiatry,' in A. Scull (ed.), *Madhouses, Mad-doctors, and Madmen: The Social History of Psychiatry in the Victorian Era*, Philadelphia: University of Pennsylvania Press, 1981, pp. 105–18. This reference is on p. 107.

9 Foucault, *Madness and Civilization*, p. 68.

10 Ibid., pp.74–5.

11 Ibid., pp. 68–78; Scull, 'Moral treatment reconsidered,' pp. 106–10.

12 Dr de la Rive's remarks are translated from the original French which was quoted in Jones, *History of Mental Health Services*, p. 49.

13 *Regolamento dei Regi Spedali di Santa Maria Nuova di Bonifazio*. Hospital regulations prepared under the supervision of Vincenzo Chiarugi in 1793. Quoted in Mora, 'Historical and theoretical trends,' p. 55.

14 Daquin, J., *La Philosophie de la folie*, Chambéry, 1791, cited in Mora, 'Historical and theoretical trends,' p. 57.

15 Mora, 'Historical and theoretical trends,' p. 54.

16 Jones, *History of Mental Health Services*, p. 44.

17 Ferriar, J., *Medical Histories and Reflections* (3 vols), London: Cadell & Davies, vol. 2, pp. 111–12. Quoted in Scull, 'Moral treatment reconsidered,' p. 106.

18 Mora, 'Historical and theoretical trends,' pp. 58–9.

19 Ibid., p. 54.

20 Hobsbawm, E.J., *The Age of Revolution 1789–1848*, New York: New American Library, p. 37.

21 Ibid., p. xv.

22 Ibid., p. 46.

23 Ibid., p. 38.

24 Ibid., pp.40, 103.

25 Ibid., pp. 72, 77.

26 Tuma, E.H., *European Economic History: Tenth Century to the Present*, Palo Alto, California: Pacific Books, 1979, p. 202.

27 Hobsbawm, *Age of Revolution,* p. 79.

28 Inglis, B., *Poverty and the Industrial Revolution,* London: Panther Books, 1972, p. 78; Piven, F.F. and Cloward, R.A., *Regulating the Poor: The Functions of Public Welfare,* New York: Vintage Books, 1972, p. 21.

29 Ashton, T.S., *The Industrial Revolution 1760–1830,* Oxford: Oxford University Press, 1968, p. 46.

30 Ibid., p. 46.

31 Hobsbawm, *Age of Revolution,* pp. 93, 212.

32 Maidstone Poor Law authorities. Quoted in Jones, *History of Mental Health Services,* p. 18.

33 Jones, *History of Mental Health Services,* p. 18.

34 Ibid., pp. 10–12.

35 Parry-Jones, *Trade in Lunacy,* p. 30.

36 Scull, A., *Museums of Madness: The Social Organization of Insanity in Nineteenth-Century England,* London: Allen Lane (New York: St Martin's Press), 1979, p. 39.

37 Ibid., pp. 27–34, 247; Jones, *History of Mental Health Services,* pp. 88–9.

38 Foucault, *Madness and Civilization,* p. 232.

39 Ibid., pp. 234–40.

40 Parry-Jones, *Trade in Lunacy,* p. 204.

41 Scull, *Museums of Madness,* pp. 71–3; Scull, 'Moral treatment reconsidered', pp. 112–15.

42 Lancashire Quarter Sessions Records. Quoted in Allderidge, P., 'Hospitals, madhouses and asylums: Cycles in the care of the insane,' *British Journal of Psychiatry,* 134: 321–34, 1979, p. 327.

43 Best, G., *Mid-Victorian Britain 1851–70,* Bungay, Suffolk: Fontana, 1979, p. 161.

44 Scull, *Museums of Madness,* pp. 224, 244.

45 Jones, *History of Mental Health Services,* pp. 48, 123.

46 Ibid., pp. 93–6.

47 Thurnam, *Statistics of Insanity,* pp. 138–9.

48 Walton, J., 'The treatment of pauper lunatics in Victorian England: The case of Lancaster Asylum, 1816–1870,' in Scull, *Madhouses, Mad-doctors, and Madmen,* pp. 166–97. This reference is on p. 168. Jones, *History of Mental Health Services,* pp. 114–21.

49 Walton, 'Pauper lunatics in Victorian England,' p. 180.

50 Ibid., pp. 186–91; Scull, *Museums of Madness,* pp. 214–18.

51 Parry-Jones, *Trade in Lunacy,* p. 290.

52 Ibid., p. 288.

53 Ibid., p. 177.

54 Ibid., p. 175.

55 Ibid., pp. 175, 185.

56 Ibid., pp. 154, 185–6.

57 Thurnam, *Statistics of Insanity,* p. 36.

58 Ibid., calculated from Table 12.

59 Tuke, D.H., *Chapters in the History of the Insane in the British Isles,* London: Kegan Paul, Trench, 1882, p. 491.

60  Walton, 'Pauper lunatics in Victorian England,' p. 182.
61  For a discussion of the standard of living debate see: Taylor, A.J. (ed.), *The Standard of Living in Britain in the Industrial Revolution*, London: Methuen, 1975.
62  Harrison, J.F.C., *Early Victorian Britain 1832–51*, Bungay, Suffolk: Fontana, 1979, p.34; Hobsbawm, E.J., *Labouring Men: Studies in the History of Labour*, London: Weidenfeld & Nicolson, 1968, pp. 72–82.
63  Mayhew, H., *London Labour and the London Poor II*, p. 338. Quoted in E.P. Thompson, *The Making of the English Working Class*, New York: Vintage Books, 1966, p. 250.
64  Hobsbawm, E.J., *Industry and Empire*, Harmondsworth, Middlesex: Penguin, 1969, p. 161.
65  Church, R.A., *The Great Victorian Boom 1850–1873*, London: Macmillan, 1975, pp. 72–3.
66  Piven and Cloward, *Regulating the Poor*, pp. 32–8.
67  Flinn, M.W., *British Population Growth 1700–1850*, London: Macmillan, 1970, p. 57; Kemmerer, D.L. and Hunter, M.H., *Economic History of the United States*, Totowa, New Jersey: Littlefield, Adams, 1967, pp. 61, 65; Boorstin, D.J., *The Americans: Volume II: The National Experience*, Harmondsworth, Middlesex: Penguin, p. 46.
68  Boorstin, *The National Experience*, p. 51.
69  Hunt, E.H., *British Labour History 1815–1914*, London: Weidenfeld & Nicolson, 1981, p. 108; Tucker, R.S., 'Real wages of artisans in London, 1729–1935,' in Taylor, *Standard of Living in the Industrial Revolution*, p. 33.
70  Rothman, D.J., *The Discovery of the Asylum: Social Order and Disorder in the New Republic*, Boston: Little, Brown, 1971, p. 158.
71  Ibid., p. 160.
72  Ibid., pp. 160, 205.
73  Garraty, J.A., *Unemployment in History: Economic Thought and Public Policy*, New York: Harper, 1979, p. 109.
74  This material on the corporate asylums is drawn from Scull, A., 'The Discovery of the Asylum revisited: Lunacy reform in the new American republic,' in Scull, *Madhouses, Mad-doctors and Madmen*, pp. 144–65; and Rothman, *Discovery of the Asylum*, pp. 130–54.
75  For example, see Caplan, R.B., *Psychiatry and the Community in Nineteenth-Century America*, New York: Basic Books, 1969, p. 4.
76  Mora, 'Historical and theoretical trends,' p. 62.
77  Rothman, *Discovery of the Asylum*, p. 277.
78  Ibid., p. 151.
79  Dain, N., *Disordered Minds: The First Century of Eastern State Hospital in Williamsburg, Virginia 1766–1866*, Williamsburg, Virginia: Colonial Williamsburg Foundation, 1971, pp. 66, 107.
80  The Boston Prison Discipline Society report. Quoted in Dain, *Disordered Minds*, p. 62.
81  Dain, *Disordered Minds*, pp. 43, 127.
82  Grob, G.N., *Mental Institutions in America: Social Policy to 1875*, New York: Free Press, 1973, p. 392.
83  Rothman, *Discovery of the Asylum*, pp. 144–51; Dain, N., *Concepts of Insanity in*

the United States, 1789–1865, New Brunswick, New Jersey: Rutgers University Press, p. 128.

84 Bockoven, J.S., 'Moral treatment in American Psychiatry,' *Journal of Nervous and Mental Disease*, 124: 167–94, 292–321, 1956, p. 181.

85 Thurnam, *Statistics of Insanity*, Table 16.

86 Rothman, *Discovery of the Asylum*, p. 149.

87 Dickens, C., *American Notes for General Circulation*, Harmondsworth, Middlesex: Penguin, 1972, p. 97.

88 Ibid., p. 122.

89 Ibid., p. 140.

90 Dickens and Wills, 'A curious dance,' p. 386–91.

91 Dickens, *American Notes*, p. 141.

92 Rothman, *Discovery of the Asylum*, p. 283.

93 Ibid., pp. 144–6.

94 Caplan, *Psychiatry and the Community*, p. 43.

95 Ibid., pp. 37–8; Grob, *Mental Institutions in America*, p. 179.

96 Hall, B., *Travels in North America in the Years 1827 and 1828*, Edinburgh: Cadell, 1829. Quoted in Bromberg, W., *From Shaman to Psychotherapist: A History of the Treatment of Mental Illness*, Chicago: Henry Regnery, 1975, p. 124; and cited in Caplan, *Psychiatry and the Community*, p. 90; and in Tourney, G., 'A history of therapeutic fashions in psychiatry, 1800–1966,' *American Journal of Psychiatry*, 124: 784–96, 1967. According to Scull in 'Discovery of the Asylum Revisited,' p. 164. E.S. Abdy made similar remarks in his *Journal of a Residence and Tour in the United States of North America*, London: Murray, 1835.

97 Bromberg, *Shaman to Psychotherapist*, pp. 124–5; Dain, *Disordered Minds*, p. 115; Grob, *Mental Institutions in America*, p. 182.

98 Quoted in Bromberg, *Shaman to Psychotherapist*, p. 125.

99 Deutsch, A., *The Mentally Ill in America*, New York: Columbia University Press, 1949, ch. 11.

100 See Caplan, *Psychiatry and the Community*, pp. 90–1 for a detailed list of the flaws in the recovery statistics.

101 Bromberg, *Shaman to Psychotherapist*, p. 124; Parry-Jones, *Trade in Lunacy*, pp. 202–5.

102 Thurnam, *Statistics of Insanity*, p. 57.

103 Ibid., Table 6.

104 Pliny Earle published his views on the curability of insanity as an article in 1876, and later in book form: *The Curability of Insanity: A Series of Studies*, Philadelphia: Lippincott, 1887. See Rothman, *Discovery of the Asylum*, p. 268; Caplan, *Psychiatry and the Community*, p. 92; Bromberg, *Shaman to Psychotherapist*, p. 126.

105 Bockoven, J.S., *Moral Treatment in Community Mental Health*, New York: Springer, 1972, ch. 5.

106 Rothman, *Discovery of the Asylum*, p. 357.

107 Bockoven, *Moral Treatment*, p. 67.

108 An exception would be Grob, *Mental Institutions in America*, pp. 184–5. After reviewing Dr Park's follow-up study of Dr Woodward's patients, Grob concludes that it indicates 'a record that compares quite favorably with mid-

twentieth century discharge rates from mental hospitals.'
109 Ray, I., *American Journal of Insanity*, 16: 1–2, 1861–2. Quoted in Caplan, *Psychiatry and the Community*, pp. 73–4.
110 Rothman, *Discovery of the Asylum*, p. 266.
111 Ibid., p. 281; Scull, 'Discovery of the Asylum Revisited,' pp. 157–9.
112 Scull, 'Discovery of the asylum revisited,' p. 159.
113 Mora, 'Historical and theoretical trends,' p. 73.
114 'The German asylum tradition issued more from the prison than the monastery, and this is, according to Kirchhof, the reason for their tremendous use of coercive measures.' Ellenburger, H.F., 'Psychiatry from ancient to modern times,' in S. Arieti (ed.) *American Handbook of Psychiatry*, vol. I, New York: Basic Books, 1974, pp. 3–27. This reference is on p. 22.

6 **Labor, Poverty and Schizophrenia**
1 Brenner, M.H., *Mental Illness and the Economy*, Cambridge, Massachusetts: Harvard University Press, 1973, p. 207.
2 Scull, A. T., *Decarceration: Community Treatment and the Deviant—A Radical View*, Englewood Cliffs, New Jersey: Prentice-Hall, 1977, p. 157; Sharfstein, S.S. and Nafziger, J.C., 'Community care: Costs and benefits for a chronic patient,' *Hospital and Community Psychiatry*, 27: 170–3, 1976; Murphy, J.G. and Datel, W.E., 'A cost-benefit analysis of community versus institutional living,' *Hospital and Community Psychiatry*, 27: 165–70, 1976.
3 All quotations in this paragraph are drawn from Marsden, D. and Duff, E., *Workless: Some Unemployed Men and Their Families*, Baltimore: Penguin, 1975, pp. 191–202.
4 Eisenberg, P. and Lazarsfeld, P.F., 'The psychological effects of unemployment,' *Psychological Bulletin*, 35: 358–90, 1938; The Pilgrim Trust, *Men Without Work*, New York: Greenwood Press, 1968, p. 143 et seq.
5 Bemporad, J.R. and Pinsker, H., 'Schizophrenia: The manifest symptomatology,' in S. Arieti and E.B. Brody (eds), *American Handbook of Psychiatry*, vol. III, New York: Basic Books, 1974, pp. 525–50. The quotation is on p. 540.
6 Marsden and Duff, *Workless*, p. 211.
7 Israeli, N., 'Distress in the outlook of Lancashire and Scottish unemployed,' *Journal of Applied Psychology*, 19: 67–9, 1935.
8 Ibid., p. 67.
9 Brenner, *Mental Illness and the Economy*, pp. 38, 56, 169.
10 Brown, G.W., Birley, J.L.T. and Wing, J.K., 'Influence of family life on the course of schizophrenic disorders: A replication,' *British Journal of Psychiatry*, 121: 241–58, 1972; Vaughn, C.E. and Leff, J.P., 'The influence of family and social factors on the course of psychiatric illness,' *British Journal of Psychiatry*, 129: 125–37, 1976.
11 Leff, J., 'Preventing relapse in schizophrenia,' presented at the World Psychiatric Association Regional Meeting, New York City, October 30–November 3, 1981.
12 Brown, G.W., Bone, M., Dalison, B. et al., *Schizophrenia and Social Care*, London: Oxford University Press, 1966.
13 Wing, J.K. and Brown, G.W., *Institutionalism and Schizophrenia*, London:

Cambridge University Press, 1970.

14 Huessy, H.R., 'Discussion,' *Schizophrenia Bulletin*, 7: 178–80, 1981.

15 Brown, G.W. and Birley, J.L.T., 'Crises and life changes and the onset of schizophrenia,' *Journal of Health and Social Behavior*, 9: 203–14, 1968.

16 Engels, F., *The Condition of the Working Class in England*, London: Granada, 1969, p. 117. First published in Leipzig in 1845.

17 Marx, K., *Capital*, vol. I, New York: International Publishers, 1967; reproduction of the English edition of 1887, p. 632.

18 Ibid., p. 643.

19 Ibid., pp.643–4.

20 Ibid., p. 644.

21 Ibid., pp. 644–5.

22 Mandel, E., *Marxist Economic Theory*, vol. 1, translated by B. Pearce, New York: Monthly Review Press, 1971, pp. 150–4.

23 Braverman, H., *Labor and Monopoly Capital: The Degradation of Work in the Twentieth Century*, New York: Monthly Review Press, 1974, pp. 386–401.

24 Anderson, C.H., *The Political Economy of Class*, Englewood Cliffs, New Jersey: Prentice-Hall, 1974, p. 149.

25 Silk, L., 'Stocks jump as jobs slump: So what's next?, *New York Times*, October 10, 1982, p. E1; Herbers, J., 'U.S. poverty rate highest since 1967,' *New York Times* report in the *Denver Post*, July 20, 1982, pp. 1, 12; 'Disintegration of black families threatens gains of decades,' *New York Times*, November 20, 1983, pp. 1, 36.

26 Mora, G., 'Historical and theoretical trends in psychiatry,' in H.I. Kaplan, A.M. Freedman and B.J. Sadock (eds), *Comprehensive Textbook of Psychiatry-III*, Baltimore: Williams & Wilkins, 1980, pp. 4–98. The material in this paragraph is from pp. 73–91.

27 Scull, A.T., *Museums of Madness: The Social Organization of Insanity in Nineteenth Century England*, London: Allen Lane (New York: St Martin's Press), 1979, pp. 196–9.

28 Clark, D.H., *Social Therapy in Psychiatry*, Baltimore: Penguin, 1974, p. 23.

29 Mora, 'Historical and theoretical trends,' pp. 80, 90.

30 Among those making an ideological switch in tune with the economy was psychiatrist Werner Mendel, nationally recognized in the 1970s for his advocacy of community treatment of schizophrenia. Appearing for the City and County of Denver, the defendants in the case, Dr Mendel modified his earlier views and testified that community care and vocational rehabilitation for schizophrenics just do not work. In his deposition of May 7, 1983, for the Probate Court (case number 81–MH–270) and the District Court (civil action number 81–CV–6961) of the City and County of Denver, he claimed that it would be just as well for schizophrenics if the whole mental health profession disappeared overnight. His pessimistic appraisal grew largely out of his own research and experience with a program treating psychotic patients in Los Angeles through a period of increasing unemployment and declining mental health funds.

31 For positive evaluations of the efficacy of psychosocial treatment and community support systems see Mosher, L.R. and Keith, S.J., 'Psychosocial treatment: Individual, group, family, and community support approaches,' *Schizophrenia*

*Bulletin*, 6: 11–41, 1980; Stein, L.I. and Test, M.A., 'Alternative to mental hospital treatment: I. Conceptual model, treatment program, and clinical evaluation,' *Archives of General Psychiatry*, 37: 392–7, 1980; Weisbrod, B.A., Test, M.A. and Stein, L.I., 'Alternative to mental hospital treatment: II. Economic benefit-cost analysis,' *Archives of General Psychiatry*, 37: 400–5, 1980; Test, M.A. and Stein, L.I., 'Alternative to mental hospital treatment: III. Social cost,' *Archives of General Psychiatry*, 37: 409–12, 1980; Pasamanick, B., Scarpitti, F. and Dinitz, S., *Schizophrenics in the Community: An Experimental Study in the Prevention of Hospitalization*, New York: Appleton-Century-Crofts, 1967; Mosher, L.R., Menn, A.Z. and Mathews, S., 'Soteria: Evaluation of a home-based treatment for schizophrenia,' *American Journal of Orthopsychiatry*, 45: 455–69, 1975; Polak, P.R. and Kirby, M.W., 'A model to replace psychiatric hospitals,' *Journal of Nervous and Mental Disease*, 162: 13–22, 1976.

32 Aronson, E., *The Social Animal*, 2nd edn, San Francisco: W.H. Freeman, 1976, pp. 186–9.

33 Clark, *Social Therapy in Psychiatry*, ch. 2.

34 Carstairs, G.M., 'Advances in psychological medicine,' *Practitioner*, Symposium on Advances in Treatment, 187: 495–504, 1961. Quoted in Jones, K., *A History of the Mental Health Services*, London: Routledge & Kegan Paul, 1972, p. 292.

35 Star, S., 'The public's idea of mental illness,' presented at National Association for Mental Health meeting, Chicago, Illinois, November 1955; Cumming, E. and Cumming, J., *Closed Ranks: An Experiment in Mental Health Education*, Cambridge, Massachusetts: Harvard University Press, 1957; Nunally, J.C., *Popular Conceptions of Mental Health*, New York: Holt, Rinehart & Winston, 1961.

36 Lemkau, P.V. and Crocetti, G.M., 'An urban population's opinion and knowledge about mental illness,' *American Journal of Psychiatry*, 118: 692–700, 1962; Meyer J.K., 'Attitudes towards mental illness in a Maryland community,' *Public Health Reports*, 79: 769–72, 1964.

37 D'Arcy, C. and Brockman, J., 'Changing public recognition of psychiatric symptoms? Blackfoot revisited,' *Journal of Health and Social Behavior*, 17: 302–10, 1976; Olmsted, D.W. and Durham, K., 'Stability of mental health attitudes: A semantic differential study,' *Journal of Health and Social Behavior*, 17: 35–44, 1976.

38 Jones, *History of Mental Health Services*, p. 291.

39 Ibid., pp. 283, 289–91, 304.

40 Dickens, C., *American Notes for General Circulation*, Harmondsworth Middlesex: Penguin, 1972; first published 1842, p. 100.

41 Clark, *Social Therapy in Psychiatry*, p. 21.

42 Brenner, *Mental Illness and the Economy*, pp. 170–2.

43 Thurnam, J., *Observations and Essays on the Statistics of Insanity*, London: Simpkin, Marshall, 1845; reprint edn, New York, Arno Press, 1976, p. 27.

44 Ödegard, Ö., 'A statistical study of factors influencing discharge from psychiatric hospitals,' *Journal of Mental Science*, 106: 1124–33, 1960.

45 Beck, J.C., 'Social influences on the prognosis of schizophrenia,' *Schizophrenia Bulletin*, 4: 86–101, 1978.

46 World Health Organization, *Schizophrenia: An International Follow-up Study*,

Chichester: Wiley, 1979, pp. 162, 273, 278, 286.

47  Brenner, *Mental Illness and the Economy*, p. 170.
48  Henry, A.F. and Short, J.F., *Suicide and Homicide*, Glencoe, Illinois: Free Press, 1954.
49  Brenner, *Mental Illness and the Economy*, p. 53.
50  Cooper, B., 'Social class and prognosis in schizophrenia: Parts I and II,' *Journal of Preventive and Social Medicine*, 15: 17–30, 31–41, 1961.
51  Ibid., p. 36.
52  Brooke, E.M., 'Report on the Second International Congress for Psychiatry, Zurich,' vol. III, 1957, p. 52. Cited in Cooper, 'Social class and prognosis in schizophrenia,' p. 19.
53  Hollingshead, A.B. and Redlich, F.C., *Social Class and Mental Illness*, New York: Wiley, 1958.
54  Myers, J.K. and Bean, L.L., *A Decade Later: A Follow-up of Social Class and Mental Illness*, New York: Wiley, 1968.
55  Astrachan, B.M., Brauer, L., Harrow, M. et al., 'Symptomatic outcome in schizophrenia,' *Archives of General Psychiatry*, 31: 155–60, 1974.
56  World Health Organization, *Schizophrenia*, p. 288.
57  Wing, J.K., Denham, J. and Munro, A.B., 'Duration of stay of patients suffering from schizophrenia,' *British Journal of Preventive and Social Medicine*, 13: 145–8, 1959; Carstairs, G.M., Tonge, W.L., O'Connor, N. et al., *British Journal of Preventive and Social Medicine*, 9: 187 et seq., 1955, cited in Cooper, 'Social class and prognosis in schizophrenia,' p. 19.
58  Ödegard, 'Discharge from psychiatric hospital,' pp. 1127–9.
59  Astrachan, Brauer, Harrow et al., pp. 159–60.
60  Ciompi, L., 'Catamnestic long-term study on the course of life and aging of schizophrenics,' *Schizophrenia Bulletin*, 6: 606–18, 1980.
61  Mitchell, B.R., *European Historical Statistics 1750–1970*, abridged edn, New York: Columbia University Press, 1978.
62  Ciompi, 'Life and aging of schizophrenics,' p. 615.
63  Ellman, M., *Socialist Planning*, Cambridge: Cambridge University Press, 1979, p. 257.
64  Ibid., p. 161.
65  Barker, D., 'Moscow mayor has his say on jobless,' *Guardian*, July 11, 1983.
66  Wing, J.K., *Reasoning About Madness*, Oxford: Oxford University Press, 1978; Field, M.G. and Aronson, J., 'Soviet community mental health services and work therapy: A report of two visits,' *Community Mental Health Journal*, 1: 81–90, 1965; Hein, G., 'Social psychiatric treatment of schizophrenia in the Soviet Union,' *International Journal of Psychiatry*, 6: 346–62, 1968.
67  World Health Organization, *Schizophrenia*, p. 160.

## 7  Schizophrenia in the Third World

1  Gunderson, J.G. and Mosher, L.R., 'The cost of schizophrenia,' *American Journal of Psychiatry*, 132: 901–6, 1975.
2  Collomb, H., 'Bouffées délirantes en psychiatrie Africaine,' *Transcultural Psychiatric Research*, 3: 29–34, 1966, p. 29.
3  Schwartz, R., 'Beschreibung einer ambulanten psychiatrischen Patienten-

population in der Grossen-Kabylie (Nordalgerien): Epidemiologische und Klinische Aspekte,' *Social Psychiatry* (West Germany), 12: 207–18, 1977.

4 Smartt, C.G.F., 'Mental maladjustment in the East African,' *Journal of Mental Science*, 102: 441–66, 1956.

5 Opler, M.K., 'The social and cultural nature of mental illness and its treatment,' in S. Lesse, (ed.), *An Evaluation of the Results of the Psychotherapies*, Springfield, Illinois: C.C. Thomas, 1968, p. 280–91.

6 Tewfik, G.I., 'Psychoses in Africa,' in *Mental Disorders and Mental Health in Africa South of the Sahara*, CCTA/CSA-WFMH-WHO meeting of specialists on mental health, Bukavu, London: 1958.

7 Field, M.J., *Search for Security: An Ethno-psychiatric Study of Rural Ghana*, Chicago: Northwestern University Press, 1962.

8 Fortes, M. and Mayer, D.Y., 'Psychosis and social change among the Tallensi of northern Ghana,' in S.H. Foulkes and G.S. Prince (eds) *Psychiatry in a Changing Society*, London: Tavistock, 1969, pp. 33–73.

9 Berne, E., 'Some oriental mental hospitals,' *American Journal of Psychiatry*, 106: 376–83, 1949; Seligman, C.G., 'Temperament, conflict and psychosis in a stone-age population,' *British Journal of Medical Psychology*, 9: 187–202, 1929; Jilek, W.G. and Jilek-Aall, L., 'Transient psychoses in Africans,' *Psychiatrica Clinica* (Basel), 3: 337–64, 1970.

10 Murphy, H.B.M., 'Cultural factors in the genesis of schizophrenia,' in D. Rosenthal and S.S. Kety (eds), *The Transmission of Schizophrenia*, Oxford: Pergamon, 1968, p. 138.

11 American Psychiatric Association, *Diagnostic and Statistical Manual of Mental Disorders (DSM - III)*, Washington, DC: 1968.

12 Wintrob, R.M., 'Malaria and the acute psychotic episode,' *Journal of Nervous and Mental Disease*, 156: 306–17, 1973.

13 Rin, H. and Lin, T., 'Mental illness among Formosan aborigines as compared with the Chinese in Taiwan,' *Journal of Mental Science*, 108: 134–46, 1962.

14 De Wet, J.S. Du T., 'Evaluation of a common method of convulsion therapy in Bantu schizophrenics,' *Journal of Mental Science*, 103: 739–57, 1957, p. 745.

15 Laubscher, B.J.F., *Sex, Custom and Psychopathology: A Study of South African Pagan Natives*, London: Routledge & Kegan Paul, 1937; Simons, H.J. 'Mental disease in Africans: Racial determinism,' *Journal of Mental Science*, 104: 371–88, 1958.

16 Westermeyer, J., 'Psychosis in a peasant society: Social outcomes,' *American Journal of Psychiatry*, 137: 1390–4, 1980, p. 393.

17 Ibid.

18 Westermeyer, J. and Wintrob, R., ' "Folk" criteria for diagnosis of mental illness in rural Laos: On being insane in sane places,' *American Journal of Psychiatry*, 136: 755–61, 1979, p. 755.

19 Westermeyer, J., 'Dr. Westermeyer replies,' *American Journal of Psychiatry*, 138: 699, 1981.

20 Brown, G.W., Bone, M., Dalison, B. and Wing, J.K., *Schizophrenia and Social Care*, London: Oxford University Press, 1966.

21 Kulhara, P. and Wig, N.N., 'The chronicity of schizophrenia in North West India: Results of a follow-up study,' *British Journal of Psychiatry*, 132: 186–90,

1978.

22 Murphy, H.B.M. and Raman, A.C., 'The chronicity of schizophrenia in indigenous tropical peoples,' *British Journal of Psychiatry*, 118: 489–97, 1971.

23 Waxler, N.E., 'Is outcome for schizophrenia better in nonindustrial societies? The case of Sri Lanka,' *Journal of Nervous and Mental Disease*, 167: 144–58, 1979.

24 Lo, W.H. and Lo, T., 'A ten-year follow-up study of Chinese schizophrenics in Hong Kong,' *British Journal of Psychiatry*, 131: 63–6, 1977.

25 World Health Organization, *Schizophrenia: An International Follow-up Study*, Chichester, England: Wiley, 1979.

26 Harris, M., *Culture, Man and Nature: An Introduction to General Anthropology*, New York: Thomas Y. Crowell, 1971, p. 480.

27 Lambo, T., 'The importance of cultural factors in psychiatric treatment,' in I. Al-Issa and W. Dennis (eds), *Cross-Cultural Studies of Behavior*, New York: Holt, Rinehart & Winston, 1970, pp. 548–52.

28 World Health Organization, *Schizophrenia*, p. 104.

29 Wing, J.K., 'The social context of schizophrenia,' *American Journal of Psychiatry*, 135: 1333–9, 1978.

30 World Health Organization, *Schizophrenia*, p. 104.

31 Sahlins, M., *Stone Age Economics*, Chicago: Aldine-Atherton, 1972, pp. 63–4; Neff, W.S., *World and Human Behavior*, Chicago: Aldine, 1968; Sharp, L., 'People without politics,' in V.F. Ray (ed.), *Systems of Political Control and Bureaucracy in Human Societies*, Seattle: University of Washington Press, 1958, p. 6.

32 Lee, R.E., *The !Kung San: Men, Women and Work in a Foraging Society*, New York: Cambridge University Press, 1979.

33 Richards, A.I., *Land, Labour and Diet in Northern Rhodesia*, London: Oxford University Press, 1961, appendix E; Guillard, J., 'Essai de mesure de l'activité d'un paysan Africain: Le Toupouri,' *L'Agronomie Tropicale*, 13: 415–28, 1958. Both works are cited in Sahlins, *Stone Age Economics*, pp. 62–4.

34 Eyer, J. and Sterling, P., 'Stress-related mortality and social organization,' *The Review of Radical Political Economics*, 9: 1–44, 1977, p. 15.

35 Fei, H. and Chang, C., *Earthbound China: A Study of Rural Economy in Yunnan*, Chicago: University of Chicago Press, 1945, pp. 30–4, 145; Eyer and Sterling, 'Stress-related mortality,' p. 15.

36 Sahlins, *Stone Age Economics*, ch. 2.

37 Chayanov, A.V., *The Theory of Peasant Economy*, Homewood, Illinois: Richard D. Irwin, 1966, p. 77, cited in Sahlins, *Stone Age Economics*, p. 89.

38 Richards, *Land, Labour and Diet*, p. 402; Douglas, M., 'Lele economy as compared with the Bushong,' in G. Dalton and P. Bohannen, *Markets in Africa*, Evanston, Illinois: Northwestern University Press, 1962, p. 231, cited in Sahlins, *Stone Age Economics*, pp. 52–4.

39 Linn, J.F., *Cities in the Developing World: Policies for Their Equitable and Efficient Growth*, New York: World Bank/Oxford University Press, 1983, pp. 36–42; Squire, L., *Employment Policy in Developing Countries*, New York: World Bank/Oxford University Press, 1981, pp. 66–75, 83–90.

40 World Health Organization, *Schizophrenia*, ch. 10.

41 Doyal, L., *The Political Economy of Health*, Boston: South End Press, 1981, pp. 112–13; Fortes and Mayer, 'Psychosis among the Tallensi.'

42 World Health Organization, *Schizophrenia*, pp. 271, 283.

43 Squire, *Employment Policy in Developing Countries*, p. 71.

44 World Health Organization, *Schizophrenia*, p. 283.

45 Ibid., pp. 287–8.

46 McGoodwin, J.R., 'No matter how we asked them, they convinced us that they suffer,' *Human Organization*, 37: 378–83, 1978.

47 Paul, B.D., 'Mental disorder and self-regulating processes in culture: A Guatemalan illustration,' in R. Hunt (ed.), *Personalities and Cultures: Readings in Psychological Anthropology*, Garden City, New York: Natural History Press, 1967.

48 Gelfand, M., 'Psychiatric disorders as recognized by the Shona,' in A. Kiev (ed.), *Magic, Faith and Healing*, New York: Free Press, 1964, pp. 156–73.

49 Collomb, 'Bouffées délirantes en psychiatrie Africaine,' p. 30.

50 Rogler, L.H. and Hollingshead, A.B., *Trapped: Families and Schizophrenia*, New York: Wiley, 1965, p. 254.

51 Erinosho, O.A. and Ayonrinde, A., 'Educational background and attitude to mental illness among the Yoruba in Nigeria,' *Human Relations*, 34: 1–12, 1981.

52 D'Arcy, C. and Brockman, J., 'Changing public recognition of psychiatric symptoms? Blackfoot revisited,' *Journal of Health and Social Behavior*, 17: 302–10, 1976.

53 Ibid.

54 Binitie, A.O., 'Attitude of educated Nigerians to psychiatric illness,' *Acta Psychiatrica Scandinavica*, 46: 391–8, 1970.

55 Colson, A.C., 'The perception of abnormality in a Malay village,' in N.N. Wagner and E. Tan (eds), *Psychological Problems and Treatment in Malaysia*, Kuala Lumpar: University of Malaya Press, 1971.

56 Leff, J., *Psychiatry Around the Globe: A Transcultural View*, New York: Marcel Dekker, 1981, p. 19.

57 Westermeyer and Wintrob, ' "Folk" diagnosis in rural Laos;' Westermeyer, J. and Kroll, J., 'Violence and mental illness in a peasant society: Characteristics of violent behaviors and "folk" use of restraints,' *British Journal of Psychiatry*, 133: 529–41, 1978.

58 Edgerton, R.B., 'Conceptions of psychosis in four East African societies,' *American Anthropologist*, 68: 408–25, 1966.

59 Edgerton, R.B., *The Individual in Cultural Adaption*, Berkeley: University of California Press, 1971, p. 188.

60 Edgerton, 'Psychosis in four East African societies.'

61 Ibid., p. 417.

62 Rin and Lin, 'Mental illness among Formosan aborigines.'

63 Waxler, N.E., 'Is mental illness cured in traditional societies? A theoretical analysis,' *Culture, Medicine and Psychiatry*, 1: 233–53, 1977, p. 242.

64 World Health Organization, *Schizophrenia*, p. 105.

65 Levy, J.E., Neutra, R. and Parker, D., 'Life careers of Navajo epileptics and convulsive hysterics,' *Social Science and Medicine*, 13: 53–66, 1979.

66 Sontag, S., *Illness as Metaphor*, New York: Vintage Books, 1979.

67 Eliade, M., *Shamanism: Arachaic Techniques of Ecstasy*, Princeton: Princeton

University Press/Bollingen Paperback, 1972; Black Elk, *The Sacred Pipe*, Baltimore: Penguin, 1971.

68 Rogler and Hollingshead, *Trapped: Families and Schizophrenia*, p. 254.

69 Ozturk, O.M., 'Folk treatment of mental illness in Turkey,' in Kiev, *Magic, Faith and Healing*, p. 349.

70 Benedict, R., *Patterns of Culture*, Boston: Houghton-Mifflin, 1934, pp. 267–8.

71 Ackernecht, E.H., 'Psychopathology, primitive medicine and primitive culture,' *Bulletin of the History of Medicine*, 14: 30–67, 1943; and Silverman, J., 'Shamans and acute schizophrenia,' *American Anthropologist*, 69: 21–31, 1967.

72 Torrey, E.F., *The Mind Game: Witchdoctors and Psychiatrists*, New York: Emerson Hall, 1972; Torrey, E.F., *Schizophrenia and Civilization*, New York: Jason Aronson, 1980.

73 Silverman, 'Shamans and acute schizophrenia.' p. 29.

74 Linton, R., *Culture and Mental Disorders*, Springfield, Illinois: Charles C. Thomas, 1956.

75 Mischel, W. and Mischel, F., 'Psychological aspects of spirit possession,' *American Anthropologist*, 60: 249–60, 1958.

76 Prince, R., 'Indigenous Yoruba psychiatry,' in Kiev, *Magic, Faith and Healing*, pp. 84–120.

77 Messing, S.D., 'Group therapy and social status in the Zar cult of Ethiopia,' in J. Middleton (ed.), *Magic, Witchcraft and Curing*, Garden City, New York: Natural History Press, 1967, pp. 285–93.

78 Fox, J.R., 'Witchcraft and clanship in Cochiti therapy,' in Middleton, *Magic, Witchcraft and Curing*, pp. 255–84.

79 Dawson, J., 'Urbanization and mental health in a West African community,' in Kiev, *Magic, Faith and Healing*, pp. 305–42.

80 Benedict, *Patterns of Culture*, p. 72.

81 Kaplan, B. and Johnson, D., 'The social meaning of Navajo psychopathology and psychotherapy,' in Kiev, *Magic, Faith and Healing*, pp. 203–29; Leighton, A.H. and Leighton, D.C., 'Elements of psychotherapy in Navaho religion,' *Psychiatry*, 4: 515–23, 1941.

82 Waxler, 'Is mental illness cured in traditional societies?,' p. 241.

83 World Health Organization, *Schizophrenia*, p. 288.

84 Hare, E.H., 'Mental illness and social conditions in Bristol,' *Journal of Mental Science*, 102: 349–57, 1956; Stein, L., ' "Social class" gradient in schizophrenia,' *British Journal of Preventive and Social Medicine*, 11: 181–95, 1957; Cooper, B., 'Social class and prognosis in schizophrenia: Part I,' *British Journal of Preventive and Social Medicine*, 15: 17–30, 1961; Jaco, E.G., 'The social isolation hypothesis and schizophrenia,' *American Sociological Review*, 19: 567–77, 1954.

85 Levi-Strauss, C., *Structural Anthropology*, Harmondsworth, Middlesex: Penguin, 1972, p. 180.

86 Warner, W.L., *A Black Civilization*, New York: Harper, 1937, pp. 241–2.

87 Beiser, M. and Collomb, H., 'Mastering change: Epidemiological and case studies in Senegal, West Africa,' *American Journal of Psychiatry*, 138: 455–9, 1981.

88 El-Islam, M.F., 'A better outlook for schizophrenics living in extended families,' *British Journal of Psychiatry*, 135: 343–7, 1979.

89 Wig, N.N., Menon, D.K. and Bedi, H., 'Coping with schizophrenic patients in developing countries: A study of expressed emotions in the relatives,' presented at the Seventh World Congress of Psychiatry, Vienna, July 11–16, 1983; Leff, *Psychiatry Around the Globe*, p. 157.


## 8 The Schizophrenic in Western Society

1 Kraft, S. and Shulins, N., 'Cardboard is home for box people,' Associated Press release in the *Boulder Daily Camera*, January 17, 1982, p. 5.
2 Hopper, K., Baxter, E. and Cox, S., 'Not making it crazy: The young homeless patients in New York City,' *New Directions for Mental Health Services*, no. 14: 33–42, 1982.
3 US Department of Health and Human Services, *Toward a National Plan for the Chronically Mentally Ill*, Report to the Secretary by the Steering Committee on the Chronically Mentally Ill, Washington, DC: Department of Health and Human Services Publication Number (ADM) 81–1077, 1981, part 2, p. 11.
4 Reich, R. and Siegel, L., 'The emergence of the Bowery as a psychiatric dumping ground,' *Psychiatric Quarterly*, 50: 191–201, 1978; Reich, R. and Siegel, L., 'The chronically mentally ill shuffle to oblivion,' *Psychiatric Annals*, 3: 35–55, 1973.
5 Spitzer, R.L., Cohen, G., Miller, D.J. and Endicott, J., 'The psychiatric status of 100 men on Skid Row,' *International Journal of Social Psychiatry*, 15: 230–4, 1969.
6 Baxter, E. and Hopper, K., 'The new mendicancy: Homeless in New York City,' *American Journal of Orthopsychiatry*, 52: 393–408, 1982, p. 398.
7 Ibid., pp. 398–400.
8 Hopper, Baxter and Cox, 'Not making it crazy,' p. 34.
9 Priest, R.G., 'A USA-UK comparison,' *Proceedings of the Royal Society of Medicine*, 63: 441–5, 1970.
10 Bogue, D.J., *Skid Row in American Cities*, Chicago: Community and Family Study Center, University of Chicago, 1963, p. 208.
11 Farr, R., unpublished mimeograph, 1983.
12 Torrey, E.F., 'The real twilight zone,' *Washington Post*, August 26, 1983.
13 Colorado Bar Association, Report concerning the implementation of the Colorado Act for the Care and Treatment of the Mentally Ill, submitted to the Board of Governors of the Colorado Bar Association by the Disability Law Committee on July 31, 1981, p. 22.
14 Recent news reports place the number of homeless men, women and children in the United States during the winter of 1982–3 at 2 million. This number, however, includes many who are not to be found in the downtown, urban Skid Row areas and many who are recently and, perhaps, temporarily impoverished. At the other end of the scale, in *Skid Row*, Bogue estimated that 100,000 American men were homeless in the Skid Row districts of forty-one cities in 1950. For a more recent and accurate picture we must add Skid Row women and the effects of general population growth and urbanization, deepening depression with increasing unemployment and the dumping of state hospital patients on the streets. Bogue's estimate of the number of homeless in New

York City, for example, has since trebled. We can justifiably conclude that 200,000–400,000 American men and women live on Skid Row.

Fifty thousand to 100,000 schizophrenics, then, are likely to be among the nation's Skid Row homeless; but more may well exist among the remaining 1.5 million or more homeless who are not in the Skid Row districts.

15 Freeman, S.J.J., Formo, A., Alumpur, A.G. and Sommers, A.F., 'Psychiatric disorder in a Skid-Row mission population,' *Comprehensive Psychiatry*, 20: 454–62, 1979.

16 Edwards, G., Williamson, V., Hawker, A. et al., 'Census of a Reception Centre,' *British Journal of Psychiatry*, 114: 1031–9, 1968.

17 Tidmarsh, D. and Wood, S., 'Psychiatric aspects of destitution: A study of the Camberwell Reception Centre,' in J.K. Wing and A.M. Hailey (eds), *Evaluating a Community Psychiatric Service: The Camberwell Register 1964–1971*, London: Oxford University Press, 1972.

18 Patch, I.C.L., 'Homeless men,' *Proceedings of the Royal Society of Medicine*, 63: 437–41, 1970.

19 Priest, R.G., 'The Edinburgh homeless: A psychiatric survey,' *American Journal of Psychotherapy*, 25: 191–213, 1971.

20 Her Majesty's Stationery Office, *Homeless Single Persons*, London: 1966.

21 Rollin, H., 'From patients to vagrants,' *New Society*, January 15, 1970, pp. 90–3.

22 Lim, M.H., 'A psychiatric emergency clinic: A study of attendances over six months,' *British Journal of Psychiatry*, 143: 460–6, 1983.

23 Swank, G.E. and Winer, D., 'Occurrence of psychiatric disorder in a county jail population,' *American Journal of Psychiatry*, 133: 1331–3, 1976; Petrich, J., 'Rate of psychiatric morbidity in a metropolitan county jail population,' *American Journal of Psychiatry*, 133: 1439–44, 1976; Lamb, H.R. and Grant, R.W., 'The mentally ill in an urban county jail,' *Archives of General Psychiatry*, 39: 17–22, 1982.

24 Warner, R., 'Psychotics in jail,' presented at the Mental Health Center of Boulder County Symposium on Controversial Issues in Community Care, Boulder, Colorado, March 27, 1981.

25 Service, A.L., Koval, J.S. and Pursey-Day, C., *Final Report: Mental Health Systems Study*, Submitted to the Joint Budget Committee of the Colorado General Assembly, December 1, 1981.

26 Cherry, A.L., 'On jailing the mentally ill,' *Health and Social Work*, 3: 189–92, 1978.

27 Roth, L.H. and Ervin, F.R., 'Psychiatric care of federal prisoners,' *American Journal of Psychiatry*, 128: 424–30, 1971; Kaufman, E., 'The violation of psychiatric standards of care in prisons,' *American Journal of Psychiatry*, 137: 566–70, 1980; James, J.F., Gregory, D., Jones, R.K. and Rundell, O.H., 'Psychiatric morbidity in prisons,' *Hospital and Community Psychiatry*, 31: 674–7, 1980.

28 Stelovich, S., 'From the hospital to the prison: A step forward in deinstitution-alization?' *Hospital and Community Psychiatry*, 30: 618–20, 1979.

29 Goldfarb, R., *Jails: The Ultimate Ghetto*, Garden City, New York: Anchor Press, 1975, p. 89.

30 Ibid.

31 Ibid.
32 Kaufman, 'Violation of psychiatric standards,' p. 567.
33 Ibid., p. 568.
34 Velde, R.W., associate administrator of the Law Enforcement Assistance Administration of the US Department of Justice, writing in *The Correctional Trainer,* Newsletter for Illinois Correctional Staff Training, Fall 1979, p. 109.
35 Goldfarb, *Jails;* Kaufman, 'Violation of psychiatric standards.'
36 Waldron, R.J. and Pospichal, T.J., 'The relationship between unemployment rates and prison incarceration rates,' NCJRS microfiche, 1980; Jankovic, I., 'Labor market and imprisonment,' *Crime and Social Justice,* 8: 17–31, 1977; Carlson, K., Evans, P. and Flanagan, J., *American Prisons and Jails: Volume II: Population Trends and Projections,* Washington, DC: US Department of Justice, National Institute of Justice, 1980; Greenberg, D.G., 'The dynamics of oscillatory punishment processes,' *Journal of Criminal Law and Criminology,* 68: 643–51, 1977; Brenner, M.H., *Estimating the Social Costs of National Economic Policy: Implications for Mental and Physical Health and Criminal Aggression,* Washington, DC: US Government Printing Office, 1976; Nagel, J.H., 'Crime and incarceration: A reanalysis,' NCJRS microfiche, 1977; Nagel, W.G., 'A statement on behalf of a moratorium on prison construction,' proceedings of the 106th Annual Congress of the American Correctional Association, Denver, August 1976, pp. 79–87.
37 Warner, R., 'The effect of the labor market on mental hospital and prison use: An international comparison,' *Administration in Mental Health,* 10: 239–58, 1983.
38 US DHHS, *Toward a National Plan,* part 2, p. 20.
39 A study of the chronically mentally ill in Los Angeles board and care homes found two-thirds to be schizophrenic: see Lehman, A.F., Ward, A.C. and Linn, L.S., 'Chronic mental patients: The quality of life issue,' *American Journal of Psychiatry,* 139: 1271–6, 1982.
40 US DHHS, *Toward a National Plan,* Part 2, p. 19. Minkoff, K., 'A map of the chronic mental patient,' in J.A.Talbott (ed.), *The Chronic Mental Patient,* Washington, DC: American Psychiatric Association, 1978, pp. 18–19.
41 Gunderson, J.G. and Mosher, L.R., 'The cost of schizophrenia,' *American Journal of Psychiatry,* 132: 901–5, 1975; Minkoff, 'Map of the chronic mental patient,' p. 13.
42 Minkoff ('Map of the chronic mental patient,' p. 13) calculates that there were about 1.1 million schizophrenics in treatment in 1977–8. The figure is derived from the prevalence statistic in the Monroe County case register of 4.78 per 1,000 of the general population. The commonly cited figure of 2 million Americans with schizophrenia is a crude *lifetime* prevalence estimate. Here we are concerned with *active* cases of schizophrenia and the lower point-prevalence rate is the appropriate figure.

The estimate of 1.1 million schizophrenics, however, refers to patients *in treatment* in the course of a year. This is a reasonably suitable figure for the purposes of this paper since most of the schizophrenics located in different settings are actively in treatment. As we have seen, however, close to 100,000 schizophrenics may be on Skid Row or in jail. Perhaps half or more of these psychotics receive no active treatment in the course of a year. To account for these persons we should adjust the number of American schizophrenics upwards to 1.2 million.

43 Binder, R.L., 'The use of seclusion on an inpatient crisis intervention unit,' *Hospital and Community Psychiatry*, 30: 266–9, 1979.
44 Wadeson, H. and Carpenter, W.T., 'The impact of the seclusion room experience,' *Journal of Nervous and Mental Disease*, 163: 318–28, 1976.
45 Telintelo, S., Kuhlman, T.L. and Winget, C., 'A study of the use of restraint in a psychiatric emergency room,' *Hospital and Community Psychiatry*, 34: 164–5, 1983.
46 Soloff, P.H., 'Behavioral precipitants of restraint in the modern milieu,' *Comprehensive Psychiatry*, 19: 179–84, 1978, p. 182.
47 Mattson, M.R. and Sacks, M.H., 'Seclusion: Uses and complications,' *American Journal of Psychiatry*, 135: 1210–13, 1978, p. 1211.
48 Colorado Bar Association Report, pp. 9–10. Subsequently, conditions at the two Colorado State Hospitals have substantially improved.
49 'In Your Community,' radio program in the series 'Breakdown.' Produced at Seven Oaks Productions, Boulder, Colorado, by R. Warner and K. Kindle.
50 Anonymous, 'On being diagnosed schizophrenic,' *Schizophrenia Bulletin*, 3: 4, 1977.
51 Star, S., 'The public's idea about mental illness,' presented at the National Association for Mental Health meeting, Chicago, Illinois, November 1955.
52 Cumming, E. and Cumming, J., *Closed Ranks: An Experiment in Mental Health Education*, Cambridge: Harvard University Press, 1957.
53 Nunally, J.C., *Popular Conceptions of Mental Health: Their Development and Change*, New York: Holt, Rinehart & Winston, 1961, p. 46.
54 Ibid., p. 51.
55 Ibid., p. 233.
56 Lemkau, P.V. and Crocetti, G.M., 'An urban population's opinions and knowledge about mental illness,' *American Journal of Psychiatry*, 118: 692–700, 1962; Meyer, J.K., 'Attitudes toward mental illness in a Maryland community,' *Public Health Reports*, 79: 769–72, 1964; Bentz, W.K., Edgerton, J.W. and Kherlopian, M., 'Perceptions of mental illness among people in a rural area,' *Mental Hygiene*, 53: 459–65, 1969; Crocetti, G., Spiro, H.R. and Siassi, I., 'Are the ranks closed? Attitudinal social distance and mental illness,' *American Journal of Psychiatry*, 127: 1121–7, 1971.
57 Cockerham, W.C., *Sociology of Mental Disorder*, Englewood Cliffs, New Jersey: Prentice-Hall, 1981, pp. 295–9.
58 Olmsted, D.W. and Durham, K., 'Stability of mental health attitudes: A semantic differential study,' *Journal of Health and Social Behavior*, 17: 35–44, 1976.
59 D'Arcy, C. and Brockman, J., 'Changing public recognition of psychiatric symptoms? Blackfoot revisited,' *Journal of Health and Social Behavior*, 17: 302–10 1976.
60 Miller, D. and Dawson, W.H., 'Effects of stigma on re-employment of ex-mental patients,' *Mental Hygiene*, 49: 281–7, 1965.
61 Aviram, U. and Segal, S.P., 'Exclusion of the mentally ill: Reflection of an old

problem in a new context,' *Archives of General Psychiatry*, 29: 126–31, 1973.

62 Tringo, J.L., 'The hierarchy of preference towards disability groups,' *Journal of Special Education*, 4: 295–306, 1970.

63 Lamy, R.E., 'Social consequences of mental illness,' *Journal of Consulting Psychology*, 30: 450–5, 1966.

64 Lamb, H.R., 'Roots of neglect of the long-term mentally ill,' *Psychiatry*, 42: 201–7, 1979.

65 Munoz, R.A. and Morrison, J.R., '650 private psychiatric patients,' *Journal of Clinical Psychiatry*, 40: 114–16, 1979.

66 Page, S., 'Social responsiveness toward mental patients: The general public and others,' *Canadian Journal of Psychiatry*, 25: 242–6, 1980.

67 Serban, G., 'Mental status, functioning, and stress in chronic schizophrenic patients in community care,' *American Journal of Psychiatry*, 136: 948–52, 1979, p. 951.

68 Ibid., p. 951.

69 Scheper-Hughes, N., *Saints, Scholars and Schizophrenics: Mental Illness in Rural Ireland*, Berkeley: University of California Press, 1979, p. 89.

70 Giovannoni, J.M. and Ullman, L.P., 'Conceptions of mental health held by psychiatric patients,' *Journal of Clinical Psychology*, 19: 398–400, 1963; Manis, M., Houts, P.S. and Blake, J.B., 'Beliefs about mental illness as a function of psychiatric status and psychiatric hospitalization,' *Journal of Abnormal and Social Psychology*, 67: 226–33, 1963; Crumpton, E., Weinstein, A.D., Acker, C.W. and Annis, A.P., 'How patients and normals see the mental patient,' *Journal of Clinical Psychology*, 23: 46–9, 1967.

71 Bentinck, C., 'Opinions about mental illness held by patients and relatives,' *Family Process*, 6: 193–207, 1967; Swanson, R.M. and Spitzer, S.P., 'Stigma and the psychiatric patient career,' *Journal of Health and Social Behavior*, 11: 44–51, 1970.

72 Scheff, T.J., *Being Mentally Ill: A Sociological Theory*, Chicago: Aldine, 1966.

73 Phillips, D.L., 'Public identification and acceptance of the mentally ill,' *American Journal of Public Health*, 56: 755–63, 1966.

74 Rosenhan, D.L., 'On being sane in insane places,' *Science*, 179: 250–8, 1973.

75 Gove, W.R., 'Labelling and mental illness,' in W.R. Gove (ed.), *The Labelling of Deviance: Evaluating a Perspective*, New York: Halsted, 1975.

76 Strauss, J.S. and Carpenter, W.T., *Schizophrenia*. New York: Plenum, 1981, p. 128.

77 Festinger, L., *A Theory of Cognitive Dissonance*, Stanford, California: Stanford University Press, 1957; Festinger, L. and Carlsmith, J.M., 'Cognitive consequences of forced compliance,' *Journal of Abnormal and Social Psychology*, 58: 203–10, 1959.

78 Van Putten, J., Crumpton, E. and Yale, C., 'Drug refusal in schizophrenia and the wish to be crazy,' *Archives of General Psychiatry*, 33: 1443–6, 1976.

79 Lamb, H.R. and Goertzel, V., 'Discharged mental patients—Are they really in the community?' *Archives of General Psychiatry*, 24: 29–34, 1971; Wing, J.K., 'The social context of schizophrenia,' *American Journal of Psychiatry*, 135: 1333–9, 1978.

80 Doherty, E.G., 'Labeling effects in psychiatric hospitalization: A study of diverging patterns of inpatient self-labeling processes,' *Archives of General Psychiatry*, 32: 562–8, 1975.

81 McGlashan, T.H. and Carpenter, W.T., 'Does attitude toward psychosis relate to outcome?' *American Journal of Psychiatry*, 138: 797–801, 1981.

82 Pattison, E.M., DeFrancisco, D., Wood, P. et al., 'A psychosocial kinship model for family therapy,' *American Journal of Psychiatry*, 132: 1246–51, 1975; Cohen, C.I. and Sokolovsky, J., 'Schizophrenia and social networks: Ex-patients in the inner city,' *Schizophrenia Bulletin*, 4: 546–60, 1978; Pattison, E.M. and Pattison, M.L., 'Analysis of a schizophrenic psychosocial network,' *Schizophrenia Bulletin*, 7: 135–43, 1981; Lipton, F.R., Cohen, C.I., Fischer, E. and Katz, S.E., 'Schizophrenia: A network crisis,' *Schizophrenia Bulletin*, 7: 144–51, 1981; Minkoff, 'Map of the chronic mental patient,' p. 25.

83 Lipton et al., 'A network crisis.'

84 Westermeyer, J. and Pattison, E.M., 'Social networks and mental illness in a peasant society,' *Schizophrenia Bulletin*, 7: 125–34, 1981.

85 Cohen and Sokolovsky, 'Schizophrenia and social networks.'

86 Yarrow, M., Clausen, J. and Robbins, P., 'The social meaning of mental illness,' *Journal of Social Issues*, 11: 33–48, 1955.

87 Kreisman, D.E. and Joy, V.D., 'Family response to the mental illness of a relative: A review of the literature,' *Schizophrenia Bulletin*, issue 10: 34–57, 1974.

88 Hatfield, A., 'Psychological costs of schizophrenia to the family,' *Social Work*, 23: 355–9, 1978, p. 358.

89 Creer, C., 'Living with schizophrenia,' *Social Work Today*, 6: 2–7, 1975.

90 Grinspoon, L., Courtney, P.H. and Bergen, H.M., 'The usefulness of a structured parents' group in rehabilitation,' in M. Greenblatt, D.J. Levinson and G.L. Klerman, *Mental Patients in Transition: Steps in Hospital-Community Rehabilitation*, Springfield, Illinois: Charles C. Thomas, 1961, p. 245.

91 Maddox, S., 'Profiles: Tom Hansen,' *Boulder Monthly*, January 1979, p. 19.

92 Brown, G.W., Birley, J.L.T. and Wing, J.K., 'Influence of family life on the course of schizophrenic disorders: A replication,' *British Journal of Psychiatry*, 121: 241–58, 1972; Vaughn, C.E. and Leff, J.P., 'The influence of family and social factors on the course of psychiatric illness,' *British Journal of Psychiatry*, 129: 125–37, 1976.

93 Marx, K., *The Economic and Philosophic Manuscripts of 1844*, New York: International Publishers, 1964; Novack, G., 'The problem of alienation,' in E. Mandel and G. Novack, *The Marxist Theory of Alienation*, New York: Pathfinder Press, 1973, pp. 53–94; Ollman, B., *Alienation: Marx's Conception of Man in Capitalist Society*, Cambridge: Cambridge University Press, 1971.

94 Henry, J., *Culture Against Man*, New York: Random House, 1964.

95 Berreman, G.D., 'Structure and function of caste systems,' in G. DeVos and H. Wagatsuma, *Japan's Invisible Race: Caste in Culture and Personality*, Berkeley, California: University of California Press, 1972, pp. 277–307. The reference is to p. 288.

96 Harris, M., *Culture, Man, and Nature*, New York: Thomas Y. Crowell, 1971, ch. 18.

9   The Prevalence of Schizophrenia

1   Torrey, E.F., *Schizophrenia and Civilization*, New York: Jason Aronson, 1980.

2   Leff, J., *Psychiatry Around the Globe: A Transcultural View*, New York: Marcel Dekker, 1981, p. 102.

3   Babigian, H.M., 'Schizophrenia: Epidemiology,' in H.I. Kaplan, A.M. Freedman and B.J. Sadock (eds), *Comprehensive Textbook of Psychiatry - III*, Baltimore: Williams & Wilkins, 1980, pp. 1113–21. The reference is to p. 1115; Wing, J.K., 'Epidemiology of schizophrenia,' *British Journal of Psychiatry*, 9: 25–31, 1975.

4   Taylor, M.A. and Abrams, R., 'The prevalence of schizophrenia: A reassessment using modern diagnostic criteria,' *American Journal of Psychiatry*, 135: 945–8, 1978; Helzer, J., 'Prevalence studies in schizophrenia,' presented at the World Psychiatric Association Regional Meeting, New York, October 30–November 3, 1981; Endicott, J., Nee, J., Fleiss, J. et al., 'Diagnostic criteria for schizophrenia: Reliabilities and agreement between systems,' *Archives of General Psychiatry*, 39: 884–9, 1982.

5   The studies included in Table 9.1 are listed in the general bibliography.

6   Lin, T., 'A study of the incidence of mental disorder in Chinese and other cultures,' *Psychiatry*, 16: 313–36, 1953.

7   Rin, H. and Lin, T., 'Mental illness among Formosan aborigines as compared with the Chinese in Taiwan,' *Journal of Mental Science*, 108: 134–46, 1962.

8   Leff, *Psychiatry Around the Globe*, p. 89.

9   Lin, 'Incidence of mental disorder in Chinese,' table 3.

10  Leff, *Psychiatry Around the Globe*, p. 89.

11  Rin and Lin, 'Mental illness among Formosan aborigines,' p. 139.

12  Lin, 'Incidence of mental disorder in Chinese,' p. 321.

13  Torrey, *Schizophrenia and Civilization*, p. 141.

14  Lin, T., Rin, H., Yeh, E. et al., 'Mental disorders in Taiwan, fifteen years later: A preliminary report,' in W. Caudill and T. Lin (eds), *Mental Health Research in Asia and the Pacific*, Honolulu: East-West Center Press, 1969, pp. 66–91. Dr Torrey uses what appears to be a misprint in this article to argue that the prevalence rate for schizophrenia in this 1961–3 Taiwanese Chinese sample is actually 2.1 per 1,000 instead of the authors' figure of 1.4 per 1,000. The other figures in the text clearly indicate, however, that Dr Torrey is mistaken.

15  Ibid., pp. 70–4.

16  Murphy, H.B.M. and Taumoepeau, B.M., 'Traditionalism and mental health in the South Pacific: A re-examination of an old hypothesis,' *Psychological Medicine*, 10: 471–82, 1980.

17  Wilson, L.G., Fisher, R.B. and Dale, P.W., 'Initiating community psychiatry in Micronesia,' presented at the Second Pacific Congress of Psychiatry, Manila, Philippines, May 12–16, 1980.

18  Dale, P.W., 'Prevalence of schizophrenia in Micronesia,' presented at the Second Pacific Congress of Psychiatry, Manila, Philippines, May 12–16, 1980.

19  Beaglehole, E., 'Pathology among peoples of the Pacific,' in S.C. Plog and R.B. Edgerton (eds), *Changing Perspectives in Mental Illness*, New York: Holt, Rinehart & Winston, 1969, pp. 200–17. The reference is to pp. 213–14.

20  Ibid., p. 205.

21  Torrey, *Schizophrenia and Civilization*, p. 67.

22 Ibid., p. 69.
23 Ibid., p. 71.
24 Jayasundera, M.G., 'Mental health surveys in Ceylon,' in Caudill and Lin, *Mental Health Research in Asia and the Pacific,* pp. 54–65.
25 Dube, K.C. and Kumar, N., 'Epidemiological study of schizophrenia,' *Journal of Biosocial Science,* 4: 187–95, 1972.
26 Sethi, B.B., Gupta, S.C. and Kumar, R., '300 urban families: A psychiatric study,' *Indian Journal of Psychiatry,* 9: 280–302, 1967; Sethi, B.B., Gupta, S.C., Kumar, R. and Kumari, P., 'A psychiatric survey of 500 rural families,' *Indian Journal of Psychiatry,* 14: 183–96, 1972.
27 Doyal, L., *The Political Economy of Health,* Boston: South End Press, 1981, p. 113.
28 Fortes, M. and Mayer, D.Y., 'Psychosis and social change among the Tallensi of Northern Ghana,' in S.H. Foulkes and G.S. Prince (eds), *Psychiatry in a Changing Society,* London: Tavistock, 1969, pp. 33–73. The quotation is from pp. 44–5.
29 Ibid., p. 62.
30 Ibid., p. 53.
31 Field, M.J., 'Chronic psychosis in rural Ghana,' *British Journal of Psychiatry,* 114:31–3, 1968, p. 31.
32 Murphy, H.B.M., 'The evocative role of complex social tasks,' in A.R. Kaplan, *Genetic Factors in Schizophrenia,* Springfield, Illinois: Charles C. Thomas, 1972, pp. 407–22.
33 Ibid., p. 409; van Loon, F.H., 'The problem of lunacy in Acheen,' *Meededeelingen van den burgerlijken Geneeskundigen Dienst in Nederlandsch-Indië,* 10: 2–49, 1920.
34 Siegel, J.T., *The Rope of God,* Berkeley: University of California Press, 1969, pp. 53–5, 90–6.
35 Hurd, H.M. (ed.), *The Institutional Care of the Insane of the United States and Canada,* vol. 1, Baltimore: Johns Hopkins University Press, 1916. The reference, which is to p. 381, is cited in Torrey, *Schizophrenia and Civilization,* p. 49.
36 Ackerknecht, E.H., 'Psychopathology, primitive medicine, and primitive culture,' *Bulletin of the History of Medicine,* 14: 30–67, 1943, cited in Torrey, *Schizophrenia and Civilization,* p. 50.
37 Seligman, C.G., 'Temperament, conflict and psychosis in a stone-age population,' *British Journal of Medical Psychology,* 9: 187–202, 1929.
38 Roy, C., Choudhuri, A. and Irvine, D., 'The prevalence of mental disorders among Saskatchewan Indians,' *Journal of Cross-Cultural Psychology,* 1: 383–92, 1970.
39 Teicher, M.I., 'Three cases of psychosis among the Eskimos,' *Journal of Mental Science,* 100: 527–35, 1954.
40 Sampath, H.M., 'Prevalence of psychiatric disorders in a Southern Baffin Island Eskimo settlement,' *Canadian Psychiatric Association Journal,* 19: 363–7, 1974.
41 Honigmann, J.J., 'American sub-Arctic cultures,' in *The New Encyclopaedia Britannica: Macropaedia,* vol. 1. Chicago: Encyclopaedia Britannica, 1982, pp. 694–8.

42 Graburn, N.H.H., *Eskimos Without Igloos: Social and Economic Development in Sugluk,* Boston: Little, Brown, 1969, pp. 154–7.

43 Ibid., pp. 158–9.

44 Australian Information Service, *Australia Handbook 1975,* Canberra: Australian Government Publishing Service, 1975.

45 Rowley, C.D., *Outcastes in Australia: Aboriginal Policy and Practice,* vol. 2, Canberra: Australian National University Press, 1971, p. 336.

46 Berndt, R.M. and Berndt, C.H., *The First Australians,* Sydney: Ure Smith, 1967, pp. 153–6; Abbie, A.A., *The Original Australians,* New York: American Elsevier Publishing, 1969, pp. 230–46.

47 Long, J.P.M., *Aboriginal Settlements: A Survey of Institutional Communities in Eastern Australia,* Canberra: Australian National University Press, 1970, pp. 147–53.

48 Eastwell, H., 'Schizophrenic typology in Aboriginal Land,' unpublished paper cited in Torrey, *Schizophrenia and Civilization,* pp. 144–5.

49 Kidson, M.A. and Jones, I.H., 'Psychiatric disorders among Aborigines of the Australian Western Desert,' *Archives of General Psychiatry,* 19: 413–17, 1968; Jones, I.H., 'Psychiatric disorders among Aborigines of the Australian Western Desert (II),' *Social Science and Medicine,* 6: 263–7, 1972; Jones, I.H. and Horne, D.J. de L., 'Psychiatric disorders among Aborigines of the Australian Western Desert: Further data and discussion,' *Social Science and Medicine,* 7: 219–28, 1973.

50 Kidson, M.A., 'Psychiatric disorders in the Walbiri, Central Australia,' *Australia and New Zealand Journal of Psychiatry,* 1: 14–22, 1967.

51 Cawte, J.E., 'Ethnopsychiatry in Central Australia: I. "Traditional" illnesses in Eastern Aranda people,' *British Journal of Psychiatry,* 111: 1069–77, 1965.

52 Cawte, J.E., *Cruel, Poor and Brutal Nations,* Honolulu: University of Hawaii Press, 1972, p. 60.

53 Dawson, W.R., 'The relation between the geographical distribution of insanity and that of certain social and other conditions in Ireland,' *Journal of Mental Science,* 57: 571–97, 1911, p. 580.

54 Walsh, D., O'Hare, A., Blake, B. et al. 'The treated prevalence of mental illness in the Republic of Ireland—The three county case register study,' *Psychological Medicine,* 10: 465–70, 1980.

55 Ibid., pp. 589, 591; Murphy, H.B.M., 'Alcoholism and schizophrenia in the Irish: A review,' *Transcultural Psychiatric Research Review,* 12: 116–39, 1975, p. 118.

56 Kelleher, M.J., Copeland, J.R.M. and Smith, A.J., 'High first admission rates for schizophrenia in the west of Ireland,' *Psychological Medicine,* 4: 460–2, 1974.

57 Murphy, 'Alcoholism and schizophrenia in the Irish,' p. 123.

58 Curtis, E., *A History of Ireland,* London: Methuen, 1961; Woodham-Smith, C., *The Great Hunger: Ireland 1845–9,* London: New English Library, 1965.

59 Woodham-Smith, *The Great Hunger,* p. 27.

60 Ibid., pp. 70–2.

61 Finnane, M., *Insanity and the Insane in Post-Famine Ireland,* London: Croom Helm, 1981, ch. 1.

62 McCaffrey, L.J., *Ireland from Colony to Nation State,* Englewood Cliffs, New

Jersey: Prentice-Hall, 1979, pp. 77, 172, 157–8; Inglis, B., *The Story of Ireland*, 2nd edn, London: Faber & Faber, 1965, pp. 202, 228–32; Curtis, *History of Ireland*, p. 389; Tuma, E.H., 'Land reform and tenure,' in *The New Encyclopaedia Britannica: Macropaedia*, vol. 10, Chicago: Encyclopaedia Britannica, 1982, p. 638.

63  Scheper-Hughes, N., *'Saints, Scholars, and Schizophrenics: Mental Illness in Rural Ireland,'* Berkeley: University of California Press, 1979.

64  Walsh, D. and Walsh, B., 'Mental illness in the Republic of Ireland: First admissions,' *Journal of the Irish Medical Association*, 63: 365–70, 1970.

65  Anonymous, 'Lunatic asylums in Ireland,' *American Journal of Insanity*, 4: 298–300, 1864.

66  Murphy, 'Alcoholism and schizophrenia in the Irish,' p. 126.

67  Tuma, 'Land reform and tenure,' p. 638; Lenti, L., 'Italy,' in *The New Encyclopaedia Britannica: Macropaedia*, vol. 9, Chicago: Encyclopaedia Britannica, 1982, pp. 1085–1114.

68  Kogan, N., *A Political History of Postwar Italy: From the Old to the New Center-Left*, New York: Praeger, 1981, pp. 131–2.

69  Ibid., pp. 12–13.

70  Arieti, S., *The Interpretation of Schizophrenia*, 2nd edn, New York: Basic Books, 1974, pp. 497–8.

71  Ibid., pp. 500–1.

72  Ibid., pp. 501–3.

73  Hostetler, J.A., *'Hutterite Society,'* Baltimore: Johns Hopkins University Press, 1974, p. 1.

74  Ibid., p. 182.

75  Ibid., p. 184.

76  Ibid., p. 264.

77  Eaton, J.W. and Weil, R.J., *Culture and Mental Disorders*, Glencoe, Illinois: Free Press, 1955.

78  Hostetler, J.A., *Amish Society*, revised edn, Baltimore: Johns Hopkins University Press, 1968.

79  Egeland, J.A. and Hostetter, A.M., 'Amish study, I: Affective disorders among the Amish, 1976–1980,' *American Journal of Psychiatry*, 140: 56–61, 1983; Hostetter, A.M., Egeland, J.A. and Endicott, J., 'Amish study, II: Concensus diagnoses and reliability results,' *American Journal of Psychiatry*, 140: 62–6, 1983; Egeland, J.A., Hostetter, A.M. and Eshelman, S.K., 'Amish study, III: The impact of cultural factors on diagnosis of bipolar illness,' *American Journal of Psychiatry*, 140: 67–71, 1983.

80  Egeland and Hostetter, 'Amish study, I,' p. 59.

81  Leff, *Psychiatry Around the Globe*, pp. 100–1; Gruenberg, E.M. and Turns, D.M., 'Epidemiology,' in A.M. Freedman, H.I. Kaplan and B.J. Sadock, (eds), *Comprehensive Textbook of Psychiatry-II*, vol. 1, Baltimore: Williams & Wilkins, 1975.

82  Sneznevskij, A.V., 'Dispensary method of registering psychiatric morbidity and the Soviet system of psychiatric service,' *Living Conditions and Health*, 1: 236–41, 1959.

83  Crocetti, G.M., Kulčar, Ž., Kesić, B. and Lemkau, P.V., 'Differential rates of

schizophrenia in Croatia, Yugoslavia,' *American Journal of Public Health*, 54: 196–206, 1964; Crocetti, G.M., Lemkau, P.V., Kulčar, Ž. and Kesić, B., 'Selected aspects of the epidemiology of psychoses in Croatia, Yugoslavia: III. The cluster sample and the results of the pilot survey,' *American Journal of Epidemiology*, 94: 126–34, 1971.

84 Böök, J.A., 'A genetic and neuropsychiatric investigation of a North Swedish population,' *Acta Genetica et Statistica Medica*, 4: 1–100, 1953; Böök, J.A., Wetterberg, L. and Modrzewska, K., 'Schizophrenia in a North Swedish geographical isolate, 1900–1975: Epidemiology, genetics and biochemistry,' *Clinical Genetics*, 14: 373–94, 1978.

85 Murphy, H.B.M., *Comparative Psychiatry: The International and Intercultural Distribution of Mental Illness*, New York: Springer-Verlag, 1982, p. 69.

86 Bell, R.M., 'The transformation of a rural village: Istria, 1870–1972,' *Journal of Social History*, 7: 243–70, 1974; St Erlich, V., *Family in Transition: A Study of 300 Yugoslav Villages*, Princeton, New Jersey: Princeton University Press, 1966.

87 Väisänen, E., 'Psychiatric disorders in Finland,' *Acta Psychiatrica Scandinavica*, supplement 263: 22–33, 1975.

88 Andersen, T., 'Physical and mental illness in a Lapp and Norwegian population,' *Acta Psychiatrica Scandinavica*, supplement 263: 47–56, 1975; Ingold, T., *The Skolt Lapps Today*, Cambridge: Cambridge University Press, 1976, chs 8, 9, 10.

89 Böök, 'A North-Swedish population,' ch. 1; Böök, 'A North-Swedish geographical isolate,' p. 375.

90 Rose, A.M., 'The prevalence of mental disorders in Italy,' *International Journal of Social Psychiatry*, 10: 87–100, 1964.

91 Rao, S., 'Caste and mental disorders in Bihar,' *American Journal of Psychiatry*, 122: 1045–55, 1966.

92 Nandi, D.N., Mukherjee, S.P., Boral, G.C. et al., 'Socio-economic status and mental morbidity in certain tribes and castes in India: A cross-cultural study,' *British Journal of Psychiatry*, 136: 73–85, 1980.

93 Dube and Kumar, 'Epidemiological study of schizophrenia.'

94 Elnagar, M.N., Maitra, P. and Rao, M.N., 'Mental health in an Indian rural community,' *British Journal of Psychiatry*, 118: 499–503, 1971.

95 Squire, L., *Employment Policy in Developing Countries: A Survey of Issues and Evidence*, New York: World Bank/Oxford University Press, 1981.

96 Rao, 'Caste and mental disorders,' p. 1053.

97 Nandi et al., 'Socio-economic status and mental morbidity,' p. 82.

98 Lin, 'Incidence of mental disorder in Chinese,' pp. 326–7; Lin, Rin and Yeh et al., 'Mental disorders in Taiwan,' pp. 82–7.

99 Arieti, *The Interpretation of Schizophrenia*, p. 494; Leff, *Psychiatry Around the Globe*, p. 163.

100 US Department of Health, Education and Welfare, *Vital Statistics of the United States*, Washington, DC: US Government Printing Office, 1923; Malzberg, B., 'A statistical study of mental diseases among natives of foreign white parentage in New York State,' *Psychiatric Quarterly*, 10: 127–42, 1936; Malzberg, B., *Social and Biological Aspects of Mental Disease*, Utica, New York: State Hospital Press, 1940; Malzberg, B., 'Are immigrants psychologically disturbed?' in S.C. Plog and R.B. Edgerton (eds), *Changing Perspectives in Mental Illness*, New York: Holt,

347

Rinehart & Winston, 1969, pp. 395–421.

101 Eitinger, L., 'The incidence of mental disease among refugees in Norway,' *Journal of Mental Science*, 105: 326–38, 1959.

102 Hemsi, L.K., 'Psychiatric morbidity of West Indian immigrants,' *Social Psychiatry*, 2: 95–100, 1967.

103 Cochrane, R., 'Mental illness in immigrants to England and Wales: An analysis of mental hospital admissions, 1971,' *Social Psychiatry*, 12: 25–35, 1977.

104 Cade, J.F.J. and Krupinski, J., 'Incidence of psychiatric disorders in Victoria in relation to country of birth,' *Medical Journal of Australia*, 49: 400–4, 1962.

105 Halevi, H.S., 'Frequency of mental illness among Jews in Israel,' *International Journal of Social Psychiatry*, 9: 268–82, 1963.

106 Cochrane, 'Mental illness in immigrants to England and Wales.'

107 Malzberg, 'Are immigrants psychologically disturbed?,' pp. 416–17.

108 Cochrane, R. and Stopes-Roe, M., 'Psychological and social adjustment of Asian immigrants to Britain: A community survey,' *Social Psychiatry*, 12: 195–206, 1977.

109 Bagley, C. and Binitie, A., 'Alcoholism and schizophrenia in Irishmen in London,' *British Journal of Addiction*, 65: 3–7, 1970; Clare, A.W., 'Alcoholism and schizophrenia in Irishmen in London: A reassessment,' *British Journal of Addiction*, 69: 207–12, 1974.

110 Bagley, C., 'The social aetiology of schizophrenia in immigrants groups,' *International Journal of Social Psychiatry*, 17: 292–304, 1971.

111 Arieti, *The Interpretation of Schizophrenia*, pp. 499–501.

112 Ödegard, Ö., 'Emigration and insanity,' *Acta Psychiatrica et Neurologica Scandinavica*, supplement 4, 1932.

113 Clare, 'Alcoholism and schizophrenia in Irishmen;' Walsh, O'Hare, Blake et al., 'Mental illness in the Republic of Ireland.'

114 'Relationships between aging and schizophrenia now being studied,' *Clinical Psychiatry News*, September, 1982, pp. 1, 24; Strauss, J.S. and Carpenter, W.T., *Schizophrenia*, New York: Plenum, 1981, p. 73.

115 US Bureau of the Census, *Historical Statistics of the United States: Colonial Times to 1970*, Washington, DC: 1975, Series D 29–41, p. 131 and Series D 87–101, p. 135.

116 US Bureau of the Census, *Social Indicators 1976*, Washington, DC: 1977, Table 8/5, pp. 372–3.

117 These figures are cited in Torrey, *Schizophrenia and Civilization*, pp. 155–6.

118 Thurnam, J., *Observations and Essays on the Statistics of Insanity*, London: Simpkin, Marshall, 1845, table A, appendix 1.

119 Goldhamer, H. and Marshall, A.W., *Psychosis and Civilization*, Glencoe, Illinois: Free Press, 1949, p. 65.

120 Ibid., ch. 3; Torrey, *Schizophrenia and Civilization*, p. 155.

121 Hare, E., 'Was insanity on the increase?' *British Journal of Psychiatry*, 142: 439–5, 1983.

**10 Antipsychotic Drugs: Use, Abuse and Non-use**

1 Davis, J.M., 'Antipsychotic drugs,' in H.I. Kaplan, A.M. Freedman and B.J. Sadock (eds), *Comprehensive Textbook of Psychiatry - III*, Baltimore: Williams &

Wilkins, 1981, p. 2257.

2 Gardos, G. and Cole, J.O., 'Maintenance antipsychotic therapy: Is the cure worse than the disease?' *American Journal of Psychiatry*, 133: 32–6, 1976.

3 Rogers, *v.* Okin, Federal District Court, Boston, Civil Action 75–1610–T (D. Mass. 1979); Rennie *v.* Klein, 462 F. Supp. 1131 (D. N.J. 1978); Goedecke *v.* State of Colorado, Supreme Court of Colorado, Civil Action 28179, 1979.

4 Past president of the American Psychiatric Association, Alan Stone, speaking at the 1978 Annual Meeting of the Southern Psychiatric Association. Quoted in Ford, M.D., 'The psychiatrist's double bind: The right to refuse medication,' *American Journal of Psychiatry*, 137: 332–9, 1980, p. 332.

5 Gutheil, T.G., 'In search of true freedom: Drug refusal, involuntary medication, and "rotting with your rights on." ' *American Journal of Psychiatry*, 137: 327–8, 1980.

6 Chouinard, G., Annable, L., Ross-Chouinard, A. and Nestoros, J.N., 'Factors related to tardive dyskinesia,' *American Journal of Psychiatry*, 136: 79–83, 1979; Fann, W.E., Davis, J.M. and Janowsky, D.S., 'The prevalence of tardive dyskinesia in mental hospital patients,' *Diseases of the Nervous System*, 33: 182–6, 1972; Smith, J.M., Kucharski, L.T., Oswald, W.T. and Waterman, L.J., 'A systematic investigation of tardive dyskinesia in inpatients,' *American Journal of Psychiatry*, 136: 918–22, 1979.

7 Chouinard et al., 'Factors related to tardive dyskinesia,' p. 79.

8 Singh, M.M. and Kay, S.R., 'Dysphoric response to neuroleptic treatment in schizophrenia: Its relationship to autonomic arousal and prognosis,' *Biological Psychiatry*, 14: 277–94, 1979; Van Putten, T., May, P.R.A. and Marder, S.R., 'The hospital and optimal chemotherapy in schizophrenia,' *Hospital and Community Psychiatry*, 30: 114–17, 1979.

9 Leff, J.P. and Wing, J.K., 'Trial of maintenance therapy in schizophrenia,' *British Medical Journal*, 3: 559–604, 1971.

10 Cole, J.O., Goldberg, S.C. and Klerman, G.L., 'Phenothiazine treatment in acute schizophrenia,' *Archives of General Psychiatry*, 10: 246–61, 1964.

11 Pasamanick, B., Scarpetti, F. and Dinitz, S., *'Schizophrenics in the Community: An Experimental Study in the Prevention of Rehospitalization,'* New York: Appleton-Century-Crofts, 1967; Goldberg, S.C., Schooler, N.R., Hogarty, G.E. and Roper, M., 'Prediction of relapse in schizophrenic outpatients treated by drug and sociotherapy,' *Archives of General Psychiatry*, 34: 171–84, 1977; Hogarty, G.E. and Ulrich, R.F., 'Temporal effects of drug and placebo in delaying relapse in schizophrenic outpatients,' *Archives of General Psychiatry*, 34: 297–307, 1977.

12 For thorough reviews of current research on the dopamine hypothesis of schizophrenia see Meltzer, H.Y. and Stahl, S.M., 'The dopamine hypothesis of schizophrenia: A review,' *Schizophrenia Bulletin*, 2: 19–76, 1976; and Haracz, J.L., 'The dopamine hypothesis: An overview of studies with schizophrenic patients,' *Schizophrenia Bulletin*, 8: 438–69, 1982.

13 Smythies, J.R. and Adey, W.R., *The Neurological Foundation of Psychiatry*, New York: Academic Press, 1966, pp. 150–7.

14 Melamud, N., 'Psychiatric disorder with intracranial disorders of the limbic system,' *Archives of Neurology* (Chicago), 17: 113–24, 1967; Horowitz, M.J. and

Adams, J.E., 'Hallucinations on brain stimulation: Evidence for revision of the Penfield hypothesis,' in W. Keup (ed.), *Origins and Mechanisms of Hallucinations*, New York: Plenum Publishing, 1970, pp. 13–22; Torrey, E.F. and Peterson, M.R., 'Schizophrenia and the limbic system.' *Lancet*, 2: 942–6, 1974.

15  Meltzer and Stahl list nine studies on this topic, the large majority of which show that HVA (homovanillic acid) and 5HIAA (5-hydroxyindolacetic acid) are not elevated in the cerebrospinal fluid of schizophrenics.

16  Bowers, M.B., 'Central dopamine turnover in schizophrenic syndromes,' *Archives of General Psychiatry*, 31: 50–4, 1974.

17  Three groups of researchers have found elevated dopamine binding capacity in the limbic system of both drug-treated and drug-free schizophrenics; the elevation is greater in the drug-treated patients. These studies are: Owen, F., Cross, A.J., Crow, T.J. et al., 'Increased dopamine receptor sensitivity in schizophrenia,' *Lancet*, 2: 223–6, 1978; Lee, T. and Seeman, P., 'Elevation of brain neuroleptic/dopamine receptors in schizophrenia,' *American Journal of Psychiatry*, 137: 191–7, 1980; and Reisine, T.D., Rossor, M., Spokes, E. et al., 'Opiate and neuroleptic receptor alterations in human schizophrenic brain tissue,' *Advances in Biochemical Psychopharmacology*, 21: 443–50, 1980. Studies from two other laboratories show elevation of dopamine binding capacity in drug-treated schizophrenics only. These studies include: Reynolds, G.P., Riederer, P., Jellinger, K. and Gabriel, E., 'Dopamine receptors and schizophrenia: The neuroleptic drug problem,' *Neuropharmacology*, 20: 1319–20, 1981: and Mackay, A.V.P., Iverson, L.L., Rossor, M. et al., 'Increased brain dopamine and dopamine receptors in schizophrenia,' *Archives of General Psychiatry*, 39: 991–7, 1982.

18  Goldberg, M.E. and Salama, A.I., 'Tolerance to drum stress and its relationship to dopamine turnover,' *European Journal of Pharmacology*, 17: 202–7, 1972.

19  Bowers, 'Central dopamine turnover.'

20  Burt, D.R., Creese, I. and Snyder, S.H., 'Antischizophrenic drugs: Chronic treatment elevates dopamine receptor binding in brain,' *Science*, 196: 326–8, 1977; Muller, P. and Seeman, P., 'Brain neurotransmitter receptors after long-term haloperidol: Dopamine, acetylcholine, serotonin, α-noradrenergic and naloxone receptors,' *Life Sciences*, 21: 1751–8, 1977.

21  See footnote 17 in this chapter.

22  Goldberg et al., 'Prediction of relapse:' in two groups of schizophrenic outpatients on drugs the relapse rates were 35 per cent and 48 per cent after two years. Pasamanick, Scarpetti and Dinitz, *Schizophrenics in the Community:* 23 per cent of drug-treated patients relapsed in one-and-a-half years. Englehardt, D.M., Rosen, B., Freedman, N. and Margolis, R., 'Phenothiazines in prevention of psychiatric hospitalization. IV: Delay on prevention of hospitalization —a reevaluation,' *Archives of General Psychiatry*, 16: 98–101, 1967: 21 per cent of patients on chlorpromazine relapsed during a four-year period.

23  Hogarty and Ulrich, 'Temporal effects of drug and placebo,' p. 299.

24  Schooler, N.R., Levine, J., Severe, J.B. et al., 'Prevention of relapse in schizophrenia: An evaluation of fluphenazine decanoate,' *Archives of General Psychiatry*, 37: 16–24, 1980; Rifkin, A., Quitkin, F., Rabiner, C.J. and Klein, D.F., 'Fluphenazine decanoate, fluphenazine hydrochloride given orally and

placebo in remitted schizophrenics,' *Archives of General Psychiatry*, 34: 43–7, 1977.

25 Chouinard, G. and Jones, B., 'Neuroleptic-induced supersensitivity psychosis: Clinical and pharmacological characteristics,' *American Journal of Psychiatry*, 137: 16–21, 1980. For further discussion of drug-induced supersensitivity psychosis see Davis, K.L. and Rosenberg, G.S., 'Is there a limbic system equivalent of tardive dyskinesia?' *Biological Psychiatry*, 14: 699–703, 1979; and Chouinard, G., Jones, B.D. and Annable, L., 'Neuroleptic-induced supersensitivity psychosis,' *American Journal of Psychiatry*, 135: 1409–10, 1978.

26 Rosen, B., Engelhardt, D.M., Freedman, N. and Margolis, R., 'The hospitalization proneness scale as a predictor of response to phenothiazine treatment. I: Prevention of psychiatric hospitalization,' *Journal of Nervous and Mental Disease*, 146: 476–80, 1968.

27 Rosen, B., Engelhardt, D.M., Freedman, N. et al., 'The hospital proneness scale as a predictor of response to phenothiazine treatment. II: Delay of psychiatric hospitalization,' *Journal of Nervous and Mental Disease*, 152: 405–11, 1971.

28 Goldstein, M.J., 'Premorbid adjustment, paranoid status, and patterns of response to phenothiazine in acute schizophrenia,' *Schizophrenia Bulletin*, 3: 24–37, 1970; Evans, J.R., Rodnick, E.H., Goldstein, M.J. and Judd, L.L., 'Premorbid adjustment, phenothiazine treatment, and remission in acute schizophrenics,' *Archives of General Psychiatry*, 27: 486–90, 1972.

29 Judd, L.L., Goldstein, M.J., Rodnick, E.H. and Jackson, N.L.P., 'Phenothiazine effects in good premorbid schizophrenics divided into paranoid-non paranoid status,' *Archives of General Psychiatry*, 29: 207–11, 1973.

30 Goldstein, M.J., Rodnick, E.H., Evans, J.R. et al., 'Drug and family therapy in the aftercare of acute schizophrenics,' *Archives of General Psychiatry*, 35: 1169–77, 1978.

31 Rappaport, M., Hopkins, H.K., Hall, K. et al. 'Are there schizophrenics for whom drugs may be unnecessary or contraindicated?' *International Pharmaco-psychiatry*, 13: 100–11, 1978, p. 107.

32 Carpenter, W.T., McGlashan, T.H. and Strauss, J.S., 'The treatment of acute schizophrenia without drugs: An investigation of some current assumptions,' *American Journal of Psychiatry*, 134: 14–20, 1977, p. 19.

33 Klein, D.F. and Rosen, B., 'Premorbid asocial adjustment and response to phenothiazine treatment among schizophrenic inpatients,' *Archives of General Psychiatry*, 29: 480–5, 1973.

34 Goldberg et al. 'Prediction of relapse,' p. 171.

35 May, P.R.A., Tuma, A.H. and Dixon, W.J. 'Schizophrenia—A follow-up study of results of treatment. I: Design and other problems,' *Archives of General Psychiatry*, 33: 474–8, 1976; May, P.R.A., Tuma, A.H. and Dixon, W.J., 'Schizophrenia: A follow-up study of the results of five forms of treatment,' *Archives of General Psychiatry*, 38: 776–84, 1981.

36 Schooler, N.R., Goldberg, S.C., Boothe, H. and Cole, J.O., 'One year after discharge: Community adjustment of schizophrenic patients,' *American Journal of Psychiatry*, 123: 986–95, 1967.

37 Pasamanick, Scarpetti and Dinitz, *Schizophrenics in the Community*.

351

38 National Institute of Mental Health Psychopharmacology Service Center Collaborative Study Group, 'Phenothiazine treatment in acute schizophrenia,' *Archives of General Psychiatry*, 10: 246–61, 1964.

39 Mosher, L.R. and Menn, A.Z., 'Community residential treatment for schizophrenia: Two-year follow-up,' *Hospital and Community Psychiatry*, 29: 715–23, 1978, p. 722.

40 Matthews, S.M., Roper, M.T., Mosher, L.R. and Menn, A.Z., 'A non-neuroleptic treatment for schizophrenia: Analysis of the two-year postdischarge risk of relapse,' *Schizophrenia Bulletin*, 5: 322–33, 1979.

41 Davis, J., 'Overview: Maintenance therapy in psychiatry. 1: Schizophrenia,' *American Journal of Psychiatry*, 132: 1237–45, 1975.

42 Brown, G.W. and Birley, J.L.T., 'Crises and life changes and the onset of schizophrenia,' *Journal of Health and Social Behavior*, 9: 203–14, 1968; Birley, J.L.T. and Brown, G.W., 'Crises and life changes preceding the onset or relapse of acute schizophrenia: Clinical aspects,' *British Journal of Psychiatry*, 116: 327–33, 1970; Strahilevitz, M., 'Possible interaction of environmental and biological factors in the etiology of schizophrenia,' *Canadian Psychiatric Association Journal*, 19: 207–17, 1974; Jacobs, S.C. and Myers, J., 'Recent life events and acute schizophrenic psychosis: A controlled study,' *Journal of Nervous and Mental Disease*, 162: 75–87, 1976; Leff, J.P. and Vaughn, C.E., 'The interaction of life events and relatives' expressed emotion in schizophrenia and depressive neurosis,' *British Journal of Psychiatry*, 136: 146–53, 1980; Dohrenwend, B.P. and Egri, G., 'Recent stressful life events and episodes of schizophrenia,' *Schizophrenia Bulletin*, 7: 12–23, 1981; Spring, B., 'Stress and schizophrenia: Some definitional issues,' *Schizophrenia Bulletin*, 7: 24–33, 1981.

43 Wing, J.K., 'The social context of schizophrenia,' *American Journal of Psychiatry*, 135: 1333–9, 1978, p. 1335.

44 Brown, G.W., Birley, J.L.T. and Wing, J.K., 'Influence of family life on the course of schizophrenic disorders: A replication,' *British Journal of Psychiatry*, 121: 241–58, 1972; Vaughn, C.E. and Leff, J.P., 'The influence of family and social factors on the course of psychiatric illness: A comparison of schizophrenic and depressed neurotic patients,' *British Journal of Psychiatry*, 129: 125–37, 1976.

45 Leff, J.P. and Vaughn, C.E., 'The role of maintenance therapy and relatives' expressed emotion in relapse of schizophrenia: A two-year follow-up,' *British Journal of Psychiatry*, 139: 102–4, 1981.

46 Leff and Vaughn, 'Interaction of life events and expressed emotion.'

47 Sturgeon, D., Kuipers, L., Berkowitz, R. et al., 'Psychophysiological responses of schizophrenic patients to high and low expressed emotion relatives,' *British Journal of Psychiatry*, 138: 40–5, 1981.

48 Tarrier, N., Vaughn, C.E., Lader, M.H. and Leff, J.P., 'Bodily reaction to people and events in schizophrenics,' *Archives of General Psychiatry*, 36: 311–15, 1979.

49 Paul, G.L., Tobias, L.L. and Holly, B.L., 'Maintenance psychotropic drugs in the presence of active treatment programs: A "triple-blind" withdrawal study with long-term mental patients,' *Archives of General Psychiatry*, 27: 106–15, 1972.

50 Ibid.
51 Paul, G.L. and Lentz, R.J., *Psychosocial Treatment of Chronic Mental Patients: Milieu versus Social Learning Programs*, Cambridge: Harvard University Press, 1977.
52 Goldberg et al., 'Prediction of relapse.'
53 Hogarty, G.E., Goldberg, S.C., Schooler, N.R. and the Collaborative Study Group, 'Drug and sociotherapy in the aftercare of schizophrenic patients. III: Adjustment of nonrelapsed patients,' *Archives of General Psychiatry*, 31: 609–18, 1974.
54 Hogarty, G.E., Goldberg, S.C., Schooler, N.R. et al., 'Drug and sociotherapy in the aftercare of schizophrenic patients. II: Two-year relapse rates,' *Archives of General Psychiatry*, 31: 603–8, 1974.
55 Goldberg et al., 'Prediction of relapse,' p. 171.
56 Leff, J.P., 'Preventing relapse in schizophrenia,' presented at the World Psychiatric Association Regional Meeting, New York, October 30–November 3, 1981; Berkowitz, R., Kuipers, L., Eberlein-Fries, R. and Leff, J.P., 'Lowering expressed emotion in relatives of schizophrenics,' *New Directions in Mental Health Services*, 12: 27–48, 1981.
57 Falloon, I.R.H., Boyd, J.L., McGill, C.W. et al., 'Family management in the prevention of exacerbations of schizophrenia: A controlled study,' *New England Journal of Medicine*, 306: 1437–40, 1982.
58 Schmidt, L.J., Reinhardt, A.M. Kane, R.L. and Olsen, D.M., 'The mentally ill in nursing homes: New back wards in the community,' *Archives of General Psychiatry*, 34: 687–91, 1977.
59 Sheehan, S., 'A reporter at large,' *New Yorker*, May 25, June 1, June 8, June 15, 1981.
60 *In the interest of Edmiston*, Civil Action 80 MH 378 (Denver Probate Court, December 17, 1980).
61 Jick, H., 'Reserpine and breast cancer: A perspective,' *Journal of the American Medical Association*, 233: 896, 1975; Schyve, P.M., Smithline, F. and Meltzer, H.Y., 'Neuroleptic-induced prolactin level elevation and breast cancer: An emerging clinical issue,' *Archives of General Psychiatry*, 35: 1291–1301, 1978.
62 Quitkin, F., Rifkin, A. and Klein, D.F., 'Very high dosage versus standard dosage fluphenazine in schizophrenia,' *Archives of General Psychiatry*, 32: 1276–81, 1975; McGlashan, T.H. and Carpenter, W.T., 'Postpsychotic depression in schizophrenia,' *Archives of General Psychiatry*, 33: 231–9, 1976; Van Putten, T. and May, P.R.A., ' "Akinetic depression" in schizophrenia,' *Archives of General Psychiatry*, 35: 1101–7, 1978; Hogarty, G.E., Schooler, N.R., Ulrich, R. et al., 'Fluphenazine and social therapy in the aftercare of schizophrenic patients: Relapse analyses of a two-year controlled study of fluphenazine decanoate and fluphenazine hydrochloride,' *Archives of General Psychiatry*, 36: 1283–94, 1979; Goldstein et al., 'Drug and family therapy.'
63 Hirsh, S., 'Do neuroleptics cause depression in the schizophrenias?' presented at the World Psychiatric Association Regional Meeting, New York, October 30–November 3, 1981; Moller, H. and von Zerssen, D., 'Depressive states occurring during clinical treatment of 280 schizophrenic inpatients,' presented at the World Psychiatric Association Regional Meeting, New York, October

30–November 3, 1981.
64 Hartlage, L.C., 'Effects of chlorpromazine on learning,' *Psychological Bulletin*, 64: 235–45, 1965; Bruening, S.E., Davis, V.J., Matson, J.L. and Ferguson, D.G., 'Effects of thioridazine and withdrawal dyskinesias on workshop performance of mentally retarded young adults,' *American Journal of Psychiatry*, 139: 1447–54, 1982.
65 Gardos and Cole, 'Maintenance antipsychotic therapy.'
66 Phillips, L., 'Case history data and prognosis in schizophrenia,' *Journal of Nervous and Mental Disease*, 117: 515–25, 1953; Stephens, J.H., Astrup, C. and Mangrum, J.C., 'Prognostic factors in recovered and deteriorated schizophrenics,' *American Journal of Psychiatry*, 122: 1116–21, 1966; Marder, S.R., van Kammen, D.P., Docherty, J.P. et al., 'Predicting drug-free improvement in schizophrenic psychosis,' *Archives of General Psychiatry*, 36: 1080–5, 1979.
67 Bromet, E., Harrow, M. and Kasl, S., 'Premorbid functioning and outcome in schizophrenics and nonschizophrenics,' *Archives of General Psychiatry*, 30: 203–7, 1974; Strauss, J.S. and Carpenter, W.T., 'The prognosis of schizophrenia: Rationale for a multidimensional concept,' *Schizophrenia Bulletin*, 4: 56–77, 1978; Bland, R.C., Parker, J.H. and Orn, H., 'Prognosis in schizophrenia: Prognostic predictors and outcome,' *Archives of General Psychiatry*, 35: 72–7, 1978.
68 Harrow, M., Bromet, E. and Quinlan, D., 'Predictors of post-hospital adjustment in schizophrenia: Thought disorders and schizophrenic diagnosis,' *Journal of Nervous and Mental Disease*, 158: 25–32, 1974; Strauss, J.S. and Carpenter, W.T., 'Characteristic symptoms and outcome in schizophrenia,' *Archives of General Psychiatry*, 30: 429–34, 1974; Carpenter, W.T., Bartko, J.J., Strauss, J.S. and Hawk, A.B., 'Signs and symptoms as predictors of outcome: A report from the International Pilot Study of Schizophrenia,' *American Journal of Psychiatry*, 135: 940–5, 1978.
69 Strauss, J.S. and Carpenter, W.T., 'The prediction of outcome in schizophrenia. I: Characteristics of outcome,' *Archives of General Psychiatry*, 27: 739–46, 1972; Hawk, A.B., Carpenter, W.T. and Strauss, J.S., 'Diagnostic criteria and five-year outcome in schizophrenia: A report from the International Pilot Study of Schizophrenia,' *Archives of General Psychiatry*, 32: 343–7, 1975.
70 Strauss, J.S. and Carpenter, W.T., 'The prediction of outcome in schizophrenia. II: Relationships between predictor and outcome variables: A report from the WHO International Pilot Study of Schizophrenia,' *Archives of General Psychiatry*, 31: 37–42, 1974; Strauss, J.S. and Carpenter, W.T., 'Prediction of outcome in schizophrenia. III: Five-year outcome and its predictors,' *Archives of General Psychiatry*, 34: 159–63, 1977; Mintz, J., O'Brien, C.P. and Luborsky, L., 'Predicting the outcome of psychotherapy for schizophrenics: Relative contributions of patient, therapist, and treatment characteristics,' *Archives of General Psychiatry*, 33: 1183–6, 1976.
71 Kant, O., 'The incidence of psychoses and other mental abnormalities in the families of recovered and deteriorated schizophrenic patients,' *Psychiatric Quarterly*, 16: 176–86, 1942; Vaillant, G.E., 'Prospective prediction of schizophrenic remission,' *Archives of General Psychiatry*, 11: 509–18, 1964; Welner, J. and Strömgen, E., 'Clinical and genetic studies on benign schizophreni-

form psychoses based on a follow-up, *Acta Psychiatrica Scandinavica* 33: 377–99, 1958; McCabe, M.S., Fowler, R.C., Cadoret, R.J. and Winokur, G., 'Familial differences in schizophrenia with good and poor prognosis,' *Psychological Medicine*, 1: 326–32, 1971; Fowler, R.C., McCabe, M.S., Cadoret, R.J. and Winokur, G., 'The validity of good prognosis schizophrenia,' *Archives of General Psychiatry*, 26: 182–5, 1972; Taylor, M.A. and Abrams, R., 'Manic-depressive illness and good prognosis schizophrenia,' *American Journal of Psychiatry*, 132: 741–2, 1975.

72  Fowler et al., 'The validity of good prognosis schizophrenia,' p. 182.

73  Ibid., p. 183; McCabe, 'Familial differences in schizophrenia,' pp. 327, 331.

74  Taylor and Abrams, 'Manic-depressive illness and good prognosis schizophrenia,' p.742.

75  Robins, E. and Guze, S.B., 'Establishment of diagnostic validity in psychiatric illness, Its application in schizophrenia,' *American Journal of Psychiatry*, 126: 983–7, 1970.

76  Hirschowitz, J., Casper, R., Garver, D.L. and Chang, S., 'Lithium response in good prognosis schizophrenia,' *American Journal of Psychiatry*, 137: 916–20, 1980.

77  Mosher, L.R., Menn, A. and Matthews, S.M., 'Soteria: Evaluation of a home-based treatment for schizophrenia,' *American Journal of Orthopsychiatry*, 45: 455–67, 1975, p. 458.

78  Ibid., pp. 460–1.

79  Ibid., p. 458.

80  Taylor, D.P., Riblet, L.A., Stanton, H.C. et al., 'Dopamine and anti-anxiety activity,' *Pharmacology, Biochemistry and Behavior*, vol. 17, supplement 1, pp. 25–35, 1982; Haefely, W.E., 'Behavioral and neuropharmacological aspects of drugs used in anxiety and related states,' in M.A. Lipton, A. DiMascio and K.F. Killam (eds), *Psychopharmacology: A Generation of Progress*, New York: Raven Press, 1978; Nestoros, J.N., 'Benzodiazepines in schizophrenia: A need for a reassessment,' *International Pharmacopsychiatry*, 15: 171–9, 1980; Bunney, B.S. and Aghajanian, G.K., 'The effect of antipsychotic drugs on the firing of dopaminergic neurons: A reappraisal,' in G. Sedvall, B. Uvnäs and Y. Zotterman, *Antipsychotic Drugs: Pharmacodynamics and Pharmacokinetics*, New York: Pergamon, 1976.

81  Feldman, P.E., 'An analysis of the efficacy of diazepam,' *Journal of Neuropsychiatry*, 3, supplement 1: S62–S67, 1962; Pignatoro, F.P., 'Experience with chemotherapy in refractory psychiatric disorders,' *Current Therapeutic Research*, 4: 389–98, 1962; Maculans, G.A., 'Comparison of diazepam, chlorprothixene and chlorpromazine in chronic schizophrenic patients,' *Diseases of the Nervous System*, 25: 164–8, 1964; Kramer, J.C., 'Treatment of chronic hallucinations with diazepam and phenothiazines,' *Diseases of the Nervous System*, 28: 593–4, 1967; Irvine, B.M. and Schaecter, F., ' "Valium" in the treatment of schizophrenia,' *Medical Journal of Australia*, i: 1387, 1969; Trabucchi, M. and Ba, G., 'Are benzodiazepines antipsychotic agents?' *Lancet*, ii: 868, 1975; Lipsius, L.H., 'Chlordiazepoxide as an antipsychotic agent,' *Southern Medical Journal*, 72: 636, 1979; Ansari, J.M.A., 'Lorazepam in the control of acute psychotic symptoms and its comparison with flupenthixol,' in E. Usdin, H. Eckert and I.S. Forrest (eds), *Phenothiazines and*

*Structurally Related Drugs,* New York: Elsevier/North-Holland, 1980; Beckman, H. and Haas, S., 'High-dose diazepam in schizophrenia,' *Psychopharmacology,* 71: 79–82, 1980; Lingjaerde, O., 'Effect of the benzodiazepine derivative estazolam in patients with auditory hallucinations: A multicentre double-blind, cross-over study,' *Acta Psychiatrica Scandinavica,* 65: 339–54, 1982; 'Diazepam shown to reduce many schizophrenic symptoms,' *Psychiatric News,* August 20, 1982; Haas, S., Emrich, H.M. and Beckmann, H., 'Analgesic and euphoric effects of high-dose diazepam in schizophrenia,' *Neuropsychobiology,* 8: 123–8, 1982. Several similar studies are listed in the review article—Nestoros, 'Benzodiazepines in schizophrenia'—which draws the conclusion that benzo-diazepines have generally positive effects in schizophrenia.

82 The following studies yield equivocal results: Hollister, L.E., Bennett, J.L., Kimbell, I. et al., 'Diazepam in newly admitted schizophrenics,' *Diseases of the Nervous System,* 24: 746–50, 1963; Kellner, R., Wilson, R.M., Muldawer, M.D. and Pathak, D., 'Anxiety in schizophrenia: The responses to chlordiazepoxide in an intensive design study,' *Archives of General Psychiatry,* 32: 1246–54, 1975; Jimerson, D.C., Van Kammen, D.P., Post, R.M. et al., 'Diazepam in schizophrenia: A preliminary double-blind trial,' *American Journal of Psychiatry,* 139: 489–91, 1982. Clearly negative results are reported in: Lehmann, H.E. and Ban, T.A., 'Notes from the log-book of a psychopharmacological research unit II,' *Canadian Psychiatric Association Journal,* 9: 111–13, 1964; Weizman, A., Weizman, S., Tyano, S. et. al., 'The biphasic effect of gradually increased doses of diazepam on prolactin secretion in acute schizophrenic patients,' *Israeli Annals of Psychiatry,* 17: 233–40, 1979; Ruskin, P., Averbukh, I., Belmaker, R.H. and Dasberg, H., 'Benzodiazepines in chronic schizophrenia,' *Biological Psychiatry,* 14: 557–8, 1979; Karson, C.N., Weinberger, D.R., Bidelow, L. and Wyatt, R.J., 'Clonazepam treatment of chronic schizophrenia: Negative results in a double-blind, placebo-controlled trial,' *American Journal of Psychiatry,* 139: 1627–8, 1982. For a generally negative review of the value of the benzodiazepines in schizophrenia, see Greenblatt, D.J. and Shader, R.I., *Benzodiazepines in Clinical Practice.* New York: Raven Press, 1974, ch. 4.

83 Beckman and Haas, 'High-dose diazepam in schizophrenia;' Feldman, 'The efficacy of diazepam;' Maculans, 'Diazepam in chronic schizophrenic patients;' and 'Diazepam shown to reduce many schizophrenic symptoms,' *Psychiatric News,* August 20, 1982.

## 11 Work

1 Tuke, S., *Description of the Retreat,* London: Dawson, 1964, facsimile of 1813 edn. Quoted in Scull, A.T., *Museums of Madness: The Social Organization of Insanity in Nineteenth-Century England,* London: Allen Lane (New York: St Martin's Press), 1979, p. 69.

2 Ellis, W.C., *A Treatise on the Nature, Symptoms, Causes, and Treatment of Insanity,* London: Samuel Holdsworth, 1838, p. 197.

3 Todd, E., unpublished letter in the Institute of Living archives, Hartford, Connecticut, 1830. Quoted in Braceland, F.J., 'Rehabilitation,' in S. Arieti (ed.), *American Handbook of Psychiatry,* 2nd edn, vol. 5, New York: Basic Books, 1975, pp. 683–700. The quotation is on p. 684.

4  Browne, W.A.F., *What Asylums Were, Are, and Ought to Be: Being the Substance of Five Lectures Delivered before the Managers of the Montrose Royal Lunatic Asylum*, Edinburgh: Black, 1837, pp. 229–31. Quoted in Scull, *Museums of Madness*, pp. 105–6.

5  Carlyle, T., Inaugural address at Edinburgh University, 1866, in M. Strauss (ed.), *Familiar Medical Quotations*, Boston: Little, Brown, 1968.

6  Freud, S., *Civilization and Its Discontents*, in J. Strachey (ed.), *Standard Edition of the Complete Psychological Works of Sigmund Freud*, vol. 21, London: Hogarth Press, 1953–1966. First published in 1930.

7  Wansbrough, N. and Cooper, P., *Open Employment after Mental Illness*, London: Tavistock, 1980, pp. 2–4; Fairweather, G.W., Sanders, D.H., Maynard, H. et al., *Community Life for the Mentally Ill*, Chicago: Aldine, 1969, pp. 13–14; Patterson, C.H., 'Evaluation of the rehabilitation potential of the mentally ill patient,' in L.P. Blum and R.K. Kujoth (eds), *Job Placement of the Emotionally Disturbed*, Metuchen, New Jersey: Scarecrow Press, 1972, pp. 188–215. The reference is to pp. 189–91.

8  Stringham, J.A., 'Rehabilitating chronic neuropsychiatric patients,' *American Journal of Psychiatry*, 108: 924–8, 1952.

9  Cohen, L., 'Vocational planning and mental illness,' *Personnel and Guidance Journal*, 34: 28–32, 1955.

10  Brown, G.W., Carstairs, G.M. and Topping, G., 'Post-hospital adjustment of chronic mental patients,' *Lancet*, ii: 685–9, 1958.

11  Freeman, H.E. and Simmons, O.G., *The Mental Patient Comes Home*, New York: Wiley, 1963, ch. 4.

12  Fairweather et al., *Community Life for the Mentally Ill*, ch. 12.

13  Walker, R., Winick, W., Frost, E.S. and Lieberman, J.M., 'Social restoration of hospitalized psychiatric patients through a program of special employment in industry,' *Rehabilitation Literature*, 30: 297–303, 1969.

14  Anthony, W.A., Buell, G.W., Sharatt, S. and Althoff, M.E., 'The efficacy of psychiatric rehabilitation,' *Psychological Bulletin*, 78: 447–56, 1972.

15  Barbee, M.S., Berry, K.L. and Micek, L.A., 'Relationship of work therapy to psychiatric length of stay and readmission,' *Journal of Consulting and Clinical Psychology*, 33: 735–8, 1969.

16  Wing, J.K. and Brown, G.W., *Institutionalism and Schizophrenia: A Comparative Study of Three Mental Hospitals 1960–68*, Cambridge: Cambridge University Press, 1970; Peffer, P.A., 'Money: A rehabilitation incentive for mental patients,' *American Journal of Psychiatry*, 110: 84–92, 1953. Two similar examples are given in Linn, L., 'Occupational therapy and other activities,' in H.I. Kaplan, A.M. Freedman and B.J. Sadock (eds), *Comprehensive Textbook of Psychiatry-III*, Baltimore: Williams & Wilkins, 1980, pp. 2382–90. The reference is to pp. 2385–6.

17  Johnson, R.F. and Lee, H., 'Rehabilitation of chronic schizophrenics: Major results of a three-year program,' *Archives of General Psychiatry*, 12: 237–40, 1965.

18  Kunce, J.T., 'Is work therapy really therapeutic?' *Rehabilitation Literature*, 31: 297–9, 320, 1970.

19  Miles, A., 'Long-stay schizophrenic patients in hospital workshops: A comparative

study of an industrial unit and an occupational therapy department,' *British Journal of Psychiatry*, 119: 611–20, 1971; Miles, A., 'The development of interpersonal relationships among long-stay patients in two hospital workshops,' *British Journal of Medical Psychology*, 45: 105–14, 1972.

20 Ellis, R.H. and Young, C., 'Cost savings associated with sheltered workshop employment,' Brief Report no. 2, Colorado Division of Mental Health Evaluation Services, February 25, 1983.

21 Poindexter, W.R., 'Screening ex-patients for employability,' in Blum and Kujoth, *Job Placement of the Emotionally Disturbed*, pp. 152–7. The quotation is on pp. 155–6.

22 Lowe, C.M., 'Prediction of posthospital work adjustment by the use of psychological tests,' in Blum and Kujoth, *Job Placement of the Emotionally Disturbed*, pp. 239–48; Patterson, 'Evaluation of rehabilitation potential,' p. 196; Freeman and Simmons, *The Mental Patient Comes Home*, p. 61; Brown, Carstairs and Topping, 'Post-hospital adjustment of chronic mental patients.'

23 Glasscote, R.M., Cumming, E., Rutman, I. et al., *Rehabilitating the Mentally Ill in the Community*, Washington, DC: Joint Information Service of the American Psychiatric Association and the National Association for Mental Health, 1971, p. 200; US Department of Labor, *Sheltered Workshop Study, Volume II: Study of Handicapped Clients in Sheltered Workshops and Recommendations of the Secretary*, Washington, DC: 1979, p. 31.

24 Wansbrough and Cooper, *Open Employment after Mental Illness*, p. 48.

25 Black, B. *Industrial Therapy for the Mentally Ill in Western Europe*, New York: Altro Service Bureau, 1966.

26 Wansbrough and Cooper, *Open Employment after Mental Illness*, p. 38.

27 Ibid., pp. 36–8.

28 Fairweather et al., *Community Life for the Mentally Ill*.

29 Backer, T.E. and Glaser, E.M. (eds), *Case Studies of Fairweather Hospital-Community Treatment Program*, Los Angeles: Human Interaction Research Institute, 1979.

30 Wansbrough and Cooper, *Open Employment after Mental Illness*, pp. 50–4.

31 Glasscote et al., *Rehabilitating the Mentally Ill*, p. 54.

32 Wansbrough and Cooper, *Open Employment after Mental Illness*, p. 44.

33 Blacker and Glaser, *Case Studies of Fairweather Programs*, pp. 58, 90.

34 Wansbrough and Cooper, *Open Employment after Mental Illness*, p. 37.

35 Fairweather et al., *Community Life for the Mentally Ill*, pp. 140–1.

36 Wansbrough and Cooper, *Open Employment after Mental Illness*, pp. 53–4.

37 Ibid., p. 37.

38 Backer and Glaser, *Case Studies of Fairweather Programs*, p. 46.

39 Details of the Boulder Transitional Employment Program, and other material in this chapter, were provided by Ruth Arnold, Coordinator of Vocational Services at the Mental Health Center of Boulder County, Colorado.

40 Glasscote et al., *Rehabilitating the Mentally Ill*, p. 55.

41 Wansbrough and Cooper, *Open Employment after Mental Illness*, pp. 46–50.

42 Walker et al., 'Social restoration of hospitalized patients.'

43 Wansbrough and Cooper, *Open Employment after Mental Illness*, p. 47.

44 Glasscote et al., *Rehabilitating the Mentally Ill*, pp. 55, 134.

45 Wansbrough and Cooper, *Open Employment after Mental Illness*, p. 50.
46 Keys, L.M., 'Former patients as volunteers in community agencies: A model work rehabilitation program,' *Hospital and Community Psychiatry*, 33: 1017–18, 1982.
47 Glasscote et al., *Rehabilitating the Mentally Ill*, pp. 87, 133.
48 The material throughout this section on Soviet work therapy is drawn from the following sources: Field, M.G. and Aronson, J., 'The institutional framework of Soviet psychiatry,' *Journal of Nervous and Mental Disease*, 138: 305–22, 1964; Field, M.G. and Aronson, J., 'Soviet community mental health services and work therapy: A report of two visits,' *Community Mental Health Journal*, 1: 81–90, 1965; Auster, S.L., 'Impressions of psychiatry in one Russian city,' *American Journal of Psychiatry*, 124: 538–42, 1967; National Institute of Mental Health, Special Report: The First U.S. Mission on Mental Health to the U.S.S.R., Chevy Chase, Maryland: US Department of Health, Education, and Welfare, 1969; Gorman, M., 'Soviet psychiatry and the Russian citizen,' *International Journal of Psychiatry*, 8: 841–57, 1969.
49 Gorman, 'Soviet psychiatry,' p. 846.
50 Auster, 'Impression of psychiatry,' p. 540.
51 Ellman, M., *Socialist Planning*, Cambridge: Cambridge University Press, 1979, p. 158.
52 Ibid., pp. 158–61.
53 Lindblom, C.E., *Politics and Markets: The World's Political-Economic Systems*, New York: Basic Books, 1977, pp. 43–4; Thurow, L.C., *The Zero-Sum Society: Distribution and the Possibilities for Economic Change*, Harmondsworth, Middlesex: Penguin, 1980, ch. 7.
54 Thurow, *The Zero-Sum Society*, pp. 203–7.
55 Hawkins, K., *Unemployment: Facts, Figures and Possible Solutions for Britain*, Harmondsworth, Middlesex: Penguin, 1979, p. 96; Scott, M. and Laslett, R.A., *Can We Get Back to Full Employment?*, New York: Holmes & Meier, 1979, p. 113.
56 Samuelson, P.A., *Economics*, 11th edn, New York: McGraw-Hill, 1980, p. 780.
57 Ibid., p. 777; Friedman, M., 'The role of monetary policy,' *American Economic Review*, 58: 1–17, 1968; Phelps, E.S., 'Phillips curve, expectations of inflation, and optimal unemployment over time,' *Economica*, 34: 254–81, 1967.
58 Samuelson, *Economics*, p. 777.
59 Ibid., p. 780.
60 Ibid., p. 780.
61 Ibid., pp. 780–1.
62 Hawkins, *Unemployment*, pp. 94–6, 129–31.
63 Scott and Laslett, *Can We Get Back to Full Employment?*, pp. 113–15.
64 Jay, P., *A General Hypothesis of Employment, Inflation and Politics*, London: Institute of Economic Affairs, Occasional Paper 46, 1976, pp. 33–4.
65 Bluestone, B. and Harrison, B., *The Deindustrialization of America*, New York: Basic Books, 1982, ch. 8.
66 Heilbroner, R.L., *Business Civilization in Decline*, Harmondsworth, Middlesex: Penguin, 1977.
67 Hawkins, *Unemployment*, pp. 68–71.

## 12 Desegregating Schizophrenia

1 The Mental Health Center of Boulder County, Inc., is a comprehensive community mental health center which offers a full range of psychiatric services to the 190,000 residents of the mixed urban and rural region of Boulder County, Colorado. Clients' fees are on a sliding scale and services for the indigent are free. The Center sees about 3,200 clients a year; over 1,200 cases are active at any one time and about 250 of these suffer from functional psychoses.

The Center employs 141 part-time and full-time staff (85 full-time equivalent employees). Sixty-two full-time equivalent employees provide clinical services and 23 full-time equivalent staff have administrative and clerical duties.

The Center's budget for 1982–3 was $2.9 million. The sources of revenue were as follows:

| | |
|---|---|
| Federal government | $73,000 |
| State government | $1,584,000 |
| Local government (cities and county) | $531,000 |
| Fees, insurance payments and other earnings | $704,000 |

2 Turner, J.C. and Tenhoor, W.J., 'The N.I.M.H. community support program: Pilot approach to a needed social reform,' *Schizophrenia Bulletin*, 4: 319–48, 1978.

3 Lamb, H.R., 'Structure: The neglected ingredient of community treatment,' *Archives of General Psychiatry*, 37: 1224–8, 1980.

4 Brook, B.D., Cortes, M., March, R. and Sundberg-Stirling, M., 'Community families: An alternative to psychiatric hospital intensive care,' *Hospital and Community Psychiatry*, 27: 195–7, 1976.

5 Stein, L.I. and Test, M.A., 'Alternative to mental hospital treatment: I. Conceptual model, treatment program, and clinical evaluation,' *Archives of General Psychiatry*, 37: 392–7, 1980.

6 Test, M.A. and Stein, L.I., 'Alternative to mental hospital treatment: III. Social cost,' *Archives of General Psychiatry*, 37: 409–12, 1980.

7 To this number we should add a dozen psychotic patients who have been placed in the forensic unit of the state hospital by the Boulder County criminal courts. Other psychotic patients from Boulder County receive inpatient and outpatient care in the private sector. It is not possible to say how many of these patients would be in hospital treatment if they were under the care of the mental health center. One may safely assume, however, that virtually none of the private sector psychotics is a candidate for long-term hospital care—such patients rapidly pass the point of being able to pay for private hospital treatment, the limited provisions of their health insurance having been exhausted.

8 Sandall, H., Hawley, T.T. and Gordon, G.C., 'The St. Louis community homes program: Graduated support for long-term care,' *American Journal of Psychiatry*, 132: 617–22, 1975.

9 Morris, B., 'Residential units,' in J.K. Wing and B. Morris (eds), *Handbook of Psychiatric Rehabilitation Practice*, Oxford: Oxford University Press, 1981, pp. 99–121. The reference is to p. 109.

10 Ibid., p. 106.

11 Barker, R.G., *Ecological Psychology: Concepts and Methods for Studying the*

*Environment of Human Behavior,* Stanford: Stanford University Press, 1968, ch. 7.

12 Ibid.

13 Vash, C.L., *Sheltered Industrial Employment,* Washington, DC: Institute of Research Utilization, 1977.

14 Thurow, L.C., *The Zero-Sum Society: Distribution and the Possibilities for Economic Change,* New York: Penguin, 1981, p. 211.

15 The median income of American males in 1980 was $12,530; the mean income of the same group was $15,340. See US Bureau of the Census, *Statistical Abstract of the United States: 1982,* Washington, DC: 1982, p. 438.

16 Ekdawi, M.K., 'The role of day units in rehabilitation,' in Wing and Morris, *Handbook of Psychiatric Rehabilitation,* pp. 95–8. The quotation is from p. 98.

17 Lamb, H.R., 'An educational model for teaching living skills to long-term patients,' *Hospital and Community Psychiatry,* 27: 875–7, 1976.

18 Strauss, J.S. and Carpenter, W.T., *Schizophrenia,* New York: Plenum, 1981, p. 194.

19 Ibid., p. 173.

20 Rosenhan, D.L., 'On being sane in insane places,' *Science,* 179: 250–8, 1973.

21 Mosher, L.R. and Keith, S.J., 'Research on the psychosocial treatment of schizophrenia: A summary report,' *American Journal of Psychiatry,* 136: 623–31, 1979.

22 Leff, J., Kuipers, L. and Berkowitz, R., 'Prevention of relapse in schizophrenia: A combined social and pharmacological approach,' presented at the World Psychiatric Association Regional Meeting, New York, October 30–November 3, 1981; Berkowitz, R., Kuipers, L., Eberlein-Fries, R. and Leff, J., 'Lowering expressed emotion in relatives of schizophrenics,' in M. Goldstein (ed.), *New Directions for Mental Health Services: New Developments in Interventions with Families of Schizophrenics,* no. 12, San Francisco: Jossey-Bass, December 1981, pp. 27–48.

23 Falloon, I.R.H., Boyd, J.L., McGill, C.W. et al., 'Family management in the prevention of exacerbations of schizophrenia: A controlled study,' *New England Journal of Medicine,* 306: 1437–40, 1982.

24 Mosher and Keith, 'Psychosocial treatment of schizophrenia,' pp. 626–7.

25 Wig, N.N., Menon, D.K. and Bedi, H., 'Coping with schizophrenic patients in developing countries,' presented at the Seventh World Congress of Psychiatry, Vienna, July 11–16, 1983.

26 Pyke-Lees, P., 'The National Schizophrenia Fellowship,' in Wing and Morris, *Handbook of Psychiatric Rehabilitation,* pp. 126–9.

27 *Breakdown,* a series of eight, 15-minute programs produced at Seven Oak Productions, Boulder, by Richard Warner and Konnie Kindle. Copies of the tapes for local broadcasting may be obtained by writing to the author at the Mental Health Center of Boulder County, 1333 Iris Avenue, Boulder, Colorado 80302, USA.

# Bibliography

**Studies of the Outcome of Schizophrenia in Table 3.1**

Ackner, B. and Oldham, A.J., 'Insulin treatment of schizophrenia: A three-year follow-up of a controlled study,' *Lancet,* i: 504–6, 1962.

Astrup, C., Fossum, A. and Holmboe, R., *'Prognosis in Functional Psychoses,'* Springfield, Illinois: Charles C. Thomas, 1963.

Astrup, C. and Noreik, K., *Functional Psychoses: Diagnostic and Prognostic Models,* Springfield, Illinois: Charles C. Thomas, 1966.

Beck, M.N., 'Twenty-five and thirty-five year follow up of first admissions to mental hospitals,' *Canadian Psychiatric Association Journal,* 13: 219–29, 1968.

Bland, R.C. and Orn, H., 'Fourteen-year outcome in early schizophrenia,' *Acta Psychiatrica Scandinavica,* 58: 327–38, 1978.

Bland, R.C., Parker, J.H. and Orn, H., 'Prognosis in schizophrenia,' *Archives of General Psychiatry,* 35: 72–7, 1978.

Bleuler, E., *Dementia Praecox, or the Group of Schizophrenias,* New York: International Universities Press, 1950.

Bleuler, M., *The Schizophrenic Disorders: Long-term Patient and Family Studies,* New Haven: Yale University Press, 1978.

Bond, E.D., 'Results in 251 cases five years after admission to a hospital for mental diseases,' *Archives of Neurology and Psychiatry,* 6: 429–39, 1921.

Bond, E.D. and Braceland, F.J., 'Prognosis in mental disease,' *American Journal of Psychiatry,* 94: 263–74, 1937.

Braatöy, T., 'The prognosis in schizophrenia, with some remarks regarding diagnosis and therapy,' *Acta Psychiatrica et Neurologica Scandinavica,* 11: 63–102, 1936.

Briner, O., 'Zentralblatt für die gesamte Neurologie und Psychiatrie,' 162: 582, cited in E. Guttman, W. Mayer-Gross and E. Slater, 'Short-distance prognosis of schizophrenia,' *Journal of Neurological Psychiatry,* 2: 25–34, 1939.

Brown, G.W., Bone, M., Dalison, B. and Wing, J.K., *Schizophrenia and Social Care,* London: Oxford University Press, 1966.

Carter, A.B., 'The prognostic factors of adolescent psychosis,' *Journal of Mental Science,* 88: 31–81, 1942.

Cheney, C.O. and Drewry, P.H., 'Results of non-specific treatment in dementia praecox,' *American Journal of Psychiatry,* 95: 203–17, 1938.

Cole, N.J., Brewer, D.L. and Branch, C.H.H., 'Socioeconomic adjustment of a sample of schizophrenic patients,' *American Journal of Psychiatry,* 120: 465–71, 1963.

Cottman, S.B. and Mezey, S.B., 'Community care and the prognosis of schizophrenia,'

*Acta Psychiatrica Scandinavica*, 53: 95–104, 1976.

Eitinger, L., Laane, C.L. and Langfeldt, G., 'The prognostic value of the clinical picture and the therapeutic value of physical treatment in schizophrenia and the schizophreniform states,' *Acta Psychiatrica et Neurologica Scandinavica*, 33: 33–53, 1958.

Errera, P.A., 'Sixteen-year follow-up of schizophrenic patients seen in an outpatient clinic,' *Archives of Neurology and Psychiatry*, 78: 84–8, 1957.

Evensen, H., *Dementia Praecox*, Oslo: Kristiania, 1904.

Freyhan, F.A., 'Course and outcome of schizophrenia,' *American Journal of Psychiatry*, 112: 161–7, 1955.

Fröshaug, H. and Ytrehus, A., 'The problems of prognosis in schizophrenia,' *Acta Psychiatrica Scandinavica*, supplement 169: 176–87, 1963.

Fromenty, L., 'Les remissions dans la schizophrénie statistique sur leur fréquence et leur durée avant l'insulinthérapie,' *Encephale*, 1: 275–86, 1937.

Gerloff, W., 'Über Verlauf und Prognose der Schizophrenie,' *Archiv für Psychiatrie und Nervenkrankheiten*, 106: 585–98, 1936.

Guttman, E., Mayer-Gross, W. and Slater, E., 'Short-distance prognosis of schizophrenia,' *Journal of Neurological Psychiatry*, 2: 25–34, 1939.

Hall, J.C., Smith, K. and Shimkunas, A., 'Employment problems of schizophrenic patients,' *American Journal of Psychiatry*, 123: 536–40, 1966.

Harris, A., Linker, I., Norris, V. and Shepherd, M., 'Schizophrenia: A prognostic and social study,' *British Journal of Social and Preventive Medicine*, 10: 107–14, 1956.

Harrow, M., Grinker, R.R., Silverstein, M.L. and Holzman, P., 'Is modern-day schizophrenia outcome still negative?' *American Journal of Psychiatry*, 135: 1156–62 1978.

Hastings, D.W., 'Follow-up results in psychiatric illness,' *American Journal of Psychiatry*, 114: 1057–65, 1958.

Henisz, J., 'A follow-up study of schizophrenic patients,' *Comprehensive Psychiatry*, 7: 524–8, 1966.

Hoenig, J. and Hamilton, M.W., 'Schizophrenia in an extramural service,' *Comprehensive Psychiatry*, 7: 81–9, 1966.

Holmboe, R. and Astrup, C., 'A follow-up study of 255 patients with acute schizophrenia and schizophreniform psychoses,' *Acta Psychiatrica et Neurologica Scandinavica*, supplement 125, 1957.

Holmboe, R., Noreik, K. and Astrup, C., 'Follow-up of functional psychoses at two Norwegian mental hospitals,' *Acta Psychiatrica Scandinavica*, 44: 298–310, 1968.

Horwitz, W.A. and Kleiman, C., 'Survey of cases of dementia praecox discharged from the Psychiatric Institute and Hospital,' *Psychiatric Quarterly*, 10: 72–85, 1936.

Huber, G., Gross, G. and Schuttler, R., 'A long-term follow-up study of schizophrenia: Psychiatric course of illness and prognosis,' *Acta Psychiatrica Scandinavica*, 52: 49–57, 1975.

Hunt, R.C., Feldman, H. and Fiero, R.P., 'Spontaneous remission in dementia praecox,' *Psychiatric Quarterly*, 12: 414–25, 1938.

Johanson, E., 'A study of schizophrenia in the male: A psychiatric and social study based on 138 cases with follow-up,' *Acta Psychiatrica et Neurologica Scandinavica*, supplement 125, 1958.

Johnstone, E.C., Frith, C.D., Gold, A. and Stevens, M., 'The outcome of severe acute schizophrenic illness after one year,' *British Journal of Psychiatry*, 134: 28–33, 1979.

Kelly, D.H.W. and Sargant, W., 'Present treatment of schizophrenia,' *British Medical Journal*, 1: 147–50, 1965.

Kraepelin, E., *Dementia Praecox and Paraphrenia*, Edinburgh: Livingstone, 1919.

Langfeldt, G., 'The prognosis in schizophrenia and factors influencing the course of the disease,' *Acta Psychiatrica et Neurologica Scandinavica*, supplement 13, 1939.

Leiberman, D.M., Hoenig, J. and Auerbach, I., 'The effect of insulin coma and E.C.T. on the 3 year prognosis of schizophrenia,' *Journal of Neurology, Neurosurgery and Psychiatry*, 20: 108–13, 1957.

Lemke, R., 'Untersuchungen über die soziale Prognose der Schizophrenie unter besonders Beruchsicktigung des encephalographischen Befundes,' *Archiv für Psychiatrie und Nervenkrankheiten*, 104: 89–136, 1935.

Levenstien, S., Klein, D.F. and Pollack, M., 'Follow-up study of formerly hospitalized voluntary psychiatric patients: The first two years,' *American Journal of Psychiatry*, 122: 1102–9, 1966.

Leyberg, J.T., 'A follow-up study on some schizophrenic patients,' *British Journal of Psychiatry*, 111: 617–24, 1965.

Malamud, W. and Render, I.N., 'Course and prognosis in schizophrenia,' *American Journal of Psychiatry*, 95: 1039–57, 1939.

Mandelbrote, B.M. and Folkard, S., 'Some factors related to outcome and social adjustment in schizophrenia,' *Acta Psychiatrica Scandinavica*, 37: 223–35, 1961.

Masterson, J.F., 'Prognosis in adolescent disorders: Schizophrenia,' *Journal of Nervous and Mental Disease*, 124: 219–32, 1956.

Mayer-Gross, W., 'Die schizophrenie,' in O. Bumke (ed.), *Handbuch der Geisteskrankheiten*, vol. 9, Berlin: Springer, 1932, p. 534.

Müller, V., 'Katamnestische Erhebungen über den Spontanverlauf der Schizophrenie,' *Monatsschrift für Psychiatrie und Neurologie*, 122: 257–76, 1951.

Murdoch, J.H., 'Crime in schizophrenic reaction types,' *Journal of Mental Science*, 79: 286–97, 1933.

Niskanen, P. and Achté, K.A., 'Prognosis in schizophrenia: A comparative follow-up study of first admissions for schizophrenic and paranoid psychoses in Helsinki in 1950, 1960 and 1965,' *Psychiatria Fennica Year Book 1971*, 1971, pp. 117–26.

Norton, A., 'Mental hospital ins and outs: A survey of patients admitted to a mental hospital in the past 30 years,' *British Medical Journal*, 1: 528–36, 1961.

Otto-Martiensen, J., *Zeitschrift für Psychiatrie*, 77: 295 et seq., 1921, cited in R. Lemke 'Untersuchungen über die soziale Prognose der Schizophrenie unter besonders Beruchsichtigung des encephalographischen Befundes,' *Archiv für Psychiatrie und Nervenkrankheiten*, 104: 89–136, 1935.

Rennie, T.A.C., 'Follow-up study of 500 patients with schizophrenia admitted to the hospital from 1913–1923,' *Archives of Neurology and Psychiatry*, 42: 877–91, 1939.

Romano, J. and Ebaugh, F.G., 'Prognosis in schizophrenia,' *American Journal of Psychiatry*, 95: 583–96, 1938.

Rosanoff, A.J., 'A statistical study of prognosis in insanity,' *Journal of the American Medical Association*, 62: 3–6, 1914.

Rupp, C. and Fletcher, E.K., 'A five to ten year follow-up study of 641 schizophrenic cases,' *American Journal of Psychiatry*, 96: 877–88, 1940.

Stalker, H., 'The prognosis in schizophrenia,' *Journal of Mental Science*, 85: 1224–40, 1939.

Stearns, A.W., 'The prognosis in dementia praecox,' *Boston Medical and Surgical Journal*, 167: 158–60, 1912.

Stephens, J.H., 'Long-term course and prognosis in schizophrenia,' *Seminars in Psychiatry*, 2: 464–85, 1970.

Strecker, E.A. and Willey, G.F., 'Prognosis in schizophrenia,' *Journal of Mental Science*, 73: 9–39, 1927.

Tsuang, M.T., Woolson, R.F. and Fleming, J.A., 'Long-term outcome of major psychoses: I. Schizophrenia and affective disorders compared with psychiatrically symptom-free surgical conditions,' *Archives of General Psychiatry*, 36: 1295–1301, 1979.

Vaillant, G.E. and Funkenstein, D.H., 'Long-term follow-up (10–15 years) of schizophrenic patients with Funkenstein (adrenalin-mecholyl) tests,' in P.H. Hoch and J. Zubin (eds), *Psychopathology of Schizophrenia*, New York: Grune & Stratton, 1966.

Vaillant, G.E., Semrad, E.V. and Ewalt, J.R., 'Current therapeutic results in schizophrenia,' *New England Journal of Medicine*, 271: 280–3, 1964.

Wirt, R.D. and Simon, W., *Differential Treatment and Prognosis in Schizophrenia*, Springield, Illinois: Charles C. Thomas, 1959.

Wootton, L.H., Armstrong, R.W. and Lilly, D., 'An investigation into the after-histories of discharged mental patients,' *Journal of Mental Science*, 81: 168–72, 1935.

World Health Organization, *Schizophrenia: An International Follow-Up Study*, Chichester, England: Wiley, 1979.

### Studies of the Prevalence of Schizophrenia in Table 9.1

Akimoto, H., Shimazaki, T., Okada, K. and Tatetsu, M, 'Chihō shōtoshi ni okeru minseigaku-teki oyobi seishinigaku-teki chosa,' *Seishin Shinkei Gaku Zasshi*, 47: 1–24, 1943, cited in E.F. Torrey, *Schizophrenia and Civilization*, New York: Jason Aronson, 1980.

Baasher, T., 'Survey of mental illness in Wadi Halfa,' presented at the Sixth International Congress on Mental Health, Paris, September, 1961, cited in J. Racy, 'Psychiatry in the Arab East,' *Acta Psychiatrica Scandinavica*, supplement 211: 1–171, 1970, pp. 92–3.

Böök, J.A., 'A genetic and neuropsychiatric investigation of a North-Swedish population,' *Acta Genetica et Statistica Medica*, 4: 1–100, 1953.

Böök, J.A., Wetterberg, L. and Modrzewska, K., 'Schizophrenia in a North Swedish geographical isolate, 1900–1977: Epidemiology, genetics and biochemistry,' *Clinical Genetics*, 14: 373–94, 1978.

Bremer, J., 'A social psychiatric investigation of a small community in northern Norway,' *Acta Psychiatrica et Neurologica Scandinavica*, supplement 62: 1–166, 1951.

Brugger, C., 'Versuch einer Geisteskrankenzahlung in Thuringen,' *Zeitschrift für Psychiatrie und Neurologie*, 133: 352–90, 1931.

Brugger, C., 'Gebiete eines medizinish-anthropologischen Zensus in der Nähe von Rosenheim,' *Zeitschrift für Psychiatrie und Neurologie,* 160: 189–201, 1937.

Carstairs, G.M. and Kapur, R.L., *The Great Universe of Kota: A Study of Stress, Change, and Mental Disorder in an Indian Village,* Berkeley: University of California Press, 1976.

Crocetti, G.M., Lemkau, P.V., Kulčar, Ž. and Kesič, B., 'Selected aspects of the epidemiology of psychoses in Croatia, Yugoslavia: III. The cluster sample and the results of the pilot survey,' *American Journal of Epidemiology,* 94: 126–34, 1971.

Dube, K.C. and Kumar, N., 'Epidemiological study of schizophrenia,' *Journal of Biosocial Science,* 4: 187–95, 1972.

Eastwell, H., 'Schizophrenic typology in Aboriginal Australia: Observations from Arnhem Land,' unpublished paper dated 1975 cited in Torrey, *Schizophrenia and Civilization,* pp. 144–5.

Eaton, J.W. and Weil, R.J., *Culture and Mental Disorders,* Glencoe, Illinois: Free Press, 1955.

Egeland, J.A. and Hostetter, A.M., 'Amish study, I: Affective disorders among the Amish, 1976–1980,' *American Journal of Psychiatry,* 140: 56–61, 1983.

Elnager, M.N., Maitra, P. and Rao, M.N., 'Mental health in an Indian rural community,' *British Journal of Psychiatry,* 118: 499–503, 1971.

Essen-Moller, E., 'Individual traits and morbidity in a Swedish rural population,' *Acta Psychiatrica et Neurologica Scandinavica,* supplement 100: 1–160, 1956.

Fremming, K.H., *The Expectations of Mental Infirmity in a Sample of the Danish Population,* London: Cassell, 1951.

Fugelli, P., 'Mental health and living conditions in a fishing community in northern Norway,' *Acta Psychiatrica Scandinavica,* 51, supplement 263: 39–42, 1975.

Hagnell, O., *A Prospective Study of the Incidence of Mental Disorder,* Lund, Sweden: Norstedts-Bonniers, 1966.

Helgason, T., 'Epidemiology of mental disorder in Iceland,' *Acta Psychiatrica Scandinavica,* supplement 173, 1964.

Hollingshead, A.B. and Redlich, F.C., *Social Class and Mental Illness,* New York: Wiley, 1958.

Japanese Ministry of Health and Welfare, Nationwide prevalence survey of mental disorders in 1954, Tokyo: 1955. Unpublished mimeograph cited in M. Kato, 'Psychiatric epidemiological surveys in Japan: The problem of case finding,' in W. Caudill and T. Lin (eds), *Mental Health Research in Asia and the Pacific,* Honolulu: East-West Center Press, 1969, pp. 92–104.

Japanese Ministry of Health and Welfare, Wagakuni ni okeru seishin-shōgai no genjō. Tokyo: Kōsei-shō Kōshū Eisei Kyoku, 1965. Cited in M. Kato, 'Psychiatric epidemiological surveys in Japan: The problem of case finding,' in M. Caudill and T. Lin (eds), *Mental Health Research in Asia and the Pacific,* Honolulu: East-West Center Press, 1969, pp. 92–104.

Jayasundera, M.G., 'Mental health surveys in Ceylon,' in W. Caudill and T. Lin, *Mental Health Research in Asia and the Pacific,* Honolulu: East-West Center Press, 1969, pp. 54–65.

Jones, I.H. and Horne, D. J. de L., 'Psychiatric disorders among Aborigines of the Australian Western Desert: Further data and discussion,' *Social Science and Medicine,* 7: 219–28, 1973.

Kaila, M., 'Über die Durchschnittshäufigkeit der Geisteskrankheiten und des Schwachsinns in Finland,' *Acta Psychiatrica et Neurologica Scandinavica*, 17: 47–67, 1942.

Kato, M., 'Psychiatric epidemiological surveys in Japan: The problem of case finding,' in W. Caudill and T. Lin (eds), *Mental Health Research in Asia and the Pacific*, Honolulu: East-West Center Press, 1969, pp. 92–104.

Kramer, M., 'Population changes and schizophrenia, 1970–1985,' in L.C. Wynn, R.L. Cromwell and S. Matthyse (eds), *The Nature of Schizophrenia: New Approaches to Research and Treatment*, New York: Wiley, 1978, pp. 545 et seq.

Larsson, T. and Sjögren, T., 'A methodological, psychiatric, and statistical study of a large Swedish rural population,' *Acta Psychiatrica et Neurologica Scandinavica*, supplement 89: 1–250, 1954.

Leighton, D.C., Harding, J.S., Macklin, D.B. et al., *The Character of Danger: The Stirling County Study of Psychiatric Disorder and Sociocultural Environment. Volume III. Psychiatric Symptoms in Selected Communities*, New York: Basic Books, 1963.

Lemkau, P.V., Tietze, C. and Cooper, M., 'Mental hygiene problems in an urban district,' *Mental Hygiene*, 25: 624–46, 1942.

Lemkau, P.V., Tietze, C. and Cooper, M., 'Mental hygiene problems in an urban district: Second paper,' *Mental Hygiene*, 26: 100–19, 1943.

Lin, T., 'A study of the incidence of mental disorder in Chinese and other cultures,' *Psychiatry*, 16: 313–36, 1953.

Lin, T., Rin, H., Yeh, E. et al., 'Mental disorders in Taiwan, fifteen years later: A preliminary report,' in W. Caudill and T. Lin (eds), *Mental Health Research in Asia and the Pacific*, Honolulu: East-West Center Press, 1969.

Mayer-Gross, W., 'Mental health survey in a rural area,' *Eugenics Review*, 40: 140–8, 1948.

Murphy, H.B.M. and Lemieux, M., 'Quelques considerations sur le taux élevé de schizophrénie dans un type de communauté canadienne-francaise, *Canadian Psychiatric Association Journal*, 12: S71–S81, special number, 1967.

Murphy, H.B.M. and Taumoepeau, B.M., 'Traditionalism and mental health in the South Pacific: A re-examination of an old hypothesis,' *Psychological Medicine*, 10: 471–82, 1980.

Murthy, R.S., Kala, R. and Wig, N.N., 'Mentally ill in a rural community: Some initial experiences in case identification and management,' *Indian Journal of Psychiatry*, 20: 143–7, 1978.

Nandi, D.N., Ajmany, S., Granguli, H. et al., 'Psychiatric disorders in a rural community in West Bengal: An epidemiological study,' *Indian Journal of Psychiatry*, 17: 87–99, 1975.

Nandi, D.N., Mukherjee, S.P., Boral, G.C. et al., 'Socio-economic status and mental morbidity in central tribes and castes in India: A cross-cultural study,' *British Journal of Psychiatry*, 136: 73–85, 1980.

Nielsen, J. and Nielsen, J.A., 'A census study of mental illness in Samso,' *Psychological Medicine*, 7: 491–503, 1977.

Primrose, E.J.R., *Psychological Illness: A Community Study*, London: Tavistock, 1962.

Rin, H. and Lin, T., 'Mental illness among Formosan aborigines as compared with the Chinese in Taiwan,' *Journal of Mental Science*, 108: 134–46, 1962.

Roth, W.F. and Luton, F.H., 'The mental health program in Tennessee,' *American*

*Journal of Psychiatry*, 99: 662–75, 1943.

Roy, C., Choudhuri, A. and Irvine, D., 'The prevalence of mental disorders among Saskatchewan Indians,' *Journal of Cross-Cultural Psychology*, 1: 383–92, 1970.

Sato, I., 'Seishin-byōin no tachiba kara,' *Seishin Igaku*, 8: 6–10, 1966, cited in M. Kato, 'Psychiatric epidemiological surveys in Japan: The problem of case finding,' in W. Caudill and T. Lin (eds), *Mental Health Research in Asia and the Pacific*, Honolulu: East-West Center Press, 1969, p. 92–104.

Sethi, B.B., Gupta, S.C. and Kumar, R., '300 urban families: A psychiatric study,' *Indian Journal of Psychiatry*, 9: 280–302, 1967.

Sethi, B.B., Gupta, S.C., Mahendru, R.K. and Kumari, P., 'Migration and mental health,' *Indian Journal of Psychiatry*, 14: 115–21, 1972a.

Sethi, B.B., Gupta, S.C., Kumar,. R. and Kumari, P. 'A psychiatric survey of 500 rural families,' *Indian Journal of Psychiatry*, 14: 183–96, 1972b.

Sethi, B.B., Gupta, S.C., Mahendru, R.K. and Kumari, P., 'Mental health and urban life: A study of 850 families,' *British Journal of Psychiatry*, 124: 243–6, 1974.

Sjögren, T., 'Genetic-statistical and psychiatric investigations of a West Swedish population,' *Acta Psychiatrica et Neurologica*, supplement 52, 1948.

Strömgren, E., 'Beiträge zur psychiatrischen Erblehre,' *Acta Psychiatrica et Neurologica*, supplement 19, 1938, cited in P. Lemkau, C. Tietze and M. Cooper, 'Survey of statistical studies on the prevalence and incidence of mental disorder in sample populations,' *Public Health Reports*, 58: 1909–27, 1943.

Surya, N.C., Datta, S.P., Krishna, R.G. et al., 'Mental morbidity in Pondicherry (1962–1963),' *Transaction* (All Indian Institute of Mental Health, Bangalore), 4: 50–61, 1964.

Thacore, V.R., Gupta, S.C. and Suraiya, M., 'Psychiatric morbidity in a north Indian community,' *British Journal of Psychiatry*, 126: 364–9, 1975.

Tsugawa, B., 'Daitoshi ni okeru seishin-shikkan no hassei-hindo ni kansuru kenkyū,' *Seishin Shinnkei Gaku Zasshi*, 47: 204 et seq., 1942, cited in E.F. Torrey, *Schizophrenia and Civilization*, New York: Jason Aronson, 1980.

Uchimura, Y., 'Hachijō-jima ni okeru seishin-shikkan no hassei-hindo ni kansuru kenkyū,' *Minzoku Eisei*, 10: 1 et seq., 1940, cited in M. Kato, 'Psychiatric epidemiological surveys in Japan: The problem of case finding,' in W. Caudill and T. Lin (eds), *Mental Health Research in Asia and the Pacific*, Honolulu: East-West Center Press, 1969, pp. 92–104.

Vaisanen, E., 'Psychiatric disorders in Finland,' *Acta Psychiatrica Scandinavica*, 51, supplement 263: 22–33, 1975.

Verghese, A., Beig, A., Senseman, L.A. et al., 'A social and psychiatric study of a representative group of families in Vellore town,' *Indian Journal of Medical Research*, 61: 608–20, 1973.

Walsh, D., O'Hare, A., Blake, B. et al., The prevalence of mental illness in Ireland: Of the three county case register study, Dublin: Medico-Social Research Board, 1979. Unpublished mimeograph cited in E.F. Torrey, *Schizophrenia and Civilization*. New York: Jason Aronson, 1980.

Wijesinghe, C.P., Dissanayake, S.A.W. and Dassanayake, P.V.L.N., 'Survey of psychiatric morbidity in a semi-urban population in Sri Lanka,' *Acta Psychiatrica Scandinavica*, 58: 413–41, 1978.

# Index

Aarhus (Denmark), 147, 155, 157
aboriginal populations, *see* Australian
  Aborigines; Taiwan, aborigines
Abrams, Richard, 261
Accra (Ghana), 22
Adler, Alfred, 139
affect, *see* emotional expression
Africa, *see* East Africa; West Africa; *individual*
  *countries*
Age of Reason, *see* Enlightenment
Agnews State Hospital (California), 88, 249
Agra (India), 155, 157, 160, 206, 225
agrarian lifestyle, 158–60, 215–17, 226; *see*
  *also* Amish; Hutterites; schizophrenia,
  prevalence, urban and rural
Alabama, 175
Alaska, 276
alcohol consumption, 39, 41, 42, 52; *see also*
  stress
alcoholism, 222
Algeria, 149
alienation, 49–51, 144, 161–2, 168, 188– 90,
  216, 217, 275
Alliances for the mentally ill, *see* Boulder
  Alliance for the Mentally Ill; National
  Alliance for the Mentally Ill; National
  Schizophrenia Fellowship
altered states of consciousness, 166
Aluthgama (Sri Lanka), 205
ambivalence, 14
American Indians (including Canada),
  162–3, 165; healing, 167, 168;
  schizophrenia, prevalence, 195–8, 199,
  209, 210–11, 218; suicide, 55
*American Journal of Insanity*, 216
*American Journal of Psychiatry*, 181
*American Notes for General Circulation*
  (Dickens), 118
American Psychiatric Association, *see*
  *Diagnostic and Statistical Manual*
Ami, 201
Amish, 195–8, 199, 219–21
Ampeng (Taiwan), 201
amphetamines, 8, 242
Amsterdam (Netherlands), 84–5
Anchorage (Alaska), 276
Anderson, Charles H., 136
anergy, 133
angina pectoris, *see* heart disease

Anthony, William A., 271
antipsychotic drugs, 1, 3, 16, 19, 29, 59,
  62–8, 70, 72–3, 76, 77, 95; antidotes, 241;
  impact, 81–4, 85–7, 93, 98, 141;
  introduction (1950s), 80; side effects,
  240–1, 243–4, 250, 258–9; tolerance to,
  246–7; types (*see* Chlorpromazine;
  Promazine); use, 183, 239, 240, 241,
  247–53, 254, 255, 256, 257, 258, 259,
  264, 292, 297, 307
anxiety, 52, 61, 133
apartment programs, *see* independent living
Appalachia (US), 52
Arieti, Sylvano, 217, 230
Armenians, 209
Ashton, T.S., 106
asylums, 13–14, 87, 102, 107, 108, 110, 113,
  114, 126, 268; expenditure on, 129–30;
  mortality rate, 110, 111, 112, 117, 118;
  recovery rate, 111–13, 116, 117, 123
Atayal, 201
Atjehnese, 208–9
Auster, Simon L., 280
Australia, 19, 43, 95, 96–7, 228, 308–9
Australian Aborigines, 169, 195–8, 199,
  211–12, 218
autism, 10–13, 14
automatic obedience, 10–13
Awl, William, 121

*Baa*, 151, 164
bachelorhood, 216
Baffin Island (Canada), 210
Bagley, Christopher, 229
Baksa area (Taiwan), 201
Baltimore (Maryland), 35, 175
Bangladesh, 232
Banias, 225
Bantu, 151
barbiturate coma, 62–8
Barker, Roger G., 296
Bassuk, Ellen L., 87
Bateson, Gregory, 28
Beaglehole, Ernest, 204
Bean, L.L., 145
Beck, James C., 143
Belgium, 94
Bell, George, 84
Bemba, 159

369

Maine Insane Hospital, 116, 117, 118
malaria, 150, 202
Malaya, *see* Malaysia
Malays, 208
Malaysia, 163, 232
malnutrition, 33, 34
Manchester Lunatic Asylum (England), 104, 107
Manhattan State Hospital (New York), 115
manic-depressive illness, 8, 9, 17–18, 73, 192, 219, 220, 221, 222, 239, 240, 288; treatment, 18–19; *see also* schizophrenia, compared to manic-depressive illness
Maoris, 204
Mapperley Hospital (Nottingham), 82, 84
marriage, 39, 42, 216, 223, 252
Marshall, James R., 55
Marx, Karl, 49, 135–6, 189
Marxist theory, 42; *see also* alienation; Marx, Karl; materialist approach
Maryland, 35, 38, 40, 116, 118, 175
Maryland State Hospital, 116
Massachusetts, 35, 48, 82, 92, 114, 116, 117, 120, 121, 122, 123, 124, 126, 175, 232, 278
Massachusetts Mental Health Center, 188
materialist approach, 2
Maudsley Hospital (London), 174
Mauritius, 152–4, 156, 157
May, Philip R.A., 251
Mayer, Doris Y., 149, 207, 208
Mayhew, Henry, 113
Mazatlan (Mexico), 161
Medicaid (US), 90, 95
Medical Research Council (London), 169–70, 254
Medicare (US), 90
megalomania, 149
melancholia, 234
Member Employee Program, 272
Mende, 168
Menn, Alma Z., 252
Mental Health Center of Boulder County (Colorado), 274, 277, 278, 285, 286, 287, 293, 304, 360 n.1
Mental health centers, *see* United States
*Mental Health of the Industrial Worker* (Kornhauser), 50
mental hospitals, 292–4; admissions and economy, 41, 54–5, 128, 137, 144, 145 (*see also* schizophrenia, and economy); beds, 293–4, 308–9; expenditure, 128–31, 139, 176, 179; expenditure and recovery, 131; use, 95–9, 130
mental illness: folk criteria, 152, 161–9; and homelessness, 172–4, 178, 258, 286, 289, 337–8 n. 14; mortality rate (*see* asylums; Great Britain; United States); recovery, 119–25, 137–40, 142, 328–9 n. 108; and society, 137, 138, 139, 140, 141, 167–9 (*see also* United States, mental illness, attitude toward)
*Mental Illness and the Economy* (Brenner), 54, 128

*Mental Patient Comes Home, The* (Freeman and Simmons), 270
Mescaline, 26
mesocortical tract, 242
Mesolimbic system, 27, 242, 244, 247
Mexico, 161
Meyer, Adolf, 138
Michigan, 50
Micronesia, 204
middle class, *see* social class
migration, 34, 38, 43, 160, 191, 216, 224, 228–30; *see also* labor market, migrant; rural-urban migration
milieu therapy, 93
Mills, Hannah, 102
Milwaukee (Wisconsin), 35
Minnesota, 230
Missouri, 35, 39, 40, 41, 55, 294
Modecate, *see* Fluphenazine
Mondays, 48, 54, 319–20 n. 114
Monoamine oxidase, 26
Monroe County (New York), 231
Montrose Royal Asylum (Scotland), 268
Mora, George, 104, 115, 117
moral management, *see* moral treatment
moral treatment, 101–2, 103–6, 107–13, 114, 117, 125–7, 137, 138, 266, 268, 288, 307; and Open Door Movement, 109–10
Mornington Island (Australia), 212
mortality rates: and economy, 39, 41, 42, 43, 44–7; and workplace, 48; *see also* infant mortality; suicide; *under* asylum; schizophrenia; *individual countries*
Moscow (Soviet Union), 146, 147, 155, 156, 157, 221
Mosher, Loren R., 252, 256, 263
Munda, 225
Murphy, H.B.M., 150, 154, 203, 204, 216, 223
*Museums of Madness* (Scull), 107
Myers, Jerome K., 145
myocardial infarction, *see* heart disease

Nandi, D.N., 225, 226
narcosis, 62–8
National Alliance for the Mentally Ill, 305, 306
National Health Service Act (1948) (Great Britain), 141
National Institute of Mental Health (NIMH), US, 241, 250, 251, 256, 285
National Schizophrenia Fellowship (Great Britain), 305, 306
Navajo Indians, 165
Nebraska, 35
negativism, 10–13
negativity, 133
neologisms, 10–13
Netherlands, 84–5, 93, 94
Netherne Hospital (London), 84
neuroleptic drugs, *see* antipsychotic drugs
neurosis, 52, 61, 139
New England, 181; *see also individual states*
New Hampshire, 276